CAREER OPPORTUNITIES IN FORENSIC SCIENCE

CAREER OPPORTUNITIES IN FORENSIC SCIENCE

SUSAN ECHAORE-McDAVID AND RICHARD A. McDAVID

Checkmark Books®
An imprint of Infobase Publishing

Career Opportunities in Forensic Science

Checkmark Books
An imprint of Infobase Publishing
132 West 31st Street
New York NY 10001

ISBN-10: 0-8160-6157-2
ISBN-13: 978-0-8160-6157-0

Library of Congress Cataloging-in-Publication Data

Echaore-McDavid, Susan.
  Career opportunities in forensic science / Susan Echaore-McDavid and Richard A. McDavid.
    p. cm.
  Includes bibliographical references and index.
  ISBN-13: 978-0-8160-6156-3 (hc : alk. paper)
  ISBN-10: 0-8160-6156-4 (hc : alk. paper)
  ISBN-13: 978-0-8160-6157-0 (pb : alk. paper)
  ISBN-10: 0-8160-6157-2 (pb : alk. paper) 1. Forensic sciences—Vocational guidance. 2. Criminal investigation—Vocational guidance. I. McDavid, Richard A. II. Title.
  HV8073.E34 2008
  363.25023—dc22   2007016012

Checkmark Books are available at special discounts when purchased in bulk quantities for businesses, associations, institutions, or sales promotions. Please call our Special Sales Department in New York at (212) 967-8800 or (800) 322-8755.

You can find Ferguson on the World Wide Web at http://www.fergpubco.com

Cover design by Takeshi Takahashi

Printed in the United States of America

VB Hermitage 10 9 8 7 6 5 4 3 2 1

This book is printed on acid-free paper and contains 30% post-consumer recycled content.

To our brothers—
Santiago Echaore Jr. and Douglas McDavid

CONTENTS

INDUSTRY OUTLOOK

Whenever you read or hear about seemingly unsolvable crimes that are indeed solved, or about suspects being found and apprehended months after the crime was committed, do you wonder how it is that such cases come to rest?

When you read about missing persons who are found and identified years after they died, or hear about how fires were deliberately set and what incendiary devices were used to set them, do you wonder who was able to unravel such mysteries?

Various professionals contribute to solving crimes and bringing suspects to justice. Usually most people think of police officers, detectives, special agents, lawyers, and judges. However, many more professionals contribute their efforts. Key among these professionals are forensic scientists and forensic experts. They work in forensic laboratories, police departments, universities, archaeology digs, coroner's offices, hospitals, government offices, courtrooms, and many other settings.

These men and women are responsible for examining and analyzing evidence that is found at crime scenes. They study evidence that ranges from the physical (such as broken glass, tire marks, or documents) to the biological (such as blood, sweat, and tears). They scrutinize trace evidence, such as fibers and pollen, that is barely visible to the naked eye. They examine evidence that is found on computers, videotapes, and recording devices.

By analyzing evidence, forensic experts are able to reconstruct events or reveal the appearance of unidentified remains prior to death. Forensic specialists also analyze how individuals behave or how persons use language. The list of evidence that forensic experts examine is long, diverse, and growing—financial accounts, personnel records, musical compositions, medical records, health studies, surveying plats, and weather patterns, to name just a few more.

With the analyses and conclusions that these forensic professionals make, law enforcement officers are able to solve cases and prosecuting attorneys are able to convict criminal suspects.

What Is Forensic Science?

What exactly is this thing we call forensics or forensic science? We may define "forensics" as a noun meaning the application of scientific methods to settling questions about legal disputes. This word derives from the Latin word "forensis," which means "in an open court" or "public." In our modern usage, the word *forensic* is often coupled with *science* to form the phrase *forensic science*.

Many, but not all, forensic experts are indeed scientists by training. They apply the scientific principles and techniques of their disciplines to their forensic examinations and analyses. Forensic experts who are not scientists per se use scientific methods to conduct their work.

Probably the most recognizable forensic scientists are the criminalists. They are the latent print examiners, forensic chemists, DNA analysts, firearms experts, bloodstain analysts, and others who work in the crime labs that are part of law enforcement agencies and prosecuting attorneys' offices. Other familiar forensic scientists are the pathologists and toxicologists who work in coroners' and medical examiners' offices. Then there are the forensic scientists who approach their work from the standpoint of numerous occupations that may seem at first glance unrelated to criminal justice, or even science.

According to the American Academy of Forensic Sciences (AAFS), any science that is used for the purposes of law is a forensic science. Additionally, AAFS states that forensic science may be broadly defined as the application of scientific, technical, or other specialized knowledge to legal issues. Hence, today, we have forensic experts with backgrounds in fields as diverse as medicine, art, microbiology, architecture, videography, engineering, language, anthropology, social work, information technology, mental health, construction, the environment, and many more.

Television CSI Shows

Many of us are familiar with some of the television crime shows that portray various forensic professionals. In fact, some people, perhaps like you, got interested in exploring forensic science as a possible career because of these entertaining shows. These programs introduce the viewer to crime scene investigation and other forensic specialties. On the one hand, this serves a positive end: that individuals who might not otherwise be exposed to these occupations can understand them on a fundamental level. On the other hand, popular television crime investigation programs tend to sensationalize and simplify what forensic specialists do in their line of work.

Real forensic professionals rarely, if ever, conveniently solve crimes within a matter of an hour's time. Moreover, very few forensic professionals perform more than one forensic investigative task, as do many of the heroes of network television.

Most importantly, forensic scientists are not crime scene investigators nor are they criminal investigators. These three occupations each can fulfill distinct roles. Many forensic scientists do not go to crime scenes. They work primarily in laboratories and offices where they carefully examine and analyze evidence that was collected by crime scene investigators. The conclusions that forensic scientists form help criminal investigators determine if there is sufficient proof to arrest suspects for a crime.

Furthermore, many forensic experts never directly investigate crimes or testify in court because their professional responsibilities involve such diverse tasks as accident reconstruction, vocational rehabilitation, or weather pattern analysis, among others, that are not portrayed on television. Certainly, television does not fully present a realistic examination of forensic science. Keep that in mind as you watch your favorite crime shows.

Historical Background

Forensic science as it is known today is a little over a century old. Prior to the 19th century, forensic science developed rather slowly. During the 1800s, the various forensic disciplines became more highly developed in parallel fashion to the advances that came with the Industrial Age. However, it was only within the past several decades that forensic science has rapidly grown more sophisticated and more pervasively useful to law and law enforcement.

Certain aspects of forensic science have been known and used throughout the ages and in many cultures. Perhaps the earliest recognition that fingerprints were unique to individuals was in ancient Babylon, where tablets used to record business transactions were marked with fingerprints. Around 700 B.C. in China, people frequently marked their written documents and clay sculptures with fingerprints to denote who created them. In 250 B.C., a Greek doctor named Erasistratus noticed that his patients' hearts beat faster when they were not telling the truth. This doctor used his observations as what is believed to be the first lie detection method. About two hundred years later, the Roman doctor Antistius noticed that out of 23 stab wounds on the body of assassinated emperor Julius Caesar, only one chest wound was the decisive blow.

In Rome during the 11th century A.D., an attorney named Quintilian demonstrated that someone tricked a blind man to leave his palm prints in blood at the scene of his mother's murder. In China, in 1248, a book (titled *Hsi Duan Yu*) explained how to tell the difference between death by drowning or by strangulation. Not long afterwards, the Bolognese surgeon Bartolomeo da Varignana performed a medical autopsy in a murder case. In 1507, during the reign of the bishop of Bamberg, the book *Constitutio Bambergen-sis Criminalis* noted how doctors were helpful in legal cases involving injuries and infanticide.

In 17th century France, Francois DeMelle wrote the first publication that covered the subject of the examination of documents in systematic detail. Also during that century, English doctor Sir Thomas Browne, one of the first forensic archaeologists, discovered adipocere, a fatty substance formed by decaying flesh; and a citizen of Bologna, Italy, anatomy professor Marcello Malpighi, made note of the various loops, spirals, and ridges in fingerprints.

Great advances in forensic science characterized the 18th, 19th, and 20th centuries. Among the numerous major milestones in modern forensic science:

- 1784—the murder conviction of one John Toms in Lancaster, England, based on matching bits of newspaper in his pocket and in his pistol
- 1810—the establishment of the first detective force in Paris and the first known use of questioned document analysis in Germany
- 1828—the polarizing light microscope, which opened the door to numerous uses in forensic science invented by William Nicol
- 1835—the first use of bullet comparison to solve a murder, credited to Henry Goddard of Scotland Yard
- 1880—the publication of an article by Henry Faulds in which he described his use of fingerprints to exonerate a burglary suspect and identify the perpetrator in Tokyo
- 1892—Argentina became the first nation to use a fingerprint classification system, which was developed by Juan Vucetich, a police researcher
- 1905—President Theodore Roosevelt authorized the establishment of the Federal Bureau of Investigation (FBI)
- 1910—the first police crime lab, established in France by Edmund Locard (who is known for the Locard's Exchange Principle, the forensic science principle that states whenever a person comes into contact with another person or a place, materials are usually exchanged between the two people or the person and the place)
- 1921—the portable polygraph designed by John Larson and Leonard Keeler
- 1937—the first university criminology program established at the University of California by Paul Kirk
- 1941—the technique of voiceprint identification initiated by Murray Hill of Bell Labs
- 1950—the American Academy of Forensic Sciences formed in Chicago, Illinois
- 1954—the Breathalyzer field sobriety test invented by R. F. Borkenstein
- 1960—gas chromatography as a method to identify petroleum products first described by Douglas Lucas in Canada

- 1975—the Federal Rules of Evidence enacted by the United States Congress, establishing the relevancy standard of admissible evidence
- 1977—the development of the "Superglue" fuming method of detecting latent fingerprints by Masato Soba in Japan
- 1984—the first DNA profiling test, developed by Sir Alec Jeffreys, who used the method to both identify a murderer and exonerate a suspect in 1986
- 1991—the development of the Integrated Ballistics Identification System by Walsh Automation, Inc. in Montreal
- 1996—the Automated Fingerprint Identification System (AFIS), a computerized fingerprint database introduced by the FBI

Modern Forensic Occupations

Forensic experts are employed both within and outside the law enforcement community. Forensic scientists who work in public crime labs, forensic units, and coroners' (or medical examiners') offices may be law enforcement officers or civilians. Depending on the structure, size, needs, and other factors of a police department or sheriff's office, officers may work full time or part time in performing their forensic duties. Some opportunities in these settings are also available for criminalists, forensic pathologists, forensic photographers, audio forensics experts, computer forensics specialists, accident reconstruction specialists, forensic toxicologists, forensic nurses, and forensic anthropologists.

Law enforcement agencies, coroners' offices, and prosecuting attorneys' offices also seek forensic experts who work in the private sector and in academic institutions on a contractual basis. They might, for example, consult with forensic archaeologists, forensic sculptors, forensic palynologists, forensic entomologists, forensic accountants, fraud examiners, forensic psychologists, and forensic linguists.

Due to the pervasiveness of popular TV crime shows, many of us think that forensic applications are used for the sole purpose of solving crime. That, however, is not the case. Increasingly, attorneys, the courts, insurance companies, corporations, government agencies, and other organizations retain forensic experts for assistance with issues related to civil litigation, insurance claims, contractual disputes, regulatory compliance, and other legal matters.

Expert Witnesses

Serving as expert witnesses in civil or criminal trials is a crucial role for these professionals, as it is their investigative and analytical conclusions about the evidence that must be used to convince judges and juries of the guilt or innocence of criminals, or of the veracity of claims made by civil litigants. Expert witness testimony differs from that of ordinary fact witnesses, who may only relate the circumstances of an event as they personally experienced it. Expert witnesses also offer facts about a case but, in addition, present unbiased opinions based on their examination and testing of the evidence.

Forensic scientists arrive at their conclusions by using very technical methods and, as a consequence, their opinions may be complicated. Their role as expert witnesses is to present their opinions in terms that judges and juries can comprehend from their nontechnical standpoint.

Expert witnesses may be hired by either prosecutors or defenders but may not take sides in any case. Regardless of their unbiased opinion, these forensic scientists face intense scrutiny by cross-examination. Opposing attorneys may try to challenge or discredit the expert's testimony. Therefore, a characteristic common to expert forensic witnesses is their calm, unbiased, and professional composure.

A court determines whether forensic scientists qualify as expert witnesses before they can give testimony. They meet the requirements of qualification through educational background, professional experience, membership in professional associations, and published work. They also must be well versed in the rules of how evidence must be acceptable in court. Forensic scientists train to become expert witnesses by participating in mock trials.

Job Outlook

Forensic scientists are employed in both the public and private sectors. They work for law enforcement agencies, medical examiners' offices, private forensic laboratories, government agencies, colleges and universities, research institutes, hospitals, engineering firms, forensic consulting companies, and other organizations. Many of them are independent practitioners.

Opportunities for job seekers in forensic science vary from one occupation to another, just as in any other career category. In general, however, forensic science is a vital, growing field with promise of expanding career horizons. More forensic disciplines are emerging and becoming accepted by law enforcement and the courts. Moreover, technology advancements help in the growth and development of new forensic disciplines. For example, microbial forensics, forensic epidemiology, forensic palynology, forensic archaeology, forensic statistics, child abuse pediatrics, and forensic radiology are just a few disciplines that have emerged in recent years.

In law enforcement agencies, crime labs, and coroners' offices, many forensic positions are held by police officers and deputy sheriffs. They conduct latent print examination, forensic video analysis, forensic photography, forensic art, computer forensics examination, forensic hypnosis, and medicolegal death investigations, for example. In recent years, particularly with many of the crime lab positions, the trend has been to hire civilians with strong scientific backgrounds. According to the U.S. Bureau of Labor Statistics, employment for forensic science technicians is expected to increase by 27 percent or more through 2014.

Forensic Education and Training

Most, if not all, forensic scientists and experts possess bachelor's, master's, doctoral, or professional degrees in their disciplines, including chemistry, biology, anthropology, psychology, law, and medicine, for example. Obtaining a degree in forensic science was rare for a long time. With the rise in popularity in the field, increasingly more courses and degree programs in the forensic sciences are being established at two-year colleges, four-year colleges, and universities across the United States.

Whether forensic experts work within law enforcement or other occupations, they acquire their skills and abilities through specialized training beyond that required of their basic profession. Much of this training is provided on the job. For example, entry-level forensic scientists in crime labs generally work under the supervision and guidance of experienced staff members for two to three or more years, depending on the discipline, before they handle cases on their own.

Many forensic medical experts and academicians who perform forensic consulting tasks obtain their training by earning degrees or becoming certified in their particular forensic field. For example, forensic anthropologists are trained in anthropology at the university level, with qualifications that range from a bachelor's degree in anthropology to a doctoral degree in physical anthropology to experience with assisting reputable forensic anthropologists with their casework. They may fulfill additional requirements by studying for and passing written and practical exams to earn certification from the American Board of Forensic Anthropology.

Continuing education plays an important part in the continued development of individuals' professions. Throughout their careers, forensic scientists are involved in independent study and networking with colleagues to increase their knowledge and improve their skills. They also enroll in courses, attend workshops and seminars, and participate in professional meetings and conferences.

In This Book

In *Career Opportunities in Forensic Science*, you will learn about 82 career options that are available in the forensics field. This book contains profiles of occupations found in crime scene investigations, criminal investigations, criminalistics, medicolegal death investigations, art and multimedia, health and medicine, the natural sciences, math and computer science, engineering and construction, the behavioral sciences, language and speech, business, jurisprudence, and education and research.

Most of the job profiles in this book cover different forensic experts. Many of them may be unfamiliar to you, such as forensic sculptors, forensic nurses, forensic architects, forensic hypnotists, forensic economists, forensic entomologists, and forensic chiropractic examiners. Other occupational profiles describe occupations that support forensic scientists or work closely with these professionals. As you read about the different opportunities that are available in forensic science, you just may find one or several that interest you.

A Note to High School Students

Now is the time to start preparing for your future career, whether it is in forensic science or another area that interests you. While you are in high school, take courses that can help you succeed in college. For any college program, you need a foundation in English, mathematics, science, history, and social science. If you are planning to major in forensic science, or in a science or engineering discipline, it would be a good idea to take as many science and math classes as you can to help you handle a college curriculum.

Other courses that can help you meet the challenges of college include computer, public speaking, and foreign language classes. Also be sure to develop your writing, critical thinking, and problem-solving skills, which will be essential to performing well in college as well as in your future jobs.

You can start getting an idea of what lies ahead in college by checking out various college catalogs. (School and public libraries usually carry catalogs of different colleges and universities.) These catalogs describe the school enrollment process, the different academic departments and majors, and campus life.

Also be sure to talk with your high school counselor or teachers. Let them know about your interest in going to college and perhaps pursuing a career in the forensic sciences. They can help you choose appropriate courses, as well as advise you on the different college and career options that are available.

Start Exploring Your Options

Career Opportunities in Forensic Science provides you with basic information about 82 professions. When you come across occupations that look intriguing, take the time to learn more about them. The references mentioned throughout the book and in the appendixes can help you further research careers that interest you. In addition, here are a few other things you might do to explore a profession or field in more depth:

- read books about the profession or field
- read professional and trade magazines, journals, newspapers, and other print and online periodicals

- visit Web sites of professional societies, trade associations, businesses, and other organizations related to your desired occupation
- talk with professionals who work in those jobs that interest you
- visit settings where professionals work, if possible
- enroll in courses related to the profession
- browse through career resources that are available at libraries and career centers
- obtain part-time, seasonal, volunteer, or internship positions at forensic labs, law enforcement agencies, law firms, courts, or other organizations

As you explore various occupations, you will discover the kind of careers you might like—and will not like. You will also be gaining valuable knowledge and experience. Furthermore, you will be building a network of contacts who may be able to help with your next steps—obtaining further education and training, as well as future jobs.

Remember, only you can make your career goals and dreams come true. Go for it!

ACKNOWLEDGMENTS

We could not have done this book without the help of many people who took the time out of their busy schedules to help us. We would especially like to thank the following individuals:

Suzanne Baldon, M.A. (Anthropology), Sociology and Anthropology Department, University of Texas at Arlington; Hayden B. Baldwin, Director, Forensic Enterprises, Inc. (http://www.feinc.net); Kathleen Bergeron, HEB Engineers (North Conway, New Hampshire); Michael Bloomenfeld, The Art Engineering Company (Menlo Park, California); Phil Breuser, Professional Meteorologist; Vaughn M. Bryant, Director, Palynology Laboratory, Department of Anthropology, Texas A&M University.

Nancy Clark, C.T.P.E., Forensic Specialist, Downey Police Department (Downey, California); Melissa Connor, Ph.D., Director, Forensic Science Program, Nebraska Wesleyan University (Lincoln, Nebraska); Dr. Owen Davis, Department of Geosciences, University of Arizona (Tucson, Arizona); Craig De Wilde, Ph.D., School of Music, Conservatorium, Monash University (Melbourne, Australia); Timothy S. Duerr, Forensic Scientist, Miami Valley Regional Crime Laboratory (Dayton, Ohio).

Gerald Eskelin, Ph.D., Forensic Musicologist; Nadine M. Filipiak, M.S., Director, Communications, American Society for Clinical Pathology; Emalee G. Flaherty, M.D., Medical Director, Protective Service Team, Children's Memorial Hospital and Associate Professor of Pediatrics, Northwestern Feinberg School of Medicine (Chicago); Trooper Sarah Foster, Forensic Artist, Michigan State Police Detroit Post (Detroit, Michigan); John Fudenberg, Assistant Coroner, Clark County (Las Vegas, Nevada).

Susan J. Garcia, C.L.P.E., President of Southern California Association of Fingerprint Officers; Dr. Malcolm Getz, Department of Economics and Business Administration, Vanderbilt University (Nashville, Tennessee); Ben Gibson, D.D.S., M.A., Executive Director, American Society of Forensic Odontology; Fred Ginsburg, C.A.S., C.F.V., Ph.D., Executive Director, National Association of Forensic Video; Richard A. Gould, Ph.D., Professor of Anthropology, Brown University (Providence, Rhode Island) and Director and Team Leader, Forensic Archaeology Recovery; David Grimes, Professional Land Surveyor, Grimes Surveying and Mapping, Inc. (Los Angeles and Ventura, California).

Robert A. Hayes, C.P.G., President and Principal Forensic Geologist, GeoForensics, Inc. (Williamston, Michigan);

Richard W. Hurst, Ph.D., Professor of Geology and Geochemistry, CSU, Los Angeles and President, Hurst and Associates, Inc. (Thousand Oaks, California); Gretchen D. Jones, Ph.D., USDA Agriculture Research Service, Areawide Pest Management Research Unit.

John P. Kenney, D.D.S., M.S., D-ABFO, President, American Board of Forensic Odontology 2006–07 and Deputy Coroner/Director Identification Services, Coroner's Office, DuPage County, Illinois; Judy LaDuc, B.S., HTL (ASCP); Joseph T. Latta, Executive Director, International Association for Property and Evidence, Inc.; Joyce A. Lauterbach; Robert A. Leonard, Ph.D., Professor of Linguistics and Director of the Forensic Linguistics Project, Hofstra University (Long Island, New York); Ed Lum; Leo Limuaco, P.A. (ASCP); Deborah Lowen, M.D., Medical Director, Children's Justice Center, Pediatric Residency Program Director, OU College of Medicine—Tulsa (Tulsa, Oklahoma).

Mona Lisa R. Maynard, International Association for Identification Tenprint Certification Board Chairperson; Brady W. Mills, Supervising Forensic Scientist, DNA, Texas DPS Austin Crime Lab; Ann C. Morland, Forensic Facial Reconstruction Specialist and Director of the Academy of Forensic Facial Reconstruction (Millbrook, Alabama); Stephen Nawrocki, Ph.D., DABFA, University of Indianapolis Archaeology and Forensics Laboratory Services; James O'Donnell, Pharm.D., M.S., FCP, ABCP, FACN, CNS, Associate Professor of Pharmacology, Rush Medical College (Chicago) and Private Consultant, Pharmaconsultant Inc. (http://www.pharmaconsultantinc.com).

Thomas J. Owen, Owl Investigations, Inc. (Colonia, New Jersey); Carrie Stuart Parks, Forensic Artist, Stuart Parks Forensic Associates (http://www.stuartparks.com); Ioana G. Petrisor, Ph.D., Managing Editor, *Environmental Forensics Journal*; Laura Pettler, Director, Carolina Forensics (Waxhaw, North Carolina); Gene Poole, D.C.; Norman Reeves, BPA Consulting (Tucson, Arizona); Howard C. Rile Jr., Forensic Document Examiner; Randall Robbins, President, Association of Forensic Quality Assurance Managers.

Ervin B. Shaw, M.D., Pathology Associates of Lexington, P.A. (http://www.palpath.com); Dr. Gary Skoog, President, National Association of Forensic Economics 2007–08 and President, Legal Econometrics, Inc.; Suzanne E. Smith, Audit Program Manager, Quality Assurance and Training Unit; Sergeant Daniel Sollitti, Forensic Artist, Jersey City (New Jersey) Police Department; David Sylvester, Deputy

Chief Scientist, National Forensic Science Technology Center; Richard Tesoriero, D.C.

Cathy Valceschini, President, California State Coroner's Association, Chief Deputy Coroner, Nevada County Sheriff's Office; Lloyd B. Ward, Barnwell County Coroner and President, South Carolina Coroner's Association; Dr. Joseph Warren; Earl Wells, Laboratory Director, South Carolina Law Enforcement Division Forensic Services Laboratory; Stephen Wistar, Certified Consulting Meteorologist, Accu-Weather (State College, Pennsylvania).

We also want to express our gratitude to the editorial and production staff at Ferguson Publishing, and in particular our editor James Chambers for believing in us. Thank you, Jim!

HOW TO USE THIS BOOK

In *Career Opportunities in Forensic Science*, you will learn about 82 occupations that are available in this field. The majority of these job profiles are about various forensic scientists and forensic consultants. Some profiles are about professions that work very closely with forensic specialists.

Career Opportunities in Forensic Science provides basic information about each of the 82 occupations. You will read about what the occupations are like and which job requirements are needed. You will also get a general idea of the salaries, job markets, and advancement prospects for each occupation.

Sources of Information

The information presented in *Career Opportunities in Forensic Science* comes from a variety of sources—forensic scientists, forensic experts, educators, professional societies, trade associations, government agencies, and others. In addition, books and periodicals related to the different occupations were read by the authors along with research reports, pamphlets, and other materials created by professionals, professional associations, federal agencies, businesses, and others. Job descriptions, work guidelines, and other work-related materials for the different occupations were also studied by the authors.

The World Wide Web was also a valuable information source. The authors visited a wide range of Web sites to learn about each of the occupations that are described in this book. These Web sites included academic departments, societies, government agencies, forensic consulting firms, and online periodicals, among others.

How This Book Is Organized

Career Opportunities in Forensic Sciences is designed to be easy to use and read. Altogether there are 82 job profiles in 14 sections. A section may have as few as two profiles or as many as 10 profiles, and the profiles are usually two or three pages long. All profiles follow the same format so that you may read the profiles or sections in whatever order you prefer.

Section one of this book covers careers involving crime scene investigation and criminal investigation. Sections two and three discuss forensic scientists who work in the crime lab. Section four describes career options in the coroner's (or medical examiner's) office. Sections five through 12 cover various forensic examiners in a wide range of disciplines, including art, medicine, geology, business, psychol-

ogy, language, and statistics, among others. The final two sections describe a few career options in jurisprudence and education.

The Job Profiles

Each of the 82 profiles starts with the *Career Profile*—a summary of the job's major duties, salary, job outlook, and opportunities for promotion. It also sums up general requirements and special skills needed for the job, as well as personality traits that successful professionals may share. The *Career Ladder* section is a visual presentation of a typical career path.

The rest of each occupational profile is divided into the following parts:

- The "Position Description" describes what an occupation is and its major responsibilities and duties.
- "Salaries" presents a general range of the wages that professionals may earn.
- "Employment Prospects" provides a general survey of the job market for an occupation.
- "Advancement Prospects" discusses some options in which individuals may advance in their careers.
- "Education and Training" describes the type of education and training that may be required to enter a profession.
- "Special Requirements" covers any professional license, certification, or registration that may be required for an occupation.
- "Experience, Skills, and Personality Traits" generally covers the job requirements needed for entry-level positions. It also describes some basic employability skills that employers expect job candidates to have. In addition, this part describes some personality traits that successful professionals have in common.
- "Unions and Associations" provides the names of some professional associations and labor unions that professionals are eligible to join.
- "Tips for Entry" offers general advice for gaining work experience, improving employability, and finding jobs. It also gives suggestions for finding more information on the World Wide Web.

Additional Resources

At the end of the book are four appendixes that provide additional resources for the occupations described in *Career Opportunities in Forensic Sciences*. Appendix I provides

Web resources for you to learn about educational programs for some of the professions described in this book. Appendix II is a list of some professional certification programs for the different occupations profiled in this book. Appendix III presents contact information for professional unions and associations that were mentioned in this book. In Appendix IV, you will find a listing of resources on the World Wide Web that can help you learn more about the various occupations in this book.

In addition, there is a glossary that defines some of the terms used in this book. Furthermore, you will find a bibliography that lists titles of periodicals and books to help you learn more about the professions that interest you.

The World Wide Web

Throughout *Career Opportunities in Forensic Science*, Web site addresses for online resources are provided so that you can learn more on your own. All the Web sites were accessible as this book was being written. Keep in mind that Web site owners may change Web site addresses, remove the web pages to which you have been referred, or shut down their Web sites completely. Should you come across a URL that is unavailable, you may still be able to find the Web site by entering its title or the name of the organization or individual into a search engine.

This Books Is Yours

Career Opportunities in Forensic Science is your reference book. Use it to read about jobs you have often wondered about. Use it to learn about professions in the forensic science world that you never knew existed. Use it to start your search for the career of your dreams.

Good luck!

CRIME SCENE AND CRIMINAL INVESTIGATION PERSONNEL

CRIME SCENE INVESTIGATOR (CSI)

CAREER PROFILE

Duties: Collect and process physical evidence from crime scenes; may provide expert witness testimony; perform other duties as required

Alternate Title(s): Crime Scene Technician, Evidence Technician, Forensic Investigator, Crime Scene Examiner

Salary Range: $20,000 to $50,000+

Employment Prospects: Fair

Advancement Prospects: Poor for civilian employees

Prerequisites:

Education or Training—Requirements vary with the different agencies

Experience—Requirements vary for civilian and law enforcement CSI positions; previous crime scene experience preferred

Special Skills and Personality Traits—Interpersonal, teamwork, communication, writing, and self-management skills; detail-oriented, observant, meticulous, objective, honest, and ethical

Special Requirements—Peace officer certificate may be required

CAREER LADDER

```
┌─────────────────────────────────────┐
│  Senior Crime Scene Investigator     │
└─────────────────────────────────────┘

┌─────────────────────────────────────┐
│     Crime Scene Investigator         │
└─────────────────────────────────────┘

┌─────────────────────────────────────┐
│            Trainee                   │
└─────────────────────────────────────┘
```

Position Description

Wherever crimes are committed, various types of physical evidence—such as bloodstains, hair strands, bullets, fiber, fingerprints, glass fragments, and documents—are left behind. It is crucial that all evidence is properly handled as soon as possible after the crime occurred. The evidence must be categorized, inventoried, and collected for further analysis. The crime scene technicians known as Crime Scene Investigators (CSIs) do this work. These forensic specialists are involved with the crime scene investigation of burglaries, robberies, homicides, assaults, arson, and all other types of crime. CSIs might also collect evidence at autopsies and at non-crime scenes such as serious car accidents.

CSIs are among the first professionals to arrive at the scene of a crime. A crime scene may encompass several locations including a suspect's or victim's home or place of work, or any place where a crime's evidence can be found. A bullet that lodged in a passing vehicle may travel miles away from where the firearm was discharged. It is still part of the crime scene.

Wherever they are assigned to gather evidence, CSIs follow specific procedures that involve three basic stages of crime scene processing. The first stage is scene recognition. CSIs walk through and look at a crime scene to establish the area's extent and which items in the area can be used as physical evidence. They observe minute details of an area. They interview law enforcement personnel and the crime victim to determine what happened. They decide which equipment they will need to gather evidence. Whereas they do not perform the analytical work on the evidence, they possess an understanding of how each item of evidence will be analyzed.

The second stage of processing is scene documentation. CSIs take written notes, make sketches, and take photographs of the crime scene as well as of the various items of evidence. They might also take video recordings.

It is important for CSIs to make an accurate record of the appearance and location of everything within the scene before any evidence is moved to the crime lab for further analysis. Furthermore, when a crime case is brought to court, the crime must be accurately reconstructed. The sketches record the location of everything that is used for evidence; photographs taken from various distances and angles, including close-ups of serial numbers or tags, provide information vital to solving the case; and written notes offer facts about the crime scene that are untainted by opinion or judgment.

The third stage of processing is the collection of physical evidence. CSIs gather everything that may be pertinent to identifying both the perpetrator and victim of the crime. This work requires careful attention to detail. They survey the entire area to find everything they can that will serve as evidence. Some evidence is clearly visible, such as weapons, bullet casings, documents, bloodstains, or anything that is out of place. Trace evidence includes smaller items such as hair, tool marks, paint chips, glass fragments, and fibers. Other evidence, such as fingerprints or footprints, is invisible to the eye.

CSIs package evidence in sealed bags or envelopes and deliver them to crime laboratories for analysis and preparation for use in court proceedings. In some law enforcement units, CSIs bring analysis kits or mobile crime labs to the crime scene so that they may test blood samples or gunpowder residue on the spot. They may also fingerprint deceased victims found at the scene of the crime.

Crime Scene Investigators are employees of law enforcement agencies. They may be police officers or civilians. Their background is in science, particularly biology or chemistry. CSIs also undergo intensive on-the-job training to learn crime scene processing, latent fingerprint processing, photography, and other areas of crime scene investigation.

Their duties vary according to where they work, as well as their experience and skill levels. For example, they may be responsible for:

- securing crime scenes with tape, barricades, or police personnel and providing specific areas for spectators, work areas for investigators, and the crime scene itself
- working and cooperating with victims and witnesses
- surveying a scene and reconstructing the events of a crime
- taking accurate measurements of the crime scene to be noted on sketches
- formulating plans of action for processing and surveying crime scenes
- providing expert testimony in court hearings
- leading and informing other crime scene investigators
- training new technicians
- writing detailed reports

- processing film or digital images and maintaining photographic equipment
- communicating with the public about their work by answering their questions, handling complaints, and describing investigative procedures
- giving presentations at community events such as job fairs or crime watch meetings

All CSIs are responsible for keeping up to date with laws, criminal cases, and their agency's regulations. Their work is often physically demanding, as they must climb, kneel, or stoop to collect evidence. Heavy lifting is frequently required. Consequently, CSIs need to be in excellent physical condition.

They may work either indoors or outdoors to investigate crime scenes. They can be exposed to physical or chemical hazards. In such situations, they may be required to use respirators or other protective equipment.

Law enforcement officers are assigned to their crime scene investigation unit on a full-time or part-time basis, depending on the needs of their agency. In many agencies, law enforcement officers perform this detail in addition to their primary duties as patrol officers, detectives, supervisors, or administrators. Civilian CSIs usually work full time.

CSIs are assigned to rotating shifts, which may include working nights, weekends, and holidays. They are expected to respond to emergency calls on an around-the-clock basis.

Salaries

Salaries for Crime Scene Investigators vary, depending on such factors as their experience, position, education, employer, and geographic location. Law enforcement officers typically earn higher incomes than civilian employees. According to the May 2006 *Occupational Employment Statistics* survey by the U.S. Bureau of Labor Statistics, the estimated annual salary for most police and sheriff patrol officers ranged between $27,310 and $72,450. The International Crime Scene Investigators Association Web site (http://www.icsia.org) reports that the average annual salary for CSIs ranges from $20,000 to more than $50,000.

Law enforcement officers usually earn supplementary compensation for performing special detail duties such as crime scene investigation. Many also receive additional pay for working overtime, weekends, holidays, and late-night shifts.

Employment Prospects

CSIs work in city and state police departments as well as in county sheriffs' offices. Job opportunities are usually better for law enforcement officers than for civilians as many agencies do not hire full-time civilian CSIs. Law enforcement agencies that serve populations of over 25,000 typically hire full-time CSIs.

Openings become available as CSIs retire, transfer to other jobs, or advance to higher positions. Many agencies require that law enforcement officers commit a minimum number of years when they are chosen for crime scene duty.

Advancement Prospects

Within the crime scene unit, CSIs may advance to the position of unit commander.

Law enforcement officers have more advancement opportunities than civilian employees. Officers can develop a career according to their interests and ambitions. They can rise through the ranks as detectives, sergeants, lieutenants, and so on, up to chief of police. They can also seek positions in other special details that interest them, such as their agency's air support unit, bomb squad, SWAT team, or K9 unit. In addition, they can pursue supervisory and managerial positions. In some agencies, officers in higher administrative positions are limited in their ability to volunteer for special details.

Education and Training

Educational requirements vary with the different law enforcement agencies. Some agencies require candidates to have only a high school diploma or general equivalency diploma, while others prefer to hire applicants with an associate or bachelor's degree in law enforcement, criminal justice, or another related discipline.

Many colleges and universities offer degree or certificate programs in crime scene investigation, including online and distance learning programs. Some programs require their students to successfully complete an internship or apprenticeship in which they gain practical experience in crime scene investigations.

Novice CSIs typically receive on-the-job training, in which they work under the supervision and guidance of experienced CSIs. Many agencies also provide formal classroom training in crime scene response, evidence collection, latent fingerprint processing, forensic photography, blood splatter interpretation, and arson investigation, among other areas.

Throughout their careers, CSIs enroll in courses, workshops, seminars, and other educational and training programs to update their skills and increase their knowledge in their field.

Special Requirements

In agencies in which CSIs are law enforcement officers, applicants must possess a basic peace officer standards and training certificate. These agencies may hire candidates without a certificate on the condition they complete the necessary law enforcement academy program to obtain the certificate.

Law enforcement officers must successfully complete annual training to maintain their certification.

Experience, Special Skills, and Personality Traits

Qualifications vary for civilian and law enforcement CSI positions. In general, applicants should have some experience working with crime scenes. Law enforcement officers are usually eligible to apply for their agency's crime scene detail after meeting the minimum requirement for working patrol duty. (Many agencies have a one- to five-year minimum requirement.)

CSIs must be able to work well with team members, law enforcement officers, and others. Hence, they need excellent interpersonal, teamwork, and communication skills. They also must have strong writing skills as well as effective self-management skills such as the ability to work independently, understand and follow instructions, handle stressful situations, and prioritize multiple tasks.

Successful CSIs share similar personality traits, including being detail-oriented, observant, meticulous, objective, honest, and ethical. They also have the state of mind to handle highly unpleasant and shocking situations.

Unions and Associations

Many CSIs belong to professional associations that serve the specific interests of their profession. Three such organizations at the national level are the International Crime Scene Investigators Association, the International Association for Identification, and the Association for Crime Scene Reconstruction. (For contact information, see Appendix III.) By joining societies, CSIs can take advantage of networking opportunities, professional publications, training programs, certification, and other professional services and resources.

Some CSIs belong to a union that represents them in contract negotiations with their employers for better terms regarding pay, benefits, and working conditions.

Tips for Entry

1. To learn more about the crime scene investigation field, read books about the subject and talk with CSIs about their work.
2. Take a basic course in photography. Having fundamental photography skills may improve your chances of obtaining a CSI job.
3. To enhance their employability as well as advancement opportunities, CSIs might obtain professional certification from recognized organizations. For some certification programs, see Appendix II.
4. Contact agencies for which you wish to work for current information about their qualifications for CSIs, selection process, and job vacancies.
5. Use the Internet to learn more about CSIs and their work. You might start by visiting the International Crime Scene Investigators Association Web site at http://www.icsia.org. For more links, see Appendix IV.

CRIME SCENE SUPERVISOR

Duties: Oversee the collection and processing of physical evidence at crime scenes; supervise crime scene technicians; perform other duties as required

Alternate Title(s): None

Salary Range: $40,000 to $104,000

Employment Prospects: Poor

Advancement Prospects: Poor

Prerequisites:

Education or Training—Requirements vary with the different agencies

Experience—Two or more years of work experience as crime scene technicians; supervisory experience preferred

Special Skills and Personality Traits—Leadership, teamwork, interpersonal, communication, organizational, problem-solving, presentation, and writing skills; courteous, fair, honest, respectful, dependable, calm, and encouraging

Special Requirements—Peace officer certificate may be required

---

Crime Scene Unit Manager

Crime Scene Supervisor

Crime Scene Investigator

Position Description

Investigating crime scenes is exacting, time consuming, and detailed work. Several crime scene investigators may work on categorizing, collecting, and documenting the physical evidence—fingerprints, bloodstains, bullets, tool marks, fiber, glass fragments, bodily fluids, and so on. To ensure the integrity and quality of their work, they are overseen and monitored by Crime Scene Supervisors. These professionals supervise at such crime scenes as murders, burglaries, robberies, arson, terrorist incidents, and others. They may also direct the collection and processing of evidence at accident scenes. Crime Scene Supervisors exercise their ability to make independent decisions and utilize common sense to provide leadership to their staff, plan their activities, and check their job performance.

Local and state law enforcement agencies are mostly responsible for crime scene investigations. Crime Scene Supervisors may be law enforcement officers or civilian employees. They report directly to their superiors within their law enforcement agency through work reviews and results summaries.

These men and women possess more expertise than the technicians that work under them. They are knowledgeable about the techniques of crime scene investigations, related technologies, and new trends in their field. They understand every process of investigation, and know all the ways to search for evidence. In addition, Crime Scene Supervisors stay current with all laws and law enforcement practices, particularly the procedures used by their local law enforcement agency. They are similar to supervisors in other vocations in that they are knowledgeable about such principles of supervision as maintaining budgets, tracking employee performance, planning work schedules, and establishing goals. They also serve as a resource for instruction and training for their subordinates.

Crime Scene Supervisors generally work alongside their staff to process crime scenes. They fulfill the same functions as the crime scene technicians that they oversee. Supervisors visually inspect the scene to determine what transpired during the commission of the crime and what items at the scene may be used as evidence to solve the crime. They write detailed notes about all their observations. They take photographs of the crime scene in general, shots of individual items of evidence, and close-ups of fingerprints, powders, or fibers. They make sketches of the scene to indicate the location of each item, including accurate measurements and diagrams. They lift fingerprints and make casts of impressions from shoes or vehicle tires. They might also conduct field tests of gunpowder residue, drugs, and other substances. These supervisors gather evidence in the proper fashion for delivery to the crime lab for analysis.

As unit leaders, Crime Scene Supervisors provide guidance and direction to their team members. It is their job to establish and maintain solid working relationships within their unit. Supervisors also instruct and provide technical knowledge to their subordinates. They perform a variety of supervisory duties: They plan work schedules and assign duties to their team members. They monitor their employees' performance to make sure that they follow correct procedures and safety standards; for example they review documents and photographs that their subordinates produce. They perform employee evaluations on a regular basis, as well as prepare and submit clearly written employee evaluations and monthly reports of their unit's activities.

Crime Scene Supervisors perform various other duties, such as:

- testify in court as expert witnesses
- inspect, maintain, and repair equipment in compliance with safety standards and official regulations
- maintain an adequate supply of all needed materials
- develop or assist in the development of new investigative techniques
- oversee darkroom activity and review the production of photography
- create composite drawings of suspects
- manage unit payrolls
- help with budget planning
- assist in the hiring of subordinate staff
- receive and take action on complaints from the public

Crime Scene Supervisors are responsible for keeping up to date with developments in their field by taking courses and attending training seminars as well as reading publications.

These professionals maintain contact with a wide variety of people every day, including subordinates, law enforcement officers, governmental employees, and the general public, among others.

Crime Scene Supervisors spend much of their time working in offices, but also work at indoor or outdoor crime scenes. They need to be in good physical condition to withstand the demands on their bodies from climbing, stooping, or kneeling as well as lifting heavy weights on occasion. They may be exposed to hazardous chemicals, bodily fluids, or other substances and consequently may be required to use respirators or other protective gear.

Crime Scene Supervisors put in 40 hours per week, but are available for service at all hours and every day of the year. They may be assigned to work specific shifts.

Salaries

Salaries for Crime Scene Supervisors vary, depending on such factors as their experience, education, employer, and geographic location. Law enforcement officers typically earn higher incomes than civilian employees. Formal salary information for this occupation is unavailable. One expert in the field estimates that the annual salary range for Crime Scene Supervisors is between $40,000 and $100,000. According to the May 2006 *Occupational Employment Statistics* survey by the U.S. Bureau of Labor Statistics, the estimated annual salary for most first-line supervisors of police and detectives ranged between $41,260 and $104,410.

Employment Prospects

Crime Scene Supervisors work for local and state law enforcement agencies. There are usually more job opportunities for law enforcement officers than for civilians. Openings become available as individuals advance to higher positions, transfer to other jobs, or retire.

Advancement Prospects

Supervisors may be promoted to manage crime scene units. They may also pursue higher management positions in forensic sections of law enforcement agencies. However, these types of opportunities are usually limited.

Unlike civilian employees, law enforcement officers have more advancement opportunities. They can rise through the ranks as detectives, sergeants, and so on, up to police chiefs. They can also seek positions in other law enforcement special details that interest them. They can also pursue supervisory and managerial positions within their agency.

Education and Training

Educational requirements vary with the different law enforcement agencies. Some agencies require that candidates have at least a high school diploma or high school equivalency diploma, while others require that applicants have a minimum number of hours of college course work. Some agencies prefer to hire applicants who possess a bachelor's degree in forensic science, biology, biochemistry, chemistry, or another related field.

Some agencies also like candidates to have completed training programs in crime-scene processing and evidence collection. They may hire strong candidates without this qualification if they successfully complete appropriate training programs within a certain time frame.

Special Requirements

In agencies in which Crime Scene Supervisors are law enforcement officers, applicants must possess a basic peace officer standards and training certificate. These agencies may hire candidates without a certificate on the condition they complete the necessary law enforcement academy program to obtain the certificate.

Law enforcement officers must successfully complete annual training to maintain their certification.

Experience, Special Skills, and Personality Traits

Applicants need two to five years of work experience as a crime scene technician, depending on the requirements of a law enforcement agency. Many employers also prefer that candidates have some supervisory experience.

To perform well at their job, Crime Scene Supervisors must have strong leadership, teamwork, interpersonal, and communication skills. They also need effective organizational, problem-solving, presentation, and writing skills. Being courteous, fair, honest, respectful, dependable, calm, and encouraging are some personality traits that successful Crime Scene Supervisors have in common.

Unions and Associations

Many Crime Scene Supervisors belong to professional associations to take advantage of networking opportunities, professional publications, training programs, certification, and other professional services and resources. Three national societies that serve the interests of crime scene personnel are the International Crime Scene Investigators Association, the International Association for Identification, and the Association for Crime Scene Reconstruction. For contact information, see Appendix III.

Tips for Entry

1. Many agencies prefer to hire candidates who have completed course work in photography, criminalistics, and physical science.
2. To enhance their employability, some individuals obtain professional certification in crime investigation from recognized organizations such as the International Association for Identification. For a list of some certification programs, see Appendix II.
3. Learn more about the field of crime scene investigation on the Internet. One Web site you might visit is Crime Scene Investigation at http://www.crime-scene-investigator.net. For more links, see Appendix IV.

PATROL OFFICER

CAREER PROFILE

Duties: Enforce laws, preserve peace, protect life and property, investigate criminal incidents, apprehend criminals, provide community service, and perform other duties as required

Alternate Title(s): Police Officer, Deputy Sheriff, State Trooper, or other title that reflects a particular job

Salary Range: $27,000 to $72,000

Employment Prospects: Good

Advancement Prospects: Excellent

Prerequisites:

Education or Training—Educational requirements vary with different agencies; police academy training; field training

Experience—Prior experience may not be necessary

Special Skills and Personality Traits—Observational, problem-solving, critical thinking, teamwork, math, writing, computer, interpersonal, communication, and self-management skills; honest, trustworthy, dedicated, dependable, levelheaded, courteous, tactful, friendly, and composed

Special Requirements—Peace officer certificate required; meet certain requirements; hold a valid driver's license

CAREER LADDER

```
┌─────────────────────────────────────┐
│  Special Assignments, Detective, or  │
│              Sergeant                │
└─────────────────────────────────────┘

┌─────────────────────────────────────┐
│           Patrol Officer             │
└─────────────────────────────────────┘

┌─────────────────────────────────────┐
│              Recruit                 │
└─────────────────────────────────────┘
```

Position Description

Patrol Officers are usually the first law enforcement officers to arrive at a crime scene, a location where a burglary, robbery, assault, murder, or another criminal incident has taken place. They may have happened upon an incident as it was occurring, or they may have responded to a call from a citizen, a police dispatcher, or another law enforcement officer. If possible, they apprehend and arrest criminal suspects. It is also their duty to prevent the destruction of physical evidence at the crime scene.

Patrol Officers are uniformed officers who work for local, state, and federal law enforcement agencies. They are police officers, sheriff's deputies, state troopers, conservation officers (also known as park rangers), and other law enforcement officers.

Patrol Officers make up the basic units of their agencies. They are assigned beats, or geographical areas, within their agency's jurisdiction that may include neighborhoods, business sections, schools, airports, rural areas, highways, shorelines, harbors, parks, or remote locations. It is their job to enforce laws, preserve the peace, protect life and property, investigate crime, apprehend criminals, and provide community service within their beats. Many of them are also responsible for enforcing the traffic laws within their jurisdiction. They make regular rounds throughout their work shift, while keeping an eye open for suspicious activities and public hazards as well as responding to citizens' requests for help. These officers may work alone or with partners, and may cover their beats on foot, in marked vehicles, or on bicycles, motorcycles, horses, or boats.

As first responders at crime scenes, Patrol Officers follow certain procedures while they deal with a number of things. They always assume that criminal activity is still taking place; hence, officers carefully assess the area as they enter it. They note who is there, how it looks, and what is happening, as well as watch for persons or vehicles leaving the area and for potential physical evidence. Their first priority is the safety and physical well being of themselves, other officers, and people who are in and around the crime scene. They identify and control any dangerous persons and situations, such as gas leaks, bombs, or hazardous wastes, and inform all people at the scene. Patrol Officers contact appropriate personnel for assistance or backup. These officers also assess victims' medical needs and call for medical assistance if required.

First responders determine what is the primary scene of a crime as well as secondary sites, such as vehicles or other locations where the crime took place. In addition, they physically secure the primary and secondary crime scenes as well as exit and entry paths to these areas with flags, traffic cones, barrier tape, or other means to ensure that bystanders do not access the area and destroy evidence. These officers also separate suspects, victims, and witnesses so that they cannot talk amongst each other. The first responders obtain identifications and take initial statements from them.

Along with interviewing bystanders, first responders are responsible for documenting the crime scene. They write notes about who called for help, who was at the scene, the location of people and objects, how things looked, how things were moved, and environmental conditions, among other details. When the appropriate authorities appear on the scene, Patrol Officers release the crime scene to those authorities as well as brief them about the information that the first responders have acquired. The authorities may request that the Patrol Officers stay on to assist with controlling or processing the crime scene.

Patrol Officers may be assigned to perform other duties besides patrol duty, depending on their experience, skills, and interests as well as their agency's needs. For example, they may be assigned to process crime scenes, investigate traffic accidents, assist in criminal investigations, guard prisoners, escort government officials or other very important people, direct traffic at special events, or present crime prevention workshops. Patrol Officers also perform duties that are specific to their agency's mission and jurisdiction. For example, conservation officers may be responsible for issuing hunting licenses, inspecting game farms, and responding to public complaints about wildlife in urban areas.

Patrol Officers keep a daily logbook of their activities and complete accurate reports of all criminal and noncriminal incidents to which they responded. They may be called upon to testify at court trials. Occasionally, Patrol Officers work on assignments with law enforcement officers from other local, state, or federal jurisdictions.

Patrol Officers normally work rotating shifts that may include nights, weekends, and holidays. They are on call 24 hours a day, every day of the year.

Salaries

Salaries for Patrol Officers vary, depending on such factors as their experience, rank, education, employer, and geographic location. According to the May 2006 *Occupational Employment Statistics* (OES) survey by the U.S. Bureau of Labor Statistics (BLS), the estimated annual salary for most police and sheriff patrol officers ranged between $27,310 and $72,450.

Patrol Officers may earn additional compensation for working overtime, holidays, and late-night shifts. Many also receive extra pay for working special details, such as the bomb squad, aviation unit, or SWAT team.

Employment Prospects

Employers of Patrol Officers include city police departments, county sheriffs' offices, state police offices, and state fish and game departments, as well as special police departments such as campus police departments and airport police departments. At the federal level, Patrol Officers are employed by the U.S. Capitol, National Park Service, Federal Protective Service, Bureau of Indian Affairs, and Department of Veterans Affairs, among others. The BLS reported in its May 2006 OES survey that an estimated 624,380 police and sheriff's Patrol Officers were employed in the United States. About 85 percent were employed by local governments.

According to the BLS, employment for police officers is expected to increase by 9 to 17 percent through 2014. In addition to job growth, openings will become available as officers retire, transfer to other jobs, or advance to higher positions. Opportunities in any agency can vary from year to year, depending on the availability of funds.

The competition for jobs is particularly keen among federal and state agencies as well as in police departments in affluent communities. Opportunities are usually better in special police departments and in communities where salaries are generally low or the crime rate is high.

Advancement Prospects

Law enforcement officers can advance in any number of ways, depending on their personal interests and ambitions. After serving one or more years of patrol duty, officers can apply for voluntary positions on special details that their agency may offer, such as the bike patrol, the canine unit, the SWAT team, the bomb squad, the aviation unit, or the crime scene investigation unit. They may also pursue a career in criminal investigations, which requires passing a competitive detective exam. Those interested in supervisory or administrative duties can pursue such positions.

In addition, Patrol Officers can rise through the ranks as sergeant, lieutenant, captain, and so on, up to police chief. This usually requires passing competitive exams and reviews as well as obtaining additional education and experience.

Law enforcement officers normally can retire with a pension after serving 20 to 25 years on their force. (Federal agencies usually require law enforcement officers to retire at the age of 57.) Many officers retire and pursue second careers in law enforcement, security, or other fields that interest them.

Education and Training

Educational requirements for law enforcement recruits vary with the different law enforcement agencies. Some agencies require that applicants possess at least a high school or general equivalency diploma. Some agencies hire high school graduates if they also possess a minimum number of college credits in an appropriate field of study. In other agencies, the minimum educational requirement is an associate or bachelor's degree in law enforcement, criminal justice, police science, or another related discipline.

Recruits complete three to six months or more of basic training at a law enforcement academy. They study law, investigative procedures, self-defense, use of firearms, and first aid, among other subjects. Upon successful completion of their training, they are assigned to work under the supervision of field training officers or senior Patrol Officers.

Throughout their careers, law enforcement officers enroll in workshops, seminars, and courses to update their skills and knowledge.

Special Requirements

Local and state law enforcement officers must hold a current peace officer certificate, which is earned upon completing basic training at a law enforcement academy.

Most, if not all, law enforcement agencies require that applicants be U.S. citizens. In addition, they must not have a criminal record, and they must meet age, residency, weight, height, vision, medical, and other requirements. Agencies usually require candidates to possess a valid driver's license.

Experience, Special Skills, and Personality Traits

Many agencies hire candidates without any experience for entry-level positions. Some agencies, however, prefer to hire candidates who have one or more years of law enforcement experience. They may have gained their experience through internships, volunteer work, work-study programs, or employment with law enforcement agencies.

To perform well at their work, Patrol Officers must have excellent observational, problem-solving, critical thinking, and teamwork skills as well as strong math, writing, and computer skills. They also need effective interpersonal and communication skills, as they must be able to work well with colleagues, supervisors, and the general public. Furthermore, their job requires that they have superior self-management skills, such as the ability to work independently, handle stressful situations, prioritize multiple tasks, and understand and follow instructions.

Some personality traits that successful Patrol Officers share include being honest, trustworthy, dedicated, dependable, levelheaded, courteous, tactful, friendly, and composed.

Unions and Associations

Many Patrol Officers join professional associations to take advantage of networking opportunities, educational programs, and other professional services and resources. These societies are available at the local, state, national, and international levels. They can join organizations that serve the general interests of all law enforcement officers such as the American Federation of Police and Concerned Citizens, or the Fraternal Order of Police. Special-interest societies are also available such as the International Association of Women Police, the National Black Police Association, the American Deputy Sheriffs' Association, the National Troopers Coalition, or the North American Wildlife Enforcement Officers Association. For contact information, see Appendix III.

Many law enforcement officers belong to a union that represents them in contract negotiations with their employers for better terms regarding pay, benefits, and working conditions. The union also handles any grievances that officers may have against their employers.

Tips for Entry

1. Are you a high school student? Join a law enforcement Explorer unit if one is available. Check with your local law enforcement agencies.
2. Gain experience by doing volunteer work at a police department or sheriff's office.
3. For information about job vacancies and selection processes, contact a law enforcement agency directly. You may be able to find such information at an agency's Web site.
4. Being proficient in a second language that is common within the community where you wish to work may enhance your employability.
5. Use the Internet to learn more about a law enforcement agency for which you would like to work. Most law enforcement agencies have a presence on the Internet. To find the Web site for an agency where you would like to work, enter its name into a search engine. For some links about the law enforcement field in general, see Appendix IV.

CRIMINAL INVESTIGATOR

CAREER PROFILE

Duties: Enforce local, state, or federal criminal laws; investigate criminal cases; perform other duties as required

Alternate Title(s): Detective, Special Agent; a title that reflects a specific occupation such as FBI Special Agent

Salary Range: $34,000 to $93,000

Employment Prospects: Good

Advancement Prospects: Good

Prerequisites:

Education or Training—Educational requirements vary with every agency; new investigators complete criminal investigation training as well as on-the-job training

Experience—One or more years of law enforcement or criminal investigation experience required

Special Skills and Personality Traits—Analytical, problem-solving, teamwork, interpersonal, crisis management, interviewing, research, writing, and communication skills; calm, perceptive, self-motivated, honest, and trustworthy

Special Requirements—Peace officer certificate may be required; meet certain requirements; hold a valid driver's license

CAREER LADDER

```
┌─────────────────────────────────┐
│   Senior Criminal Investigator   │
└─────────────────────────────────┘

┌─────────────────────────────────┐
│      Criminal Investigator       │
└─────────────────────────────────┘

┌─────────────────────────────────┐
│   Criminal Investigator Trainee  │
└─────────────────────────────────┘
```

Position Description

People sometimes confuse crime scene investigators with Criminal Investigators. Crime scene investigators are responsible for examining crime scenes to gather and process physical evidence that may link suspects to the crime scenes. Criminal Investigators, on the other hand, are responsible for conducting intensive probes into criminal cases and solving them. They find sufficient proof—through witnesses, physical evidence, and other sources—to arrest and prosecute suspects.

These law enforcement officers perform challenging and dangerous work. Some Criminal Investigators are engaged in cases in which criminal laws, such as those pertaining to burglary, robbery, assault, murder, stalking, domestic violence, kidnapping, fraud, arson, vice, narcotics, and terrorism, have been broken. Other investigators work on criminal cases that involve violations of civil rights, environmental, postal, tax, social security, and other laws.

Criminal Investigators work in city police departments, sheriffs' offices, special jurisdiction departments (such as campus and airport police departments), state police departments and attorney generals' offices, and tribal police departments. At the federal level, Criminal Investigators work in numerous agencies, including the Federal Bureau of Investigation, Drug Enforcement Administration, Immigration and Customs Enforcement, U.S. Postal Service, Internal Revenue Service, Social Security Administration, and Environmental Protection Agency. Criminal Investigators are also employed by local, state, and federal wildlife or natural resource conservation agencies.

Some Criminal Investigators work in offices of inspectors general, which are part of local, state, or federal government agencies. These inspectors investigate cases that involve employees who are suspected of violating rules or committing crimes.

Criminal Investigators work on several cases at a time. Regardless of their work setting, they conduct investigations for each case in a similar fashion. They develop plans on how they will conduct their investigations. They gather information about cases by examining crime scenes for facts and evidence. They interview suspects, witnesses, and others for pertinent information regarding their cases. They sometimes interview individuals several times during their investigations. These investigators also review police, crime lab, medical examiner reports, and other relevant reports, records, and files.

Criminal Investigators analyze information and evidence to develop leads for their cases. They verify facts to ensure they have correct and accurate information about their cases. On some cases, they might conduct surveillance on suspects or perform undercover work. They might also serve search warrants to individuals in order to perform a search of their property for specific items that may be proof that a crime has been committed.

When Criminal Investigators are sure they have sufficient evidence that suspects have committed specific crimes, they may arrest suspects or request that the suspects be arrested. Criminal Investigators also assist attorneys in preparing cases for court trials. Investigators may be asked to provide testimony at depositions and trials about their findings.

Criminal Investigators maintain files on all their cases. They keep detailed notes as well as prepare written reports of their findings. They make sure their documents are accurate and precise, as they may be entered as evidence in court trials.

Their job requires them to carry and use firearms in the performance of their duties. They may be assigned to handle a case alone or with a partner. On occasion, Criminal Investigators are assigned to work on cases with other law enforcement agencies. Cases may take several weeks, months, or years to solve. Some cases are never solved.

Criminal Investigators are scheduled to work 40 hours a week but often put in additional hours to complete their duties. They often work nights, weekends, and holidays. Many of them are assigned to rotating shifts. Criminal Investigators are usually on call 24 hours a day.

Investigators may travel to other cities, states, and countries to work on their cases. Federal investigators may be reassigned to other field offices within their agencies, which may be in the United States or in other countries.

Salaries
Salaries for Criminal Investigators vary, depending on such factors as their education, experience, employer, and geographic location. Federal agency employees generally earn more than employees of local and state agencies. According to the May 2006 *Occupational Employment Statistics* survey by the U.S. Bureau of Labor Statistics (BLS), the estimated annual salary for most detectives and Criminal Investigators ranged between $34,480 and $92,590.

Federal investigators earn a salary based on the general schedule (GS), a federal pay schedule that covers many federal employees. Depending on the agency, entry-level investigators may start at the GS-5, GS-7, or GS-9 level. Full-performance, or journey, investigators can progress to either the GS-12 or GS-13 level. In 2007, the annual basic pay rates for law enforcement officers (at the GS-5 to GS-10 levels) ranged from $31,601 to $57,005.

Employment Prospects
Opportunities for Criminal Investigators are available with local, state, federal, and tribal law enforcement agencies, as well as parks, fish and game departments, and other government agencies. Qualified candidates typically outnumber the positions that are vacant. The BLS reports that employment of law enforcement officers is expected to increase by 9 to 17 percent through 2014. In addition to job growth, openings for Criminal Investigators become available as individuals advance to higher positions, transfer to other jobs, or retire. A law enforcement agency may create additional investigator positions to meet growing demands when funding becomes available.

Advancement Prospects
Criminal Investigators can advance in numerous ways. As they gain experience, they can seek assignments of their choice. For example, they can ask for a transfer to a particular office or geographical location, or they can specialize in a particular area of investigations, such as homicide or technology crime.

They can also pursue supervisory, managerial, or executive positions. Those at the local and state levels can rise through the ranks as lieutenants, captains, and so on, up to the police chief's or sheriff's position. Executive-level positions are either appointed by executive bodies or elected by voters.

Education and Training
Educational requirements for Criminal Investigators vary with the different law enforcement agencies. Many local and state agencies require that candidates have some college background or possess a college degree (which may be an associate or a bachelor's degree) in law enforcement, criminal justice, or another related field. At some local and state agencies, the minimum requirement is a high school or general equivalency diploma.

At the federal level, the minimum requirement for entry-level applicants is a bachelor's degree in a field that a federal law enforcement agency prefers. For example, the FBI seeks candidates who hold a degree in law, accounting, computer science, criminal justice, or another related discipline.

New investigators undergo a training program that may last several weeks or months, depending on the law enforcement agency. Local and state trainees usually attend a local law enforcement academy. Many federal agencies send trainees to the Federal Law Enforcement Training Center in Glynco, Georgia.

New Criminal Investigators normally receive on-the-job training while working under the supervision and guidance of experienced investigators.

Throughout their careers, Criminal Investigators enroll in continuing education programs and training programs to update their skills and knowledge.

Special Requirements

Local and state law enforcement officers must hold a current peace officer certificate, which is earned upon completing basic training at a law enforcement academy.

Most, if not all, law enforcement agencies require that applicants be U.S. citizens and that they do not have a criminal record. Applicants must also meet certain vision, weight, and height requirements. Age requirements vary with the different agencies. For example, to apply for most federal positions, an applicant may not be older than 36 years old at the time of their appointment. Agencies usually require candidates to possess a valid driver's license.

Experience, Special Skills, and Personality Traits

Depending on their agency's requirements, police officers, deputy sheriffs, state police, and conservation workers generally must have completed one or more years of patrol duty before they are eligible to apply for a Criminal Investigator, or detective, position.

Requirements vary for the different federal agencies. In general, applicants should have prior experience working in law enforcement, preferably in criminal investigations. Some agencies accept candidates without any law enforcement experience for entry-level positions if they have three years of progressively responsible work experience.

Criminal Investigators need excellent analytical, problem-solving, teamwork, interpersonal, and crisis management skills to be effective at their work. In addition, they need strong interviewing, research, writing, and communication skills. Being calm, perceptive, self-motivated, honest, and trustworthy are some personality traits that successful Criminal Investigators share.

Unions and Associations

Many Criminal Investigators are members of a union that represents them in negotiations with employers for better contractual terms regarding pay, benefits, and working conditions. In addition, the union handles any grievances that officers may have against their employers.

Criminal Investigators are also eligible to join professional associations to take advantage of networking opportunities, continuing education, professional certification, and other professional resources and services. Professional societies are available for officers locally, statewide, nationally, and internationally. Some national societies that serve the various special interests of Criminal Investigators include:

- American Deputy Sheriffs' Association
- Federal Criminal Investigators Association
- Federal Law Enforcement Officers Association
- Fraternal Order of Police
- High Technology Crime Investigation Association
- International Association of Arson Investigators
- International Association of Women Police
- International Homicide Investigators Association
- National Black Police Association

For contact information, see Appendix III.

Tips for Entry

1. Agencies hire candidates with a clean personal record. Having past arrests, convictions, drug or alcohol problems, financial debts, or terminations may disqualify you for a law enforcement career.
2. While in high school or college, you can gain experience by volunteering or obtaining an internship with a local law enforcement agency.
3. If you are interested in working for a federal agency, contact it directly to learn about specific qualifications, job vacancies, and their application process.
4. A willingness to relocate may enhance your employability.
5. Use the Internet to learn more about criminal investigations. To find relevant Web sites, enter the keywords *criminal investigations* or *criminal investigators* in a search engine. For some links, see Appendix IV.

FIRE INVESTIGATOR

CAREER PROFILE

Duties: Conduct investigations to determine origin and cause of fire incidents; may also conduct arson investigations; perform other duties as required

Alternate Title(s): Arson Investigator, Fire Marshal

Salary Range: $30,000 to $75,000

Employment Prospects: Fair

Advancement Prospects: Good

Prerequisites:

Education or Training—Educational requirements vary; complete employer training programs

Experience—Several years of service as a firefighter or law enforcement officer

Special Skills and Personality Traits—Critical-thinking, problem-solving, interviewing, research, writing, interpersonal, teamwork, and communication skills; honest, trustworthy, dependable, detail-oriented, self-motivated, persistent, and conscientious

Special Requirements— Peace officer certificate may be required

CAREER LADDER

```
┌─────────────────────────────┐
│   Senior Fire Investigator  │
└─────────────────────────────┘

┌─────────────────────────────┐
│      Fire Investigator      │
└─────────────────────────────┘

┌─────────────────────────────┐
│         Firefighter         │
└─────────────────────────────┘
```

Position Description

When fires occur—whether they are structural or wildland fires—professionals known as Fire Investigators are sent out to examine them. It is the job of these investigators to identify the origin and cause of a fire and to seek ways to prevent such a fire from occurring again. These highly trained men and women generally begin their investigations with the premise that a fire started accidentally or naturally. If Fire Investigators determine that it was arson (a fire set deliberately for malicious reasons) or it was due to criminal negligence, the inquiry turns into a criminal investigation.

Most Fire Investigators are public employees who work at the local, state, and federal government levels. They may be employed by fire departments, law enforcement agencies (such as sheriffs' offices), or fire marshals' offices.

The composition of fire investigation teams varies widely across the United States. They may be composed of volunteer firefighters who are trained in fire investigation. Some teams may consist of full-time or part-time Fire Investigators who are cross-trained in firefighting and law enforcement.

These investigators may be sworn peace officers that have the authority to carry firearms, serve warrants, and arrest arson suspects. Other teams may be made up of Fire Investigators, who conduct cause-and-origin investigations, and arson investigators, who concentrate on criminal investigations. In other departments, when Fire Investigators determine that arson or criminal negligence is involved, they release their cases to arson investigators in a law enforcement agency; they provide technical assistance to the arson investigators as needed.

Fires can be started in any number of ways—faulty wiring, gas leaks, cooking mishaps, burning cigarette butts, sparks from campfires, or lightning, for example. Hence, Fire Investigators are well informed in many areas, including the basics of fire behavior, burn patterns, construction of various structures, building materials, electricity, and human behavior, among other areas. They are also knowledgeable about appropriate laws, regulations, and codes. In addition, Fire Investigators are knowledgeable about the techniques of collecting and preserving evidence and ignition sources at fire-incident scenes.

Fire Investigators follow certain protocols and standards as they conduct their investigations. Their job is often complicated by the fact that fire—as well as the task of putting out the fire—can destroy ignition sources, evidence, and other data needed to determine the origin and cause of a fire.

These investigators are responsible for carefully examining the fire scenes to which they are assigned. When they arrive at an incident scene, they talk with the fire commander to gather facts about a fire—what has happened, the current status of the fire, what public safety personnel is at the scene (such as firefighters, emergency medical technicians, police officers, and hazardous materials personnel), safety conditions, issues, and so on.

Fire investigators then inspect the area and adjacent areas to determine the fire's perimeter, fire patterns, and damage. They document the incident scene and evidence thoroughly by writing detailed notes, taking measurements, making sketches, and taking photographs. Some of them also take video recordings.

Their job also involves developing a witness list that includes names of fire personnel, first responders, law enforcement officers, property owners and managers, the persons who reported the fire, occupants, neighbors, and bystanders. Investigators will contact these witnesses at a later time to interview them about their observations.

Fire Investigators are responsible for the collection and preservation of fire debris evidence—metal fragments, charred wood, or accelerant residue, for example. They are also trained to recognize other physical evidence, such as bloodstains, shoe prints, and trace evidence, which they may collect or call the appropriate personnel to collect. Investigators follow specific policies and procedures for processing evidence to prevent its contamination and to establish a proper chain of custody to ensure the integrity of the evidence. They place evidence into proper containers, and label them appropriately and accurately. The evidence is sent to forensic labs to be analyzed. Investigators will review the results to help them determine the cause of a fire.

Their investigations also involve testing sites and materials with proper equipment to determine facts such as burn patterns and flash points (the lowest temperature at which a vapor will ignite). They examine floor plans, architectural or engineering drawings, and other relevant diagrams and drawings related to the incident scene. After completing their analyses, Fire Investigators prepare and submit detailed reports about their findings.

Fire Investigators who are assigned to arson cases are additionally responsible for conducting criminal investigations. These investigators are usually sworn peace officers. Their duty is to find sufficient evidence to link suspects to crime scenes. Arson investigators analyze information from fire reports, police records, crime lab reports, and other documents to develop leads for suspects. They interview suspects and witnesses to obtain pertinent information. They might conduct surveillance or perform undercover work. They prepare accurate and precise notes and records of their cases, which may be entered as evidence at trials.

Because they are law enforcement officers, arson investigators have the authority to carry firearms, serve warrants, and arrest arson suspects. They are also responsible for assisting attorneys in preparing cases for court trial. They may also be asked to provide testimony about their findings at depositions and trials.

Fire Investigators perform other duties, which vary from agency to agency. For example, they may be involved in developing and coordinating fire prevention activities and programs for their communities; providing technical assistance to governmental officials on the interpretation of codes, regulations, and ordinances; reviewing construction plans in regard to compliance with fire safety laws and regulations; or conducting internal investigations of fire department employees who have violated laws. Senior investigators may be responsible for providing supervision and training to staff members.

Fire Investigators work a 40-hour schedule, but they put in additional hours as needed to complete their tasks. They often work nights, weekends, and holidays. Many of them are assigned to rotating shifts. Some investigators are on call 24 hours a day. Their investigations may involve exposure to fire, fire debris, hazardous substances, heavy equipment, and all types of weather conditions.

Salaries

Salaries for Fire Investigators vary, depending on such factors as their experience, education, employer, and geographic location. Investigators in the private sector usually earn higher wages than public service employees. The estimated annual salary for most Fire Investigators ranged from $29,840 to $74,930, according to the May 2006 *Occupational Employment Statistics* (OES) survey by the U.S. Bureau of Labor Statistics (BLS). The annual mean salary was $51,320 for investigators working at the local government level, and $43,560 for those working at the state government level.

Employment Prospects

According to the May 2006 OES survey by the BLS, an estimated 13,360 Fire Investigators were employed in the United States. The majority of them worked in public service at the local government level.

As public service employees, these investigators are hired by local fire and police departments as well as by state and federal agencies such as state fire marshals' offices, the U.S. Forest Service, and the U.S. Bureau of Alcohol, Tobacco, Firearms and Explosives. Fire Investigators also work in the private sector. They are employed by insurance companies, private investigation firms, and nonprofit organizations that are involved in the area of fire service and fire protection. Some Fire Investigators are self-employed as independent contractors.

Opportunities generally become available as Fire Investigators transfer to other jobs, advance to higher positions, or retire.

Advancement Prospects

As Fire Investigators gain experience, they are assigned to more complex cases as well as receive greater responsibilities. Individuals with supervisory and managerial ambitions can pursue such positions, but opportunities are generally limited. In addition, Fire Investigators can pursue careers as trainers or educators. Many Fire Investigators measure success through job satisfaction, higher incomes, and professional recognition. Fire Investigators in fire departments and law enforcement agencies can also advance in rank.

Education and Training

Educational requirements vary with the different employers. Some employers require that applicants hold at least a high school or general equivalency diploma, while others require applicants to have a bachelor's degree in an appropriate field.

Many Fire Investigators possess a bachelor's degree in such diverse fields as criminal justice, fire science, and engineering. While moving up through the ranks at their agency, many of them enroll in fire-investigator training programs on their own time to gain basic knowledge and skills for their future work. These programs are sponsored by colleges, professional associations, such as the National Association of Fire Investigators, and other organizations, such as the National Center for Forensic Science.

Employers typically provide novice investigators with formal and on-the-job training programs. Throughout their careers, Fire Investigators enroll in continuing education programs and training programs on a voluntary basis to update their skills and knowledge.

Special Requirements

Being law enforcement officers, arson investigators must possess a basic peace officer standards and training certificate. Agencies may hire candidates without a certificate on the condition they complete the necessary law enforcement academy program to obtain the certificate. Law enforcement officers must successfully complete annual training to maintain their certification.

Experience, Special Skills, and Personality Traits

Employment requirements vary with the different employers. In general, applicants must complete several years of service as firefighters or law enforcement officers before they are eligible to apply for Fire (or arson) Investigator positions.

To perform effectively at their job, Fire Investigators need strong critical-thinking, problem-solving, interviewing, research, and writing skills. They must also have excellent interpersonal, teamwork, and communication skills, as they must be able to work well with colleagues, officials, public safety officers, and others from diverse backgrounds. Being honest, trustworthy, dependable, detail-oriented, self-motivated, persistent, and conscientious are some personality traits that successful Fire Investigators share.

Unions and Associations

Many Fire Investigators belong to various firefighting and law enforcement societies to take advantage of networking opportunities, training programs, professional certification, and other professional services and resources. Some national associations that serve the particular interests of Fire Investigators include the National Association of Fire Investigators, the International Association of Arson Investigators, and the National Fire Protection Association. For contact information, see Appendix III.

Tips for Entry

1. While in school, volunteer at your local fire department to start gaining valuable experience.
2. Some Fire Investigators obtain professional certification to enhance their employability. For some certification programs, see Appendix II.
3. Employers generally are not interested in hiring applicants who have a police record, have a poor financial history, or have been fired from a job due to poor work performance or an act of violence.
4. Contact prospective employers and ask them about special skills that they are seeking in new employees, such as fluency in a second language. If you have such skills, be sure to mention them on your application or resume.
5. Use the Internet to learn more about fire investigations. You might start by visiting these Web sites: National Association of Fire Investigators, http://www.nafi.org; and interFIRE online, http://www.interfire.org. For more links, see Appendix IV.

FINGERPRINT TECHNICIAN

CAREER PROFILE

Duties: Classify and identify fingerprints; process fingerprints; may collect fingerprints at crime scenes; perform other duties as required

Alternate Title(s): Fingerprint Examiner, Fingerprint Specialist, Fingerprint Identification Expert

Salary Range: $25,000 to $50,000

Employment Prospects: Poor

Advancement Prospects: Fair

Prerequisites:

Education or Training—Educational requirements vary with agencies; fingerprint classification training

Experience—One or more years of general clerical experience, preferably in a law enforcement setting; previous fingerprinting experience preferred

Special Skills and Personality Traits—Interpersonal, teamwork, communication, and self-management skills; observant, perceptive, precise, cooperative, and courteous

Special Requirements—Peace officer certificate may be required

CAREER LADDER

Senior Fingerprint Technician

Fingerprint Technician

Fingerprint Technician (Entry-Level)

Position Description

Every human being has one characteristic that distinguishes himself or herself from every other human being—fingerprints. No two fingerprints are identical. The patterns of ridges and grooves on our finger pads that make us unique can be used to identify us. In the realm of forensic science, this is a proven factor in solving crimes of all descriptions. Forensic professionals who study, identify, and classify fingerprints are called Fingerprint Technicians.

In local and state law enforcement agencies, Fingerprint Technicians work within fingerprint identification units. They may be law enforcement officers or civilian employees.

These identification technicians work with fingerprints found at crime scenes as well as those submitted by suspects as they are arrested and booked. Fingerprint Technicians take fingerprints from individuals by applying ink to their fingers and impressing them upon cards that are filed or transferred to fingerprint databases. Cards that include all of a person's fingerprints are known as ten cards. These technicians also take fingerprints of law-abiding individuals for employment or other purposes.

People have known about the uniqueness of fingerprints for many centuries, but it has only been within the last century that they have been thoroughly classified. There are three basic types of fingerprint patterns: arches, loops, and whorls. Each of these patterns can be further classified in subgroups. Within each subgroup, fingerprints vary from one another. Millions of fingerprints are kept in files and databases by law enforcement agencies at the local, state, and federal levels. A computerized system called the automated fingerprint identification system (AFIS) can scan hundreds of thousands of fingerprints per second to find a match for prints found at a crime scene. Fingerprint Technicians are thus able to identify criminal suspects quite rapidly and consistently. Without the AFIS, it would take decades for these professionals to identify each print. AFIS systems are used in specific law enforcement jurisdictions within municipalities, states, or regions. The integrated automated fingerprint identification system (IAFIS) is a nationwide database that is maintained by the FBI.

When we touch or hold objects, our fingers leave impressions that may or may not be readily noticeable. Three types of fingerprints are left at crime scenes: patent prints, such as those left when fingers coated with dirt or blood touch a surface; plastic prints, which are left when fingers come in contact with such soft substances as dust, soap, or putty; and latent prints, which are invisible to unaided eyesight, but leave sweat or oily secretions from fingers on dry surfaces.

Patent and plastic fingerprints can be photographed and matched against print databases. Several methods are used for lifting latent fingerprints from crime scenes. Some latent prints can be discerned by shining lights on surfaces that are thought to carry fingerprints. Some may become visible by dusting powder on the surface, or spraying various chemicals, such as cyanoacrylate vapor (the main ingredient of Super Glue), iodine fumes, ninhydrin, and silver nitrate. All of these substances render latent prints visible enough to record photographically. Prints that are partial or unclear can be digitally enhanced.

Fingerprint Technicians work at several levels of expertise. They learn their profession as on-the-job trainees, while working under the close supervision of experienced technicians. Trainees are often assigned to take fingerprints of job candidates and license applicants. They learn to classify fingerprints and search files for prior records of the prints they have been assigned to investigate. Trainees also assist others in their agency by gathering information related to criminal cases such as suspect arrest records. In addition, they maintain fingerprint files and other records.

As Fingerprint Technicians proceed to more advanced levels of expertise, their responsibilities increase and they work more independently. They accept more complex assignments and fulfill the full range of functions pertaining to fingerprint processing. Where required, they obtain AFIS certification and maintain that qualification throughout their careers.

Journey-level technicians become more familiar with using the AFIS. They compare fingerprints to existing files to verify that they match. They also enter new data as well as substitute old images with new ones when needed to update the information. They correct problems with the system and keep it in good running order. They also perform a variety of specific tasks, such as:

- converting ten cards and other print records to digital format for input into the AFIS
- sorting print cards and sending them to appropriate sections of their agency or other agencies
- classifying cards by comparing them to prints on their AFIS database
- reporting confirmed fingerprint matches to clients
- examining fingerprints, deciding whether they can be classified, and returning unacceptable prints to the sender
- interpreting official classifications for their agency

- assessing criminal histories and their AFIS data for accuracy
- testifying in court as an expert witness
- maintaining records and preparing reports, letters, and other documents
- working on special projects

Senior Fingerprint Technicians perform more complex assignments. They write training or procedures manuals, court documents, agency reports, and other documents. They review ten cards and digital fingerprint records for accuracy and compliance with regulations. They train junior employees in classrooms or on the job. Some senior technicians also perform supervisory duties. Their responsibilities include directing their staff performance by assigning work, setting priorities, and resolving problems. They also ensure that their staff performs within established standards and in compliance with local, state, and federal regulations.

Fingerprint Technicians work in offices where they sit at tables, desks, or computer terminals. Their work requires them to sit for extended periods and closely examine minutely detailed images. They occasionally work with various types of office equipment such as copy machines, fax machines, or laminators that require a measure of manual dexterity to operate. They may face another type of physical demand when they need to lift boxes weighing up to 55 pounds and carry them for distances up to 200 feet.

Fingerprint Technicians come in contact with a variety of people in addition to their fellow employees. They communicate with sworn law enforcement officers, court personnel, and the general public to provide fingerprint information or testify in court.

These professionals are often required to work either rotating or fixed shifts and irregular hours. Their assignments may include weekends and holidays.

Salaries

Salaries for Fingerprint Technicians vary, depending on such factors as their education, experience, job duties, employer, and geographic location. Formal salary information for this occupation is unavailable. One expert in the field reports that estimated annual salaries for Fingerprint Technicians in Florida range from $25,000 to $40,000, while those in California earn estimated annual salaries between $35,000 and $50,000. Another expert estimates that Fingerprint Technicians generally earn an annual salary between $25,000 and $40,000.

Employment Prospects

One expert in the field reports that a growing number of law enforcement agencies are hiring civilians to be Fingerprint Technicians.

Opportunities are generally created to replace Fingerprint Technicians who have advanced to higher positions, transferred to other jobs, or left the workforce for various reasons. Job competition is keen. An expert in the field reports that the number of openings for this occupation has decreased in recent years because technology advancements allow for fewer people to perform the work.

Advancement Prospects

Fingerprint Technicians can advance to lead and supervisory positions within their units, but opportunities are limited. With additional education (or training) and experience, they can pursue careers as crime scene investigators, latent print examiners, criminalists, or forensic scientists. Civilian employees may also choose to become law enforcement officers.

Law enforcement officers can develop a career according to their interests and ambitions. They can rise through the ranks as detectives, sergeants, and so on, up to chief of police. They can also seek positions in other special details that interest them, such as their agency's air support unit, bomb squad, or K9 unit. In addition, they can pursue supervisory and managerial positions.

Education and Training

Minimally, entry-level applicants need a high school or general equivalency diploma. Some employers may also require that applicants have completed a minimum number of credits of college course work. Some employers prefer to hire candidates who have completed a course or training in fingerprint classification.

Employers typically provide entry-level Fingerprint Technicians with training programs, which may include both on-the-job training and formal classroom training. Novices work under the supervision and direction of experienced Fingerprint Technicians.

Throughout their careers, Fingerprint Technicians enroll in continuing education programs and training programs to update their skills and keep up with advancements in their field.

Special Requirements

In agencies in which Fingerprint Technicians are law enforcement officers, applicants must possess a basic peace officer standards and training certificate. These agencies may hire candidates without a certificate on the condition they complete the necessary law enforcement academy program to obtain the certificate.

Law enforcement officers must successfully complete annual training to maintain their certification.

Experience, Special Skills, and Personality Traits

Requirements for entry-level positions vary with the different employers. In general, civilian applicants need one or more years of general clerical experience, preferably in law enforcement settings. Employers typically prefer to hire candidates who have previous experience taking fingerprints, classifying them, and searching fingerprint files.

Fingerprint Technicians need keen eyesight to be able to compare the fine details of fingerprints precisely and accurately. Some essential skills that they need to perform their work well are interpersonal, teamwork, and communication skills. They also need strong self-management skills such as the ability to understand and follow instructions, prioritize multiple tasks, work independently, and meet deadlines.

Some personality traits that successful Fingerprint Technicians share include being observant, perceptive, precise, cooperative, and courteous.

Unions and Associations

Fingerprint Technicians can join professional associations to take advantage of networking opportunities, professional certification, and other professional services and resources. One national society that serves their interests is the International Association for Identification. For contact information, see Appendix III.

Some Fingerprint Technicians belong to a union that represents them in contract negotiations with their employers for better terms regarding pay, benefits, and working conditions.

Tips for Entry

1. You may be asked at your job interview to demonstrate your knowledge about the law enforcement agency and the community it serves.
2. Find out if a law enforcement agency maintains a register of eligible candidates for Fingerprint Technicians. As openings become available, the agency will select candidates from that register. Learn how you can apply for it.
3. Some agencies require that you apply online for openings. Be sure to make a copy of your application for your own file. You may be asked to bring a copy of it to your interview.
4. Use the Internet to learn more about fingerprinting. You might start by visiting this Web site: Ridges and Furrows, http://www.ridgesandfurrows.homestead. com. For more links, see Appendix IV.

EVIDENCE CUSTODIAN

CAREER PROFILE

Duties: Receive, store, and release physical evidence found at crime scenes as well as abandoned, found, stolen, or seized property; perform duties as required

Alternate Title(s): Evidence Clerk, Evidence Officer, Property and Evidence Specialist, Property/Evidence Technician

Salary Range: $25,000 to $40,000+

Employment Prospects: Poor

Advancement Prospects: Poor for civilian employees

Prerequisites:

Education or Training—High school diploma

Experience—One or more years of experience in warehousing, inventory control, clerical work, or another related area

Special Skills and Personality Traits—Computer, math, writing, problem-solving, communication, interpersonal, customer-service, and self-management skills; organized, methodical, dependable, trustworthy, tactful, discreet, and cooperative

Special Requirements—Peace officer certificate may be required

CAREER LADDER

```
┌─────────────────────────────────┐
│   Senior Evidence Custodian     │
└─────────────────────────────────┘

┌─────────────────────────────────┐
│      Evidence Custodian         │
└─────────────────────────────────┘

┌─────────────────────────────────┐
│ Evidence Custodian (Entry-Level)│
└─────────────────────────────────┘
```

Position Description

Once a crime scene has been isolated and thoroughly examined, physical evidence is collected and stored for future analysis by crime labs. The evidence is also preserved for later presentation in court as exhibits. When evidence is no longer needed, it is returned to its owner or it is auctioned or destroyed. Men and women called Evidence Custodians do the work of keeping track, storing, releasing, and disposing of these articles of evidence.

They are also responsible for handling and processing property that is seized by law enforcement officers, as well as stolen, abandoned, or found property. Such property can range in size from handheld objects to vehicles. It includes narcotics, weapons, currency, hazardous substances, documents, computers, and automobiles, among many other items.

Evidence Custodians may be law enforcement officers or civilian employees. They work in law enforcement sections called property/evidence units. These units range in size from small storage areas to large warehouses. Evidence Custodians are accountable for each item of physical evidence and property. Everything in Evidence Custodians' trust must be properly received, efficiently processed, labeled, securely stored, made readily available for use in court cases, and disposed of properly—all in compliance with the law.

These professionals use either manual inventory records or automated bar code systems to keep accurate inventories as well as to track incoming and outgoing movements of each item or groups of items. With automated systems, each item is assigned a bar code upon receipt. That code is registered with every transaction or inventory count. Evidence Custodians ensure that their records are complete at all times. It is also their responsibility to maintain the chain of custody on every item of evidence to make sure that it has not been tampered with or contaminated. If the chain of custody has been violated on an item of physical evidence, it may not be admitted in court.

Evidence Custodians are trained in and knowledgeable about all aspects of their function. They understand the principles of warehouse operations including receiving, storing, and dispensing inventory with a particular focus on working with evidence in a strict security environment. They are also knowledgeable about procedures of quality control, record-keeping, office duties, and the use of material handling equipment. They possess a familiarity with all laws and regulations pertinent to their occupation.

Their duties vary, depending on their experience and skills. For example, Evidence Custodians may be assigned to:

- maintain the operational function of the automated bar code system
- create chain of custody records and keep them current
- perform physical inventories
- photograph property and evidence for cross-reference to chain of custody records
- deliver evidence for laboratory analysis or for use in court proceedings
- perform quality control assessments on property and evidence inventories
- prepare items for shipment
- clear evidence and property for destruction or for auction
- destroy hazardous materials, weapons, or narcotics
- confirm amounts of impounded currency
- consult with law enforcement personnel including police and probation officers, attorneys, and other court officials about the status of active cases
- assist law enforcement personnel with the transport of evidence and property items to court or crime labs and back to storage
- testify in court in regard to chain of evidence issues
- arrange for and maintain personal and telephone communication with members of the public to field their questions about property and evidence
- prepare written documents, including quarterly and annual reports of activities and statistics of their unit
- train new Evidence Custodians in classroom or on-the-job settings

Some Evidence Custodians help with the collection and documentation of physical evidence at crime scenes. Some also assist in the capacity of fingerprint identification specialists, sketch artists, or photographers. Senior custodians may be assigned such lead person duties as supervising team members, assigning tasks, and evaluating the job performance of subordinates.

Evidence Custodians work in office settings to manage inventory records. Their unit's storage areas may include confined spaces. In storage and warehouse areas, Evidence Custodians may need to access inventory items by climbing ladders, operating order pickers, or using forklifts. Their work environment is occasionally subject to extremes in temperature, and may be dusty and noisy. They are sometimes required to stand for extended periods and perform a moderate level of lifting, including above head-level. From time to time, they handle hazardous materials, weapons, or human tissues and fluids, which requires them to wear protective clothing or equipment.

Evidence Custodians work for 40 hours per week, but put in extra hours as needed. Their schedules may include rotating shifts, weekends, nights, and holidays. They may be called in to work on an emergency basis.

Salaries

Salaries for Evidence Custodians vary, depending on such factors as their education, experience, employer, and geographic location. Formal salary information for this occupation is unavailable. One expert in the field states that Evidence Custodians generally earn about $25,000 to $40,000 per year. Another expert estimates that civilian employees could earn hourly wages that begin at minimum wage for entry-level positions and go to $20 to $30 per hour for experienced personnel.

Employment Prospects

Evidence Custodians work for local and state police departments as well as for sheriffs' offices. Civilians are mostly employed in this occupation on the west coast of the United States. On the east coast, particularly the northeast, sworn officers take turns fulfilling this role for their agencies.

Civilian opportunities generally become available as Evidence Custodians transfer to other jobs, advance to higher positions, or leave the workforce for various reasons. One expert in the field reports that job prospects are few in number.

Advancement Prospects

Promotional opportunities for Evidence Custodians are limited to lead and supervisory positions within their units. With additional education (or training) and experience, they can pursue careers as crime scene investigators, latent print examiners, criminalists, or forensic scientists. Civilian employees may also choose to become law enforcement officers.

Law enforcement officers can develop a career according to their interests and ambitions. They can rise through the ranks as detectives, sergeants, and so on, up to chief of police. They can also seek positions in other special details that interest them, such as their agency's air support unit, or SWAT team. In addition, they can pursue supervisory and managerial positions.

Education and Training

Minimally, applicants for civilian positions must possess a high school or general equivalency diploma. Some agencies may prefer to hire candidates who have an associate degree in forensic science, law enforcement, or another related discipline, or who have taken some course work in forensic science.

Entry-level Evidence Custodians receive on-the-job training while working under the guidance and direction of experienced personnel.

Special Requirements

In agencies in which Evidence Custodians are law enforcement officers, applicants must possess a basic peace officer standards and training certificate. These agencies may hire candidates without a certificate on the condition they complete the necessary law enforcement academy program to obtain the certificate.

Law enforcement officers must successfully complete annual training to maintain their certification.

Experience, Special Skills, and Personality Traits

Requirements for civilian positions vary with the different employers. In general, applicants should have one or more years of experience in warehousing, inventory control, clerical work, or another related area. Most employers prefer to hire candidates who have experience working in law enforcement settings.

Evidence Custodians need strong computer, math, writing, and problem-solving skills to perform well at their job. They also must have effective communication, interpersonal, and customer-service skills, as they must be able to establish and maintain good working relationships with colleagues, law enforcement officers, the public, and others. In addition, Evidence Custodians need excellent self-management skills, including the ability to prioritize multiple tasks, understand and follow instructions, work independently, and work well under pressure. Being organized, methodical, dependable, trustworthy, tactful, discreet, and cooperative are some personality traits that successful Evidence Custodians have in common.

Unions and Associations

Evidence Custodians can join professional associations to take advantage of networking opportunities, training programs, and other professional services and resources. One national society that serves their interests is the International Association for Property and Evidence. For contact information, see Appendix III.

Tips for Entry

1. Learn how to type or use a keyboard. These skills are helpful for any job.
2. Employers usually require that civilian applicants possess a valid driver's license by their date of hire.
3. Contact employers' personnel or human resources office directly about job openings.
4. Many employers prefer to hire candidates who have previous experience working in law enforcement settings. If an Evidence Custodian job is unavailable, apply for other jobs for which you qualify.
5. Use the Internet to learn more about property/evidence units in law enforcement agencies. You might start by visiting the International Association for Property and Evidence Web site at http://www.iape.org. For more links, see Appendix IV.

POLYGRAPH EXAMINER

CAREER PROFILE

Duties: Develop and administer a polygraph test on criminal suspects to determine if they are being truthful about facts related to a criminal investigation; perform other duties as required

Alternate Title(s): Polygraphist, Forensic Psychophysiologist

Salary Range: $27,000 to $72,000

Employment Prospects: Fair

Advancement Prospects: Poor

Prerequisites:

Education or Training—Educational requirements vary; completion of training programs

Experience—Several years of investigative experience

Special Skills and Personality Traits—Interviewing, communication, interpersonal, organizational, and self-management skills; calm, levelheaded, tenacious, trustworthy, and impartial

Special Requirements—Professional license or certification may be required; peace officer certification may be required

CAREER LADDER

> **Senior Polygraph Examiner**

> **Polygraph Examiner**

> **Polygraph Examiner (Entry-level)**

Position Description

In criminal investigations, Polygraph Examiners play a role in finding links between suspects and crime scenes. They develop and administer tests on polygraphs to determine whether suspects, victims, witnesses, or informants are being misleading about particular issues in criminal cases. Criminal investigators use the results of polygraph examinations to help them with such matters as confirming allegations that cannot be disproved by evidence, developing investigative leads, and establishing probable cause to obtain search warrants.

Polygraph Examiners are trained to operate analog or digital equipment, which are commonly known as lie detectors. Polygraphs are medical devices that monitor the changes in individuals' respiratory rate, blood pressure, pulse rate, and sweat gland activity as they answer questions. However, polygraphs cannot determine if a person is lying. These instruments can only detect if a person is showing deceptive behavior.

Polygraph Examiners are expected to follow strict procedures and protocols when they conduct their examinations.

They address only those issues about a case that criminal investigators require. Prior to conducting their tests, Polygraph Examiners collect information about a case, the issues to be tested, and the examinees (the individuals to be tested). They review case files and other pertinent documents as well as talk with criminal investigators and other sources. The examiners then develop a set of questions for each separate issue about which they will ask examinees. For example, if an examinee was involved in two robberies, the Polygraph Examiner designs a set of questions about each robbery.

The polygraph examination has two phases. The pretest interview is the first stage. Polygraph Examiners describe the test procedure to the examinees—how the polygraph works and what the testing entails—as well as explain their legal rights. The examiners also review the questions they would be asking the examinees. Polygraph Examiners make sure that the examinees understand the proceedings before continuing to the testing phase.

In the second stage, examiners connect the examinees to the polygraphs. They then ask the examinees a series of questions. The polygraphs record the examinees' physiological activities as they answer the questions. Polygraph Examiners may ask the same set of questions more than once.

After the polygraph examination, the examiners score, analyze, and interpret the polygraph charts. They determine one of three conclusions: the examinee was answering the questions truthfully or not truthfully, or the test results were inconclusive. If the results were questionable, the examiners decide whether to conduct another examination.

Upon completion of an examination, Polygraph Examiners prepare and submit reports of their findings and conclusions to the proper authorities. These professionals may be asked to testify in court as expert witnesses.

Many Polygraph Examiners also perform polygraph examinations on job applicants for law enforcement officer and civilian positions at their agencies.

In some local law enforcement agencies, Polygraph Examiners are peace officers who have volunteered to be part of the polygraph detail. They conduct polygraph examinations in addition to their primary duties as detectives, patrol officers, supervisors, or other roles.

Polygraph Examiners work in offices. They often sit for long periods of time. Their job requires them to do some lifting and moving of heavy objects. In addition to polygraphs, they use computers, copiers, and other office machines while performing their work.

They may be on call 24 hours a day.

Salaries

Salaries for Polygraph Examiners vary, depending on such factors as their education, experience, job duties, employer, and geographic location. Specific salary information for this occupation is unavailable. A general idea can be gained by looking at the earnings for law enforcement officers. According to the May 2006 *Occupational Employment Statistics* survey by the U.S. Bureau of Labor Statistics, the estimated annual salary for most patrol officers ranged from $27,310 to $72,450.

Employment Prospects

Opportunities are available with local, state, and federal law enforcement agencies. Polygraph Examiners may be civilian employees or law enforcement officers. Most employers require law enforcement officers to commit to a minimum number of years for assignment in their polygraph examination unit.

Polygraph Examiners can also find employment with attorneys' offices (both public and private), parole and probation departments, and other legal organizations. Security and other firms that offer polygraph examination services employ Polygraph Examiners as well. Some Polygraph Examiners are self-employed or independent contractors.

In general, employers hire Polygraph Examiners to replace individuals who advance to higher positions, transfer to other jobs, retire, or leave the workforce for various reasons. Employers will create additional positions as long as funding is available.

Advancement Prospects

As law enforcement officers, Polygraph Examiners can advance according to their personal interests and ambitions. They can advance in terms of pay as well as rank. They can apply for voluntary positions on special details within their agency, such as the SWAT team, bomb squad, aviation unit, or crime scene investigation division. They may also pursue a career in criminal investigations, which requires passing a competitive detective exam. Those interested in supervisory or administrative duties can pursue such positions.

Civilian employees in law enforcement agencies have few opportunities. They may be promoted to supervisory and management positions, which are limited.

Entrepreneurial Polygraph Examiners can pursue careers as independent contractors or business owners of polygraph examination services.

Education and Training

Educational requirements vary with the different employers. Many law enforcement agencies prefer to hire candidates who have an associate or bachelor's degree (or have completed a minimum amount of course work) in criminal justice, law, police science, or another related field. Some employers may require civilian applicants to have completed certified training from a polygraph school accredited by a recognized organization such as the American Polygraph Association.

Novice examiners usually complete a certified training program as well as on-the-job training under the supervision of a senior Polygraph Examiner.

Throughout their careers, Polygraph Examiners enroll in seminars, workshops, and courses to update their skills and keep up with advancements in their field.

Special Requirements

In 2007, Polygraph Examiners were required to possess a professional license or certificate in 29 states and three counties, according to the American Polygraph Association Web site. To qualify for professional certification or licensure in some states, a bachelor's degree may be needed. Depending on the jurisdiction, individuals may be required to complete an internship and successfully pass an examination.

In agencies in which Polygraph Examiners are law enforcement officers, applicants must possess a basic peace officer standards and training certificate. These agencies may hire candidates without a certificate on the condition they complete the necessary law enforcement academy program to obtain the certificate.

Law enforcement officers must successfully complete annual training to maintain their certification.

Experience, Special Skills, and Personality Traits

Requirements vary with the different agencies. In general, applicants for entry-level positions need to have several years of criminal investigation experience.

Polygraph Examiners must have excellent interviewing, communication, and interpersonal skills to work effectively with different people from diverse backgrounds. They also need strong organizational and self-management skills, such as the ability to work independently, handle stressful situations, prioritize multiple tasks, and understand and follow instructions. Being calm, levelheaded, tenacious, trustworthy, and impartial are some personality traits that successful Polygraph Examiners have in common.

Unions and Associations

Polygraph Examiners can join professional associations to take advantage of training programs, professional publications, networking opportunities, and other professional services and resources. Societies that serve the particular interests of this profession are available at the local, state, and national levels. The American Polygraph Association and the American Association of Police Polygraphists are two major national organizations. For contact information, see Appendix III.

Tips for Entry

1. Do you think you might enroll in a polygraph school? Contact employers for whom you would like to work for suggestions about reputable and accredited schools. Also talk with professional associations and various Polygraph Examiners.
2. Read job announcements carefully to determine if you meet the minimum qualifications for a position. Employers typically disqualify applicants who do not fulfill those requirements.
3. Use the Internet to learn more about Polygraph Examiners. You might start by visiting the American Polygraph Association at http://www.polygraph.org. For more links, see Appendix IV.

CRIME LAB PERSONNEL

CRIMINALIST

CAREER PROFILE

Duties: Identify, analyze, and interpret physical evidence; prepare reports of findings; provide expert witness testimony; perform other duties as required

Alternate Title(s): Forensic Scientist, Crime Lab Analyst, Forensic Science Technician; Forensic Chemist, DNA Analyst, Firearms Examiner, or other title that reflects a particular specialty

Salary Range: $28,000 to $73,000

Employment Prospects: Good

Advancement Prospects: Fair

Prerequisites:

Education or Training — Bachelor's degree in a physical or natural science discipline, forensic science, or another related field; on-the-job training

Experience — Previous lab experience usually required

Special Skills and Personality Traits — Problem-solving, organizational, teamwork, interpersonal, writing, communication, presentation, and self-management skills; methodical, detail-oriented, persistent, honest, courteous, friendly, patient

Special Requirements — Peace officer certificate may be required

CAREER LADDER

```
┌─────────────────────────────────────┐
│  Senior or Supervisory Criminalist  │
└─────────────────────────────────────┘

┌─────────────────────────────────────┐
│     Criminalist (Journey-level)     │
└─────────────────────────────────────┘

┌─────────────────────────────────────┐
│       Criminalist (Trainee)         │
└─────────────────────────────────────┘
```

Position Description

Could a hair strand, bloodstain, or a tiny piece of fabric prove that a person committed a crime? Is the bullet that was found at a crime scene from the suspect's gun? Do any of the partial fingerprints found at a crime scene belong to the perpetrator of the crime? These are a few of the types of questions criminal investigators and prosecuting attorneys ask about physical evidence collected at crime scenes. Experts known as Criminalists provide investigators and attorneys with scientific proof that may help them find a link between suspects and victims or crime scenes.

Criminalists are sometimes confused with crime scene investigators, more popularly known as CSIs. Both groups perform work involving physical evidence. CSIs work at crime scenes where they are responsible for collecting and processing all types of physical evidence — including fingerprints, bloodstains, hair, fibers, glass fragments, drugs, computer files, documents, soil, and tire tracks, among others.

Criminalists, on the other hand, work in crime laboratories (or crime labs). These professional men and women are responsible for examining physical evidence that has been brought to their labs. They apply scientific principles and methods to identify, analyze, and interpret physical evidence to reconstruct crime scenes. For example, a Criminalist might determine that the carpet fibers found on the victim and in a suspect's vehicle are similar to the fibers of the suspect's living room carpet.

Depending on their experience and the needs of their labs, Criminalists may be assigned to conduct chemical, microscopic, comparative, and other complex laboratory analyses on one or more types of physical evidence. Some of the more common forensic disciplines include:

- DNA analysis—the identification and testing of individuals' DNA samples
- drug analysis—the identification of controlled substances
- firearms and tool marks—the examination of guns and other weapons and tools
- forensic chemistry—the identification and analysis of unknown chemical substances, gun powder residue, explosives, and other chemical products
- imprint and impression evidence—the examination of footprints, tire markings, and other two- or three-dimensional impressions
- latent prints—the identification and comparison of hidden impressions from fingers, palms, or feet
- questioned documents—the analysis of documents (such as wills, checks, correspondence, and invoices) to determine if alterations have been made or if they are forged or counterfeit
- serology—the analysis of blood and other body products
- trace evidence—the examination of hair, fibers, glass fragments, soil, minerals, and other substances in very small sizes or quantities

Some Criminalists are trained to work in other specialties, such as toxicology, computer forensics, voice analysis, crime scene reconstruction, forensic photography, and forensic anthropology.

Criminalists carefully and precisely document every step they take when examining physical evidence. First, they inspect an item of evidence and note what it is, how it looks, how much it weighs, and so on. They may sketch, photograph, or record video of the evidence. Criminalists then determine what tests should be performed. Upon completion of their tests, they make sure the evidence is packaged and labeled properly and sent to storage. Criminalists then interpret the results of their tests and prepare formal reports that describe their findings and the methods they used to obtain them. Their reports must be comprehensive yet clearly understandable by law enforcement officers, attorneys, judges, and juries.

Criminalists may be called upon to testify as expert witnesses at court trials. They provide impartial and unbiased testimony on issues related to their laboratory analyses. They may also answer questions about the procedures, methods, and techniques that are used in the crime lab.

Criminalists are expected to perform their work accurately and correctly. They follow strict procedures and protocols and keep up with current laws pertinent to evidence, criminal procedures, and crime. They make sure that they maintain the chain of custody on every piece of evidence that they handle to ensure that it has not been tampered with or contaminated. Physical evidence may not be admitted in court if the chain of custody has been violated.

In addition to performing laboratory analyses, Criminalists perform other duties. For example, they develop new methodologies and techniques of laboratory analysis. They keep up with current research and technologies. They maintain laboratory equipment, instruments, and work areas. Criminalists may also assist in collecting physical evidence at crime scenes.

Criminalists may be civilian employees or law enforcement officers. Entry-level Criminalists work under the guidance and supervision of experienced staff for several months to two or three years, depending on the area of forensic investigation. During this developmental phase, Criminalists focus on learning analytical skills as well as laboratory rules, standards, procedures, and practices.

As they gain experience and knowledge, they receive more complex assignments and are able to exercise greater levels of authority. After several years, Criminalists usually reach the journey level and are competent in one or more forensic disciplines. They are assigned sensitive and highly technical casework, and may assist in training laboratory staff.

Advanced-level Criminalists are given the most difficult cases to work. They move to this level after 10 or more years. They are usually involved in training staff on a regular basis and may be assigned as lead workers. Some Criminalists are specialists in one or more forensic disciplines.

Criminalists mostly work indoors in clean, well-lit, and ventilated laboratories. They operate a variety of instruments and machines, such as lights, cameras, microscopes, and spectroscopes, for recording, measuring, and testing evidence. They are exposed to chemicals, odors, fumes, and disease; hence, they wear protective equipment.

They work 40 hours per week, and put in additional hours as needed to complete tasks and meet deadlines. Some Criminalists are on call 24 hours a day. Sworn officers are also on standby to assist with law enforcement matters at any time of the day.

Salaries

Salaries for Criminalists vary, depending on such factors as their education, experience, position, employer, and geographic location. According to the May 2006 *Occupational Employment Statistics* (OES) survey by the U.S. Bureau of Labor Statistics (BLS), the estimated annual salary for most forensic science technicians ranged between $27,530 and $73,100.

Employment Prospects

Criminalists are employed by public and private crime laboratories. The BLS reported in its May 2006 OES survey that about 12,310 forensic science technicians were employed in the United States. Nearly 80 percent of these technicians worked at the local and state government levels.

About 398 crime labs in this country are publicly funded, according to the American Society of Crime Lab Directors.

Most of these labs are connected to law enforcement agencies and prosecuting attorneys' offices in municipal, county, and state jurisdictions. The Federal Bureau of Investigation, the Drug Enforcement Administration, the U.S. Bureau of Alcohol, Tobacco, Firearms and Explosives, the Secret Service, and the U.S. Fish and Wildlife Service are a few federal agencies that have forensic laboratories.

Competition for jobs is keen. In general, job openings become available as individuals retire, transfer to other jobs, or advance to higher positions. Job growth in this field is predicted to increase by 27 percent or more through 2014, according to the BLS. Many experts in the field report that there is a continuous backlog of work in most laboratories; consequently there is a need for experienced Criminalists. Many public laboratories are unable to hire enough Criminalists due to lack of funding, but as finances become available they may create additional positions.

Advancement Prospects
Criminalists can advance in any number of ways, depending on their ambitions and interests. They can become technical specialists in particular areas such as ballistics analysis or crime scene reconstruction. They can rise through the administrative and managerial ranks as technical leaders, unit supervisors, managers, and so on, up to lab directors, which may require their transferring to other employers. Managerial opportunities are usually better in large laboratories that have several levels of management. Individuals with entrepreneurial ambitions can become independent practitioners or owners of forensic firms that offer consulting or technical services. Criminalists can also pursue opportunities as instructors and researchers in higher education institutions. To advance to higher positions or to obtain teaching jobs, they may be required to possess a master's or doctoral degree.

Law enforcement officers have additional advancement opportunities. They can rise through the ranks as detectives, sergeants, lieutenants, and so on, up to chief of police. They can also seek positions in other special details that interest them, such as their agency's air support unit, bomb squad, SWAT team, or K9 unit. In addition, they can pursue supervisory and managerial positions.

Education and Training
Employers generally require that applicants for entry-level positions possess a bachelor's degree in chemistry, biochemistry, biology, or another discipline within the physical or natural sciences. A bachelor's degree in forensic science is also often acceptable. Employers may hire applicants without a bachelor's degree for such positions as latent fingerprint examiner or fire examiner if they have enough years of qualifying experience.

Entry-level Criminalists typically complete a training period that may last several months to a few years, depending on the type of analysis they are hired to perform. Some crime labs cross-train employees in several forensic disciplines. Novice Criminalists work under the guidance and supervision of experienced Criminalists.

For sworn officer positions, Criminalists must complete three to six months or more of basic training at a law enforcement academy. They study various subjects such as law, investigative procedures, self-defense, use of firearms, and first aid.

Throughout their careers, Criminalists enroll in continuing education programs and training programs to update their skills and keep up with advancements in their fields.

Special Requirements
In agencies in which Criminalists are law enforcement officers, applicants must possess a basic peace officer standards and training certificate. These agencies may hire candidates without a certificate on the condition they complete the necessary law enforcement academy program to obtain the certificate.

Law enforcement officers must successfully complete annual training to maintain their certification.

Experience, Special Skills, and Personality Traits
Requirements vary with the different employers. Most crime labs prefer to hire candidates for entry-level positions who have previous laboratory experience, which they may have gained through internships, research assistantships, or employment in analytical, crime, or scientific research laboratories. Entry-level candidates should be able to demonstrate their knowledge about proper lab procedures and the handling of lab instruments and equipment.

To perform the various aspects of their job well, Criminalists must have excellent problem-solving, organizational, teamwork, interpersonal, writing, communication, and presentation skills. In addition, they need strong self-management skills, such as the ability to work independently, prioritize multiple tasks, meet deadlines, and handle stressful situations. Being methodical, detail-oriented, persistent, honest, courteous, friendly, and patient are some personality traits that successful Criminalists have in common.

Unions and Associations
Criminalists can join professional associations to take advantage of networking opportunities, continuing education, professional certification, and other professional resources and services. Professional societies are available locally, statewide, regionally, nationally, and worldwide. Some national societies that serve the diverse interests of Criminalists are:

- American Academy of Forensic Sciences
- American College of Forensic Examiners
- International Association for Identification
- Association of Firearms and Tool Mark Examiners
- International Association of Bloodstain Pattern Analysts
- American Society of Questioned Document Examiners
- Association of Forensic DNA Analysts and Administrators

For contact information, see Appendix III.

Many Criminalists also belong to a labor union that represents them in negotiations with employers for better contractual terms for pay, benefits, and working conditions. In addition, the union handles any grievances that members may have against their employers.

Tips for Entry

1. While in high school or college, learn as much as you can about criminalistics to determine if it is the right field for you. Read books and magazines about the field and visit Web sites of professional associations. Talk with Criminalists about their work. Attend criminal trials to listen to Criminalists give expert witness testimony.

2. Some experts in the field suggest that students obtain a bachelor's degree in a physical or natural science in their field of interest, and then get a master's degree in forensic science.

3. Law enforcement officers must usually serve one or more years as patrol officers before they can apply for positions in their agency's crime lab.

4. Individuals who are willing to relocate to other cities or states may have greater chances of obtaining a job.

5. Use the Internet to learn more about Criminalists and their work. You might start by visiting the International Association for Identification at http://www. theiai.org. For more links, see Appendix IV.

CRIME LAB TECHNICIAN

CAREER PROFILE

Duties: Provide technical support to forensic scientists; perform routine laboratory tests; perform other duties as required

Alternate Title(s): Forensic Lab Technician, Laboratory Assistant

Salary Range: $28,000 to $53,000

Employment Prospects: Poor

Advancement Prospects: Poor

Prerequisites:

Education or Training—Bachelor's degree or an equivalent combination of education, training, and work experience

Experience—Laboratory work experience usually required

Special Skills and Personality Traits—Interpersonal, teamwork, communication, computer, and writing skills; detail-oriented, accurate, diligent, reliable, honest, and adaptable

CAREER LADDER

```
┌─────────────────────────────┐
│   Senior Lab Technician     │
└─────────────────────────────┘

┌─────────────────────────────┐
│       Lab Technician        │
└─────────────────────────────┘

┌─────────────────────────────┐
│       Lab Assistant         │
└─────────────────────────────┘
```

Position Description

Crime Lab Technicians provide technical support to criminalists in crime laboratories. They assist these forensic scientists in performing complex laboratory analyses on items of physical evidence that are collected from crime scenes. For example, they might aid criminalists with identifying shell-casing markings, examining documents for authenticity, conducting analyses on DNA samples from suspects, or performing qualitative and quantitative analyses on evidence for the presence of controlled substances. The results of these scientific analyses may help investigators and attorneys to arrest and convict criminal suspects.

Crime Lab Technicians are knowledgeable about general scientific principles and methodologies. They are familiar with laboratory equipment and terminology as well as with laboratory techniques and procedures. In addition, they are trained to comply with all laboratory policies and procedures to ensure that the chain of custody and the integrity of physical evidence are maintained at all times.

Crime Lab Technicians work under the direction of experienced criminalists. They assist in the preparation of foren-

sic examinations. An example of such a task is collecting and preparing blood, DNA, or other specimens for laboratory testing. Another example is preparing chemical solutions and reagents for various analyses. These technicians also perform routine microscopic, chemical, comparative, and other tests on physical evidence. They are responsible for writing clear and comprehensive reports about their findings, which may be used as testimony in court trials. They are sometimes required to testify as expert witnesses in court to answer questions about their analyses and findings.

They perform other duties, which vary among Crime Lab Technicians according to their position, skills, and experience. Some technicians are responsible for receiving, processing, and maintaining the inventory of physical evidence in the laboratory. They may prepare items of evidence for forensic analysis or for proper storage until analysis can be performed. They may also release evidence to the proper law enforcement agencies when analyses are completed.

Some Crime Lab Technicians are assigned to assist with the collection and processing of physical evidence at crime scenes for future laboratory analysis. They may do such tasks as collecting biological evidence, performing latent fingerprint searches, making plaster casts and impressions of evidence, taking photographs of crime scenes, and interviewing victims and witnesses.

Crime Lab Technicians are usually responsible for organizing and maintaining orderly and clean laboratories. They perform maintenance and minor repairs on laboratory apparatus, instruments, and equipment. They wash and clean test tubes, beakers, flasks, and other glassware. They also disinfect workbenches and sterilize laboratory materials, supplies, and equipment. In addition, they collect, package, and arrange for the removal of hazardous chemical and biological wastes.

Other tasks that these technicians may perform include:

- keeping an inventory of laboratory supplies
- distributing and replenishing supplies
- maintaining the laboratory library and reference collections
- generating and maintaining lab records and files
- updating case files to assist the crime lab analysts
- entering data for reports and logs onto computer files
- preparing diagrams, charts, and drawings for court presentations, investigative aids, or training

Technicians mostly work indoors in well-lit, well-ventilated laboratories. They are routinely exposed to chemicals and other hazardous materials, and are required to wear protective equipment.

Crime Lab Technicians work a 40-hour per week schedule. They may be required to be on call during their off-duty hours.

Salaries

Salaries for Crime Lab Technicians vary, depending on such factors as their education, experience, job duties, employer, and geographic location. Specific salary information for Crime Lab Technicians is unavailable. A general idea can be gained by looking at salaries for similar occupations. According to the Salary.com Web site (in August 2006), the national average salary for laboratory assistants in science and research fields ranged from $28,324 to $35,730 for entry-level positions to $40,707 to $53,453 for level III positions.

Employment Prospects

Crime Lab Technicians are employed by public and private crime (or forensic) laboratories. There are nearly 400 public crime laboratories in the United States, which are part of law enforcement agencies, prosecuting attorneys' offices, and other government agencies at the local, state, and federal levels.

Opportunities are generally better in large crime labs in urban areas. Job openings typically become available as technicians transfer to other jobs, advance to higher positions, or leave the workforce for various reasons. Employers may create additional positions to meet demands, as long as funding is available. The job competition is keen for vacant positions.

Advancement Prospects

Advancement opportunities are limited for Crime Lab Technicians. They can advance by earning higher salaries and being assigned greater responsibilities. In large laboratories, they may be promoted to lead and supervisory technician positions.

Technicians who have bachelor's degrees in appropriate disciplines can use their experience as a stepping-stone to forensic scientist positions.

Education and Training

Educational requirements vary with the different employers. In general, applicants should have a combination of education, training, and experience that is equivalent to a bachelor's degree from an accredited college or university. They should have completed a minimum number of units in the natural or physical sciences. Employers usually prefer to hire candidates who hold a bachelor's degree in chemistry, biology, biochemistry, forensic science, or another related field.

Employers provide entry-level technicians with on-the-job training.

Experience, Special Skills, and Personality Traits

Employers usually seek candidates who have one or more years of work experience in laboratory assistance. Many employers prefer to hire candidates who have experience working in crime labs or with crime scene processing. Candidates should be able to demonstrate a basic knowledge of laboratory procedures, terminology, and equipment.

Because they must work well with others, Crime Lab Technicians need effective interpersonal, teamwork, and communication skills. Their work also requires that they have adequate computer and writing skills.

Some personality traits that successful Crime Lab Technicians share include being detail-oriented, accurate, diligent, reliable, honest, and adaptable.

Unions and Associations

Many Crime Lab Technicians are members of a union that represents them in negotiations with employers for better contractual terms for pay, benefits, and working conditions. In addition, the union handles any grievances that members may have against their employers.

These technicians are also eligible to join local, state, or national professional associations that serve the interests of forensic professions. These organizations offer their members networking opportunities and other professional resources and services. Two national societies they might join are the American Academy of Forensic Sciences and the American College of Forensic Examiners. For contact information, see Appendix III.

Tips for Entry

1. High school science, mathematics, and English classes can help you prepare for a future career in a crime lab.

2. Contact crime labs directly about job openings and their selection process.

3. Employers usually require that Crime Lab Technicians possess a valid driver's license.

4. If crime lab jobs are not available, seek laboratory work in medical, science research, and other settings to gain valuable work experience.

5. Use the Internet to learn about the services that crime laboratories provide. To find relevant Web sites, enter the keywords *crime labs*, *crime laboratory*, or *forensic laboratory*.

CRIME LAB SUPERVISOR

CAREER PROFILE

Duties: Oversee the daily operations of a crime lab unit; provide leadership and guidance to forensic scientists, technicians, and other support staff; perform criminalistic duties; perform other duties as required

Alternate Title(s): Supervisory Criminalist, Supervising Criminalist, Technical Leader; a title that reflects a particular laboratory unit or section such as DNA Supervisor

Salary Range: $28,000 to $73,000+

Employment Prospects: Poor

Advancement Prospects: Poor

Prerequisites:

Education or Training—Bachelor's degree in a physical or natural science discipline, forensic science, or another related field

Experience—Several years of work experience as a criminalist, including supervisory and management experience

Special Skills and Personality Traits—Leadership, teambuilding, interpersonal, communication, listening, problem-solving, organizational, time-management, customer-service, writing, and presentation skills; honest, respectful, compassionate, positive, encouraging, calm, consistent, dedicated

Special Requirements—Peace officer certificate may be required

CAREER LADDER

```
┌─────────────────────────────┐
│     Crime Lab Manager       │
└─────────────────────────────┘

┌─────────────────────────────┐
│    Crime Lab Supervisor     │
└─────────────────────────────┘

┌─────────────────────────────┐
│     Senior Criminalist      │
└─────────────────────────────┘
```

Position Description

Crime laboratories provide technical and scientific support to criminal investigators and prosecuting attorneys to help them arrest and convict criminal suspects. The criminalists at these labs perform scientific analyses on various items of physical evidence that are found at crime scenes, such as firearms, bullets, latent prints, hair, glass fragments, body fluids, controlled substances, and fire debris. Because of the different forensic disciplines, many crime labs divide the specialties into units. For example, criminalists in a crime lab might work in its firearms, latent prints, forensic biology, trace evidence, drug analysis, or forensic chemistry unit.

Crime Lab Supervisors are responsible for the day-to-day operations of crime lab units. It is their job to plan, coordinate, and manage the work activities of their units as well as to provide direction and guidance to criminalists, technicians, and clerical support workers who staff their units. They also establish and maintain effective working relationships with law enforcement officers, attorneys, and other governmental officials and personnel.

Crime Lab Supervisors work cooperatively with other unit supervisors and lab managers to continually seek ways to improve operations as well as to provide quality customer service to law enforcement agencies, attorney's offices, and other public organizations. These criminalistic supervisors assist in defining program goals, objectives, accomplishments, and problem areas. They also help develop new or improved procedures and methods to establish more efficient work processes as well as to decrease turnaround times for casework.

These supervisors are expected to be knowledgeable in many areas, including the application of scientific principles and techniques in forensic investigations; basic principles, practices, and procedures of crime lab testing; laboratory management; lab safety practice and procedures; criminal laws and rules of evidence; and research methods and techniques. In addition, they are expected to stay up to date with current techniques, procedures, and other developments in their field.

Crime Lab Supervisors are responsible for planning and making work assignments to staff members, monitoring the progress of their staffs' assignments, and reviewing the quality of their work. These supervisors are advanced-level criminalists. They oversee the analyses of physical evidence by their technical staff. Supervisors make sure that cases are processed accurately, completely, and in a timely manner. It is also their duty to ensure safe working conditions in their units as well as to maintain quality assurance standards. Supervising criminalists are also responsible for the planning and implementation of training programs, as well as the professional development of their staffs.

Supervisors are also required to perform various administrative duties. They assist lab managers with the development of laboratory procedures, policies, standards, techniques, and methods. Crime Lab Supervisors plan and administer budgets for their units, and prepare monthly and annual reports. They conduct job performance evaluations on their staff members. In addition, they coordinate and direct audits, competency tests, and other quality control procedures to ensure that their units are in compliance with standard procedures, laboratory policies, and governmental laws and regulations. Furthermore, they assist in the preparation of grant proposals and applications and make recommendations for the purchase of lab equipment and supplies.

Crime Lab Supervisors continue to perform laboratory analyses on physical evidence. They usually work on the more complex, sensitive, and highly technical examinations in their units. When requested, supervisors testify in courts as expert witnesses on questions about their laboratory analyses or to explain technical methods and procedures. Crime Lab Supervisors also conduct research into new methods and techniques for performing microscopic, comparative, chemical, or other types of examinations on physical evidence. Upon request, supervisors assist crime scene investigators in the collection and processing of physical evidence at crime scenes.

Supervising criminalists perform a wide range of tasks, which vary every day. For example, they:

- plan and schedule work and activities for their units
- assign cases and projects to staff members
- advise criminalists on their cases

- identify and resolve technical, operational, and personnel problems as they arise
- inspect and monitor laboratory equipment and instruments to make sure they meet manufacturer's specifications as well as operating and safety standards and regulations
- conduct staff meetings
- monitor special projects
- research professional journals and other publications to learn about new techniques of analysis
- consult with experts on solutions to problems involving identification or evaluation of physical evidence
- maintain communication with criminal investigators regarding cases
- provide scientific assistance to attorneys
- evaluate training needs of staff members
- review technical reports written by staff members
- prepare memos, correspondence, reports, evaluations, and other required documents
- prepare and maintain laboratory records and files

Most Crime Lab Supervisors are civilians. In some local agencies, they are sworn peace officers. Depending on the size and structure of their laboratory, they receive supervision and direction from a mid-level manager or the lab director.

Supervisory criminalists work mostly in laboratory settings, but on occasion may be asked to assist in the collection and processing of physical evidence at crime scenes. Like all criminalists, supervisors are regularly exposed to dangerous and toxic chemicals, odors, and fumes. They wear appropriate protective equipment as needed.

These supervisors work 40 hours per week, and put in additional hours as needed to complete tasks and meet deadlines. Some of them are on call 24 hours a day.

Salaries
Salaries for Crime Lab Supervisors vary, depending on such factors as their education, experience, employer, and geographic location. Specific salary information for this occupation is unavailable. In general, they receive higher salaries than journey-level and senior forensic science technicians. The estimated annual salary for most forensic science technicians ranged between $27,530 and $73,100, according to the May 2006 *Occupational Employment Statistics* survey by the U.S. Bureau of Labor Statistics.

Employment Prospects
Most Crime Lab Supervisors work in public crime laboratories that are part of local and state law enforcement agencies and prosecuting attorneys' offices. Some are employed by federal crime labs that are part of the Federal Bureau of Investigation, the U.S. Bureau of Alcohol, Tobacco, Firearms and Explosives, the U.S. Fish and Wildlife Service,

and other federal agencies. Other Crime Lab Supervisors work for private forensic laboratories.

Employers hire supervising criminalists to replace personnel who advance to higher positions, transfer to other jobs, or leave the workforce due to retirement or other reasons.

Advancement Prospects

Crime Lab Supervisors can advance to managerial positions, including crime lab directors, but opportunities are limited and often require transferring to other employers. Managerial opportunities are usually better in large laboratories that have several levels of management. Individuals with entrepreneurial ambitions can become independent practitioners or owners of forensic firms that offer consulting or technical services. Crime Lab Supervisors can also pursue opportunities as instructors and researchers in higher education institutions. To advance to higher positions or obtain teaching jobs may require possession of a master's or doctoral degree.

Law enforcement officers have additional advancement opportunities. They can rise through the ranks as detectives, sergeants, lieutenants, and so on, up to chief of police. They can also seek positions in other special details that interest them, as well as pursue supervisory and managerial positions.

Education and Training

Minimally, applicants must hold a bachelor's degree in chemistry, biochemistry, biology, forensic science, or another related discipline. Some employers prefer to hire candidates with a master's or doctoral degree in an appropriate discipline.

Throughout their careers, Crime Lab Supervisors enroll in continuing education programs and training programs to update their skills and increase their knowledge.

Special Requirements

In agencies in which supervisory criminalists are law enforcement officers, applicants must possess a basic peace officer standards and training certificate. These agencies may hire candidates without a certificate on the condition they complete the necessary law enforcement academy program to obtain the certificate.

Law enforcement officers must successfully complete annual training to maintain their certification.

Experience, Special Skills, and Personality Traits

Many employers require that applicants have five or more years of journey-level experience as criminalists. Their work history should demonstrate increasing responsibilities and include experience performing supervisory and administrative duties. In addition, applicants should have extensive experience in the forensic discipline (i.e., DNA analysis, firearms examination) for which they would be supervising.

Crime Lab Supervisors need effective leadership, team-building, interpersonal, communication, and listening skills to work well with staff members, managers, and others from diverse backgrounds. They also need excellent problem-solving, organizational, time-management, customer-service, writing, and presentation skills to perform the various aspects of their position. Being honest, respectful, compassionate, positive, encouraging, calm, consistent, and dedicated are some personality traits that successful supervisors share.

Unions and Associations

Many Crime Lab Supervisors are members of local, state, and national societies to take advantage of networking opportunities, continuing education, professional certification, and other professional resources and services. Some national professional associations that serve the general interests of forensic scientists include the American Academy of Forensic Sciences, the American College of Forensic Examiners, and the International Association for Identification. They may also join societies that serve their particular discipline such as the Association of Firearms and Tool Mark Examiners or the Association of Forensic DNA Analysts and Administrators. Supervisors in local and state laboratories are eligible to join the American Society of Crime Laboratory Directors. For contact information for these societies, see Appendix III.

Tips for Entry

1. Many employers allow applicants to substitute a master's or doctoral degree for one or more years of work experience.
2. Some employers require applicants to be U.S. citizens or U.S. permanent residents.
3. One way to demonstrate your flexibility and dedication to your work is to learn how to perform other types of analyses and jobs in the crime lab.
4. Use the Internet to learn more about different crime labs and how they are organized into different units. To find relevant Web sites, enter the keywords *crime lab*, *crime laboratory*, or *forensic laboratory*.

QUALITY MANAGER

CAREER PROFILE

Duties: Develop, implement, and maintain quality programs and activities in crime laboratories; perform other duties as required

Alternate Title(s): Quality Assurance Manager, Quality Control Manager

Salary Range: $50,000 to $90,000

Employment Prospects: Poor

Advancement Prospects: Poor

Prerequisites:

Education or Training—Bachelor's degree

Experience—Several years of work experience as a journey-level criminalist

Special Skills and Personality Traits—Self-management, organizational, time-management, writing, communication, interpersonal, and teamwork skills; observant, detail-oriented, meticulous, flexible, calm, cooperative

Special Requirements—Peace officer certificate may be required

CAREER LADDER

```
┌─────────────────────────────────┐
│       Crime Lab Manager         │
└─────────────────────────────────┘

┌─────────────────────────────────┐
│       Quality Manager           │
└─────────────────────────────────┘

┌─────────────────────────────────┐
│  Senior or Supervisory Criminalist │
└─────────────────────────────────┘
```

Position Description

Crime laboratories (or crime labs) play an essential role in linking criminal suspects to crime scenes and victims. They conduct scientific analyses on various types of physical evidence found at crime scenes to assist criminal investigators and prosecuting attorneys in arresting and convicting criminal suspects. Thus, it is imperative that the technical data and findings that these laboratories produce are accurate and trustworthy. To ensure the credibility and integrity of the forensic services that crime labs provide, many of them employ Quality Managers to develop, implement, and oversee appropriate quality measures.

Quality Managers are experienced criminalists. They may be civilian employees or law enforcement officers. Quality Managers have advanced knowledge in the principles, methods, materials, equipment, and techniques of forensic science and are highly familiar with laboratory standards, protocols, and safety. They are also well versed in law enforcement operations and procedures, and with laws and regulations pertaining to the collection, preservation, analysis, and presentation of physical evidence.

These managers design and manage a system of quality programs and activities that address a wide range of quality issues regarding management, operations, personnel, procedures, equipment, physical plant, security, health and safety, and other areas. Quality systems are generally divided into two areas—quality assurance (QA) and quality control (QC). QA programs and activities—such as laboratory policies and procedures, training programs, procedural manuals, and quality monitoring programs—establish the requirements for acceptable forensic laboratory performance. QC programs and activities are the daily practices used—such as control samples, documentation, and good laboratory practices—to ensure the reliability of the work that criminalists perform.

Quality Managers may oversee a quality system for one crime lab or for a laboratory system consisting of several crime labs in different locations. They are responsible for monitoring several technical units (such as the firearms, latent prints, or DNA units) in a crime lab to ensure that all quality measures are working properly. They examine work areas, equipment, and instruments. They monitor the work performance of personnel by reviewing completed casework as well as by observing them at work in the lab and as they testify in court. These managers also address quality issues as they arise, and develop and implement appropriate corrective actions. For example, they might recommend that laboratory staff receive certain training to improve the quality of their work.

Many crime labs choose to obtain voluntary accreditation from forensic laboratory accreditation bodies such as the American Society of Crime Lab Directors. To qualify, labs must meet strict accreditation standards as well as continue to maintain those requirements throughout their period of accreditation. Quality Managers help crime labs develop and execute quality measures to gain the accreditation they seek. Once a lab is accredited, Quality Managers are responsible for assuring that the crime lab continually maintains accreditation standards.

Quality Managers perform many duties, which vary every day. For example, they may be involved in:

- developing policies and procedures for quality programs and activities
- supervising the implementation of quality control procedures
- conducting laboratory audits
- assisting lab supervisors with preparations for inspections by a laboratory accrediting agency
- investigating and resolving technical problems
- researching ways to improve the QA and QC programs and activities
- training laboratory staff on quality procedures
- maintaining the policy and procedural manuals for their lab
- preparing reports, records, and other required documents and paperwork
- reading professional journals and other literature to stay current with the latest developments in forensic analysis, forensic lab quality measures, and technology

When requested, Quality Managers testify in court to address legal issues regarding the quality of lab policies and procedures. In some crime labs, Quality Managers are also responsible for planning, implementing, and overseeing safety programs.

Their job requires that they work cooperatively and effectively with a wide range of people, including lab managers and supervisors, criminalists, law enforcement officers, city officials, and the general public. Quality Managers may be supervised directly by a crime lab director or by another upper-level manager.

Quality Managers work full or part time, depending on the needs of their laboratories. Some Quality Managers continue performing casework in their forensic specialties. In forensic laboratory systems, Quality Managers travel to labs in different locations.

Salaries

Salaries for Quality Managers in forensic laboratories vary, depending on such factors as their education, experience, employer, and geographic location. In an informal survey conducted by the Association of Forensic Quality Assurance Managers, the approximate salary range for a forensic quality assurance manager was $50,000 to $90,000. According to the Salary.com Web site, the base pay for Quality Managers, overall, in the United States ranged between $54,687 to $70,417 in August 2006.

Employment Prospects

Quality Managers work for both public and private criminal laboratories. There are nearly 400 local, state, and federal government laboratories in the United States. In general, job openings become available as individuals retire, transfer to other jobs, or advance to higher positions.

Local and state crime labs create Quality Manager positions to comply with accreditation requirements of the American Society of Crime Laboratory Directors (ASCLD). Hence, more opportunities become available as labs seek ASCLD accreditation.

Advancement Prospects

Quality Managers can advance to other managerial positions, such as unit manager or crime lab director. Opportunities, however, are limited and often require that they transfer to other employers. Individuals can also pursue opportunities as instructors and researchers in higher education institutions. Those with entrepreneurial ambitions can become independent practitioners or owners of forensic firms that offer consulting or technical services. To advance to higher positions or to obtain teaching jobs, they may be required to possess a master's or doctoral degree.

Law enforcement officers have additional advancement opportunities. They can rise through the ranks as detectives, sergeants, and so on, up to chief of police. They can also seek positions in other special details that interest them, as well as pursue supervisory and managerial positions.

Education and Training

Minimally, applicants need a bachelor's degree in chemistry, biology, biochemistry, toxicology, forensic science, or another related field.

Throughout their careers, Quality Managers enroll in continuing education programs and training programs to update their skills and increase their knowledge.

Special Requirements

In agencies in which Quality Managers are law enforcement officers, applicants must possess a basic peace officer standards and training certificate. These agencies may hire candidates without a certificate on the condition they complete the necessary law enforcement academy program to obtain the certificate.

Law enforcement officers must successfully complete annual training to maintain their certification.

Experience, Special Skills, and Personality Traits

Requirements vary with the different employers. In general, applicants must have several years of work experience as a journey-level criminalist. Some employers allow applicants to substitute an advanced degree in an appropriate discipline for one or more years of work experience. Employers also prefer to hire candidates who have a few years of experience working in a lead or supervisory position.

To be effective at their job, Quality Managers need strong self-management skills, such as the ability to prioritize multiple tasks, follow and understand instructions, meet deadlines, and work independently. Other essential skills are organizational, time-management, writing, communication, interpersonal, and teamwork skills. Being observant, detail-oriented, meticulous, flexible, calm, and cooperative are some personality traits that successful Quality Managers share.

Unions and Associations

Many Quality Managers belong to professional associations at the local, state, or national level to take advantage of networking opportunities and other professional resources and services. They may join general forensic societies such as the American Academy of Forensic Sciences, the American College of Forensic Examiners, and the International Association for Identification. Some managers belong to the Association of Forensic Quality Assurance Managers. For contact information for these groups, see Appendix III.

Tips for Entry

1. To obtain any job in forensics, you must be prepared to go through an intense selection process that may include any of the following steps: job application, interview, job-related aptitude and skills tests, medical examination, drug screening, psychological review, polygraph examination, and background investigation.

2. As a staff member in a crime lab, become familiar with your lab's quality programs and activities. If possible, volunteer to work on a quality program or activity.

3. Stay up to date with quality assurance and quality control issues in forensic laboratories.

4. Use the Internet to learn more about quality programs in crime laboratories. You might start by visiting the Association of Forensic Quality Assurance Managers at http://www.afqam.org. For more links, see Appendix IV.

CRIME LAB DIRECTOR

CAREER PROFILE

Duties: Oversee crime laboratory operations on a daily basis; perform administrative and managerial duties; provide staff leadership and supervision; perform other duties as required

Alternate Title(s): Crime Lab Manager, Forensic Laboratory Manager

Salary Range: $60,000 to $146,000

Employment Prospects: Poor

Advancement Prospects: Poor

Prerequisites:

Education or Training—Bachelor's degree

Experience—Several years of professional work experience in a crime lab; previous supervisory and management experience

Special Skills and Personality Traits—Leadership, team-building, communication, listening, interpersonal, organizational, conflict-resolution, time-management, personnel-management, business, customer-service, and writing skills; honest, trustworthy, decisive, calm, cooperative, flexible, inspirational, consistent, dedicated

Special Requirements—Peace officer certificate may be required

CAREER LADDER

```
┌─────────────────────────────────────────┐
│  Crime Lab Director (larger laboratory)  │
└─────────────────────────────────────────┘

┌─────────────────────────────────────────┐
│           Crime Lab Director             │
└─────────────────────────────────────────┘

┌─────────────────────────────────────────┐
│   Assistant Crime Lab Director or        │
│   Managerial (or Supervisory)            │
│   Criminalist                            │
└─────────────────────────────────────────┘
```

Position Description

Crime labs play an important role in helping link suspects with victims and crime scenes in criminal investigations as well as in the prosecution of criminal cases in courts. They provide law enforcement agencies and prosecuting attorneys' offices with scientific analyses of physical evidence—bullets, latent prints, blood, body fluids, paint, hair, fibers, and so on—that is found at crime scenes. Crime Lab Directors have the overall responsibility for the quality and timeliness of delivery of forensic services for their laboratories.

As executive managers, Crime Lab Directors oversee crime laboratory operations and make sure that they run smoothly and efficiently each day. Some crime labs are private entities, while others are part of law enforcement agencies, prosecuting attorneys' offices, or other government agencies at the local, state, or federal level.

Directors may be in charge of a single forensic lab or a laboratory system made up of several crime labs in different locations. They apply scientific and forensic principles and techniques to solve a wide range of technical problems and issues. Their job also requires that they be knowledgeable about physical security and evidence management as well as quality assurance principles and practice. In addition, these administrators employ business and management principles and practices, such as human resource management, strategic planning, financial planning, program management, and resource allocation.

A crime lab is usually divided into several technical sections that conduct particular types of forensic examinations (such as trace evidence, controlled substances, and forensic biology). Crime Lab Directors plan, organize, and coordinate the programs and activities for the various technical sections in their laboratories. They develop and implement laboratory policies, procedures, objectives, and goals as well. They also plan and maintain systems that ensure the safety and security of the physical facilities as well as the credibility and integrity of forensic laboratory services. Additionally, these managers are responsible for ensuring that crime labs comply with employers' missions and policies, forensic laboratory accreditation standards, and governmental laws and regulations.

As leaders, Crime Lab Directors are responsible for the supervision and guidance of all laboratory employees— criminalists, managers, technicians, clerical staff, and other laboratory personnel. These executive managers are engaged in planning work schedules for their staff, making work assignments, reviewing technical casework, conferring with staff about work-related problems, and evaluating their job performance. In crime labs with multiple levels of management, directors oversee managers or supervisors who in turn are responsible for the oversight of employees in their technical units.

Crime Lab Directors are also involved in the process of hiring, disciplining, and firing personnel. Further, they are responsible for the planning and implementation of training and professional development programs for the different staff members.

In addition, these executive managers handle a wide array of administrative responsibilities. Some of their duties include planning, preparing, and executing budgets; authorizing purchases; developing and submitting grant proposals; and preparing reports, memos, correspondence, and other required documents. These managers also supervise management information systems that are used in the reporting and tracking of laboratory data, evidence, inventory, statistical reports, budgeting, human resources, and other technical and operational areas.

Crime Lab Directors perform various other duties, such as:

- providing expertise to laboratory staff on forensic science issues
- researching new technologies and methods to increase the efficiency of crime lab functions
- inspecting, monitoring, and evaluating physical facilities and equipment to determine that they meet operating and safety standards, regulations, and guidelines
- providing training programs in crime scene handling and processing of physical evidence for law enforcement agencies
- representing their crime lab as well as parent agency (such as a police department) at meetings with governmental agencies, law enforcement agencies, the legislature, forensic lab accreditation bodies, the media, and other groups

Many Crime Lab Directors continue performing forensic analyses on physical evidence. They usually take on the most difficult casework. When required, they provide testimony as expert witnesses in court trials. On occasion, they are requested to assist with evidence collection and processing at crime scenes.

Crime Lab Directors keep up to date with new technologies and scientific developments in the forensic science field as well as stay abreast of current management practices. They read professional and trade publications, network with other crime lab administrators, enroll in workshops, seminars, and courses, and participate in professional societies, technical working groups, and professional conferences.

Crime Lab Directors interact with many people on a daily basis, including staff members, management, law enforcement officers, government officials, attorneys, officers of the court, vendors, and the public, among others. They are expected to develop and foster strong working relationships with the various groups of people they encounter.

These directors frequently undergo stress when handling technical issues. They deal with conflict situations, meet deadlines, and perform other tasks. Their work exposes them to hazardous chemicals and agents; thus, they are required to wear protective equipment. They spend most of their time in office and lab settings. They sometimes travel to attend meetings and conferences in other cities.

Crime Lab Directors work full time. They put in additional hours as needed to complete their duties, and may be required to work weekends and holidays. They are on call 24 hours a day.

Salaries

Salaries for Crime Lab Directors vary, depending on such factors as their education, experience, employer, and geographic location. Specific salary information for this occupation is unavailable. They generally earn salaries similar to natural sciences managers. According to the May 2006 *Occupational Employment Statistics* survey by the U.S. Bureau of Labor Statistics (BLS), the estimated annual salary for most natural sciences managers ranged between $60,300 and $145,600. One expert in the field states that starting salaries for new crime lab managers range from $35,000 to $60,000 per year.

Employment Prospects

Crime Lab Directors run private and public criminal laboratories. In the United States, there are nearly 400 government crime labs, which are part of law enforcement agencies, prosecuting attorneys' offices, and other government agencies. At the local and state levels, Crime Lab Directors may be civilian employees or law enforcement officers.

In general, job openings become available as directors retire, transfer to other jobs, or advance to higher positions.

Advancement Prospects

The Crime Lab Director is the highest position in a forensic laboratory. Most directors rise through the ranks within their laboratory system.

Directors may seek management positions in other crime labs that offer higher incomes, greater challenges, or more prestige. Individuals with entrepreneurial ambitions can become consultants or owners of forensic firms that offer management consulting or technical services.

Law enforcement officers have additional advancement opportunities. They can rise through the ranks as detectives, sergeants, lieutenants, and so on, up to chief of police. They can also seek other administrative and managerial positions within their agency.

Education and Training

Minimally, applicants need a bachelor's degree in chemistry, biology, biochemistry, forensic science, or another related field. Some employers prefer to hire candidates who possess a master's, doctoral, or medical degree.

Special Requirements

In agencies in which Crime Lab Directors are law enforcement officers, applicants must possess a basic peace officer standards and training certificate. These agencies may hire candidates without a certificate on the condition they complete the necessary law enforcement academy program to obtain the certificate.

Law enforcement officers must successfully complete annual training to maintain their certification.

Experience, Special Skills, and Personality Traits

In general, applicants must have five to seven or more years of professional experience in a crime laboratory. Depending on the employer, they must also have one or more years of supervisory and managerial experience.

Crime Lab Directors need excellent leadership, team-building, communication, listening, and interpersonal skills to work well with criminalists, technicians, managers, public agencies, attorneys, law enforcement officers, vendors, and various others from diverse backgrounds. In addition, their job requires that they have effective organizational, conflict-resolution, time-management, personnel-management, business, customer-service, and writing skills. Being honest, trustworthy, decisive, calm, cooperative, flexible, inspirational, consistent, and dedicated are some personality traits that successful Crime Lab Directors share.

Unions and Associations

Crime Lab Directors can join professional associations at the local, state, and national levels to take advantage of networking opportunities, professional certification, continuing education, job listings, and other professional resources and services. Some national societies include the American Academy of Forensic Sciences, the American College of Forensic Examiners, and the International Association for Identification. Managers of local and state laboratories can also join the American Society of Crime Laboratory Directors. For contact information for these societies, see Appendix III.

Tips for Entry

1. Employers may require that applicants be U.S. citizens or U.S. permanent residents.
2. Employers may ask for proof of your educational and professional records. Thus, keep photocopies of your college transcripts, training records, and professional certificates on hand. Also have a list of professional references with their current job titles and contact information.
3. To enhance their employability, some Crime Lab Managers obtain professional certification from societies in which they are members.
4. Enroll in management courses, workshops, and seminars to learn new skills and knowledge.
5. Learn more about crime lab management on the Internet. You might start by visiting the American Society of Crime Laboratory Directors Web site at http://www.ascld.org. For more links, see Appendix IV.

CRIMINALISTS

BLOODSTAIN PATTERN ANALYST

CAREER PROFILE

Duties: Examine and interpret bloodstain patterns at crime scenes and recreate the events that occurred; prepare reports of findings; provide expert witness testimony; perform other duties as required

Alternate Title(s): Blood Splatter Analyst; Crime Scene Analyst, Forensic Scientist, Criminalist

Salary Range: $28,000 to $73,000

Employment Prospects: Poor

Advancement Prospects: Fair

Prerequisites:

Education or Training—Educational requirements vary; on-the-job training

Experience—Several years' experience performing crime scene investigation and analysis

Special Skills and Personality Traits—Teamwork, interpersonal, communication, writing, and self-management skills; detail-oriented, precise, observant, objective, honest, trustworthy, and diligent

Special Requirements—Peace officer certificate may be required

CAREER LADDER

```
┌─────────────────────────────────┐
│  Senior Crime Scene Analyst or  │
│           Criminalist           │
└─────────────────────────────────┘

┌─────────────────────────────────┐
│    Bloodstain Pattern Analyst   │
└─────────────────────────────────┘

┌─────────────────────────────────┐
│   Crime Scene Investigator or   │
│           Criminalist           │
└─────────────────────────────────┘
```

Position Description

Assaults, murders, and other violent crimes result in the loss of blood. Victims usually lose blood in these unfortunate incidents, but sometimes so do the perpetrators. Blood splatters in all directions and lands on all nearby surfaces, including on the people involved. It leaves trails when perpetrators and victims move within and from the crime scene. These bloodstains serve as valuable evidence of the crime, and crime scene investigators take great care to preserve the stains and splatters as much as possible for analysis.

Forensic specialists known as Bloodstain Pattern Analysts closely examine these marks to interpret and help recreate the events that transpired in the commission of the crime. The information they glean from bloodstain patterns is used in combination with other conclusions that arise from crime scene investigation and analysis. They can, within reason, anticipate reaching certain conclusions from their analysis. They can determine what movement or type of weapon created the stains, where the blood originated, how many blows

were inflicted to create the wounds, and the whereabouts of the victim, perpetrator, or various objects within the scene.

Bloodstain Pattern Analysts use their knowledge of chemistry, biology, physics, and mathematics in the execution of their job. Their particular expertise lies in an understanding of how blood behaves in a variety of conditions. These crime scene analysts are trained to recognize the various patterns that blood makes as it drops, flies, scatters, and smears. They also grasp how blood behaves as it exits the body in different circumstances, such as from bullet or knife wounds and from bludgeoning with fists or blunt instruments. For example, they can distinguish how blood leaves a stain when it drips from a cut or is flung from a weapon.

In addition, Bloodstain Pattern Analysts conduct experiments to better understand what happened during violent crimes. They perform tests with blood to see how it drops on various surfaces and from a variety of angles and velocities. For example, they notice that blood forms a sphere as it falls. From a short distance at 90° and onto a smooth surface, blood creates a round stain. From a higher distance, smaller splatters surround the central round stain. When blood hits the surface at an angle, the stain is elongated, and when it drops while its source is moving, it forms a different type of elongated pattern. Stains that fall on textured surfaces differ from those that fall on smooth surfaces. Bloodstain Pattern Analysts can read these and many other types of bloodstains and can determine the circumstances that created them as well as where the sources of the blood were located.

Bloodstain Pattern Analysts are often called to crime scenes to observe and measure bloodstains. When they cannot be present at a crime scene, they do their work in a laboratory setting. In both scenarios, these forensic specialists use photographs of the stains because many bloodstains cannot be taken to the lab. The photographs include scales such as yardsticks or measuring tape placed alongside the stains that indicate the size of the stains. Both vertical and horizontal measurements are indicated, which help analysts record the sizes of each bloodstain and their distance from each other. Bloodstain Pattern Analysts also carefully write their measurements and other observations.

When they examine bloodstains at crime scenes or from the clothing of the persons involved, Bloodstain Pattern Analysts can confirm or refute assumptions concerning the events of the crime and their sequence. They can ascertain the position of the victim and read evidence of a struggle. They can also verify or disprove statements made by the principals in a case by determining whether stains found on the perpetrator's or victim's clothing are consistent with their accounts of the incident or with what witnesses claim to have occurred.

Bloodstain Pattern Analysts perform various tasks in conducting their examinations. They review victim, witness, and suspect statements along with examination records from police, medical examiners, and other forensic scientists that assist them in their evaluations. They confer with crime scene investigators about the proper procedures for collecting and preserving bloodstain evidence. They also document all of their activities and write detailed reports of their test results and conclusions. When requested by attorneys, these analysts provide unbiased testimony as expert witnesses in courts of law.

Many Bloodstain Pattern Analysts work in local and state crime laboratories associated with law enforcement agencies, attorneys' offices, or other governmental agencies. The majority of these experts perform bloodstain analysis services as part of their duties as crime scene analysts (in the crime scene investigation unit) or as forensic scientists (in the crime lab). Bloodstain pattern experts are usually senior members of their staff.

These forensic specialists work standard 40-hour schedules, but must be available at all times. Hence, they may be required to work overtime or irregular hours, including weekends and holidays. They must be prepared to deal with heavy or stressful workloads.

Salaries

Bloodstain Pattern Analysts earn salaries based on their primary role as crime scene analysts or criminalists. Their earnings vary, and depend on such factors as their education, experience, position, employer, and geographic location. According to the May 2006 *Occupational Employment Statistics* survey by the U.S. Bureau of Labor Statistics, the estimated annual salary for most forensic science technicians ranged between $27,530 and $73,100.

Employment Prospects

Some Bloodstain Pattern Analysts work for private forensic labs, and some are independent practitioners. But most bloodstain pattern experts work in public crime labs, which are associated with law enforcement agencies, prosecuting attorneys' offices, and other government agencies. They may be law enforcement officers or civilian employees.

Few government agencies specifically hire individuals to perform bloodstain pattern analysis. Instead, most employ these experts as criminalists (or forensic scientists) or crime scene analysts who are responsible for several areas of forensic expertise.

Opportunities for Bloodstain Pattern Analysts are expected to increase in the future, as more criminalists and crime scene analysts become trained in bloodstain analysis. According to the *180 Day Study Final Report* (March 2006) by the International Association for Identification, there is a growing need and demand for qualified bloodstain pattern practitioners to assist in crime scene reconstruction.

Advancement Prospects

Bloodstain Pattern Analysts can be promoted to become technical leaders, unit or section supervisors, and managers. However, opportunities are limited. Sworn officers can rise through the ranks as detectives, sergeants, lieutenants, and so on, up to chief of police.

Individuals with teaching talents and interests can seek positions as trainers as well as instructors at colleges and universities. Those with entrepreneurial ambitions can become independent practitioners or owners of forensic firms that offer consulting or technical services.

Education and Training

Educational requirements vary with the different employers as well as for the different positions. For crime lab positions, employers usually require that applicants hold a bachelor's degree in forensic science or a physical or natural science. For crime scene analysis positions, some agencies require applicants to have only a high school diploma or general equivalency diploma, while others prefer that applicants possess an associate or bachelor's degree in law enforcement, criminal justice, forensic science, or another related discipline.

To become Bloodstain Pattern Analysts, criminalists or crime scene technicians must complete a specialized training program. This usually includes formal classroom instruction and on-the-job training, in which they work under the supervision and direction of experienced personnel.

Throughout their careers, Bloodstain Pattern Analysts enroll in courses, workshops, seminars, and other educational and training programs to update their skills and increase their knowledge.

Special Requirements

In agencies in which criminalists are law enforcement officers, applicants must possess a basic peace officer standards and training certificate. These agencies may hire candidates without a certificate on the condition they complete the necessary law enforcement academy program to obtain the certificate.

Law enforcement officers must successfully complete annual training to maintain their certification.

Experience, Special Skills, and Personality Traits

Employers seek candidates who have several years of work experience in crime scene investigation and analysis and have experience conducting experiments pertaining to bloodstain pattern analysis. Many Bloodstain Pattern Analysts gained their experience by working under the helm of knowledgeable and practiced practitioners.

To perform well at their job, Bloodstain Pattern Analysts need effective teamwork, interpersonal, communication, writing, and self-management skills. Being detail-oriented, precise, observant, objective, honest, trustworthy, and diligent are some personality traits that these analysts have in common.

Unions and Associations

Many Bloodstain Pattern Analysts join professional associations to take advantage of networking opportunities, professional publications, certification programs, and other professional services and resources. One national society that serves their particular interests is the International Association of Bloodstain Pattern Analysts. Other national associations that they may join are the International Association for Identification, the Association for Crime Scene Reconstruction, the American College of Forensic Examiners, and the American Academy of Forensic Science. For contact information, see Appendix III.

Some of these forensic practitioners belong to a labor union that represents them in negotiations with employers for better contractual terms for pay, benefits, and working conditions.

Tips for Entry

1. Talk with bloodstain pattern experts to learn more about their work and how they got into that line of work.
2. As a crime scene technician or crime lab professional, express your interest to your team leader or unit supervisor about learning how to perform bloodstain pattern analysis.
3. Be sure you submit your job application for a position on time. Few employers accept applications that come in after the deadline date.
4. Many professionals obtain professional certification as a bloodstain pattern practitioner to enhance their employability and credibility. For information about certification programs, see Appendix II.
5. Use the Internet to learn more about bloodstain pattern analysis. You might start by visiting the International Association of Bloodstain Pattern Analysts Web site at http://www.iabpa.org. For more links, see Appendix IV.

DNA ANALYST

CAREER PROFILE

Duties: Identify, analyze, and interpret DNA samples of biological evidence submitted for criminal investigations or other legal matters; prepare reports of findings; provide expert witness testimony; perform other duties as required

Alternate Title(s): Criminalist, Forensic Scientist

Salary Range: $28,000 to $73,000

Employment Prospects: Good

Advancement Prospects: Fair

Prerequisites:

Education or Training—Bachelor's degree in biology, chemistry, forensic science, or another related field; on-the-job training

Experience—Six months to one or more years of work experience in a forensic lab preferred

Special Skills and Personality Traits—Self-management, critical-thinking, writing, communication, presentation, interpersonal, and teamwork skills; objective, impartial, ethical, trustworthy, detail-oriented, and diligent

Special Requirements—Peace officer certificate may be required

CAREER LADDER

```
┌─────────────────────────────────────┐
│  Senior or Supervisory DNA Analyst  │
└─────────────────────────────────────┘

┌─────────────────────────────────────┐
│            DNA Analyst              │
└─────────────────────────────────────┘

┌─────────────────────────────────────┐
│   DNA Analyst (Entry-Level) or      │
│        DNA Technologist             │
└─────────────────────────────────────┘
```

Position Description

DNA, or deoxyribonucleic acid, is what makes us "us." We, like all organisms, are composed of cells. Each of our cells contains threads of material called chromosomes, and along each chromosome are nearly 30,000 genes that instruct our cells to create proteins that determine such characteristics as our eye color or hair texture. Each gene is contained within DNA, and that carries our genetic information. Every one of us has unique DNA.

DNA analysis is used for the identification of unknown individuals or living organisms in legal, medical, and other matters. For example, DNA analysis helps us to identify victims of accidents, settle questions regarding paternity or other family relationships, match organ donors to recipients, identify endangered species, find pollution-causing bacteria, verify the authenticity of various foods such as wine or caviar, or establish the lineage of livestock breeds. Crimes are sometimes solved by the identification of suspects through their DNA.

DNA is found in all the cellular structures, or tissues, of our bodies including our saliva, blood, hair follicles, muscles, bones, teeth, fingernails, and skin. Perpetrators may leave some of their tissue behind at crime scenes or, if perpetrators come into contact with them, on victims. Forensic scientists known as DNA Analysts specialize in examining DNA samples from biological evidence that is found at crime scenes. Their analyses help identify crime suspects as well as exonerate persons who have been wrongly accused or convicted of crimes.

DNA Analysts apply the principles and techniques of biochemistry, molecular biology, genetics, and statistics to their work. They understand that DNA molecules are composed of repeating components called nucleotides consisting of four bases: adenine, guanine, cytosine, and thymine. These bases pair up in a regular repeating pattern to help form a spiral-shaped double helix, the DNA molecule. Each DNA molecule in a person is distinguished from the DNA molecules in other persons by the order of its bases.

DNA Analysts use several methods to work with these base patterns to identify crime suspects. These methods involve cutting sections of DNA by using special enzymes, then comparing their base patterns with the patterns contained within control DNA samples. Analysts use special equipment to perform these procedures. Each of these methods are useful in different circumstances, but all allow DNA Analysts to match the repeating base patterns between DNA samples found at crime scenes with DNA samples extracted from suspects. DNA is taken from suspects by swabbing the inside of their cheeks. DNA is also extracted from convicted criminals. Additionally, these analysts examine samples taken from dead bodies, dried semen deposits, or decomposed bloodstains.

DNA Analysts have access to a database of DNA profiles known as the Combined DNA Index System (CODIS). This is a software program that maintains municipal, state, and federal databases of DNA profiles of convicted criminals. DNA Analysts use CODIS to match suspect DNA profiles with those in the database.

DNA Analysts work under close supervision and divide their duties to fulfill certain functions. The majority of their time is spent working with DNA evidence that is submitted to their lab. They look at and study physical evidence, remove DNA from the samples, and conduct various tests for analysis and profiling on CODIS. Upon completion of their examinations, they prepare and submit reports of their findings. The rest of their time is allocated to research, preparing for and performing expert witness duties, or updating their training or providing training to law enforcement, health care, or educational personnel. Furthermore, they maintain and calibrate their equipment, prepare chemical solutions, order supplies, and perform other related tasks.

DNA Analysts begin their careers as trainees. They focus on developing their knowledge and skills as well as their understanding of the laws and regulations, as well as the standards and practices of their employers. They are given assignments with specific directions and clearly defined objectives, and perform their work under the guidance and supervision of senior forensic scientists.

After DNA Analysts complete their training period, they are then assigned casework that they perform under the supervision of experienced personnel. As DNA Analysts gain experience, they are assigned more complex responsibilities. For instance, they prepare analytical reports of a more confidential nature; they conduct advance research and perform technical reviews of current cases; they provide technical and scientific consultation to other investigators; and they testify in court as expert witnesses.

Senior or advanced analysts may assume the function of team leader or unit supervisor. They lead others by providing technical advice, assigning work to team members, monitoring their work, and contributing to employee performance evaluations. These advanced professionals maintain supplies and equipment, participate in the hiring and training processes for new employees, and help to set goals and objectives for their unit's activities. They are also assigned other responsibilities. For example, they might assist in the development of a DNA database of convicted sex offenders, which would be incorporated in the CODIS; or they might assist in overseeing quality assurance programs to ensure that their units are in compliance with policies, procedures, laws, and regulations.

In some crime labs, DNA Analysts are also assigned to perform other types of forensic work, such as serology, trace evidence, or firearms analysis.

DNA Analysts work in laboratory, office, and field settings. They work a standard 40-hour week, but may put in additional hours as needed. They may be called to work at any time of the day or night, as well as on weekends and holidays. They must be prepared to report for duty within an hour's notification. When they work at crime scenes, they must be able to negotiate rough terrain or climb up and down embankments.

Salaries

Salaries for DNA Analysts vary, depending on such factors as their education, experience, employer, and geographic location. Specific salary information for this occupation is unavailable. However, the U.S. Bureau of Labor Statistics reported in its May 2006 *Occupational Employment Statistics* survey that the estimated annual salary for most forensic science technicians ranged between $27,530 and $73,000.

Employment Prospects

The major employers of DNA Analysts include local and state crime labs associated with law enforcement agencies and prosecuting attorneys' offices; crime labs run by such federal agencies as the Federal Bureau of Investigation, the U.S. Postal Inspection Service, and the U.S. Fish and Wildlife Service; and privately owned forensic laboratories. Other employers include colleges and universities. DNA Analysts are also hired by medical, scientific, and research laboratories to perform DNA analysis for noncriminal matters.

In government crime labs, DNA Analysts are mostly civilians. In local and state labs, they may be law enforcement officers.

In general, job openings become available as individuals retire, transfer to other jobs, or advance to higher positions. Job growth in the forensic science field is predicted to increase by 27 percent or more through 2014, according to the BLS. Some experts in the field report that DNA analysis is one of the fastest growing areas in forensic science. Nationwide, there is a demand for experienced DNA Analysts. Many forensic laboratories are experiencing a backlog of casework.

Opportunities for entry-level positions are generally more available with state, federal, and private labs, according to one expert. Many labs prefer to hire experienced analysts. However, the ability of a government crime lab to maintain or hire more staff depends on the availability of funding.

Advancement Prospects

Individuals with supervisory and managerial ambitions can pursue such positions, but opportunities are limited. Hence, they may need to seek positions with other employers to advance. A master's or doctoral degree may be required for higher-level management positions.

Sworn officers have additional opportunities for advancement. They can rise through the ranks as detectives, sergeants, lieutenants, and so on, up to chief of police. They can also pursue administrative and managerial positions within their agency.

Education and Training

Minimally, applicants for entry-level positions need a bachelor's degree in biology, chemistry, forensic science or another related field. Ideally, they would have completed course work in genetics, biochemistry, molecular biology, and statistics. Some employers prefer to hire candidates who hold a master's degree in an appropriate field.

Entry-level DNA Analysts undergo a training period that lasts between six and 12 months or more. They complete formal classroom instruction as well as receive on-the-job training while working under the supervision and direction of experienced DNA Analysts.

Throughout their careers, DNA Analysts update their skills and increase their knowledge by enrolling in courses, workshops, and seminars given by employers, professional associations, universities, and other organizations.

Special Requirements

In agencies in which DNA Analysts are law enforcement officers, applicants must possess a basic peace officer standards and training certificate. These agencies may hire candidates without a certificate on the condition they complete the necessary law enforcement academy program to obtain the certificate.

Law enforcement officers must successfully complete annual training to maintain their certification.

Experience, Special Skills, and Personality Traits

Requirements for entry-level positions vary with the different forensic laboratories. Many employers prefer to hire candidates who have six months to one or two years of experience working in a forensic laboratory. Candidates may have gained experience through internships, employment, or research assistantships.

Like other forensic scientists, DNA Analysts must have effective self-management skills, such as the ability to work independently, handle stressful situations, and prioritize multiple tasks. Their line of work also requires that these forensic examiners have strong critical-thinking, writing, communication, presentation, interpersonal, and teamwork skills.

Some personality traits that successful DNA Analysts have in common include being objective, impartial, ethical, trustworthy, detail-oriented, and diligent.

Unions and Associations

Some DNA Analysts are members of a labor union that represents them in negotiations with employers for better contractual terms for pay, benefits, and working conditions. In addition, the union handles any grievances that they may have against their employers.

Professional associations that serve the interests of DNA Analysts are available at the local, state, and national levels. By joining societies, they can take advantage of networking opportunities, professional certification, professional publications, and other professional resources and services. Some national societies that serve the interests of DNA examiners are the Association of Forensic DNA Analysts and Administrators, the International Association for Identification, the American Academy of Forensic Sciences, and the American College of Forensic Examiners. For contact information, see Appendix III.

Tips for Entry

1. Along with science and math courses, take classes in English, grammar, and public speaking in high school to help prepare you for a career in forensic science.
2. Talk to various DNA Analysts to learn more about their work. Also find out how they entered the field as well as ask for suggestions about how you can best prepare for a career in forensic science.
3. Some DNA Analysts started off their careers as serologists.
4. Learn as much as you can about a particular job before you go to your job interview. Employers are usually inclined to hire candidates who have a strong understanding about the job they would be performing.
5. You can learn more about forensic DNA analysis on the Internet. To get a list of relevant Web sites, enter the keywords *forensic DNA analysis* or *DNA forensics* in a search engine. For some links, see Appendix IV.

FIREARMS EXAMINER

CAREER PROFILE

Duties: Identify, compare, and analyze firearms, ammunition, and tool marks that are evidence in criminal investigations; prepare reports of findings; provide expert witness testimony; perform other duties as required

Alternate Title(s): Firearms and Tool Mark Examiner, Firearms Analyst, Forensic Scientist, Criminalist

Salary Range: $28,000 to $73,000

Employment Prospects: Good

Advancement Prospects: Fair

Prerequisites:

Education or Training—Educational requirements vary; on-the-job training

Experience—Previous lab experience usually required

Special Skills and Personality Traits—Problem-solving, organizational, teamwork, interpersonal, writing, communication, presentation, and self-management skills; impartial, ethical, trustworthy, detail-oriented, persistent, cooperative, and patient

Special Requirements—Peace officer certificate may be required

CAREER LADDER

```
┌─────────────────────────────────┐
│    Senior Firearms Examiner     │
└─────────────────────────────────┘

┌─────────────────────────────────┐
│       Firearms Examiner         │
└─────────────────────────────────┘

┌─────────────────────────────────┐
│    Firearms Examiner Trainee    │
└─────────────────────────────────┘
```

Position Description

In the crime lab, Firearms Examiners are the experts in firearms identification. They have been trained in the identification, comparison, and testing of firearms, firearm parts, ammunition, and ammunition components. Most of them are also responsible for examining tool marks, another type of physical evidence that is found at crime scenes. These forensic specialists perform their analyses and interpretations with the goal of providing criminal investigators and prosecuting attorneys with scientific proof that may help them arrest and convict criminal suspects.

Firearms and tools each produce their own unique markings. With the use of a special microscope, Firearms Examiners can compare markings of recovered bullets from a crime scene with test bullets from a specific gun that investigators have submitted. If the markings on the recovered and test bullets match, then that is positive proof the recovered bullets come from the gun in question. Firearms Examiners use a similar method to determine if tool marks recovered

from a crime scene match certain tools (such as screwdrivers, crowbars, bolt cutters, scissors, and knives) that are suspected of being used.

In the area of firearms evidence, Firearms Examiners conduct examinations for various purposes, as requested by criminal investigators or prosecuting attorneys. Depending on their skill level and expertise, their casework may involve:

- determining if bullets, cartridge cases, or other ammunition components may have been fired by a certain firearm or may have been in the firearm
- identifying the type, brand, and caliber of firearms and ammunition
- establishing how a firearm works
- determining if a firearm functions properly or if it could have discharged accidentally
- finding out at what distance a firearm was fired
- restoring serial numbers on firearms

- detecting and characterizing gunshot residue patterns on victims' garments

Some Firearms Examiners are experts in ballistics, the study of projectiles (such as bullets) in motion. These examiners assist crime scene technicians and criminal investigators with the reconstruction of shooting events at a crime scene. For example, they perform analyses to determine the path that bullets may have taken or to establish what happens when a projectile strikes a target.

Firearms Examiners mostly work in the crime lab. On occasion, they are requested to assist in the collection and preservation of firearms and tool marks evidence at crime scenes.

Firearms Examiners apply scientific principles and methods to identify, analyze, and interpret firearms and tool mark evidence. Their casework involves comparative, microscopic, chemical, and other complex laboratory analyses. In addition, these examiners follow strict procedures and protocols as well as comply with the laws and regulations concerning evidence, criminal procedures, and crime. They also make sure that they maintain the chain of custody on every piece of evidence that they handle to ensure that it has not been tampered with or contaminated. Physical evidence may not be admitted at court trials if the chain of custody has been violated.

Firearms Examiners carefully and precisely document every step they take when examining physical evidence. First, they inspect an item of evidence and take notes about what it is, how it looks, how much it weighs, and so on. They may sketch, photograph, or take a video of the evidence, which becomes part of their report. They then determine what tests should be performed. Upon completion of their tests, they evaluate the results and prepare formal reports that describe their findings and the methods they used to obtain them. Their reports must be comprehensive yet clearly understandable by law enforcement officers, attorneys, judges, and juries.

Like all criminalists, Firearms Examiners may be called upon to testify as expert witnesses at court trials. They provide impartial and unbiased testimony on issues related to their laboratory analyses as well as the crime lab procedures, methods, and techniques that they practice.

Firearms Examiners are assigned several cases at a time. They are expected to manage, plan, and prioritize assignments so that each of their cases is completed in a timely manner. They perform various other duties along with their casework. For example, they:

- prepare photographic exhibits and other visual aids for court presentations or training purposes
- conduct research on new methodologies and techniques in the examination of firearms and tool marks
- maintain accurate records on their casework

- maintain lab equipment, instruments, and work area
- assist in the development and implementation of quality assurance activities
- train subordinate staff members
- train law enforcement officers in the proper methods for seeking, collecting, and processing evidence
- stay current with new technologies, issues, and developments in their field as well as keep abreast of changing laws and rules pertaining to the collection, preservation, and submission of evidence

Firearms Examiners work a 40-hour schedule but put in additional hours as needed to complete their duties or to meet deadlines. They may be required to be on call 24 hours a day.

Salaries

Salaries for Firearms Examiners vary, depending on such factors as their education, experience, position, employer, and geographic location. According to the May 2006 *Occupational Employment Statistics* survey by the U.S. Bureau of Labor Statistics (BLS), the estimated annual salary for most forensic science technicians ranged between $27,530 and $73,100.

Employment Prospects

Firearms Examiners are employed by public and private crime laboratories. In the United States, there are nearly 400 publicly funded crime labs. Most of these labs are connected to law enforcement agencies and prosecuting attorneys' offices in municipal, county, and state jurisdictions. The Federal Bureau of Investigation, the Drug Enforcement Administration, the Bureau of Alcohol, Tobacco, Firearms and Explosives, the Secret Service, and the U.S. Postal Inspection Service are some federal agencies that employ Firearms Examiners in their forensic labs. In government crime labs, Firearms Examiners may be law enforcement officers or civilian employees.

In general, job openings become available as individuals retire, transfer to other jobs, or advance to higher positions. Agencies will create additional positions as long as funding is available. The job competition is keen, and should become even more competitive due to the increasing number of individuals who are entering the forensic science field. Job growth in this field is predicted to increase by 27 percent or more through 2014, according to the BLS.

Advancement Prospects

Administrative and managerial opportunities are available, but limited. Firearms Examiners can seek positions as technical leaders, unit supervisors, and managers. Sworn officers can rise through the ranks as detectives, sergeants, lieutenants, and so on, up to chief of police.

Opportunities are usually better in large laboratories that have several levels of management. Individuals with entrepreneurial ambitions can become independent practitioners or owners of forensic firms that offer consulting or technical services. Individuals can also pursue opportunities as forensic trainers or as instructors and researchers in higher education institutions. To advance to higher positions or obtain teaching jobs, these forensic specialists may be required to possess a master's or doctoral degree.

Education and Training
Educational requirements vary with the different employers. Many prefer to hire candidates who possess a bachelor's degree in a physical or natural science discipline, forensic science, law enforcement, or another related field. Some agencies require only a high school or general equivalency diploma, as long as candidates have qualifying work experience.

Entry-level Firearms Examiners undergo a training program that usually lasts two years. Their training includes classroom instruction as well as on-the-job training in which they work under the guidance and direction of experienced personnel.

Throughout their careers, Firearms Examiners enroll in continuing education programs and training programs to update their skills and increase their knowledge.

Special Requirements
In agencies in which Firearms Examiners are law enforcement officers, they must possess a basic peace officer standards and training certificate. These agencies may hire candidates without a certificate on the condition they complete the necessary law enforcement academy program to obtain the certificate.

Law enforcement officers must successfully complete annual training to maintain their certification.

Experience, Special Skills, and Personality Traits
Requirements vary with the different employers. For entry-level positions, most crime labs prefer to hire candidates who have previous laboratory experience, which they may have gained through internships, research assistantships, or employment in analytical, crime, or scientific research laboratories. Entry-level candidates should be able to demonstrate their knowledge about proper lab procedures and the handling of lab instruments and equipment.

To perform the various aspects of their job well, Firearms Examiners must have excellent problem-solving, organizational, teamwork, interpersonal, writing, communication, and presentation skills. In addition, they need strong self-management skills, such as the ability to work independently, prioritize multiple tasks, meet deadlines, and handle stressful situations. Being impartial, ethical, trustworthy, detail-oriented, persistent, cooperative, and patient are some personality traits that successful Firearms Examiners have in common.

Unions and Associations
Many Firearms Examiners belong to professional associations to take advantage of networking opportunities, continuing education, professional certification, and other professional resources and services. Some national societies that serve their interests include the Association of Firearms and Tool Mark Examiners, the International Association for Identification, the American Academy of Forensic Sciences, and the American College of Forensic Examiners. For contact information, see Appendix III.

Some examiners are also members of a labor union that represents them in negotiations with employers for better contractual terms for pay, benefits, and working conditions.

Tips for Entry
1. As a student, gain experience by working in a law enforcement agency, by volunteering, or by completing an internship. If possible, seek a volunteer or intern position in the agency's forensic services division.
2. Check job listings for forensic positions on the Internet. Many forensic societies post current job vacancies at their Web sites.
3. Stay current with technologies, issues, and other developments in the forensic science field. Being able to discuss such matters can impress job interviewers as well as professors and professionals who may be able to refer you to job openings.
4. Use the Internet to learn more about Firearms Examiners. You might start by visiting the Association of Firearm and Tool Mark Examiners Web site at http://www.afte.org. For more links, see Appendix IV.

FORENSIC BIOLOGIST

CAREER PROFILE

Duties: Identify, analyze, and interpret biological evidence for criminal investigations or trials; prepare reports of findings; provide expert witness testimony; perform other duties as required

Alternate Title(s): Criminalist, Forensic Scientist; a title that reflects a specialty such as DNA Analyst

Salary Range: $28,000 to $73,000

Employment Prospects: Good

Advancement Prospects: Fair

Prerequisites:

Education or Training—Bachelor's degree in microbiology, biochemistry, medical technology, forensic science, or another related field; on-the-job training

Experience—Previous lab experience usually required

Special Skills and Personality Traits—Self-management, problem solving, teamwork, interpersonal, writing, communication, and presentation skills; patient, trustworthy, non-judgmental, precise, honest, and persistent

Special Requirements—Peace officer certificate may be required

CAREER LADDER

```
┌─────────────────────────────────┐
│    Senior Forensic Biologist    │
└─────────────────────────────────┘

┌─────────────────────────────────┐
│       Forensic Biologist        │
└─────────────────────────────────┘

┌─────────────────────────────────┐
│    Forensic Biologist Trainee   │
└─────────────────────────────────┘
```

Position Description

Evidence gathered at crime scenes can be divided into two classes: physical evidence and biological evidence. Physical evidence consists of items or substances such as glass, fibers, paint chips, firearms, and documents. Biological evidence is made up of items or substances that originate with human tissue, such as fingernails, hair, skin, blood, saliva, dental pulp, and sexual fluids. Many crime labs have a forensic biology section that conducts scientific examinations on biological evidence to assist criminal investigators and prosecuting attorneys in linking suspects to crime scenes or victims.

Highly trained men and women known as Forensic Biologists are responsible for identifying, analyzing, and interpreting samples of biological evidence. Their scientific findings provide unbiased information that can help eliminate individuals as suspects, support case circumstances, disprove a suspect's alibi, determine what happened at a crime scene and in what order events occurred, and establish a location as being a crime scene.

Forensic Biologists enter this career after completing university studies with a focus on such subjects as forensic biology, forensic chemistry, forensic human pathology, and forensic DNA analysis. They round off their education with courses in mathematics, criminal justice, and other sciences. They receive training in the collection of evidence in field settings such as mock crime scenes and in the analysis of evidence in laboratory settings. Their education and training provide Forensic Biologists with knowledge about scientific principles, analytical procedures, and the use of the reagents needed to detect or measure blood and other bodily secretions. They are well versed in working in both standard and crime laboratory environments. They possess an understanding of how the criminal trial process works and are knowledgeable about standard rules of evidence.

Forensic Biologists work in forensic science laboratories where they perform analyses of tissues and bodily fluids that were left behind during criminal acts such as burglaries, homicides, or rapes. These scientists process specimens to identify their origin. The specimens are refrigerated until they are needed. Each Forensic Biologist is assigned to specific cases and works with the samples associated with those cases.

These criminalists examine the samples under microscopes or perform immunologic or biochemical tests. They identify samples of physiological evidence, and determine whether they are of human or animal origin. With some tests, they attempt to establish the age, sex, and other characteristics about the persons from whom the samples came. Forensic Biologists also determine which samples are appropriate for DNA analysis. If they are trained in that area, they conduct DNA marker typing procedures for comparison to suspect samples or to DNA entries in the Combined DNA Index System (or CODIS), the DNA databank.

After they complete their evaluations for a case, Forensic Biologists prepare and submit technical reports of their findings. They describe their procedures and analysis in language that is easily understood by criminal investigators, attorneys, and others who may not have any technical or scientific background. Forensic Biologists are often called upon to testify as expert witnesses about their findings in the courts.

Forensic Biologists perform most of their work in laboratories. Occasionally, they may assist at crime scenes to detect and collect specimens of bodily substances and fluids. At times, these specimens may be only dried stains or in trace amounts. They can be detected with the use of special lights and chemical sprays that reveal their presence. Forensic Biologists collect specimens from corpses, walls, floors, and objects at the scene by using swabs, filter papers, tweezers, special tubes, and other devices and place the samples in envelopes or plastic bags. Once collected, the samples are taken to laboratories for further analysis.

In some labs, Forensic Biologists may specialize as forensic serologists, DNA analysts, blood spatter analysts, or in some other area of concern, such as forensic entomology.

Forensic Biologists complete a variety of duties along with their casework. For example, they:

- obtain evidence from evidence officers and keep a record of its use in compliance with chain-of-custody procedures
- prepare serological or chemical reagents
- document all laboratory activities and generate detailed reports of test results and conclusions
- prepare evidence for presentation in court proceedings
- write and revise laboratory manuals
- maintain and calibrate sensitive laboratory equipment
- train laboratory technicians
- contribute to laboratory quality control programs
- confer with and train law enforcement personnel about the proper procedures for collecting and preserving evidence
- give presentations about forensics to students, other law enforcement personnel, or the general public

Forensic Biologists stand for extended periods, and are required to lift moderate to heavy weights, including corpses. They handle sharp surgical instruments. They must be able to tolerate exposure to unusual samples, including organs, tissues, and body parts. They may be exposed to hazardous materials, including chemicals and biohazards such as bodily fluids or contagious diseases, as well as noxious odors.

Forensic Biologists work on an on-call basis in addition to their regular hours. They may be called to handle emergencies or work overtime as needed.

Salaries

Salaries for Forensic Biologists vary, depending on such factors as their education, experience, position, employer, and geographic location. According to the May 2006 *Occupational Employment Statistics* survey by the U.S. Bureau of Labor Statistics (BLS), the estimated annual salary for most forensic science technicians ranged between $27,530 and $73,100.

Employment Prospects

In general, job openings become available as individuals retire, transfer to other jobs, or advance to higher positions. Employers will create additional positions to meet growing needs, as long as funding is available. According to the BLS, job growth in the forensic science field is predicted to increase by 27 percent or more through 2014.

Opportunities are usually better for experienced Forensic Biologists, as many crime labs do not have the time nor staff to train entry-level criminalists. The majority of Forensic Biologists work in crime labs that are part of law enforcement agencies, prosecuting attorneys' offices, and other governmental agencies at the local, state, and federal levels of government.

In local and state crime labs, Forensic Biologists may be civilian employees or law enforcement officers.

Advancement Prospects

Forensic Biologists can advance in any number of ways, depending on their ambitions and interests. They can become technical specialists in DNA analysis, serology examination, or other areas. They can rise through the administrative and managerial ranks as technical leaders, unit supervisors, and managers, which may require transferring to other employers. Sworn officers also have the opportunity to advance in rank as well as pursue administrative and managerial careers in their agency.

Individuals with entrepreneurial ambitions can become independent practitioners or owners of forensic firms that offer consulting or technical services. To advance to higher positions or to obtain teaching jobs, these forensic scientists may be required to hold a master's or doctoral degree.

Education and Training

In general, employers seek candidates for entry-level positions that hold a bachelor's degree in microbiology, biochemistry, medical technology, forensic science, or another related field. Some employers may prefer to hire candidates who possess a master's degree. Applicants who wish to perform DNA analysis should have completed course work in molecular biology, genetics, biochemistry, and statistics.

Entry-level Forensic Biologists undergo a training period that includes formal classroom instruction and on-the-job training. They perform routine tasks while working under the supervision and direction of experienced staff members.

Throughout their careers, Forensic Biologists enroll in continuing education programs and training programs to update their skills and keep up with advancements in their fields.

Special Requirements

In agencies in which Forensic Biologists are law enforcement officers, they must possess a basic peace officer standards and training certificate. These agencies may hire candidates without a certificate on the condition they complete the necessary law enforcement academy program to obtain the certificate.

Law enforcement officers must successfully complete annual training to maintain their certification.

Experience, Special Skills, and Personality Traits

Requirements vary with the different employers. Most crime labs prefer to hire candidates for entry-level positions who have previous laboratory experience, preferably in a forensic lab. They may have gained their experience through internships, research assistantships, or employment. Entry-level candidates should be able to demonstrate their knowledge about proper lab procedures and the handling of lab instruments and equipment.

To perform effectively at their job, Forensic Biologists must have excellent self-management, problem-solving, teamwork, interpersonal, writing, communication, and presentation skills. Being patient, trustworthy, non-judgmental, precise, honest, and persistent are some personality traits that successful Forensic Biologists have in common.

Unions and Associations

Forensic Biologists are eligible to join professional associations to take advantage of networking opportunities, continuing education, professional certification, and other professional resources and services. Professional societies are available locally, statewide, regionally, nationally, and worldwide. Some national societies that serve the diverse interests of these forensic scientists are:

- American Academy of Forensic Sciences
- American College of Forensic Examiners
- International Association for Identification
- International Association of Bloodstain Pattern Analysts
- Association of Forensic DNA Analysts and Administrators

For contact information, see Appendix III.

Some Forensic Biologists are members of a labor union that represents them in negotiations with employers for better contractual terms for pay, benefits, and working conditions. In addition, the union handles any grievances that members may have against their employers.

Tips for Entry

1. Different crime labs use general job titles such as forensic scientist, criminalist, or crime lab analyst for Forensic Biologist positions. Be sure to read all job announcements thoroughly to ensure that you do not miss job vacancies for the position you seek.
2. Answer all questions completely and thoroughly on your job applications. Do not leave any spaces blank. If a question does not apply to you, write *Not Applicable* or *N/A* in the space.
3. If a person or organization refers you to a job opening, be sure you mention that person's or group's name on your job application or cover letter.
4. Take advantage of your college career center to find job vacancies, as well as to help you improve your job search skills. Most, if not all, college career centers assist both students and alumni.
5. Use the Internet to learn more about what Forensic Biologists do. To obtain relevant Web sites, enter the keywords *forensic biology section* in a search engine. For some links, see Appendix IV.

FORENSIC CHEMIST

CAREER PROFILE

Duties: To identify and evaluate physical evidence by performing chemical analysis; prepare reports of findings; provide expert witness testimony; perform other duties as required

Alternate Title(s): Criminalist, Forensic Scientist; a title that reflects a particular job such as Forensic Drug Chemist or Forensic Toxicologist

Salary Range: $28,000 to $73,000

Employment Prospects: Good

Advancement Prospects: Fair

Prerequisites:

Education or Training—Bachelor's degree in chemistry, forensic science, or another related field; on-the-job training

Experience—Previous lab experience usually required

Special Skills and Personality Traits—Problem-solving, organizational, writing, communication, presentation, and self-management skills; detail-oriented, versatile, patient, composed, impartial, ethical, and collaborative

Special Requirements—Peace officer certificate may be required

CAREER LADDER

```
┌─────────────────────────────┐
│   Senior Forensic Chemist   │
└─────────────────────────────┘

┌─────────────────────────────┐
│      Forensic Chemist       │
└─────────────────────────────┘

┌─────────────────────────────┐
│  Forensic Chemist Trainee   │
└─────────────────────────────┘
```

Position Description

Forensic Chemists are the men and women in crime laboratories who conduct chemical analyses on physical evidence with the goal of finding links between criminal suspects and crime scenes. They assist on various cases, including homicides, assaults, robberies, arson, and vandalism, among others. They examine evidence such as hair, fiber, blood or other bodily fluids, drugs, poisons, gunshot residue, fire debris, explosive residue, inks, paints, and noxious chemicals.

Many Forensic Chemists are cross-trained to provide DNA analysis, trace evidence examination, explosives analysis, and other types of examinations for their crime labs. Some Forensic Chemists work in drug units, where they focus on identifying and analyzing illicit drugs seized by law enforcement officers. Others work in toxicology units, where they are responsible for detecting and examining living and dead human tissue for drugs or poisons.

Forensic Chemists are responsible for identifying, analyzing, and interpreting the physical evidence that they are assigned. They utilize their background in chemistry, criminalistics, and instrumental analysis, as well as physics, mathematics, and other scientific areas. Those chemists who contribute to DNA analysis work also have knowledge of microbiology, biochemistry, and genetics, while those who focus on toxicology bring an expertise about physiology to their work.

These forensic specialists follow strict practices, procedures, and standards, as well as comply with laws and regulations pertaining to the handling and processing of evidence. They study each case carefully to learn about the evidence and what kind of information criminal investigators or attorneys need. They then determine what tests, methods, and procedures to perform on the evidence to obtain the data. Their work involves the use of computers, microscopes, chromatographs, spectrographs, and other technologically advanced equipment and instruments.

Forensic Chemists perform their casework accurately and correctly and are expected to complete their work in a timely manner. They handle each item of evidence carefully to maintain the chain of custody. If any article of evidence has been tampered with or contaminated, it may not be admitted as testimony in a court of law.

Forensic Chemists prepare formal reports of their findings and conclusions and submit them to the proper authorities. They may be called upon to testify in the courts about their casework. They are qualified as expert witnesses to provide testimony about their findings and conclusions on a case, as well as to answer questions regarding the methods and techniques of performing chemical analyses.

Forensic Chemists mostly work in clean, well-lit, and ventilated laboratories. From time to time, they are called out to assist at crime scenes. They may be engaged in assisting or directing crime scene investigators with locating, collecting, and processing physical evidence.

These forensic specialists also perform other duties besides casework, which vary according to their skill levels and expertise. For example, they may be assigned such responsibilities as:

- preparing exhibits or visual aids for court presentations or training sessions
- acting as a technical resource to attorneys and law enforcement officers
- conducting research to design new or improved lab techniques, methods, and procedures
- maintaining lab areas, equipment, and instruments, according to established standards of cleanliness, safety, and efficiency
- organizing and maintaining records, logs, and files
- training crime scene technicians and law enforcement officers in the collection and processing of physical evidence
- assisting in the development and implementation of quality assurance activities and programs
- supervising entry-level examiners, technicians, and other subordinate staff members
- attending workshops, seminars, and courses to maintain proficiency certifications
- keeping up with current laws of evidence, criminal procedures, and crime, as well as new technologies, techniques, and developments in their forensic specialty

Forensic Chemists handle dangerous, toxic, and flammable chemicals and they are required to wear protective clothing and equipment. They work a standard 40-hour work schedule but are expected to put in additional hours as needed to complete tasks and meet deadlines. They are on call 24 hours a day.

Salaries

Salaries for Forensic Chemists vary, depending on such factors as their education, experience, employer, and geographic location. According to the May 2006 *Occupational Employment Statistics* survey by the U.S. Bureau of Labor Statistics (BLS), the estimated annual salary for most forensic science technicians ranged between $27,530 and $73,100.

Employment Prospects

Forensic Chemists find employment with government crime laboratories at the local, state, and federal levels. They are usually civilian employees, but in some local and state labs, they are sworn officers. Some work for private forensic laboratories or for academic labs that are associated with forensic programs.

Job growth in the forensic science field is predicted to increase by 27 percent or more through 2014, according to the BLS. In addition, opportunities become available as individuals retire, transfer to other jobs, or advance to higher positions. However, the ability of public laboratories to hire and maintain sufficient levels of staffing is contingent on the availability of funding.

The job competition is keen. Interest in forensic careers has grown in recent years, thus increasing the number of people seeking to enter the field.

Advancement Prospects

Forensic Chemists who are interested in managerial careers can rise through the ranks as technical leaders, unit supervisors, administrative managers, and so on, up to lab directors. Opportunities are limited, however. They are usually better in large laboratories that have several levels of management. Individuals with entrepreneurial ambitions can become independent practitioners or owners of forensic firms that offer consulting or technical services. Those with teaching interests and skills can become trainers or academic instructors.

Law enforcement officers have more advancement options than civilians. They can rise through the ranks as well as pursue administrative and management positions within their agency.

Education and Training

Employers seek entry-level candidates who possess a bachelor's degree in chemistry, forensic science, or another related field, preferably with course work in analytical chemistry.

Entry-level Forensic Chemists undergo a training program that includes both formal classroom instruction and on-the-job training.

Throughout their careers, Forensic Chemists enroll in continuing education programs and training programs to update their skills and increase their knowledge.

Special Requirements

In crime labs in which Forensic Chemists are law enforcement officers, applicants must possess a basic peace officer standards and training certificate. These agencies may hire candidates without a certificate on the condition they complete the necessary law enforcement academy program to obtain the certificate.

Law enforcement officers must successfully complete annual training to maintain their certification.

Experience, Special Skills, and Personality Traits

Requirements vary with the different employers. For entry-level positions, most crime labs prefer to hire applicants who have six months to one year or more of laboratory experience. They may have gained their experience through internships, research assistantships, or employment in analytical, crime, or scientific research laboratories.

Some skills that Forensic Chemists need to perform effectively are problem-solving, organizational, writing, communication, and presentation skills. They must also have excellent self-management skills, such as the ability to work independently, handle stressful situations, meet deadlines, and prioritize multiple tasks. Successful Forensic Chemists share similar personality traits, including being detail-oriented, versatile, patient, composed, impartial, ethical, and collaborative.

Unions and Associations

Some Forensic Chemists are members of a labor union, which represents them in negotiations with employers for better contractual terms for pay, benefits, and working conditions.

Many Forensic Chemists also belong to professional associations that serve the interests of forensic professionals. Some national societies are the International Association for Identification, the American Academy of Forensic Sciences, and the American College of Forensic Examiners. In addition, some Forensic Chemists join the American Chemical Society, an association that serves the general population of chemists. For contact information for these organizations, see Appendix III.

Tips for Entry

1. If you have a record of drug use or arrests, your chances of obtaining a job in a crime lab is very slim, according to some experts in the field.
2. Some higher education institutions offer a bachelor's degree program in forensic chemistry. You might consider enrolling in such a program, if one is offered at the college of your choice. Alternatively, you might take a few basic courses in such an academic program.
3. Contact employers directly about job openings.
4. Use the Internet to learn more about the forensic chemistry field. To get a list of relevant Web sites, enter any of these keywords into a search engine: *forensic chemistry*, *forensic chemists*, or *forensic chemistry lab*. For some links, see Appendix IV.

FORENSIC DRUG CHEMIST

CAREER PROFILE

Duties: Identify and analyze samples for controlled substances; prepare reports of findings; provide expert witness testimony; perform other duties as required

Alternate Title(s): Forensic Drug Analyst, Forensic Chemist, Criminalist, Forensic Scientist

Salary Range: $28,000 to $73,000

Employment Prospects: Good

Advancement Prospects: Fair

Prerequisites:

Education or Training—Bachelor's degree in chemistry, forensic science, or another related field; on-the-job training

Experience—Previous lab experience usually required

Special Skills and Personality Traits—Organizational, problem-solving, teamwork, interpersonal, self-management, writing, communication, and presentation skills; positive, collaborative, dedicated, honest, trustworthy, and persistent

Special Requirements—Peace officer certificate may be required

CAREER LADDER

```
┌─────────────────────────────────────┐
│     Senior Forensic Drug Chemist     │
└─────────────────────────────────────┘

┌─────────────────────────────────────┐
│        Forensic Drug Chemist         │
└─────────────────────────────────────┘

┌─────────────────────────────────────┐
│     Forensic Drug Chemist Trainee    │
└─────────────────────────────────────┘
```

Position Description

Many crime labs have a drug unit that specifically conducts examinations on illegal drugs that law enforcement officers have found on suspects, at crime scenes, or in drug seizures. Pills, powders, capsules, liquids, and plant material are brought to criminalists known as Forensic Drug Chemists for analysis. Their findings help criminal investigators and prosecuting attorneys arrest and convict suspects in possession of illicit drugs.

Forensic Drug Chemists do not visit crime scenes for investigative work except on rare occasions. Neither do they deal directly with criminals. They may be called upon to investigate covert drug laboratories where illegal drugs are manufactured. However, for the most part they work in government forensic services laboratories that are affiliated with local, state, and federal law enforcement agencies or with medical examiners' offices. There are also a small number of private labs that perform forensic science analyses where these scientists carry out their assignments.

Forensic Drug Chemists utilize their background in chemistry, criminalistics, and instrumental analysis. Most of the evidence that these scientists analyze is in the area of illicit drugs. These are substances that are classified by the federal government as harmful or dangerous and thus are controlled. Law forbids their use, and heavy penalties are imposed upon people who manufacture, distribute, and use them. These drugs include narcotics such as morphine or heroin, depressants such as barbiturates or tranquilizers, stimulants such as amphetamines and cocaine, and hallucinogens such as marijuana and LSD. Law enforcement units are also on the alert about other substances. Synthetic opiates such as Oxycontin or "club drugs" such as ecstasy are increasingly abused, as are some prescription drugs, anabolic steroids, and solvents. Some substances are not illegal but are abused and distributed in an illicit manner. Hence, they are often a contributing factor to criminal activity.

Drug chemists also identify the paraphernalia that drug abusers use to ingest the drugs, and they examine drug-manufacturing equipment that investigators confiscate from clandestine laboratories. The abuse of illegal drugs sometimes results in overdose and death. Forensic Drug Chemists identify the substances involved in those cases and provide assistance to coroners and medical examiners.

Forensic Drug Chemists use several testing methods to identify the substances in their laboratories. Before conducting these tests, they examine the evidence and write down their initial observations. Then they weigh the substance or substances. The weight determines the severity of the penalty for the crime. Their next step is to perform a color test. When drugs are exposed to certain chemicals, their color changes. Each color corresponds to a general category of drug.

Other compounds stimulate the growth of crystals, which serve to more specifically identify each drug. Forensic Drug Chemists carefully examine these crystals by using a polarized light microscope. When drugs are mixed with other substances, Forensic Drug Chemists use a process to separate the drugs from their diluents. The result is a pure sample of the controlled substance. They also use another testing method with which they examine a drug's characteristic absorption of ultraviolet or infrared light to identify it. They identify marijuana leaf fragments by looking through a microscope for distinctive hairs that grow on the leaves.

When they complete their casework, Forensic Drug Chemists write reports of their findings, which they submit to the proper authorities. These chemists may also function as expert witnesses to present their evidence findings in court proceedings connected to their casework.

Forensic Drug Chemists perform general duties in the course of their daily routine, which include:

- observing standard procedures for testing and analysis
- learning new procedures and approaches to analyze evidence
- maintaining solid relationships with other forensic scientists, law enforcement personnel, and employees of the court system
- conducting research
- writing concise and well-organized reports of scientific examinations
- performing data-entry tasks
- ensuring that all of their equipment and work conditions meet with operational and safety guidelines

In some crime labs, drug analysis is done by forensic chemists who also conduct analyses on other types of physical evidence, such as fire debris, gunshot residue, bodily fluids, paint chips, and soils.

Forensic Drug Chemists concentrate on performing quality work and focus on effectively managing their time. Funding for their laboratories is often limited, and the amount of evidence requiring analysis is increasing. They com-municate regularly with court officials about delays they encounter.

Forensic Drug Chemists usually work a regular 40-hour week but are on call around the clock. In large laboratory facilities, Forensic Drug Chemists are rotated on their on-call schedule.

Salaries

Salaries for Forensic Drug Chemists vary, depending on such factors as their education, experience, employer, and geographic location. According to the May 2006 *Occupational Employment Statistics* survey by the U.S. Bureau of Labor Statistics (BLS), the estimated annual salary for most forensic science technicians ranged between $27,530 and $73,100.

Employment Prospects

Forensic Drug Chemists find employment with crime laboratories that are part of local, state, and federal government agencies. In local and state labs, they may be civilian employees or law enforcement officers. Forensic Drug Chemists also work for private forensic laboratories.

Job growth in the forensic science field is predicted to increase by 27 percent or more through 2014, according to the BLS. In addition, opportunities become available as individuals retire, transfer to other jobs, or advance to higher positions. The ability of public laboratories to hire and maintain sufficient levels of staffing is contingent on the availability of funding.

Job competition is keen. Interest in forensic careers has grown in recent years, thus increasing the number of people seeking to enter the field.

Advancement Prospects

Forensic Drug Chemists with managerial ambitions can rise through the ranks as technical leaders, unit supervisors, administrative managers, and so on, up to lab directors. Opportunities are limited, however. They are usually better in large laboratories that have several levels of management. Individuals with entrepreneurial ambitions can become independent practitioners or owners of forensic firms that offer consulting or technical services.

Law enforcement officers have more advancement options than civilians. They can rise through the ranks as well as pursue administrative and management positions within their agency.

Education and Training

Employers seek candidates who possess a bachelor's degree in chemistry, forensic science, or another related field, preferably with course work in analytical chemistry.

Entry-level Forensic Drug Chemists complete a training program that includes both formal classroom instruction and on-the-job training. They perform routine tasks under the guidance and direction of experienced staff members.

Throughout their careers, Forensic Drug Chemists enroll in continuing education programs and training programs to update their skills and keep up with advancements in their field.

Special Requirements

In crime labs in which Forensic Drug Chemists are law enforcement officers, applicants must possess a basic peace officer standards and training certificate. These agencies may hire candidates without a certificate on the condition they complete the necessary law enforcement academy program to obtain the certificate.

Law enforcement officers must successfully complete annual training to maintain their certification.

Experience, Special Skills, and Personality Traits

Requirements for entry-level positions vary with the different employers. Most crime labs prefer to hire applicants who have six months to one year or more of laboratory experience. They may have gained their experience through internships, research assistantships, or employment in analytical, crime, or scientific research laboratories.

To perform well at their work, Forensic Drug Chemists must have effective organizational, problem-solving, teamwork, interpersonal, and self-management skills. They must be able to describe technical terms in ways that are understandable to legal, technical, and lay audiences; thus, it is essential that they have strong writing, communication and presentation skills. Being positive, collaborative, dedicated, honest, trustworthy, and persistent are some personality traits that successful Forensic Drug Chemists share.

Unions and Associations

The International Association for Identification, the American Academy of Forensic Sciences, and the American College of Forensic Examiners are three professional associations that are available to Forensic Drug Chemists. (For contact information, see Appendix III.) By joining a society at the local, state, or national level, these forensic scientists can take advantage of various professional services and resources such as professional certification, professional publications, and networking opportunities.

Forensic Drug Chemists may also be eligible to join a labor union that represents them in negotiations with employers for better contractual terms for pay, benefits, and working conditions. In addition, the union handles any grievances that members may have against their employers.

Tips for Entry

1. Applicants with tattoos, branding, or body piercing that cannot be covered by clothing may be disqualified for positions with law enforcement agencies.
2. If you are willing to relocate, you may have a greater chance of finding the job you want.
3. Most, if not all, employers will hire candidates upon the condition that they have passed a background check and a drug screening for illegal drugs.
4. Use the Internet to learn more about what Forensic Drug Chemists do. To obtain a list of relevant Web sites, enter the keywords *forensic drug analysis* or *crime lab drug unit* in a search engine. For some links, see Appendix IV.

FORENSIC SEROLOGIST

CAREER PROFILE

Duties: Identify, analyze, and interpret samples of blood and other forms of bodily fluids for criminal investigations; prepare reports of findings; provide expert witness testimony; perform other duties as required

Alternate Title(s): Forensic Biologist, Criminalist, Forensic Scientist

Salary Range: $28,000 to $73,000

Employment Prospects: Good

Advancement Prospects: Fair

Prerequisites:

Education or Training—Bachelor's degree in a physical or natural science discipline, forensic science, or another related field; on-the-job training

Experience—Previous lab experience usually required

Special Skills and Personality Traits—Problem-solving, organizational, teamwork, interpersonal, writing, communication, presentation, and self-management skills; methodical, detail-oriented, persistent, honest, courteous, friendly, patient

Special Requirements—Peace officer certificate may be required

CAREER LADDER

```
┌──────────────────────────────────┐
│    Senior Forensic Serologist    │
└──────────────────────────────────┘

┌──────────────────────────────────┐
│       Forensic Serologist        │
└──────────────────────────────────┘

┌──────────────────────────────────┐
│    Forensic Serologist Trainee   │
└──────────────────────────────────┘
```

Position Description

There are two approaches to investigating the blood that is left behind at crime scenes. One approach is from the standpoint of physics: blood spatter analysis. The other approach is biological: serology. The term *serology* is derived from the word *serum*, which is the clear and slightly yellow fluid within blood. Criminalists known as Forensic Serologists examine blood evidence to help criminal investigators and prosecuting attorneys find the link between a suspect and the crime scene or the victim. These professional men and women are also assigned the task of analyzing other bodily fluids (such as saliva, sweat, urine, and semen), as well as human tissue and other biological evidence.

Forensic Serologists make use of their backgrounds in biology, biochemistry, genetics, human anatomy, physiology, and statistics in addition to their training in the methodologies of forensics. Their forensics training provides them with a solid expertise in handling evidence and maintaining the chain of custody of biological and physical evidence. They also possess a familiarity with case law pertaining to forensic serology and DNA analysis, as well as with criminal law and courtroom presentation processes. Furthermore, their work involves the use of computers, photographic equipment, and scientific instruments and equipment.

While Forensic Serologists work with all bodily fluids, their foundation is in the study of blood. They have a thorough understanding about blood and its various components and how they contribute to blood typing. Blood is composed of water, cells, proteins, enzymes, and inorganic substances. The fluid part of blood is broken down into plasma, which is largely composed of water, and serum. Serum contains, among other substances, antibodies. Red blood cells make up most of the part of blood that is solid.

Forensic Serologists are mainly interested in analyzing serum and red blood cells in blood evidence. Serum is useful because it helps these professionals discern the freshness and blood type of a blood sample as well as whether the sample is of human or animal origin. Studying red blood cells also helps them identify the blood type of a blood sample. There are three basic blood types—A, B, and O, and they are also detectable in other bodily fluids. Forensic Serologists are able to prove that a sample of blood or bodily fluid found at a crime scene came from a specific segment of the population, which helps them to narrow down the field of suspects, or verify the innocence of others.

Forensic Serologists are responsible for completing their casework in a timely manner and complying with policies, procedures, standards, laws, and regulations. When a new criminal case comes before them, these criminalists study the evidence and other information about the case to determine which problems need to be solved. They closely check stain evidence for blood, or other bodily fluids. They remove any other trace evidence such as hair, paint chips, fiber, vegetable matter, soil, or glass from each sample. Forensic Serologists decide whether each sample has significance to the case at hand. They conduct their tests to determine whether samples are indeed blood and whether they are animal or human blood. If the samples are human blood, they determine blood types. They also test the samples to approximate such factors as the age, sex, or race of the individual or individuals who left the stains at the crime scene.

Upon completing their analysis for a case, Forensic Serologists prepare and submit reports of their findings and conclusions to the proper authorities. If one of their cases goes to trial, they may be requested to provide testimony as expert witnesses.

Forensic Serologists are responsible for completing certain routine tasks in addition to their normal course of activities. For example, they may:

- coordinate with evidence officers about their use of evidence and about maintaining chain-of-custody protocols
- create and sustain good relationships with co-workers and personnel from other departments or agencies and with the general public
- synchronize work assignments and responsibilities with colleagues
- keep their workplace and equipment organized and maintained
- supervise student interns or volunteer staff members
- write clear and concise reports
- maintain detailed records including chain of custody records; descriptions of evidence; documents about their observations, methods, and results; documentation of quality control issues and technical problems; and supply inventories
- stay current with criminal investigation procedures and new developments in forensic science research

Many Forensic Serologists are cross-trained to perform one or more other forensic examinations. For example, they may conduct DNA analysis, investigate bloodstain patterns, or perform trace evidence examinations. The majority of their time is spent in the laboratory. On occasion, they are called upon to assist at crime scenes. They may actually look for and recover physical evidence or supervise crime scene technicians in the collection of blood samples.

Forensic Serologists work in crime laboratories affiliated with law enforcement agencies, prosecuting attorneys' offices, and other government agencies. In law enforcement agencies, most of these scientists are employed as civilians.

They usually put in a standard 40-hour workweek but may sometimes work evenings or weekends to meet deadlines or complete work assignments. Their workload may be stressful and priorities may shift. Hence, they must be able to adapt to such conditions.

Salaries

Salaries for Forensic Serologists vary, depending on such factors as their education, experience, employer, and geographic location. The U.S. Bureau of Labor Statistics reported in its May 2006 *Occupational Employment Statistics* survey that the estimated annual salary for most forensic science technicians ranged between $27,530 and $73,100.

Employment Prospects

Forensic Serologists are employed by government and private forensic laboratories in the United States. Most government laboratories are part of law enforcement agencies and prosecuting attorneys' offices in municipal, county, and state jurisdictions. Federal crime labs are part of various federal agencies, such as the Federal Bureau of Investigation, the U.S. Bureau of Alcohol, Tobacco, Firearms and Explosives, the Secret Service, the U.S. Fish and Wildlife Service, and the U.S. Postal Inspection Service.

In local and state crime labs, Forensic Serologists may be civilian employees or law enforcement officers.

In general, job openings become available as individuals retire, transfer to other jobs, or advance to higher positions. Labs will create additional positions to meet growing needs, as long as funding is available.

Advancement Prospects

Many Forensic Serologists measure their success by receiving more complex responsibilities, earning higher incomes, and gaining professional recognition. Individuals with supervisory and managerial ambitions can advance to lead, supervisory, and managerial positions, but opportunities are limited. A master's or doctoral degree may be required for higher-level management positions.

Law enforcement officers have more advancement options than civilians. They can rise through the ranks as well as pursue administrative and management positions within their agency.

Education and Training

Minimally, applicants for entry-level positions need a bachelor's degree in biology, microbiology, chemistry, forensic science, or another related field. For positions in which they will also perform DNA analysis, applicants must have completed course work in molecular biology, genetics, biochemistry, and statistics.

Entry-level Forensic Serologists begin their career as trainees. They undergo an intense training period that includes formal classroom instruction as well as on-the-job training.

Throughout their careers, Forensic Biologists enroll in continuing education programs and training programs to update their skills and increase their knowledge.

Special Requirements

In crime labs in which Latent Print Examiners are law enforcement officers, applicants must possess a basic peace officer standards and training certificate. These agencies may hire candidates without a certificate on the condition they complete the necessary law enforcement academy program to obtain the certificate.

Law enforcement officers must successfully complete annual training to maintain their certification.

Experience, Special Skills, and Personality Traits

Requirements for entry-level positions vary with the different employers. Most crime labs prefer to hire candidates who have previous laboratory experience, which they may have gained through internships, research assistantships, or employment. Candidates should be able to demonstrate their knowledge about proper lab procedures and the handling of lab instruments and equipment.

To perform the various aspects of their job well, Forensic Serologists must have excellent problem-solving, organizational, teamwork, interpersonal, writing, communication, and presentation skills. In addition, they need strong self-management skills, such as the ability to work independently, prioritize multiple tasks, meet deadlines, and handle stressful situations. Being detail-oriented, persistent, honest, courteous, friendly, and patient are some personality traits that successful Forensic Serologists share.

Unions and Associations

Forensic Serologists can join professional associations to take advantage of networking opportunities, continuing education, and other professional resources and services. Some national societies that serve the general interests of this profession are the International Association for Identification, the American Academy of Forensic Sciences, and American College of Forensic Examiners. For contact information, see Appendix III.

Many forensic scientists belong to a labor union that represents them in negotiations with employers for better contractual terms for pay, benefits, and working conditions.

Tips for Entry

1. You may be asked to provide proof of your education when you submit a job application. Be sure to attach a copy of an official transcript that shows your major field of study. Employers usually discard any applications that do not have the requested documents attached.
2. You can sometimes download a job application at an employer's Web site. Many employers also allow applicants to submit their completed forms through the Internet.
3. Learn more about forensic serology on the Internet. To find relevant Web sites, enter the keywords *forensic serology* or *forensic serologists* into a search engine.

LATENT PRINT EXAMINER

CAREER PROFILE

Duties: Process, analyze, and identify latent print evidence; prepare reports of findings; provide expert witness testimony; perform other duties as required

Alternate Title(s): Latent Print Analyst, Criminalist, Forensic Scientist

Salary Range: $28,000 to $73,000

Employment Prospects: Good

Advancement Prospects: Fair

Prerequisites:

Education or Training—Educational requirements vary; on-the-job training

Experience—Previous work experience in fingerprinting, crime scene investigation, and latent print analysis preferred

Skills and Personality Traits—Memory, writing, communication, presentation, interpersonal, teamwork, and self-management skills; patient, objective, unbiased, trustworthy, honest, and methodical

Special Requirements—Peace officer certificate may be required

CAREER LADDER

```
┌─────────────────────────────────────┐
│    Senior Latent Print Examiner      │
└─────────────────────────────────────┘

┌─────────────────────────────────────┐
│      Latent Print Examiner           │
└─────────────────────────────────────┘

┌─────────────────────────────────────┐
│   Criminalist (Entry-Level) or       │
│     Fingerprint Technician           │
└─────────────────────────────────────┘
```

Position Description

Everyone has a unique set of prints—fingerprints, palm prints, or footprints. Thus, chances are strong that criminals can be linked to crime scenes or victims by any prints that they leave behind on tabletops, papers, glass, plastics, metal, bed sheets, rocks, cigarettes, weapons, dead bodies, or other type of surfaces. Some prints, known as latent prints, are invisible or barely visible, but oftentimes crime scene investigators can find them by shining strong flashlights on surfaces, dusting the surfaces, or using other methods. These full or partial prints are carefully preserved and sent to crime labs where Latent Print Examiners process and analyze the prints for positive identification.

Latent Print Examiners are forensic scientists who work in crime labs. They apply science principles and methodologies to the examination and analysis of latent print evidence. Their work involves the use of physical, optical, and electronic equipment and techniques. In addition, they follow specific practices, procedures, and standards as well as comply with laws and regulations pertaining to the handling and processing of evidence.

To determine the identity of a latent print, these forensic specialists compare it with known prints of suspects, victims, and other individuals to find a match. They also use a computerized system called the automated fingerprint identification system (AFIS), which can scan hundreds of thousands of fingerprints per second to obtain a list of possible matches. In addition, many examiners have access to the integrated automated fingerprint identification system (IAFIS), a nationwide database containing 47 million fingerprints that is maintained by the FBI. Latent Print Examiners evaluate each file to determine if there is a positive match with the latent print they are seeking to identify.

When these forensic specialists complete an examination, they prepare a detailed report of their findings and conclusions and submit them to the proper authorities. They may be called upon to testify as expert witnesses in court to address questions regarding their casework as well as the procedures and techniques for processing latent prints.

Latent Print Examiners perform various other duties besides their casework, which vary according to their level of expertise and skills. For example, they may be assigned to:

- take inked or digital scans of fingerprints of individuals for criminal and noncriminal matters
- take fingerprints, palm prints, or footprints of dead bodies
- organize and maintain latent print files, logs, and records
- input latent prints into the AFIS system
- maintain lab areas, equipment, and instruments according to established standards of cleanliness, safety, and efficiency
- provide training to law enforcement officers in the proper method of taking fingerprints as well as collecting and preserving physical evidence
- train, supervise, and direct the work of entry-level examiners and other subordinate staff
- keep up with current technologies and developments in their field

On occasion, Latent Print Examiners are called upon to assist at crime scenes, particularly major crimes such as homicides, sex offenses, and kidnapping. Their primary task is to locate, collect, and process latent prints. They may also be asked to aid in the collection of other physical evidence such as trace evidence or the impressions of shoe prints and tire tracks.

Latent Print Examiners can expect to handle heavy and stressful workloads. For example, they work under emotional conditions when dealing with dead bodies or victims of violent crimes. They are in daily contact with a wide range of people from different backgrounds, including professional colleagues, managers, law enforcement officers, witnesses, suspects, government employees, court officers, and the public, among others.

Their work involves occasional standing, walking, or bending for long periods of time. These forensic specialists also handle hazardous, flammable, and toxic chemicals as well as blood and other bodily fluids in the course of their work; thus, they are required to wear protective clothing and equipment.

Latent Print Examiners work standard workweeks, but must be available at all times for emergency call outs. They may be required to work shifts, weekends, and holidays.

Salaries
Salaries for Latent Print Examiners vary, depending on such factors as their education, experience, employer, and geographic location. The estimated annual salary for most forensic science technicians, including Latent Print Examiners, ranges from $27,530 to $73,100, according to the May 2006 *Occupational Employment Statistics* survey by the U.S. Bureau of Labor Statistics.

Employment Prospects
Latent Print Examiners work for local, state, and federal crime labs. They may be law enforcement officers or civilian employees. Some examiners are independent contractors or work for private practices. Job openings typically become available as individuals retire, transfer to other jobs, or advance to higher positions. Employers will create additional positions, as long as funding is available.

Advancement Prospects
Latent Print Examiners who are interested in pursuing managerial positions can be promoted to become technical leaders, unit supervisors, and managers. Opportunities, however, are limited. Managerial opportunities are usually better in large laboratories that have several levels of management. Individuals with entrepreneurial ambitions can become independent practitioners or owners of forensic firms that offer consulting or technical services.

Latent Print Examiners can also pursue opportunities as instructors and researchers in higher education institutions. To advance to higher positions or to obtain teaching jobs, these forensic specialists may be required to have a master's or doctoral degree.

Law enforcement officers have more advancement options than civilians. They can rise through the ranks as detectives, sergeants, lieutenants, captains, and so on, up to police chiefs. They also can pursue administrative and management positions within their agency.

Education and Training
Educational requirements vary with the different employers. Many prefer to hire candidates who possess a bachelor's degree in a physical or natural science discipline, forensic science, law enforcement, or another related field. Some agencies hire candidates who have only a high school or general equivalency diploma, as long as they have qualifying work experience.

Entry-level Latent Print Examiners undergo a training program that may last two to three years before they are assigned casework. Their training includes classroom instruction as well as on-the-job training. Novice examiners work under the guidance and direction of experienced personnel.

Throughout their careers, Latent Print Examiners enroll in continuing education programs and training programs to update their skills and increase their knowledge.

Special Requirements
In crime labs in which Latent Print Examiners are law enforcement officers, applicants must possess a basic peace officer standards and training certificate. These agencies may hire candidates without a certificate on the condition they complete the necessary law enforcement academy program to obtain the certificate.

Law enforcement officers must successfully complete annual training to maintain their certification.

Experience, Special Skills, and Personality Traits

Requirements for entry-level positions vary with the different employers. In general, employers seek candidates who have experience in fingerprint identification, crime scene investigation, and latent print analysis. Entry-level applicants may be required to have one to five years of work experience, depending on their level of education.

To be effective at their work, Latent Print Examiners need excellent memory, writing, communication, and presentation skills. They also must have strong interpersonal, teamwork, and self-management skills. Being patient, objective, unbiased, trustworthy, honest, and methodical are some personality traits that successful examiners have in common.

Unions and Associations

Some Latent Print Examiners are members of a labor union, which represents them in negotiations with employers for better contractual terms for pay, benefits, and working conditions.

Many examiners belong to professional associations to take advantage of networking opportunities, continuing education, professional certification, and other professional resources and services. Professional societies are available locally, statewide, regionally, nationally, and worldwide. Some societies that serve the interests of Latent Print Examiners are the American Academy of Forensic Science, the American College of Forensic Examiners, and the International Association for Identification. For contact information, see Appendix III.

Tips for Entry

1. While in high school and college, you can begin to prepare yourself for court presentations as an expert witness. For example, you can take a drama or public speaking class, or participate on the debate team or in school or community theater.

2. If you are interested in working in another city or state, use the Internet to learn about opportunities in forensic laboratories in the area. Many government agencies and private labs post job listings at their Web sites.

3. Some agencies hire Latent Print Examiners for temporary positions. Holding a temporary position allows you to gain valuable experience. Sometimes it may lead to a permanent position with an employer.

4. Learn more about fingerprints and latent print examinations on the Internet. You might start by visiting this Web site: Latent Print Examination: Fingerprints, Palmprints, and Footprints (by Ed German), http://www.onin.com/fp.

QUESTIONED DOCUMENT EXAMINER

CAREER PROFILE

Duties: Analyze documents to determine if they are authentic, counterfeit, or forgeries; prepare reports of findings; provide expert witness testimony; perform other duties as required

Alternate Title(s): Forensic Document Examiner, Criminalist, Forensic Scientist

Salary Range: $28,000 to $73,000

Employment Prospects: Fair

Advancement Prospects: Fair

Prerequisites:

Education or Training—Bachelor's degree preferred; on-the-job training

Experience—Previous work experience in a crime lab or crime scene unit preferred

Skills and Personality Traits—Self-management, interpersonal, teamwork, communication, writing, and presentation skills; observant, patient, organized, persistent, honest, and trustworthy

Special Requirements—Peace officer certificate may be required

CAREER LADDER

```
┌─────────────────────────────────────────┐
│  Senior Questioned Document Examiner     │
└─────────────────────────────────────────┘

┌─────────────────────────────────────────┐
│     Questioned Document Examiner         │
└─────────────────────────────────────────┘

┌─────────────────────────────────────────┐
│     Questioned Document Examiner         │
│              Trainee                     │
└─────────────────────────────────────────┘
```

Position Description

Is the signature on a check forged? Who is the author of a kidnapping note? Did someone alter the terms of a business contract? Oftentimes checks, contracts, correspondence, and other documents are evidence in homicides, assaults, kidnapping, hate crimes, robberies, theft, and other criminal acts. Forensic scientists known as Questioned Document Examiners are trained to analyze documents to determine if they are genuine or fake, to identify who wrote them, or to discern if they have been altered in any way. The facts that these criminalists establish about evidence can help criminal investigators and prosecuting attorneys arrest and convict criminal suspects.

Questioned Document Examiners are not the same as graphologists who study handwriting samples to deduce the character of the writers. Some graphologists use the title document examiners, thus leading to the confusion between them and Questioned Document Examiners.

These forensic examiners apply scientific principles and methodologies to the examination and analysis of evidence. They may perform physical or chemical analyses on documents. They follow specific practices, procedures, and standards as well as comply with laws and regulations pertaining to the handling and processing of evidence. Their work involves the use of computers as well as measuring devices, magnifiers, microscopes, and other specialized scientific instruments and equipment.

Questioned Document Examiners engage in many cases in which they analyze handwriting or hand printing to determine who wrote or signed a document. They also analyze documents for other legal questions such as when a document was produced, how was it produced, or if information in the document was erased. Their examinations may involve identifying inks and papers that are used for documents, or examining typewriters, printers, copy machines, or other machines that produce documents.

Generally, these forensic scientists compare a suspected document, or components of a document, with a document containing a set of known standards. They carefully examine each item for detectable characteristics; they then compare the two documents for similarities and differences pertinent to those properties. They make a conclusion based on their evaluation of the compared characteristics.

They are responsible for preparing a detailed report of their findings and conclusions for each case and submitting the report to the proper authorities. If their case goes before a court of law, Questioned Document Examiners may be summoned to testify as expert witnesses about their findings and conclusions on the case.

Questioned Document Examiners are assigned several cases at a time. They are expected to manage, plan, and prioritize assignments so that each of their cases is completed in a timely manner.

These examiners perform various other duties along with their casework. For example, they:

- prepare photographic exhibits and other visual aids for court presentations or training purposes
- conduct research on new methodologies and techniques in the examination of questioned documents
- prepare reports, correspondence, and other required paperwork
- keep records on their casework up-to-date
- maintain lab equipment, instruments, and work areas
- assist in the development and implementation of quality assurance activities
- train subordinate staff members
- provide or assist in the instruction of law enforcement officers in the proper methods for seeking, collecting, and processing document evidence
- stay current with new technologies, issues, and developments in their field as well as keep abreast of changing laws and rules pertaining to the collection, preservation, and submission of evidence

They are also expected to observe safety rules as they use forensic tools in the preparation, storage, and disposal of chemicals.

Questioned Document Examiners mostly work in crime labs. Occasionally they are called out to crime scenes to help locate and gather evidence, or to supervise in the collection of evidence. They work a 40-hour schedule but put in additional hours as needed to complete their duties or to meet deadlines. Some of them are on-call 24 hours a day.

Salaries

Salaries for Questioned Document Examiners vary, depending on such factors as their education, experience, employer, and geographic location. According to the May 2006 *Occupational Employment Statistics* survey by the U.S. Bureau of Labor Statistics, the estimated annual salary for most forensic science technicians, including these examiners, ranged between $27,530 and $73,100.

Employment Prospects

Questioned Document Examiners work for local, state, and federal crime labs. They may be law enforcement officers or civilians. Some examiners are independent contractors or employees of private forensic practices that offer questioned document examination services. Job openings usually become available as individuals retire, transfer to other jobs, or advance to higher positions. Employers will create additional positions, as long as funding is available.

Opportunities are usually available for qualified Questioned Document Examiners. One expert in the field reports that the demand is greater than the number of qualified examiners that are available. However, many government crime labs are unable to hire enough examiners because of lack of funding.

Advancement Prospects

Questioned Document Examiners can advance in any number of ways, depending on their ambitions and interests. They can rise through the administrative and managerial ranks as technical leaders, unit supervisors, and managers, which may mean transferring to other employers. Individuals with entrepreneurial ambitions can become independent practitioners or owners of forensic firms that offer consulting or technical services. These examiners can also pursue opportunities as trainers or instructors and researchers in higher education institutions. To advance to higher positions or to obtain teaching jobs, these examiners may be required to possess a master's or doctoral degree along with professional certification.

Law enforcement officers have additional advancement opportunities. They can rise through the ranks as well as pursue administrative and management positions within their agency.

Education and Training

Educational requirements vary with the different employers. Increasingly more employers are requiring that applicants hold a bachelor's degree in a physical or natural science discipline, forensic science, criminal justice, or another related field. Some agencies require only a high school or general equivalency diploma, as long as candidates have qualifying work experience.

Entry-level examiners undergo a two- to three-year apprenticeship. They work under the direction and guidance of experienced Questioned Document Examiners in a government crime lab or in a private practice. They also participate in formal classroom instruction.

Throughout their careers, Questioned Document Examiners enroll in continuing education programs and training programs to increase their knowledge and update their skills.

Special Requirements

In agencies in which Questioned Document Examiners are law enforcement officers, they must possess a basic peace officer standards and training certificate. These agencies may hire candidates without a certificate on the condition they complete the necessary law enforcement academy program to obtain the certificate.

Law enforcement officers must successfully complete annual training to maintain their certification.

Experience, Special Skills, and Personality Traits

Requirements for entry-level applicants vary with the different employers. Many employers prefer to hire candidates who have one or more years of work experience in a crime scene unit, crime lab, or another related setting. They may have gained their experience through internships, research assistantships, or employment in analytical, crime, or scientific research laboratories. Entry-level candidates should be able to demonstrate their knowledge about proper lab procedures and handling of lab instruments and equipment.

Questioned Document Examiners must have strong self-management skills, such as the ability to work independently, handle stressful situations, prioritize multiple tasks, and follow and understand instructions. Their job also requires that they have effective interpersonal, teamwork, communication, writing, and presentation skills. Being observant, patient, organized, persistent, honest, and trustworthy are some personality traits that Questioned Document Examiners share.

Unions and Associations

Many Questioned Document Examiners join professional associations to take advantage of networking opportunities, continuing education, professional certification, and other professional resources and services. Professional societies are available locally, statewide, regionally, nationally, and worldwide. Some national societies that serve their interests include the American Society of Questioned Document Examiners, the American Academy of Forensic Sciences, the International Association for Identification, and the American College of Forensic Examiners. For contact information, see Appendix III.

Some examiners belong to a labor union that represents them in negotiations with employers for better contractual terms for pay, benefits, and working conditions. In addition, the union handles any grievances that members may have against their employers.

Tips for Entry

1. If you are in high school, begin learning about the forensic document examination field. Read books and professional journals as well as visit relevant Web sites.
2. Become proficient in computers, photography, and microscopy. These are all tools you will be using on the job as a Questioned Document Examiner.
3. Some professional associations offer student memberships. Join one that interests you, and participate in its activities to meet professionals in the field. Take the opportunity to begin building a network of contacts for your future job hunt.
4. Before starting your job hunt, have an idea of what you are seeking. Ask yourself such questions as: What would be my ideal job? What jobs would I be willing to take? What jobs would I not want to take? What jobs am I most qualified for now?
5. Use the Internet to learn more about the forensic questioned document specialty. To get a list of relevant Web sites, enter either of these keywords into a search engine: *questioned documents* or *questioned document examination*. For some links, see Appendix IV.

TRACE EVIDENCE EXAMINER

CAREER PROFILE

Duties: Identify, analyze, and interpret tiny particles of physical evidence; prepare reports of findings; provide expert witness testimony; perform other duties as required

Alternate Title(s): Trace Evidence Analyst, Criminalist, Forensic Scientist

Salary Range: $28,000 to $73,000

Employment Prospects: Good

Advancement Prospects: Fair

Prerequisites:

Education or Training—Bachelor's degree in a physical or natural science discipline, forensic science, or another related field; on-the-job training

Experience—Previous lab experience usually required

Special Skills and Personality Traits—Teamwork, interpersonal, communication, writing, presentation, and self-management skills; ethical, trustworthy, persistent, and detail-oriented

Special Requirements—Peace officer certificate may be required

CAREER LADDER

Senior Trace Evidence Examiner

Trace Evidence Examiner

Trace Evidence Examiner Trainee

Position Description

Many crimes have been solved with the help of a forensic science principle known as Locard's Exchange Principle, which is attributed to Dr. Edmund Locard, a pioneer in forensic science. Dr. Locard theorized that whenever a person comes into contact with another person or a place, materials are usually exchanged between contacts. Hence, when crime scene investigators collect evidence, they look for hair, fibers, gunshot residue, soil, pollen, glass fragments, paint specks, drugs, metal flecks, and other trace evidence that may have been left by the perpetrators. These very small, and sometimes microscopic, items of evidence are sent to the crime lab where Trace Evidence Examiners perform complex chemical and physical analyses and microscopic examinations. Their findings may contribute to the arrest and conviction of criminal suspects.

These criminalists apply scientific principles and methodologies to the examination and analysis of trace evidence. Their work involves the use of computers as well as measur-

ing devices, magnifiers, microscopes, and other specialized scientific instruments and equipment.

Like all criminalists, Trace Evidence Examiners are expected to perform their casework accurately and correctly and to complete their work in a timely manner. They follow strict practices, procedures, and standards as well as comply with laws and regulations pertaining to the handling and processing of evidence. They make sure that they maintain the chain of custody on every item of evidence that they handle to ensure that it has not been tampered with or contaminated. If the chain of custody has been violated on any article of physical evidence, it may not be admitted as testimony in a court of law.

Trace Evidence Examiners are responsible for documenting every step they take when examining physical evidence. First they inspect an item of trace evidence and describe what it is, how much it weighs, how it looks, and so on. They may sketch, photograph, or take a video of the evidence. Next, they determine which tests to conduct and how many should be performed. They use various methods and techniques to identify and analyze the composition or contents and the origins of trace evidence.

Their work involves comparing the various properties of an unknown item (trace evidence) with known ones to identify a common source. For example, investigators might submit fibers found at a crime scene along with an item of clothing that belongs to a suspect. Trace Evidence Examiners would compare the unknown fibers with fibers taken from the clothing to determine if there is a match.

These forensic specialists evaluate the results of their tests and prepare a formal report of their findings and conclusions. Their reports are read by law enforcement officers and attorneys, and may be submitted as testimony to the courts. They must be able to describe technical terms in language that is clearly understood by lay people.

Trace Evidence Examiners may be called upon to testify as expert witnesses at court trials. They provide impartial and unbiased testimony on issues related to their laboratory analyses.

Besides their casework, these examiners are responsible for other duties which vary, depending on their expertise and skills. For example, they might:

- provide training to law enforcement officers in the collection and processing of trace evidence
- conduct research in the development of new methods and techniques of laboratory analyses
- assist in the development and implementation of quality assurance activities and programs
- maintain lab areas, equipment, and instruments, according to established standards of cleanliness, safety, and efficiency
- supervise and train entry-level examiners, technicians, and other subordinate staff members
- attend workshops, seminars, and courses to maintain proficiency certifications
- keep up with current laws of evidence, criminal procedures, and crime as well as new technologies, techniques, and developments in their forensic specialty

Trace Evidence Examiners are sometimes called out to assist at crime scenes. They may assist or supervise in the collection and processing of trace evidence. In some laboratories, they are cross-trained to perform examinations on other types of physical evidence such as latent prints, firearms, bloodstains, and tire and track impressions.

These specialists mostly work indoors in clean, well-lit, and ventilated laboratories. They are exposed to chemicals, odors, fumes, and disease; hence, they wear protective equipment.

Trace Evidence Examiners work 40 hours per week but put in additional hours to complete tasks and meet deadlines. They are on call 24 hours a day. They may be expected to travel away from their labs to assist with criminal investigations and legal proceedings.

Salaries

Salaries for Trace Evidence Examiners vary, depending on such factors as their education, experience, position, employer, and geographic location. According to the May 2006 *Occupational Employment Statistics* survey by the U.S. Bureau of Labor Statistics (BLS), the estimated annual salary for most forensic science technicians ranged between $27,530 and $73,100.

Employment Prospects

Trace Evidence Examiners are employed in public and private forensic laboratories. There are almost 400 government crime labs, which are part of law enforcement agencies, prosecuting attorneys' offices, medical examiners' offices, and other government agencies. In local and state labs, these forensic specialists may be civilian employees or law enforcement officers.

In general, job openings become available as individuals retire, transfer to other jobs, or advance to higher positions. Job growth in the forensic science field is predicted to increase by 27 percent or more through 2014, according to the BLS. However, the competition for jobs is strong, and public laboratories are often unable to hire sufficient levels of staffing due to lack of funding.

Advancement Prospects

Individuals with managerial ambitions can pursue supervisory and management positions. Opportunities are limited; thus, they may need to seek positions with other employers to advance.

Law enforcement officers have more advancement options than civilians. They can rise through the ranks as detectives, sergeants, and so on, up to police chiefs. They also can pursue administrative and management positions within their agency.

Education and Training

Minimally, entry-level applicants need at least a bachelor's degree in chemistry, biology, forensic science, or another related field. Some employers prefer candidates who possess a master's degree.

Entry-level Trace Evidence Examiners usually undergo a long training period that includes formal classroom instruction and on-the-job training. The training phase may last up to two years in some crime labs.

Trace Evidence Examiners enroll in continuing education programs and training programs throughout their careers to update their skills and increase their knowledge.

Special Requirements

In crime labs in which Trace Evidence Examiners are law enforcement officers, applicants must possess a basic peace officer standards and training certificate. These agencies may hire candidates without a certificate on the condition they complete the necessary law enforcement academy program to obtain the certificate.

Law enforcement officers must successfully complete annual training to maintain their certification.

Experience, Special Skills, and Personality Traits

Requirements for entry-level positions vary with the different employers. Employers usually prefer to hire candidates who have one or more years of experience working in a forensic laboratory. They should also have experience testifying as expert witnesses.

Trace Evidence Examiners need excellent teamwork, interpersonal, and communication skills, as they must be able to work well with colleagues, managers, law enforcement officers, and others from diverse backgrounds. Their job also requires that they have effective writing, presentation, and self-management skills. Being ethical, trustworthy, persistent, and detail-oriented are some personality traits that successful Trace Evidence Examiners share.

Unions and Associations

Trace Evidence Examiners may join professional associations to take advantage of networking opportunities, pro-fessional certification, professional publications, and other professional resources and services. Some national societies that serve the interests of criminalists in general are the American Academy of Forensic Sciences, the American College of Forensic Examiners, and International Association for Identification. For contact information, see Appendix III.

Some Trace Evidence Examiners belong to a labor union that represents them in negotiations with employers for better contractual terms for pay, benefits, and working conditions. In addition, the union handles any grievances that members may have against their employers.

Tips for Entry

1. Some crime labs accept an equivalent combination of experience, training, and education that provides the required knowledge, skills, and abilities for a position.
2. You might enhance your employability by obtaining professional certification from the American Board of Criminalistics. For more information, see Appendix II.
3. Many professional associations post job announcements at their Web sites.
4. Use the Internet to learn more about trace evidence examination. To find relevant Web sites, enter the keywords *trace evidence examination* or *trace evidence analysis* into a search engine. For some links, see Appendix IV.

MEDICOLEGAL DEATH INVESTIGATION PERSONNEL

CORONER

CAREER PROFILE

Duties: Investigate the cause and manner of unexplained deaths; issue death certificates; perform other duties as required

Alternate Title(s): Sheriff-Coroner

Salary Range: $28,000 to $80,000

Employment Prospects: Poor

Advancement Prospects: Poor

Prerequisites:

Education or Training—Educational requirements vary

Experience—Medicolegal death investigation, law enforcement, or medical background usually preferred

Special Skills and Personality Traits—Interpersonal, communication, leadership, teamwork, public-relations, management, investigative, and writing skills; patient, open-minded, creative, compassionate, persistent, ethical, and goal-oriented

Special Requirements—Peace officer certificate may be required

CAREER LADDER

```
┌─────────────────────────────────────┐
│   Coroner (Multiple-term Official)   │
└─────────────────────────────────────┘

┌─────────────────────────────────────┐
│              Coroner                 │
└─────────────────────────────────────┘

┌─────────────────────────────────────┐
│     Deputy Coroner, Physician,       │
│    Law Enforcement Officer, or       │
│          Other Profession            │
└─────────────────────────────────────┘
```

Position Description

There are times when people die that it is unclear as to the circumstances or causes of their deaths. By law, such deaths must be investigated, and in many local jurisdictions in the United States, the coroner's office has that authority.

Coroners are entrusted with serving and protecting their communities by investigating the cause and manner of unexplained deaths, which may be the result of a variety of circumstances including violent crimes, suicides, or accidents. Coroners also investigate deaths that occurred in police custody or within a correctional facility. They investigate any natural death that transpired without an attending doctor outside of a medical façility, or if the deceased died under suspicious or unusual circumstances. Coroners look into any death that occurred within 24 hours of a patient entering a hospital, or that took place during surgery. Furthermore, they investigate deaths from a communicable disease that may threaten the public health.

Coroners are public officials who may be elected by the voters in their jurisdiction or appointed by a local or state executive body. In some jurisdictions, the sheriff performs the role of Coroner.

Coroners have some background in biology, particularly in how human organisms function at the cellular level and how their tissues interact among themselves and with their environment. They understand basic principles of chemistry including how chemicals interact with human organisms. Their knowledge of medicine includes the methods of diagnosing and treating disease and injuries. They also possess an understanding of business and management practices, including how to provide leadership to others and plan and coordinate productive activities. Additionally, Coroners are knowledgeable about laws, agency regulations, and the political process.

The coroner's office is responsible for conducting medicolegal death scene investigations. Depending on their jurisdiction, Coroners may perform these investigations or oversee the work of death investigators, also known as coroner's investigators or deputy coroners. The coroner's office is responsible for performing certain tasks at every death scene, including:

- performing a close examination of the body to find evidence of trauma, the presence of identifying marks, scars, or tattoos, and to determine if further examination by a pathologist is needed
- observing and documenting the position and condition of the corpse as well as the environmental conditions surrounding it
- making sure that evidence found on the body is properly collected
- interviewing death scene witnesses, family members, physicians, and others to attain information that will help determine the cause of death
- establishing the identities of deceased persons
- providing an estimate of the time of the death
- collecting and preserving personal effects of the deceased, particularly those things pertinent to the death such as suicide notes or medicines
- taking custody of the body
- making arrangements to transport the corpse to a funeral parlor, morgue, or other approved facility

Some jurisdictions require Coroners to be medical doctors, and hence they have the responsibility to perform postmortem examinations, including autopsies. In other jurisdictions, Coroners hire, or contract, medical doctors or forensic pathologists to conduct postmortem examinations. However, it is the legal obligation of Coroners to provide the official cause and manner of death in all investigations.

Once bodies have been identified, the coroner's office is responsible for notifying the next of kin. This is a difficult and often emotionally trying task. If family members live in another jurisdiction, Coroners must notify the appropriate personnel in that area. At the end of death investigations, Coroners issue death certificates. This is one of their most important functions, as these documents are used to settle civil, criminal, and insurance disputes. On occasion, Coroners are requested to testify at trials, hearings, or inquests.

As executive officers, Coroners perform various administrative and managerial duties. For example, they handle budgetary and financial tasks, conduct staff meetings, prepare reports and required forms, and maintain records and files of cases, reports, death certificates, and other important documents. They also develop and implement policies, procedures, and standards, and make sure that administrative and technical operations are in compliance with appropriate laws, rules, regulations, and codes. Further, Coroners are responsible for ensuring the quality, consistency, and accuracy of death investigations, postmortem examinations, and autopsies.

As leaders, Coroners provide supervision and direction to their staffs, which may include death investigators, forensic pathologists, lab technicians and assistants, and clerical personnel, among others. Coroners are also responsible for providing their various staff members with appropriate training and mentoring. In addition, they are involved in the recruiting, selection, hiring, and firing of employees, and they conduct job performance evaluations on their staffs.

As public officials, Coroners are expected to build partnerships between their offices and law enforcement agencies, physicians, government agencies, community organizations, other public officials, the general public, and others. Coroners also provide general information about their work to courts, government agencies, educational institutions, and community groups.

Coroners perform a highly stressful job. They always have a large workload. They are on call 24 hours every day and need to continuously draw on their ability to communicate with people from all walks of life, their skill at managing difficult and unpleasant tasks, their adeptness at handling public relations, and their knowledge of legal and law enforcement issues.

Salaries

Salaries for Coroners vary from county to county. In some counties, Coroners do not receive a salary, but are paid a fee each time they provide their services. Specific salary information for Coroners is unavailable. Their earnings are similar to those of compliance officers. According to the May 2006 *Occupational Employment Statistics* survey by the U.S. Bureau of Labor Statistics, the estimated annual salary for most compliance officers ranged between $27,860 and $80,380. (This category of compliance officers does not include those who work in agriculture, construction, health and safety, and transportation.)

Employment Prospects

In the United States, 29 states (as of 2006) have coroner or coroner-sheriff systems in some or all of their counties. American Samoa, a U.S. territory, also uses a coroner system. In sheriff-coroner systems, the sheriff performs the role of Coroner.

Opportunities become available in a county when the Coroner's term of office is up, which is usually every four years. For elected positions, any individual who meets the necessary qualifications can run for office. Individuals may need to spend a lot of time and money for their campaigns to convince voters in their counties to elect them.

Advancement Prospects

Coroners are usually appointed or elected for a term of four years. They may be reappointed or they may choose to run for another term of office. In general, Coroners measure advancement through job satisfaction, the fulfillment of giving back to their community, and professional recognition.

Education and Training

There are no standard educational qualifications that an individual must meet to become a Coroner. Many Coroners have a college degree or some college training in fields of their interest. Some possess a doctor of medicine (M.D.) or doctor of osteopathy (D.O.) degree.

As elected officials or appointees, Coroners learn their duties on the job. Many enroll in courses, workshops, and seminars to develop skills and knowledge in medicolegal death investigations.

Special Requirements

In sheriff-coroner systems, Coroners must possess a basic peace officer standards and training certificate. They must successfully complete annual training to maintain their certification.

Experience, Special Skills, and Personality Traits

Requirements to become a Coroner vary from county to county. For example, some counties require that Coroners be physicians, while others have no requirements other than Coroners must be U.S. citizens and be at least a certain age.

In general, most Coroners, whether elected or appointed, have a background in law enforcement, medicine, medicolegal death investigation, or another related field.

Coroners need excellent interpersonal and communication skills, as they must be able to work well with staff, law enforcement agencies, physicians, government officials, the media, family members, the public, and others from diverse backgrounds. In addition, Coroners must have effective leadership, teamwork, public relations, management, investigative, and writing skills to perform well at their job.

Being patient, open-minded, creative, compassionate, persistent, ethical, and goal-oriented are some personality traits that successful Coroners share.

Unions and Associations

Coroners can join professional associations to take advantage of professional resources and services such as continuing education and networking opportunities. One national society that serves their interests is the International Association of Coroners and Medical Examiners. For contact information, see Appendix III.

Tips for Entry

1. As a high school or college student, obtain an internship or volunteer in a coroner's office (or medical examiner's office) to get an idea if that type of work fits you.
2. Take advantage of opportunities that allow you to develop and improve your leadership and project management skills.
3. Age, residency, and other qualifications that individuals need to run for the coroner's office vary from county to county. To obtain information, contact your county elections office or county clerk.
4. Use the Internet to learn more about Coroners and what they do. To find relevant Web sites to visit, enter any of these keywords in a search engine: *coroner* or *coroner's office*. For some links, see Appendix IV.

MEDICAL EXAMINER

CAREER PROFILE

Duties: Investigate sudden, suspicious, or violent deaths; determine the cause and manner of death; may perform autopsies; perform other duties as required

Alternate Title(s): Forensic Pathologist; Assistant Medical Examiner, Associate Medical Examiner, Deputy Medical Examiner, Chief Medical Examiner

Salary Range: $45,000 to $146,000+

Employment Prospects: Fair

Advancement Prospects: Fair

Prerequisites:

Education or Training—Bachelor's degree, medical degree, residency training; pathology training may be required

Experience—Practice in medicine; pathology practice may be required

Special Skills and Personality Traits—Leadership, teamwork, interpersonal, communication, writing, customer-service, and self-management skills; enterprising, flexible, organized, analytical, detail-oriented, ethical, and respectful

Special Requirements—Be a licensed physician; board certification in pathology may be required

CAREER LADDER

Chief Medical Examiner

Associate Medical Examiner

Assistant Medical Examiner or Forensic Pathologist

Position Description

When violent, sudden, or unexpected deaths have occurred, these deaths must be investigated according to law. In many counties and states, the authority to conduct medicolegal death investigations belongs to Medical Examiners. Their job is to determine the cause of death as well as the manner by which the death occurred. This involves performing postmortem examinations to establish if a person had died from disease, injury, or poison; if a person had died naturally; or if the death was due to an accident, suicide, or homicide.

Medical Examiners are more commonly known for investigating deaths due to criminal circumstances but they also probe into deaths that resulted from accidents and suicides. In addition, they examine natural deaths of persons who were not under a physician's care or who died under suspicious or unusual circumstances. Medical Examiners also investigate cases of persons who died of a communicable disease that has the potential to become a health threat to the general public. Furthermore, they are required by law to examine the deaths of individuals who are in police custody or in jail, prison, or another correctional facility.

Medical Examiners are physicians, and many of them are trained pathologists. They follow certain procedures and protocols for performing postmortem examinations, which involve external or internal examinations of the dead body. They are also knowledgeable about forensic principles, practices, procedures, and techniques for handling, examining, and identifying physical evidence that pertains to criminal investigations.

Usually, with cases in which the cause of death is unclear, an autopsy is performed. This is a medical procedure that involves an internal examination of the whole body. Medical Examiners inspect the heart, lungs, stomach, intestines, and other internal organs for signs of injury or natural disease processes. They analyze the different tissues and fluids as well. They may send samples of tissues, blood, or bodily fluids to other laboratories or testing agencies for consultation. For example, if Medical Examiners suspect a person died from a drug overdose, they would send blood or tissue samples to a toxicology lab to determine the type and amount of drug that the deceased had consumed.

Medical Examiners also review reports to help them establish the cause and manner of deaths. They look at medical records, and in crime-related cases, they study criminal investigation and crime lab reports.

Upon completion of their postmortem examinations, they prepare and present written and verbal medical reports of their findings. They are also responsible for signing and issuing official death certificates. Medical Examiners are expected to complete their examinations in a timely manner. They are usually able to release deceased bodies to their family members after one or two days. Autopsy reports are oftentimes available several days or weeks later, as Medical Examiners must wait for reports from laboratories, crime labs, and criminal investigators to complete their analyses and evaluations.

Medical Examiners may be requested to testify in courts as expert witnesses. In either civil or criminal trials, they provide testimony about their findings on postmortem examinations they have conducted. They might also be asked to provide expert testimony on the procedures and techniques that are used to perform autopsies and external postmortem examinations.

Medical Examiners also perform other duties, depending on their position, expertise, and skill level. For example, they may be assigned to:

- provide counsel to family members of the deceased regarding the cause and manner of the person's death
- review forensic work of subordinates for quality, accuracy, and consistency
- provide data and statistical information to news media, community agencies, social agencies, the general public, and others
- conduct research to develop new or improved procedures and techniques for performing death investigations
- perform administrative duties such as preparing budgets; developing office policies and operational procedures; and maintaining accurate and complete investigative records and reports
- supervise and train subordinate staff members

Some medical examiner's offices are associated with university hospitals; thus, they may be responsible for teaching residents and medical students.

Medical Examiners are sometimes confused with coroners, who perform a similar role in other local jurisdictions. Whereas Medical Examiners are appointed to their positions, coroners are usually elected by the voters in their jurisdiction for a term of office. Coroners are not typically physicians. In a coroner's office, autopsies are performed by forensic pathologists who may be part of the coroner's staff. Some coroners contract with forensic pathologists or a medical examiner's office in another jurisdiction to provide medical expertise and perform autopsies as needed.

Medical Examiners work for county medical examiners' offices or within state medical examiner systems. In a state system, Medical Examiners may be assigned to provide services to some or all counties within their state.

Medical Examiners work 40 hours per week but put in additional hours as needed to complete their duties or to deal with emergency situations. They are on call 24 hours a day. In large offices, they may be rotated on an on-call schedule. In statewide medical examiners' systems, Medical Examiners may be required to travel to different locations.

Salaries

Salaries for Medical Examiners vary, depending on such factors as their experience, position, employer, and geographic location. Salary information for this occupation is unavailable. An informal survey of job listings on the Internet showed salaries as high as $200,000 and more for experienced Medical Examiners. According to the May 2006 *Occupational Employment Statistics* survey by the U.S. Bureau of Labor Statistics, the estimated annual salary for most physicians (not listed by specialty) ranged between $45,160 and $145,600.

Employment Prospects

In the United States, death investigations are conducted by either a medical examiner's office or a coroner's office. In 2006, medical examiner systems were employed in 40 states. Some states have only medical examiner systems, while others have a mix of medical examiner and coroner systems. Medical Examiners work in county or district medical examiners' offices or in state medical examiner systems.

Job opportunities usually become available as Medical Examiners retire, transfer to other jobs, or advance to higher positions. Employers may create additional positions, as long as funding is available.

Advancement Prospects

Medical Examiners who have administrative and managerial ambitions can pursue such positions. However, they may need to transfer to other employers to obtain higher positions.

Many Medical Examiners measure their success through job satisfaction, higher incomes, and professional recognition. They may seek positions in other medical examiners' offices or systems to perform more challenging cases.

Some Medical Examiners enter the private sector by becoming consultants as forensic pathologists.

Education and Training

Medical Examiners must possess either a doctor of medicine (M.D.) or doctor of osteopathy (D.O.) degree. They must complete many years of study to obtain either degree. First, an individual must complete a bachelor's degree program in any field, which usually takes four or five years. This is followed by four years of medical school, and then another three to eight years of graduate medical education (or residency), depending on the medical specialty an individual has selected to enter.

Many Medical Examiners specialize in pathology, for which they are required to complete three years of training in anatomic pathology or five years of training in both anatomic and clinical pathology. Individuals complete an additional year of training in forensic pathology, if they wish to concentrate in that field.

Throughout their careers, Medical Examiners enroll in continuing education programs and training programs to update their skills and to keep up with advancements in their field.

Special Requirements

Medical Examiners must be medically licensed physicians in the state (or territory or District of Columbia) where they practice. Employers may also require that Medical Examiners be board-certified by the American Board of Pathology in anatomic pathology or anatomic/clinical pathology, as well as in forensic pathology.

Experience, Special Skills, and Personality Traits

Work qualifications vary from employer to employer. In general, applicants must have experience in the practice of medicine. They must also be knowledgeable about forensic pathology methods and techniques, standard autopsy room protocols, and rules and laws relating to the collection of forensic evidence.

To perform their job effectively, Medical Examiners need strong leadership, teamwork, interpersonal, communication, writing, and customer-service skills. They must also have excellent self-management skills, including the ability to handle stressful situations, work independently, follow and understand instructions, and prioritize multiple tasks.

Some personality traits that successful Medical Examiners share include being enterprising, flexible, organized, analytical, detail-oriented, ethical, and respectful.

Unions and Associations

Many Medical Examiners belong to professional associations to take advantage of networking opportunities, continuing education, professional certification, and other professional resources and services. Professional societies are available locally, statewide, regionally, nationally, and worldwide.

Some national societies that serve the interests of these medicolegal professionals include the National Association of Medical Examiners, the International Association of Coroners and Medical Examiners, and the American Academy of Forensic Sciences. Many physicians also join medical societies such as the American Medical Association, the College of American Pathology, or the American Society for Clinical Pathology. For contact information for these organizations, see Appendix III.

Tips for Entry

1. As a college student, obtain an internship, a volunteer position, or a job in a medical examiner's office to get an idea if you would like to work in that type of setting.
2. To enhance your employability, enroll in basic courses in death investigation that are offered by higher education institutions, professional associations, or other organizations.
3. Check the job listings at Web sites of different forensic societies, such as the National Association of Medical Examiners, the American Academy of Forensic Sciences, and the American Society of Crime Laboratory Directors. (See Appendix III for Web site addresses.)
4. Use the Internet to learn more about Medical Examiners. You might start by visiting the National Association of Medical Examiners Web site at http://www.thename.org. For more links, see Appendix IV.

MEDICOLEGAL DEATH INVESTIGATOR

CAREER PROFILE

Duties: Conduct medicolegal death investigations; examine corpses at death scenes; collect pertinent information; prepare reports; perform other duties as required

Alternate Title(s): Death Investigator, Forensic Investigator, Deputy Coroner, Coroner's Investigator

Salary Range: $28,000 to $73,000

Employment Prospects: Poor

Advancement Prospects: Poor for civilian employees

Prerequisites:

Education or Training—High school diploma; on-the-job training

Experience—Previous experience in medicolegal death investigations, law enforcement, medical, or another related field

Special Skills and Personality Traits—Interviewing, writing, problem-solving, teamwork, self-management, interpersonal, and communication skills; tactful, respectful, articulate, observant, dedicated, trustworthy, and honest

Special Requirements—Driver's license; peace officer certificate may be required

CAREER LADDER

```
┌─────────────────────────────────────┐
│ Senior Medicolegal Death Investigator │
└─────────────────────────────────────┘

┌─────────────────────────────────────┐
│   Medicolegal Death Investigator    │
└─────────────────────────────────────┘

┌─────────────────────────────────────┐
│   Medicolegal Death Investigator    │
│            (Entry-level)            │
└─────────────────────────────────────┘
```

Position Description

In every locality in the United States, a coroner's office or medical examiner's office has the authority to conduct investigations into violent, sudden, or unexpected deaths that have occurred within its jurisdiction. These offices are responsible for identifying the deceased and deciding the official cause and manner of death. In many of these offices, Medicolegal Death Investigators are employed to look into death that occurs in such situations as criminal violence, suspicious circumstances, accidents, suicides, in police custody, in a correctional facility, or when a physician did not attend to a decedent.

In coroners' offices, Medicolegal Death Investigators may go by such job titles as *coroner's investigator* or *deputy coroner*. In some states or counties, deputy sheriffs perform the role of coroner's investigator on a part-time or full-time basis.

Medicolegal Death Investigators generally have a background in criminal justice and the sciences, including medical terminology, biology, chemistry, physiology, pharmacology, and anatomy. They also have expertise in such areas as their agency's procedures, investigative techniques, counseling, and information management. Additionally, these professionals are knowledgeable about how bodies change after death, how to diagnose a body's outward appearance for evidence of disease, and how to prevent the spread of infection or contagious diseases.

Medicolegal Death Investigators proceed through a series of approved steps to carry out their investigations. It is their duty to document a decedent's social, mental health, and medical histories as well as sum up how the body was discovered and what transpired prior to the death.

When a death is reported to a coroner's or medical examiner's office, investigators immediately go to the death scene. They closely examine the body to find evidence of trauma and determine if further examination by a forensic pathologist is needed. They take note of changes in the body, such as rigor mortis, lividity, decomposition, or the presence of insects. They also take fingerprints, check photo identification, and look for identifying marks (such as scars or tattoos) to establish the decedent's identity.

These investigators interview witnesses at the death scene regarding their relationship to the decedent and their account of how the death occurred. They also obtain information about the decedent's health such as past medical history, current medical status, treatments, and suicide attempts. In addition, they study the environmental conditions and objects surrounding the deceased.

Medicolegal Death Investigators photograph the overall scene as well as the body, and make notes about whether it or any other evidence has been moved. They write notes and draw diagrams to describe the precise location of the body within the scene and how it is positioned in relation to other evidence. They ensure that evidence found on the body, such as gunshot residue, drugs, weapons, and trace evidence, is properly collected. They also gather and safeguard the decedent's possessions.

Medicolegal Death Investigators work with other investigators (such as crime scene technicians or criminal investigators) who are at the death scene. Together they review or establish safety protocols by removing all sources of potential contamination and ensure the well-being of the investigative personnel. The various investigators also exchange information such as preliminary witness information and each agency's tasks and responsibilities.

Medicolegal Death Investigators arrange for the body to be transported from the death scene. It may be taken to a funeral director or to a morgue or other authorized receiving facility for further postmortem examination. These investigators conclude their scene investigation with a "walk-through" to ensure that all the evidence has been collected and equipment has been recovered.

Medicolegal Death Investigators may need to perform follow-up activities to complete their investigations. For example, they might obtain medical and dental records and interview family members, friends, or physicians. In cases of unidentified bodies, these investigators might circulate photos and descriptions to the news media, neighborhood organizations, and community agencies. Upon completing their cases, Medicolegal Death Investigators prepare and submit clear and concise reports and other required forms that describe their findings. These investigators sometimes testify as expert witnesses in the courts regarding their cases or about the procedures and techniques they perform in medicolegal death investigations.

Medicolegal Death Investigators are in frequent contact with grieving family members or friends of the deceased. It is their job to locate and notify the deceased's next of kin. They inform the family of what needs to transpire, such as an autopsy or toxicology examination. They also provide information and resources such as counseling services or police assistance and inform the family about how to obtain or purchase death certificates and other relevant reports.

These death investigators work indoors and outdoors in a variety of physical environments. They are continuously in the presence of death and disease in disagreeable surroundings and are exposed to hazardous materials, fumes, odors, or other undesirable conditions. Investigators are required to be on their feet several hours each day. They stand, walk, crawl, bend, and stoop as well as regularly lift corpses and other objects that may weigh as much as 200 pounds or more.

Coroners' and medical examiners' offices operate around the clock every day, including holidays and weekends. Some investigators work on rotating shifts. Most, if not all, must be available on standby basis 24 hours a day.

Salaries

Salaries for Medicolegal Death Investigators vary, depending on such factors as their education, experience, employer, and geographic location. Formal salary information for this occupation is unavailable. Their wages are generally similar to those of forensic science technicians. According to the May 2006 *Occupational Employment Statistics* survey by the U.S. Bureau of Labor Statistics, the estimated annual salary for most forensic science technicians ranged between $27,530 and $73,100.

Employment Prospects

Medical examiners' offices and coroners' offices employ Medicolegal Death Investigators on a full-time or part-time basis. Some coroners' offices are part of sheriff-coroner systems in which deputy sheriffs are also the death investigators within their counties. Depending on the size of the jurisdiction, the sheriff's office may have a special unit dedicated to handling coroner's cases.

Opportunities generally become available as Medicolegal Death Investigators transfer to other jobs, advance to higher positions, or leave the workforce for various reasons. Employers will create additional positions to meet growing needs, as long as funding is available.

Job competition is strong. There are usually more applicants than jobs, according to one expert in the field.

Advancement Prospects

Medicolegal Death Investigators advance in salary and rank according to their job performance. They also receive greater responsibilities and more complex assignments as they gain experience. Promotions are limited to lead and supervisory positions.

In sheriff-coroner systems, investigators advance through the sheriff's ranks and pay schedule. Deputy sheriffs can develop a career according to their interests and ambitions. They can seek positions in other special law enforcement details that interest them, such as their agency's bomb squad,

SWAT team, or K9 unit. In addition, they can pursue supervisory and managerial positions.

Education and Training

Minimally, applicants for civilian entry-level positions must possess a high school or general equivalency diploma. Some employers prefer to hire candidates who possess an associate or bachelor's degree in criminal justice, health, physical science, nursing, or another related field.

To become a sheriff's deputy, applicants may need to have completed some college work or have earned an associate or bachelor's degree in criminal justice or another related field, depending on the agency's requirements.

Entry-level death investigators receive on-the-job training and instruction in such areas as investigating deaths; identifying decedents; securing information from governmental agencies, physicians, and others; and notifying family members. Novice investigators work under the supervision and direction of experienced Medicolegal Death Investigators.

Throughout their careers, Medicolegal Death Investigators enroll in courses, workshops, and seminars to update their skills and increase their knowledge.

Special Requirements

Employers require that Medicolegal Death Investigators possess a valid driver's license.

In coroner-sheriff systems, Medicolegal Death Investigators must possess a basic peace officer standards and training certificate. These agencies may hire candidates without a certificate on the condition they complete the necessary law enforcement academy program to obtain the certificate.

Experience, Special Skills, and Personality Traits

Job qualifications for entry-level positions vary among employers. In general, applicants must have one or more years of full-time experience working in medicolegal death investigation, law enforcement, forensic science, mortuary science, or another related field. Some death investigators work their way up through the ranks as morgue attendants, forensic pathology technicians, and similar positions within a coroner's office or medical examiner's office. Many Medicolegal Death Investigators are former law enforcement officers, criminal investigators, registered nurses, surgi-

cal technicians, emergency medical technicians, physician assistants, and medical record clerks.

To perform well at their job, Medicolegal Death Investigators must have excellent interviewing, writing, problem-solving, teamwork, and self-management skills. They also need effective interpersonal and communication skills, as they must be able to deal with colleagues, witnesses, family members, law enforcement officers, and many others from diverse backgrounds. Being tactful, respectful, articulate, observant, dedicated, trustworthy, and honest are some personality traits that successful Medicolegal Death Investigators share.

Unions and Associations

Medicolegal Death Investigators might join professional associations to take advantage of networking opportunities, continuing education, and other professional resources and services. The American Board of Medicolegal Death Investigators and the National Association of Medical Examiners are two national societies that serve this profession. For contact information, see Appendix III.

Tips for Entry

1. To prepare for a career in medicolegal death investigations, one expert in the field suggests that students take courses in biology, chemistry, forensic science, and criminal justice.
2. Gain practical experience by participating in a reserve investigator program, if one is available in your area. Reserves are volunteers that an agency trains to assist staff in conducting medicolegal death investigations.
3. The more willing and flexible you are about relocating to other parts of the country, the greater chances you have of obtaining a job.
4. To enhance their employability, some Medicolegal Death Investigators obtain professional certification that is granted by the American Board of Medicolegal Death Investigators. For contact information about this certification program, see Appendix II.
5. Use the Internet to learn more about medicolegal death investigations. To obtain a list of relevant Web sites, enter any of these keywords into a search engine: *medicolegal death investigations*, *deputy coroners*, or *medical examiner's death investigators*. For some links, see Appendix IV.

FORENSIC PATHOLOGIST

CAREER PROFILE

Duties: Perform autopsies to determine the cause and manner of death in medicolegal death investigations; prepare reports of findings; provide expert witness testimony; perform other duties as required

Alternate Title(s): Medical Examiner

Salary Range: $45,000 to $146,000+

Employment Prospects: Good

Advancement Prospects: Good

Prerequisites:

Education or Training—Bachelor's degree; medical degree; residency training

Experience—Experience performing medicolegal death investigations and autopsies

Special Skills and Personality Traits—Interpersonal, teamwork, communication, customer-service, writing, analytical, organizational, and self-management skills; detail-oriented, ethical, respectful, honest, energetic, cooperative, and flexible

Special Requirements—Be a licensed physician; board certification in pathology may be required

CAREER LADDER

```
┌─────────────────────────────────┐
│   Senior Forensic Pathologist   │
│  (or Associate Medical Examiner)│
└─────────────────────────────────┘

┌─────────────────────────────────┐
│      Forensic Pathologist       │
│ (or Assistant Medical Examiner) │
└─────────────────────────────────┘

┌─────────────────────────────────┐
│   Resident in Forensic Pathology│
└─────────────────────────────────┘
```

Position Description

Throughout the United States, coroners' offices and medical examiners' offices are required by law to investigate the cause and manner of sudden, unexpected, or violent deaths that have occurred within their jurisdictions. With some death cases, professional men and women known as Forensic Pathologists perform autopsies (internal postmortem examinations) to learn the reasons why people died.

Forensic Pathologists are licensed medical or osteopathic doctors. Forensic pathology is a subspecialty of pathology, a branch of medicine that closely examines tissues, cells, and fluids to diagnose disease and the causes of death. Forensic Pathologists also possess basic working knowledge about toxicology, forensic serology, forensic anthropology, DNA technology, and other forensic specialties such as wound ballistics and trace evidence analysis.

These medical specialists investigate deaths that may have occurred because of homicide or suicide or by accident. They also investigate cases in which the deceased died naturally but was unattended by a physician, or if the deceased died under suspicious or unusual circumstances. In addition, Forensic Pathologists examine deaths that occurred in police custody or in correctional facilities; deaths that took place within 24 hours of patients' entering a hospital, or deaths during surgery; and deaths from a communicable disease that may threaten the public health.

Their first investigative step is to obtain an account of how a death occurred and a record of the deceased's medical history. Forensic Pathologists may need to visit the death scene to gather some of this information. At a death scene, Forensic Pathologists conduct a brief preliminary examination of the body before it is moved. They also look for evidence such as bullets, hair, fibers, fingernail clippings, blood, and bodily fluids, which they collect, document, and forward to forensic specialists, such as trace evidence examiners, for identification and analysis.

In the autopsy room, Forensic Pathologists then oversee and perform a thorough examination of the body. They first closely inspect the exterior of the body and then cut open the body to obtain samples of tissues from the internal organs, which they will examine later under microscopes. They also take X-rays as well as extract bodily fluids and tissue for toxicological and chemical analysis.

Forensic Pathologists attempt to answer questions about the time of death, whether the manner of death fits one of the legal criteria, the cause of death, what type of instrument may have been used if the death was the result of injury, and whether the death occurred where the body was found or if the body was moved after death. If the identity of a body is unknown, Forensic Pathologists obtain help from other forensic specialists. For example, a forensic odontologist may be able to determine an identity by investigating dental records.

Forensic Pathologists evaluate the autopsy and lab results with the case history and draw a conclusion as to the cause and manner of death. Then they write a report that summarizes their findings and conclusions. Forensic Pathologists might meet with the family of the deceased to discuss the circumstances and cause of death. On occasion, they may be required to present their findings as expert testimony in the courts.

Law enforcement agencies sometimes request Forensic Pathologists to examine living patients to determine the cause and level of injuries due to abuse or sexual assault. These medical specialists ascertain whether such injuries correlate to known injury patterns resulting from either accidents or deliberate acts of violence.

Forensic Pathologists are responsible for completing other tasks besides performing autopsies. For example they:

- interpret medical or investigative records and reports
- confer with law enforcement personnel and attorneys about their death investigation results
- design protocol and standards for specialized death investigations such as infant deaths
- prepare and provide instruction in educational settings
- train and direct the work of subordinate pathologists, pathologist's assistants, forensic lab technicians, morgue attendants, and other support staff
- participate in community outreach and educational programs
- conduct forensic pathology research
- maintain good working relations with colleagues, law enforcement officials, attorneys, and the public
- use computers to prepare reports, charts, illustrations, and other documents
- maintain their knowledge and abilities

Forensic Pathologists work 40 hours per week, but are on call 24 hours a day, every day of the year. In large medical examiners' offices, Forensic Pathologists may be rotated on an on-call schedule.

Salaries

Salaries for Forensic Pathologists vary, depending on such factors as their experience, position, employer, and geographic location. Salary information for this occupation is unavailable. An informal survey of job listings on the Internet showed salaries as high as $200,000 and more for experienced Forensic Pathologists. According to the May 2006 *Occupational Employment Statistics* survey by the U.S. Bureau of Labor Statistics, the estimated annual salary for most physicians (not listed by specialty) ranged between $45,160 and $145,600.

Employment Prospects

Forensic Pathologists work for local and state medical examiners' offices and coroners' offices throughout the United States. Some are employed by medical schools, military services, and the federal government. Some are hired by hospitals and private firms that perform forensic autopsies on a contractual basis.

Job opportunities usually become available as Forensic Pathologists retire, transfer to other jobs, or advance to higher positions. Employers may create additional positions, as long as funding is available.

Opportunities are favorable for qualified Forensic Pathologists. According to the Wake Forest University Baptist Medical Center (Winston-Salem, North Carolina) Forensic Pathology Fellowship Program Web page, the number of physicians currently being trained in forensic pathology is fewer than the number of Forensic Pathologists who retire each year.

Advancement Prospects

As Forensic Pathologists gain experience, they receive greater responsibilities and more complex assignments. They also advance in salary and rank according to their job performance. Individuals with administrative and managerial ambitions can pursue positions as supervisors, managers, lab directors, and executive officers. Advancement opportunities, however, are limited, and candidates usually have to find positions with other employers. Those interested in teaching and conducting independent research can seek positions as academicians.

Some Forensic Pathologists choose to become independent consultants or owners of firms that offer forensic pathology services.

Education and Training

Many years of study are required for students to become Forensic Pathologists. Individuals first complete a bachelor's degree in any field, which usually takes between four and five years. They then enter medical school and complete four years of training to earn either a doctor of medicine (M.D.) or doctor of osteopathy (D.O.) degree. This is followed by graduate medical education (or residency) in pathology. Residents may choose to complete either a three-year training program in anatomic pathology or a five-year program in both anatomic and clinical pathology.

Upon finishing their residency, they complete one year of training in forensic pathology, which includes practical experience participating in medicolegal death investigations and autopsies.

Throughout their careers, Forensic Pathologists enroll in continuing education and training programs to update their skills and to keep up with advancements in their field.

Special Requirements

Forensic Pathologists must be medically licensed physicians in the state (or territory or District of Columbia) where they practice. Employers may also require that they be board-certified by the American Board of Pathology in anatomic pathology or anatomic/clinical pathology, as well as in forensic pathology.

Experience, Skills, and Personality Traits

Employers hire applicants for entry-level positions who have experience performing medicolegal death investigations and autopsies; such requirements are fulfilled through their fellowship program in forensic pathology.

Forensic Pathologists need excellent interpersonal, teamwork, communication, and customer-service skills, as they must be able to work well with colleagues, death investigators, professionals, managers, and others from diverse backgrounds. They also need effective writing, analytical, organizational, and self-management skills for their job. Being detail-oriented, ethical, respectful, honest, energetic,

cooperative, and flexible are some personality traits that Forensic Pathologists share.

Unions and Associations

Forensic Pathologists can join medical and forensic societies to take advantage of networking opportunities, continuing education, current research, and other professional resources and services. Professional associations are available locally, statewide, regionally, nationally, and worldwide. Some national societies that serve the interests of Forensic Pathologists include the National Association of Medical Examiners, the American Academy of Forensic Sciences, the American Medical Association, the College of American Pathologists, and the American Society for Clinical Pathology. For contact information for these organizations, see Appendix III.

Tips for Entry

1. Be sure pathology, and specifically forensic pathology, is the right career for you. Read books and articles about the field. Talk with professionals. Also visit a morgue or trauma center to get an idea of how you can handle unpleasant sights and stressful conditions.
2. Many employers post job announcements at their Web sites, as well as provide the opportunity to download application forms.
3. Take advantage of job and fellowship announcements that various forensic societies publish at their Web sites and in their magazines and newsletters.
4. Use the Internet to learn more about forensic pathology and about forensic autopsies. To obtain a list of relevant Web sites, enter any of these keywords into a search engine: *forensic pathology*, *forensic pathologists*, or *forensic autopsies*. For some links, see Appendix IV.

FORENSIC TOXICOLOGIST

CAREER PROFILE

Duties: Examine human tissues and fluids for the presence or absence of toxic substances; analyze and interpret findings; prepare reports; perform other duties as required

Alternate Title(s): Toxicologist

Salary Range: $35,000 to $106,000

Employment Prospects: Good

Advancement Prospects: Fair

Prerequisites:

Education or Training—Bachelor's or master's degree in chemistry, biochemistry, toxicology, or another related field

Experience—Prior work experience in toxicology laboratories required

Special Skills and Personality Traits—Writing, communication, interpersonal, teamwork, project management, math, statistics, and computer skills; organized, persistent, flexible, ethical, and trustworthy

CAREER LADDER

```
┌─────────────────────────────────┐
│  Senior or Supervisory Forensic │
│          Toxicologist           │
└─────────────────────────────────┘

┌─────────────────────────────────┐
│       Forensic Toxicologist     │
└─────────────────────────────────┘

┌─────────────────────────────────┐
│ Forensic Toxicologist (entry-level) or │
│    Toxicologist (in another setting)   │
└─────────────────────────────────┘
```

Position Description

Toxicology is the study of drugs, poisons, and other toxins and their adverse effects on living organisms. All chemicals are potentially toxic and any solid, liquid, or gaseous substance absorbed in excess can be extremely harmful. Forensic toxicology is the application of toxicology to legal matters, such as criminal investigations, medicolegal death investigations, and workplace drug testing.

Forensic Toxicologists work in any number of settings. Many of those who specialize in postmortem toxicology are employed by coroners' offices and medical examiners' offices. They assist forensic pathologists and other medicolegal death investigators in determining the cause of death of persons who have died violently, suddenly, or unexpectedly. Their function is to ascertain whether drugs or poisons are present or absent in corpses and, if they are present, to isolate, identify, and measure the amounts of toxic substances. They then provide their findings to forensic pathologists who in turn establish the cause of death in such cases as drug overdose and accidental or intentional poisoning.

Forensic Toxicologists are trained in the sciences of biology, chemistry, and, in particular, pharmacology. Their training provides a special focus on analyzing human tissues and bodily fluids and how both organic and inorganic substances interact with them. For example, they may look for either suspected substances or for substances called metabolites that the body produces when processing a drug or poison. Forensic Toxicologists possess a thorough knowledge of chemical compounds and their metabolites as well as the methods for analyzing them. They also understand how various drugs and poisons affect organisms and can thus recognize the presence of suspected substances or their metabolites in tissue samples. In addition, Forensic Toxicologists are familiar with laws, legal terms, and court processes. They are also well versed at using analytical instruments and equipment to arrive at accurate conclusions about the toxic substances they find.

In medicolegal death investigations, forensic pathologists provide Forensic Toxicologists with samples of organ tissues (such as from the liver or heart), bodily fluids, and stomach contents from the deceased to examine. They are also given reports that provide postmortem data and symptoms to review. Sometimes toxicologists are requested to analyze specimens from bodies that have been dead for a long time.

Forensic Toxicologists perform complex and precise work. When Forensic Toxicologists receive samples for testing, they first divide the specimens into acid and base fractions to extract the drug or poison. Then they utilize standard testing procedures to precisely identify the drug or poison and accurately measure the quantity of that substance. Toxicologists analyze and interpret the results of their tests, and then prepare a clear and concise written report of their findings.

Forensic Toxicologists are sometimes requested to testify as expert witnesses in the courts about their casework, or about issues related to forensic toxicology matters.

In some medical examiners' and coroners' offices, Forensic Toxicologists also provide analytical services to law enforcement agencies. For example, they may be asked to analyze tissues or bodily fluids from living persons, such as criminal suspects or traffic offenders, to determine the level of alcohol or other drugs. Some of them help doctors in hospitals to decide which drugs to administer to patients and monitor. Their knowledge about drug interactions and levels of toxicity is invaluable for making such decisions.

Forensic Toxicologists perform many duties and complete a variety of routine tasks under the supervision of a coroner or chief medical examiner. Depending on their level of expertise or seniority, they may:

- write reports about toxicological analyses
- review documents written by staff members for completeness and accuracy
- communicate regularly with coroners, medical examiners, and pathologists
- develop processes and guiding principles for laboratory activities in compliance with professional standards and legal requirements
- conduct laboratory audits
- act as technical experts in human forensic technology for their agencies
- conduct research into drug interactions and new techniques for identifying drugs as well as improving drug therapy
- provide training to new staff members
- oversee the activities of a forensic toxicology laboratory
- supervise and appraise the work of subordinate staff members

Forensic Toxicologists work in laboratory settings. They sit at lab stations but may be required to exert themselves by performing moderate lifting tasks. Forensic Toxicologists are often exposed to biohazards, toxic chemicals, and unpleasant odors emanating from bodily fluids and tissues.

Therefore, they are required to use safety equipment and exercise special precautions to minimize their exposure to hazardous substances or contagious diseases.

These professionals work a standard 40-hour week but put in additional hours as needed to complete their various duties and to meet deadlines.

Salaries

Salaries for Forensic Toxicologists vary, depending on such factors as their education, experience, employer, and geographic location. Specific salary information for this occupation is unavailable. In general, toxicologists with a doctoral degree may earn from $35,000 to $60,000 annually for entry-level positions, and from $70,000 to $100,000 for those with 10 years of experience, according to the Society of Toxicology Web site (http://www.toxicology.org).

Toxicology is considered a specialty of analytical chemistry. The estimated annual salary for most chemists ranged between $35,480 and $106,310, according to the U.S. Bureau of Labor Statistics' May 2006 *Occupational Employment Statistics* survey.

Employment Prospects

Postmortem Forensic Toxicologists are employed by medical examiners' offices and coroners' offices. Forensic Toxicologists can also find employment with crime labs associated with law enforcement agencies, prosecuting attorneys' offices, and private forensic laboratories. Local, state, and federal regulatory agencies also hire Forensic Toxicologists. Examples of federal agencies are the U.S. Food and Drug Administration, the Environmental Protection Agency, and the Occupational Safety and Health Administration. Other employers include workplace drug testing laboratories, hospitals, universities, and industry laboratories.

Some experts in the field report that opportunities in general for toxicologists are numerous, and should remain plentiful in the coming years. Job openings for Forensic Toxicologists typically become available as individuals retire, transfer to other jobs, or advance to higher positions. Employers may create additional positions if funding is available.

Advancement Prospects

Forensic Toxicologists advance in salary and rank according to their job performance. As they gain experience, they receive greater responsibilities and more complex assignments.

Individuals with administrative and managerial ambitions can pursue positions as lead persons, supervisors, and managers. Opportunities, however, are limited, and candidates usually have to find positions with other employers. Those interested in teaching and conducting independent research can seek positions as academicians. A doctorate degree is frequently required for these professionals to advance to careers in management research or teaching.

Education and Training

Depending on the employer, entry-level candidates may need a bachelor's or master's degree in toxicology, chemistry, biochemistry, biology, or another related field. Employers may prefer to hire candidates with a doctoral degree for journey positions.

Throughout their careers, Forensic Toxicologists enroll in continuing education programs and training programs to update their skills and keep up with advancements in their field.

Experience, Special Skills, and Personality Traits

Requirements for entry-level positions vary with the different employers. In general, employers prefer to hire candidates who have previous work experience in toxicology laboratories. They may have gained their experience through internships, research assistantships, postdoctoral training, or work experience.

Forensic Toxicologists need excellent writing, communication, interpersonal, and teamwork skills to work effectively at their job. They must also have strong project management, math, statistics, and computer skills. Being organized, persistent, flexible, ethical, and trustworthy are some personality traits that successful Forensic Toxicologists have in common.

Unions and Associations

Many Forensic Toxicologists join professional associations to take advantage of networking opportunities, continuing education, professional certification, and other professional resources and services. Professional societies are available locally, statewide, regionally, nationally, and worldwide. Some national societies that serve the interests of Forensic Toxicologists include the Society of Forensic Toxicologists, the International Association of Forensic Toxicologists, the Society of Toxicology, and the American Academy of Forensic Sciences. For contact information, see Appendix III.

Tips for Entry

1. As a college student, obtain an internship or part-time job in a forensic laboratory to gain valuable experience.
2. Regulatory agencies, private laboratories, hospitals, and other employers may use the job title *Toxicologist* rather than *Forensic Toxicologist* in their job announcements.
3. To enhance their employability as well as professional credibility, many Forensic Toxicologists obtain professional certification from one or more recognized organizations. For information about some certification programs, see Appendix II.
4. Use the Internet to learn more about forensic toxicology as well as the field of toxicology in general. You might start by visiting these Web sites: Society of Forensic Toxicologists, http://www.soft-tox.org; and Society of Toxicology, http://www.toxicology.org. For more links, see Appendix IV.

FORENSIC ANTHROPOLOGIST

CAREER PROFILE

Duties: Determine the manner of death; make positive identification of human remains; provide expert witness testimony; perform other duties as required

Alternate Title(s): Physical Anthropologist, Anthropology Professor; Forensic Examiner, Forensic Scientist

Salary Range: $100 to $200 or more per hour, consulting fees

Employment Prospects: Poor

Advancement Prospects: Fair

Prerequisites:

Education or Training—Advanced degree in physical anthropology or another related field

Experience—Several years of work experience

Special Skills and Personality Traits—Analytical, critical-thinking, writing, communication, and self-management skills; detail-oriented, levelheaded, flexible, trustworthy, ethical, and fair

CAREER LADDER

```
+-------------------------------------+
|    Forensic Anthropologist          |
|    (Established Expert)              |
+-------------------------------------+

+-------------------------------------+
|  Forensic Anthropology Consultant   |
+-------------------------------------+

+-------------------------------------+
|   Physical Anthropology Professor   |
+-------------------------------------+
```

Position Description

Physical (or biological) anthropology is the study of physical characteristics among humans. Some physical anthropologists apply the principles and methodologies of this field to medicolegal death investigations. These specialists are also known as Forensic Anthropologists. They are employed or contracted by coroners' and medical examiners' offices to assist with cases that involve human skeletal remains, decomposed corpses, or burned bodies of victims. Their deaths may be due to homicide, suicide, accident, natural disaster, mass fatality, or other tragedies.

In addition to anthropology, Forensic Anthropologists are trained in human osteology, the study of the human skeleton. They have acquired knowledge about the biology of human and animal skeletons, skeletal pathology, the field techniques used by archaeologists, and how cultural variations may be considered in the context of medicolegal issues.

Forensic Anthropologists do not decide the actual cause of death in medicolegal investigations. That is the function of coroners or medical examiners, who use the information that is gathered from skeletal examinations. Forensic Anthropologists are generally called upon to help these authorities identify victims, estimate when death occurred, or reconstruct what happened at the time of death as well as afterwards.

By closely examining human skeletal remains, Forensic Anthropologists can determine such factors as the gender, age, height, the health conditions, and the ethnicity of a victim or whether the victim was right- or left-handed. In addition, they can find clues about the deceased's behavioral patterns such as their habits, what kind of work they did, or what sports they played.

These forensic experts might note healed breaks or other evidence of injury and trauma and estimate when in the victim's life it was inflicted. They can often ascertain if such evidence is the result of violence, accidental injury, or surgery. They might study injuries inflicted by blunt instruments or gunshots and estimate whether the injuries occurred before death, at the time of death, or after death. They may also be able to determine what type of weapon created the injury. Furthermore, Forensic Anthropologists can provide authorities with information such as:

- whether skeletal bones are human or animal
- the original position of the body at the time of death

- any environmental forces that altered the human remains after death
- the types of tools that were used to kill victims or dismember them

Forensic Anthropologists may be requested to provide expert witness services to the courts about their findings in a medicolegal death investigation. They are expected to present information in terms that judges, juries, and attorneys can easily understand.

In addition to their contributions to crime investigation, Forensic Anthropologists are also involved with human rights and genocide issues. They work with the remains of victims found at the sites of large disasters or wars. They sift through debris to find human skeletal remains or exhume remains from mass graves. They piece fragments together to assist with the identification of unknown victims.

The vast majority of Forensic Anthropologists are academicians who work at universities as physical anthropology professors. Most of their careers are devoted to teaching and research. They provide their services to medical examiners' and coroners' offices on a consulting basis. They generally work at campus facilities that are appropriately equipped to complete their forensic anthropological casework.

These forensic consultants also offer their services to law enforcement agencies, humanitarian organizations, and other organizations. Many of them assist in the recovery of hidden, buried, or scattered human remains. Some Forensic Anthropologists have skills in facial reproduction, which can help law enforcement officers to find the identity of victims. They can make models of human skulls and show how the faces of the deceased may have appeared in life.

As professors, many Forensic Anthropologists engage in research in their specialty and other areas. They conduct studies to gain new understanding and knowledge about human skeletons and skeletal biology. Many of them are also involved in developing new methodologies and technologies for making human identification and conducting forensic investigations.

Many of the medicolegal cases that Forensic Anthropologists handle are disturbing and can have an emotional impact on them. They are expected to endure the unpleasant sights and odors that originate from decomposing flesh, maggots, and some bodily fluids. Forensic Anthropologists must be able to overcome these factors to succeed in their profession.

Academicians work long hours, which include weekends and evenings to accomplish their many duties as teachers, researchers, and consultants. They must also fulfill community service obligations at their institutions.

Salaries
Consulting Forensic Anthropologists generally earn fees that range from $100 to $200 per hour or more for their services. Salaries for academicians vary, depending on their rank,

employer, geographic location, and other factors. The estimated annual salary for most postsecondary anthropology instructors ranged between $37,590 and $109,330, according to the May 2006 *Occupational Employment Statistics* survey, by the U.S. Bureau of Labor Statistics. This agency also reports that the estimated annual salary for anthropologists in general ranged from $28,940 to $81,490.

Employment Prospects
The forensic anthropology field is a very small field. A few Forensic Anthropologist staff positions are available in medical examiners' and coroners' offices. Such opportunities are usually available in larger local jurisdictions. Most Forensic Anthropologists are independent consultants. The majority of them are employed as professors in higher education institutions. Some work in museum and research laboratories.

Some Forensic Anthropologists find employment with the military and human rights organizations that recover and identify the skeletal remains of victims of war and other atrocities.

Forensic Anthropologists are sometimes hired to other forensic positions in medical examiners' and coroners' offices as well as government and private crime labs. For example, they might be employed as medicolegal death investigators or crime scene technicians.

Advancement Prospects
As academicians, Forensic Anthropologists advance through the ranks as instructors, assistant professors, associate professors, and full professors. Individuals with managerial and administrative ambitions may seek positions as department chairs, academic deans, administrative deans, or administrative officers at their institutions.

Advancement opportunities in medical examiners' (or coroners') offices are limited to technical lead, supervisor, and manager positions.

Education and Training
Forensic Anthropologists usually possess a master's or doctoral degree in physical anthropology with a concentration in osteology and skeletal biology. For them to teach in four-year colleges and universities, a doctorate is mandatory. Obtaining a master's degree in anthropology usually involves two or more years of study after they complete a bachelor's degree program, which may be in anthropology or another field. Earning a doctorate takes them another five to eight years, and doctoral candidates must complete a dissertation on original research in forensic anthropology.

Experience, Special Skills, and Personality Traits
Forensic Anthropologists have typically worked several years in the field and are recognized as experts in their field. In order to testify as expert witnesses in the courts, they

must be able to demonstrate that they have sufficient knowledge, skills, or practical experience to address specific cases related to legal cases.

Forensic Anthropologists must have effective analytical, critical thinking, writing, communication, and self-management skills. Being detail-oriented, levelheaded, flexible, trustworthy, ethical, and fair are some personality traits that they have in common.

Unions and Associations

Many Forensic Anthropologists belong to professional associations to take advantage of networking opportunities and other professional resources and services. Some national anthropological societies that these forensic experts might join are the American Association of Physical Anthropologists and the American Anthropological Association. Some national forensic societies include the American Academy of Forensic Sciences and the American College of Forensic Examiners. For contact information for these organizations, see Appendix III.

Tips for Entry

1. If you are in high school, take classes in biology, chemistry, and physics, as they can provide a basic foundation for your future college studies. Also take an anthropology, anatomy, or physiology class, if your school offers one.

2. As a college student, gain as much practical experience as you can in the fields of anthropology and forensic science. For example, obtain a research assistantship with a professor whose field is forensic anthropology, or get an internship in a crime lab or medical examiner's office.

3. To enhance their expert credibility, some Forensic Anthropologists obtain professional certification from the American Board of Forensic Anthropology when they become eligible. For contact information about the program, see Appendix II.

4. Some activities you can do to build up your reputation as a Forensic Anthropologist include publishing your research work, conducting training workshops in forensic anthropology methods, and making presentations at professional conferences.

5. Use the Internet to learn more about forensic anthropology. You might start by visiting ForensicAnthro. com at http://www.forensicanthro.com. For more links, see Appendix IV.

FORENSIC PATHOLOGY TECHNICIAN

CAREER PROFILE

Duties: Provide technical support during autopsies in medicolegal death investigations; perform other duties as required

Alternate Title(s): Forensic Pathologist's Assistant, Forensic Autopsy Assistant, Coroner's Forensic Technician

Salary Range: $35,000 to $55,000

Employment Prospects: Good

Advancement Prospects: Fair

Prerequisites:
  Education or Training—Educational requirements vary; on-the-job training
  Experience—One or more years of laboratory experience
  Special Skills and Personality Traits—Self-management, interpersonal, teamwork, communication, analytical, problem-solving, and organizational skills; cooperative, calm, flexible, detail-oriented, honest, and innovative

CAREER LADDER

> **Senior Forensic Pathology Technician**

> **Forensic Pathology Technician**

> **Forensic Pathology Technician Trainee**

Position Description

Sometimes in medicolegal death investigations, autopsies are required to determine the cause of death due to natural, accidental, homicidal, suicidal, or undetermined circumstances. Autopsies are postmortem internal examinations, and in medicolegal death investigations, forensic pathologists usually perform them. These medical (or osteopathic) doctors are trained to closely examine and analyze tissue, cell, and blood samples of internal organs. In many coroners' and medical examiners' offices, which have the authority to conduct medicolegal death investigations in their jurisdictions, Forensic Pathology Technicians are employed to assist pathologists. While working under their direct supervision, these assistants may examine, dissect, and process organs and tissue samples from corpses of the deceased.

Forensic Pathology Technicians are highly skilled professionals. They generally possess a background in chemistry, biology, anatomy, and physiology. They are knowledgeable about medical terminology, dissection, surgical procedures, and the instruments and equipment used in surgery. They also understand the protocols of evidence handling, including chain of custody processes and the associated methods

of safeguarding and preserving evidence. Furthermore, they are aware of all the safety precautions and regulations for handling corpses, as well as maintaining the cleanliness of autopsy rooms.

Forensic Pathology Technicians follow standard procedures in handling, transporting, and preparing corpses for medicolegal autopsies. Their tasks include documenting the identity of the deceased, taking an inventory of the deceased's personal property, and storing the property. They prepare for the postmortem examinations by setting up the appropriate tools and equipment, as well as by labeling specimen containers for tissues and trace evidence. They also make sure that all the decedent's medical charts and histories are available for the pathologist to read. In addition, they clean and weigh the corpse and take X-rays of it. They may be requested to conduct a thorough examination of the body's exterior for wounds and distinguishing marks.

Under the direct supervision of forensic pathologists, these technicians perform autopsy work that is moderately complex. They open up the torso and remove the lungs, heart, stomach, intestines, and other organs. They also open the skull and remove the brain. The assistants weigh the organs and x-ray them. They also clean out the lungs, intestines, and blood vessels and remove undigested food from the stomach.

In addition, they obtain samples of various tissue, blood, and bodily fluids for histochemical, toxicological, and microscopic studies. They ensure that the specimens are properly placed in special containers, labeled, and stored. Pathologists may direct their assistants to suture and clean the body in preparation for its release to a mortician.

Forensic Pathology Technicians are usually responsible for recording data, such as the weights of the organs and anatomic observations. They also notice and record unusual conditions that could be important to a medicolegal death investigation. Additionally, they photograph a body's external surface, its organs, biological specimens, and other relevant materials. They also help pathologists examine the physical evidence that is found on or in the body, such as knives, pills, bullets, powder burns, and other objects. The assistants write the results of the evidence examination and notify the appropriate personnel.

Forensic Pathology Technicians are responsible for completing other routine tasks. For example, they may be requested to:

- refresh the inventory of supplies when needed
- sterilize surgical tools as well as clean the equipment and the entire examination area, including the walls and floors
- drive vans to and from morgue facilities to receive and deliver bodies
- complete daily accurate and concise reports of their activities
- develop photographic and X-ray film
- be of assistance to distraught and grieving friends and family of the deceased
- decide on the best action to take in stressful or emergency situations
- testify in court

The work that Forensic Pathology Technicians do is physically demanding and stressful. They are adept at lifting heavy weights, such as corpses weighing as much as 200 pounds or more. They work with bodies that are in various states of decay, that suffered traumatic injuries, or that are infested with insects or other vermin. In addition, they are exposed to hazardous conditions, substances, or diseases; thus, they are required to wear protective clothing and equipment.

Forensic Pathology Technicians work a standard 40-hour week but put in additional hours as needed. Their schedules may vary and they may be required to work different shifts, overtime, weekends, and holidays.

Salaries

Salaries for Forensic Pathology Technicians vary, depending on such factors as their education, experience, employer, and geographic location. Formal salary information for this occupation is unavailable. One expert in the field reports that salaries in his area (western United States) range between $35,000 and $55,000.

Pathology Technicians, also known as pathologists' assistants, who work in other settings can expect to receive much higher salaries.

Employment Prospects

Medical examiners' offices and coroners' offices employ Forensic Pathology Technicians to assist with medicolegal death investigations. Job openings become available to replace technicians who have advanced to higher positions, transferred to other jobs, or left the workforce for various reasons. One expert in the field states there is a shortage of qualified assistants due to the lack of training programs.

Pathologists' assistants also find employment in other settings, including hospitals, university medical centers, private pathology laboratories, and mortuaries. Opportunities for pathologists' assistants in general are numerous and are expected to remain so in the coming decade. This is a small occupation, as Forensic Pathology Technicians make up a very small percentage of the population.

Advancement Prospects

Forensic Pathology Technicians can advance to lead and supervisory positions, which are limited in government morgues. They may choose to transfer to other work settings where pathologists' assistants may have more opportunities for advancement. Another option is to continue their studies and pursue careers as forensic pathologists.

Education and Training

Educational requirements for entry-level positions vary with the different employers. Some employers require applicants to have only a high school or general equivalency diploma. Others prefer to hire candidates who have successfully completed college course work in biology, human anatomy, physiology, or criminal justice, or who graduated from a two-year college with a technical certificate or associate degree in health sciences or another related field. Still other employers require that applicants possess a bachelor's degree in biology, chemistry, or another related field.

Forensic Pathology Technicians typically learn on the job. They work under the guidance and direction of experienced Forensic Pathology Technicians, forensic pathologists, and other medicolegal death investigators. In some offices, technicians are cross-trained in histology, X-rays, and other areas.

Throughout their careers, Forensic Pathology Technicians enroll in continuing education programs and training programs to update their skills and increase their knowledge.

Experience, Special Skills, and Personality Traits

Requirements for entry-level positions vary among employers. In general, applicants should have one or more years of technical experience working in a medical or biological laboratory, morgue, mortuary, or in a similar technical setting.

To perform well at their job, Forensic Pathology Technicians must have self-management skills, such as the ability to handle stressful situations, work independently, prioritize multiple tasks, and follow and understand instructions. They need strong interpersonal, teamwork, and communication skills, as they must be able to work well on a daily basis with professionals, technicians, investigators, supervisors, and others. In addition, these forensic technicians need effective analytical, problem-solving, and organizational skills.

Some personality traits that successful Forensic Pathology Technicians share include being cooperative, calm, flexible, detail-oriented, honest, and innovative.

Unions and Associations

Some Forensic Pathology Technicians are members of a labor union that represents them in negotiations with employers. The union seeks better contractual terms for pay, benefits, and working conditions and handles any employee grievances.

Some of these technicians belong to professional associations to take advantage of certification programs, job listings, networking opportunities, and other professional resources and services. One national society that serves their general interests is the American Association of Pathologists' Assistants. For contact information, see Appendix III.

Tips for Entry

1. While in college, gain experience by volunteering or getting a job or internship in a pathology, forensic, hospital, hematology, blood bank, or other lab setting.

2. Many employers allow a combination of appropriate education, training, and work experience to substitute for either an educational or work experience requirement.

3. Some Forensic Pathology Technicians started their career path as forensic assistants or morgue attendants.

4. Some employers maintain an eligibility list of qualified applicants that they use to fill permanent and on-call temporary positions as they become available. If you are placed on a list, call the agency regularly to learn about their current employment status. Be sure to identify yourself and to remind the agency that you are on its eligibility list.

5. Use the Internet to learn more about Forensic Pathology Technicians, as well as about pathologists' assistants in general. To obtain a list of relevant Web sites, enter the keywords *forensic pathology technicians* or *pathologists' assistants* in a search engine. For some links, see Appendix IV.

HISTOLOGIST

CAREER PROFILE

Duties: Prepare tissue specimens for microscopic examinations; perform other duties as required

Alternate Title(s): Histotech, Histotechnician, Histologic Technician, Histotechnologist

Salary Range: $22,000 to $69,000

Employment Prospects: Good

Advancement Prospects: Good

Prerequisites:

 Education or Training—Educational requirements vary; a clinical lab internship or long-term training program in a histopathology lab

 Experience—Previous work experience required

 Special Skills and Personality Traits—Self-management, writing, communication, concentration, problem-solving, and teamwork skills; patient, precise, detail-oriented, cooperative, and reliable

 Special Requirements—State license and/or professional certification may be required

CAREER LADDER

```
┌─────────────────────────────────┐
│      Senior Histologist         │
└─────────────────────────────────┘

┌─────────────────────────────────┐
│         Histologist             │
└─────────────────────────────────┘

┌─────────────────────────────────┐
│    Histologist (Entry-Level)    │
└─────────────────────────────────┘
```

Position Description

Histologists play an important role in medicolegal death investigations. Their mission is to assist forensic pathologists to analyze human tissues for the effects of injury or disease that cannot be readily evident without microscopic viewing. As part of their job to determine the cause of death, forensic pathologists examine tissues for evidence of such abnormalities as disease, body dysfunction, or malignancy. They look at very thin slices of organ tissues that are prepared by the Histologists.

Histologists are laboratory technicians and technologists. Those who work in medical examiners' or coroners' offices may be designated by such job titles as *forensic histotechnician* or *forensic histotechnologist*. Histotechnologists generally have greater responsibilities than histotechnicians.

Histologists in medical examiners' offices utilize their knowledge of biology, chemistry, biochemistry, and immunology in their work. These men and women also have a background in anatomy and physiology and are comfortable with using medical terminology in their daily work. They recognize various types of cells and tissues. They understand how to use various pigments to prepare microscopic samples. Their expertise extends to technology as they use sophisticated instruments to slice thin specimens to place on microscope slides. They also use computers and digital photography equipment.

Histologists perform complex, precision work to preserve and process various tissues. They receive and prepare small samples of lungs, hearts, stomachs, kidneys, and other organs that have been obtained through autopsies. They freeze and slice sections of human tissue, mount them on slides, and stain them for visibility purposes. They use special dyes or pigments to color the slices so that various cellular structures are more visible when viewed through the microscope. The specimens they prepare must be so thin that they are transparent. They use several techniques to perform this work. For example, they may embed tissue samples in wax and then cut them into thin slices by using a special instrument called a microtome. The microtome can cut tissues into sections that are only a few microns thick.

Histologists perform a variety of routine tasks, which vary depending on their skill level, workload, or place of employment. For example, they may:

- conduct specialized testing procedures to analyze and understand the biochemistry and physiological functions of tissue samples
- collect and store the glass slides and other tissue samples for use in civil or criminal court cases
- attend to quality control procedures
- prepare for expert witness testimony at court sessions
- resolve problems
- recommend procedural changes for their laboratory
- complete preventive maintenance on histologic equipment including the sterilization of tools and instruments
- maintain a readily available supply of equipment, instruments, and materials
- prioritize work schedules
- write monthly reports outlining their activities and results
- file reports of their findings with appropriate agencies
- provide technical assistance to police departments
- provide instruction about their profession to other personnel

Many Histologists also perform tasks in morgues, as required by the medical examiner or coroner. Their assignments may include receiving and discharging bodies of the deceased, as well as weighing, fingerprinting, and photographing them. Forensic pathologists may request Histologists to assist with autopsies. Their tasks may include preparing instruments and equipment for examinations; removing internal organs from a body; obtaining blood and other fluid samples; collecting, labeling, and packaging physical evidence removed from the body; and documenting autopsy procedures.

Histologists work in clean, well-lit laboratories. Because they are exposed to chemicals, odors, fumes, and disease, they wear protective equipment and clothing to ensure their safety. The nature of their work sometimes requires them to stand for long periods of time. They generally work a standard 40-hour week but may have occasion to work overtime at night or on weekends.

Salaries

Salaries for Histologists vary, depending on such factors as their education, experience, position, employer, and geographic location. According to the American Society for Clinical Pathology, the average salary for histologic technicians ranged between $22,000 and $35,000, and for histologists (or histotechnologists), $30,000 to $50,000.

The Bureau of Labor Statistics reports in its May 2006 *Occupational Employment Statistics* survey that the estimated annual salary for medical and clinical laboratory technicians ranged between $21,830 and $50,250, and for medical and clinical laboratory technologists, between $34,660 and $69,260.

Employment Prospects

In addition to forensic laboratories, Histologists are employed by hospitals, clinics, public health organizations, private laboratories, pharmaceutical companies, veterinary laboratories, research laboratories, and universities, among others.

According to many experts in the field, the job market is healthy for histologists, in general, and is expected to remain strong for the future. Currently, there are fewer candidates available than job openings. In addition, in the next several years, many Histologists are becoming eligible for retirement, which will create more job openings.

Advancement Prospects

Histologists can advance in any number of ways, depending on their ambitions and interests. With additional education or training, histotechnicians can become histotechnologists. Histologists can also become experts in electron microscopy, immunohistochemistry, or other highly specialized areas. Those with administrative and managerial ambitions can pursue such positions, although opportunities are generally limited.

Forensic Histologists can choose to work in other settings, such as clinical, pharmaceutical, or research laboratories. Histologists can also pursue careers as repair specialists or technical service representatives in companies that sell histology equipment, supplies, or reagents. Another option is to become histology instructors in higher education programs, for which they would be required to obtain advanced degrees.

Education and Training

Educational requirements differ for histotechnicians and histotechnologists. To become histotechnicians, students must complete either an associate's degree or a certificate program in histology. To become histotechnologists, students must earn a bachelor's degree in histology or another related discipline. Employers prefer that candidates obtain their degree or certificate from a histotechnology educational program accredited by a recognized organization. The curriculum includes course work in histology, histochemistry, biology, chemistry, anatomy, immunology, laboratory mathematics, microscopy, processing techniques, and other subjects. In addition, students complete a one-year practicum (or internship) in a medical histology lab.

Alternatively, employers may hire candidates with degrees in other disciplines if they have completed a long-term training program in a histopathology lab.

Throughout their careers, Histologists enroll in continuing education programs and training programs to update their skills and knowledge.

Special Requirements

In some states, Histologists must be licensed or registered. To obtain information for the state where you wish to work, contact the board of occupational licensing or the state department of health.

Employers may require that candidates possess professional certification as histological technicians or technologists. This certification is granted by the American Society for Clinical Pathology. (For contact information for this certification program, see Appendix II.)

Experience, Special Skills, and Personality Traits

Requirements vary with the different employers. Many medical examiners' offices generally prefer to hire Histologists who have one or more years of work experience.

Histologists must have excellent self-management skills such as being able to work independently, handle stressful situations, understand and follow instructions, and prioritize multiple tasks. Having strong writing, communication, concentration, problem-solving, and teamwork skills is also essential. Being patient, precise, detail-oriented, cooperative, and reliable are some personality traits that successful Histologists have in common.

Unions and Associations

Many Histologists join professional associations to take advantage of networking opportunities, continuing education, professional certification, and other professional resources and services. One national society that serves the interests of Histologists is the National Society for Histotechnology.

Many Histologists belong to a labor union that represents them in negotiations with employers for better contractual terms for pay, benefits, and working conditions. In addition, the union handles any employee grievances that members may have.

Tips for Entry

1. One expert in the field suggests that high school students take the most challenging courses in science, math, and English that are offered at their school.
2. Do you wish to enter the field as a histotechnician or histotechnologist? Be sure you understand the difference between the two occupations in terms of educational requirements, job qualifications, job duties, salaries, and the job outlook in your area.
3. Finding an entry-level position with a medical examiners' office may be difficult. Alternatively, obtain an entry-level position in a clinical, research, or other setting to gain valuable work experience.
4. Contact medical examiners' and coroners' offices directly to ask about job openings and their selection process. If they outsource their laboratory work, ask them for the name and address of the laboratory as well as the name of a person whom you can contact.
5. Use the Internet to learn more about the histology field. You might start by visiting the National Society for Histotechnology Web site at http://www.nsh.org. For more links, see Appendix IV.

MORGUE ASSISTANT

CAREER PROFILE

Duties: Perform routine lab support and clerical duties; may assist in postmortem examinations; perform other duties as required

Alternate Title(s): Forensic Assistant, Morgue Attendant, Diener

Salary Range: $25,000 to $38,000

Employment Prospects: Fair

Advancement Prospects: Fair

Prerequisites:

Education or Training—High school diploma; on-the-job training

Experience—One or more years of work experience usually required

Special Skills and Personality Traits—Writing, communication, interpersonal, teamwork, and self-management skills; polite, cooperative, dependable, loyal, honest, detail-oriented, and self-motivated

CAREER LADDER

```
┌─────────────────────────────┐
│     Autopsy Supervisor      │
└─────────────────────────────┘

┌─────────────────────────────┐
│  Senior Morgue Assistant or │
│     Autopsy Technician      │
└─────────────────────────────┘

┌─────────────────────────────┐
│      Morgue Assistant       │
└─────────────────────────────┘
```

Position Description

In medicolegal death investigations, corpses may be transported from death scenes to a morgue that is part of a coroner's office or medical examiner's office. Many corpses are brought to a morgue for postmortem examination to determine the cause and manner of their death. Corpses are also stored at morgues until they can be identified and released to family members or others.

Many of these government morgues employ Morgue Assistants who work alongside pathologists and other staff members to attend to the disposition and processing of dead bodies. Their general functions are to receive and release bodies and perform other duties during the interim, which may include assisting with autopsies.

Morgue Assistants work under the direct authority of the morgue supervisor. Their training and background encompass basics in medical and forensic terminologies and the use of the equipment needed to perform medicolegal external examinations and autopsies. They use their writing ability to record the information that is discovered during postmortem examination procedures, which may include the preparation of diagrams. They have knowledge of photographic procedures and are familiar with different types of photographic gear. Because they are regularly required to lift or move as much as 300 pounds, Morgue Assistants are knowledgeable about body mechanics, proper lifting techniques, and the use of assistive equipment such as stretchers or hoists.

Morgue Assistants perform various duties throughout their shifts. They are responsible for receiving and releasing corpses at their facilities. It is also their duty to confirm the bodies' identities, which they enter into record logs. They may also photograph bodies for identification purposes. Morgue Assistants tag and place bodies in compartment trays for refrigerated storage, and ensure safekeeping of any personal belongings that were brought in with the deceased.

These men and women also assist with the preparations for postmortem examinations. They gather all the paperwork that pathologists need to review prior to an examination. They perform various tasks to get the corpses ready: they weigh and measure them, record their fingerprints, remove their clothing, clean them, x-ray them, and position them on the examining table. Morgue Assistants also lay out appropriate surgical instruments and other supplies, and they make preserving solutions for the pathologists.

Morgue Assistants may be requested to assist pathologists during autopsies, which are internal examinations. These assistants may do such tasks as removing internal organs from the body, weighing organs, slicing tissues, and suturing the body after the autopsy is completed.

Morgue Assistants are responsible for maintaining morgue facilities including examination areas, autopsy bays, refrigeration units, and all other areas. They also wash examination tables, sterilize instruments, sharpen knives, and replenish supplies of fresh linens and other needed items.

In addition, Morgue Assistants regularly perform routine clerical duties such as:

- answer telephones and give telephone messages to the appropriate staff members
- fill out forms and compile other paperwork for each case
- create new case files and assist with record-keeping activities
- make labels for microscope slides and file slides appropriately
- receive, sort, and distribute incoming mail
- photocopy documents

Morgue Assistants endure continually disagreeable sights, sounds, and odors, which contribute to an overall unpleasant work environment. They shoulder heavy workloads, deadlines, and the pressure of dealing with emergency situations. They encounter a degree of risk regarding safety and exposure to health hazards, and hence wear protective clothing and equipment as they work.

These assistants work a 40-hour week schedule. In large offices, they are assigned to shifts. Some of them may be required to travel to other locations to retrieve or deliver bodies.

Salaries
Salaries for Morgue Assistants vary, depending on such factors as their education, experience, employer, and geographic location. According to Salary.com, the annual base salary (as of July 2006) for morgue attendants ranged from $24,941 to $38,055.

Employment Prospects
Job openings generally become available as Morgue Assistants transfer to other jobs, advance to higher positions, or leave the workforce for various reasons. One expert in the field reports a shortage of applicants for these positions. Many people are not interested in becoming morgue attendants because of the nature of the job. Many people are also unaware of the job opportunities that are available in morgues.

Advancement Prospects
Morgue Assistants can advance in any number of ways, depending on their ambitions and interests. With experience

and additional training, they can become forensic morgue technicians who perform complex assignments as they assist forensic pathologists with postmortem examinations. Morgue Assistants who gain supervisory and administrative skills can be promoted to morgue supervisor. Morgue Assistants can also earn college degrees in fields that interest them to qualify for forensic, clinical laboratory, or law enforcement positions.

Some Morgue Assistants measure their success through higher wages and job satisfaction.

Education and Training
Minimally, applicants for entry-level positions need a high school or general equivalency diploma.

Novices typically receive on-the-job training. They work under the supervision and direction of the morgue supervisor and other senior employees.

Experience, Special Skills, and Personality Traits
Job qualifications vary with the different employers. In general, they seek candidates for entry-level positions who have one or more years of work experience that demonstrates their ability to perform well as Morgue Assistants. Candidates should have the ability to perform basic office and clerical functions, as well as have fundamental knowledge of biological and medical terminology.

To work well at their job, Morgue Assistants must have good writing and communication skills. They also need effective interpersonal and teamwork skills, as they must be able to work with supervisors, technicians, professionals, and others from different backgrounds. In addition, they need strong self-management skills, such as the ability to work independently, handle stressful situations, follow and understand directions, and handle multiple tasks. Being polite, cooperative, dependable, loyal, honest, detail-oriented, and self-motivated are some personality traits that Morgue Assistants share.

Unions and Associations
Some Morgue Assistants are members of a labor union that represents them in negotiations with employers for better contractual terms for pay, benefits, and working conditions. In addition, the union handles any grievances that members may have against their employers.

Tips for Entry
1. Some high school courses that can prepare you for a job as a Morgue Assistant are biology, chemistry, math, English, record keeping, and photography.
2. Morgue attendants need to be physically fit.

3. Do you have a current driver's license? Most, if not all, employers require Morgue Assistants to possess one.

4. Contact government morgues directly. Along with asking about job openings, ask for information about their job selection process.

5. Use the Internet to learn more about government morgues and the services they provide. To obtain a list of relevant Web sites, enter either of these keywords into a search engine: *coroner's office morgue* or *medical examiner's office morgue*.

FORENSIC EXPERTS IN ART AND MULTIMEDIA

FORENSIC PHOTOGRAPHER

CAREER PROFILE

Duties: Provide visual documentation of physical evidence, crime and accident scenes, bodily injuries of living and dead victims, and postmortem examinations; perform other duties as required

Alternate Title(s): Police Photographic Technician, Evidence Photographer

Salary Range: $16,000 to $57,000

Employment Prospects: Fair

Advancement Prospects: Fair

Prerequisites:

Education or Training—Educational requirements vary; on-the-job training

Experience—One or more years of professional photography experience

Special Skills and Personality Traits—Interpersonal, communication, self-management, writing, and computer skills; imaginative, innovative, precise, detail-oriented, patient, tactful, trustworthy, dependable, and self-motivated

Special Requirements—Peace officer certificate may be required

CAREER LADDER

```
┌─────────────────────────────────────┐
│    Senior Forensic Photographer      │
└─────────────────────────────────────┘

┌─────────────────────────────────────┐
│       Forensic Photographer          │
└─────────────────────────────────────┘

┌─────────────────────────────────────┐
│  Assistant Forensic Photographer or  │
│               Intern                 │
└─────────────────────────────────────┘
```

Position Description

Photography plays an integral role in the documentation of physical evidence found at crime and accident scenes as well as during forensic autopsies. Professional men and women known as Forensic Photographers provide their services to fulfill that role. They are highly skilled photographers who possess a particular understanding about the necessity of creating and producing quality images suitable for use as investigative aids or as demonstrative evidence in the courts.

Forensic Photographers apply their technical skills and their knowledge of anatomy and forensic requirements to take photographs that convey the information that crime scene, criminal, medicolegal, or forensic investigators need documented. These photographers are able to provide them with a permanent record of entire crime and accident scenes that shows the position of all items that can be used as evidence. They also supply clear and complete images of every

piece of evidence, including items such as fingerprints and trace evidence that are barely visible to the eye. In addition, they provide visual documentation of bodily injuries on live victims, as well as of corpses at crime scenes and autopsies.

Forensic Photographers are professionally trained in the use of photographic equipment: analog, digital, and video cameras; tripods; flash attachments and lighting fixtures; lenses; developing chemicals; and the tools used in darkrooms. They are knowledgeable about general-purpose photographic techniques but are also well versed in techniques that are unique to forensic or medicolegal photography. For example, they may work with ultraviolet or infrared photography and X-rays, or use microscope adapters and very fast strobes.

Forensic Photographers are obligated to produce photographs that are truthful and objective, as well as meet all necessary legal requirements. In other words, the images represent the facts as they appear at a crime or accident scene, as well as on living or dead victims. Their photographs are used by criminal investigators, forensic pathologists, and forensic scientists to help them with their analysis and evaluation of evidence. The photographs also become part of official law enforcement, forensic, medical, and scientific reports. Furthermore, images produced by Forensic Photographers may be submitted as evidence in criminal or civil trials.

These forensic specialists work in different settings. They may hold staff positions or provide services on a contractual basis. Many law enforcement agencies employ civilians as ʰ⁻asic Photographers to fulfill various services. In some law enforcement officers or crime scene technicians with the proper skills are assigned the role of photographer.

Forensic Photographers are among the first crime scene technicians to arrive at crime and accident scenes. They walk through a scene to obtain an overview before they begin taking photographs. They also talk with detectives and crime scene investigators to find out what items they need to have photographed in detail. They take pictures of the entire scene from every angle. They photograph victims, who may be living or dead. They take close-up shots of any injuries, wounds, bruises, bite marks, or marks created by bindings. They also document physical evidence, including fingerprints, paint chips, hairs, weapons, bloodstains, documents, tool marks, shoe imprints, and so on. Where needed, they include a scale that shows the size of small items such as bullet casings and fibers. They carefully maintain a written log of each shot that describes what the photo depicts.

Forensic Photographers in law enforcement agencies may be assigned to take photographs of physical evidence as it is being processed in crime labs. They also take "mug shots" of arrested suspects and take pictures for police lineups and public relations purposes. In addition, they may be requested to take pictures of their organization's functions such as award ceremonies and meetings or portraits of distinguished visitors.

Some Forensic Photographers work for medical examiners' offices or coroners' offices where they are responsible for taking photographs of the deceased and postmortem examinations. They take photos at death scenes as well as in the morgue. Their specific tasks include taking identifying photos of the deceased, which may be used in court, or shown to the family of the deceased.

Forensic Photographers also take pictures of cadavers prior to autopsies to document evidence. They may be responsible for cleaning the bodies, cleaning wounds, and arranging arms and legs that have contracted due to rigor mortis. On occasion they find wounds that other investigators overlooked. Photographers take shots of bodies from both the front and back, and close-up shots of wounds, bruises, and injuries. After each body is photographed, Forensic Photographers change their gloves and disinfect their cameras and other equipment.

Many self-employed Forensic Photographers provide services to attorneys, insurance companies, hospitals, and other organizations for various legal purposes. For example, personal injury attorneys or insurance companies may contract Forensic Photographers to document evidence for cases that involve medical malpractice, product liability, or negligence.

In addition to taking photographs, Forensic Photographers perform other general duties. They are responsible for processing their film in darkrooms and producing negatives, proofs, and color or black-and-white prints. Many of them also use computers and the appropriate software for processing digital photographs. It is also their responsibility to maintain, repair, and regularly inventory their equipment. Other tasks most Forensic Photographers perform include:

- writing detailed reports about their work
- preparing exhibits for court trials
- providing expert witness testimony in court proceedings
- training new personnel about photographic methods and equipment
- keeping up to date with new photographic technologies and techniques
- familiarizing themselves with forensic science terminology and information

Forensic Photographers work indoors as well as outdoors in all kinds of weather conditions. They may be required to stand or walk for long hours and lift moderately heavy objects up to 50 pounds. These photographers are exposed to a variety of hazards including chemicals, drugs, firearms, decomposing bodies, disease, and strong odors. The things they photograph may elicit strong emotions. Hence, they must be able to get accustomed to looking at and taking pictures of unpleasant subjects.

Staff photographers work a 40-hour schedule and put in additional hours as needed to complete their duties. Many of them are assigned to shifts, which include working nights, weekends, and holidays. They may be required to be available to respond to emergency or forensic situations on a 24-hour on-call basis.

Salaries

Earnings for Forensic Photographers vary, depending on their position (staff or contractual), experience, employer, geographic location, and other factors. Specific salary information is unavailable for this occupation. However, the estimated annual salary for most photographers in general ranged from $15,540 to $56,640, according to the May 2006 *Occupational Employment Statistics* survey by the U.S. Bureau of Labor Statistics.

Employment Prospects

Many medical examiners' offices and coroners' offices as well as local, state, and federal law enforcement agencies hire Forensic Photographers to staff positions. Local law enforcement agencies in large cities or metropolitan areas typically have more staff opportunities. Federal agencies usually prefer to employ highly experienced Forensic Photographers.

Some Forensic Photographers find employment with hospitals, newspapers, attorneys, and private investigators. Many of them are self-employed or work for firms that offer forensic photography services.

Job openings normally become available as replacements are needed for Forensic Photographers who have transferred to other jobs or have left the workforce for various reasons. Employers will create additional jobs to meet growing needs, as long as funding is available.

Competition for both staff and contractual positions is strong.

Advancement Prospects

In general, Forensic Photographers measure success through higher incomes, job satisfaction, and professional recognition. As staff photographers gain experience and skills, they are given increasingly greater responsibilities. Promotional opportunities are limited to lead and supervisory positions, for which they may need to move to other employers.

Forensic Photographers may also choose to become educators and teach forensic photography skills in law enforcement academies or training programs, in colleges and universities, or through professional associations and other venues.

Law enforcement officers have additional advancement options. They can rise through the ranks as detectives, sergeants, and so on, up to police chiefs. They can also seek positions in other law enforcement special details as well as pursue supervisory and managerial positions within their agency.

Education and Training

There are no standard educational requirements for individuals to fulfill to become Forensic Photographers. Minimally, they should have a high school or general equivalency diploma. Some employers prefer to hire applicants who have completed some college course work or have earned an associate or bachelor's degree in criminal justice, criminology, forensic science, physical science, or another related field. Many employers also favor candidates who have completed college-level course work in photography or who have earned an associate or bachelor's degree in photography.

Entry-level photographers receive on-the-job training while working under the direction and supervision of experienced Forensic Photographers. Some employers also provide formal instruction.

Throughout their careers, Forensic Photographers enroll in classes, seminars, and workshops to update their photography skills and keep up with advancements in crime scene investigations, medicolegal death investigations, and the other forensic areas in which they work.

Special Requirements

In agencies in which Forensic Photographers are law enforcement officers, applicants must possess a basic peace officer standards and training certificate. Officers must successfully complete annual training to maintain their certification.

Experience, Special Skills, and Personality Traits

Job qualifications for entry-level positions vary among employers. In general, they seek candidates who have one or more years of professional technical photography and photographic laboratory experience. Many employers are flexible, and allow strong candidates to substitute an equivalent combination of education or training in photography and work experience.

Forensic Photographers need effective interpersonal and communication skills, as they must be able to work well with colleagues, law enforcement officers, physicians, managers, and many others from diverse backgrounds. They must also have strong self-management skills, including the ability to handle stressful situations, work independently, prioritize multiple tasks, and follow and understand instructions. Additionally, they need adequate writing and computer skills. Being imaginative, innovative, precise, detail-oriented, patient, tactful, trustworthy, dependable, and self-motivated are some personality traits that successful Forensic Photographers share.

Unions and Associations

Forensic Photographers can join forensic and photography societies to take advantage of professional services and resources, such as training programs, professional certification, and networking opportunities. Some professional associations at the national level that serve their interests include:

- Evidence Photographers International Council
- Professional Photographers of America
- International Association for Identification
- American Academy of Forensic Sciences
- American College of Forensic Examiners
  For contact information, see Appendix III.

Tips for Entry

1. While in high school and college, gain photography experience by working on school newspapers or yearbooks.
2. Forensic Photographers can enhance their employability by obtaining professional certification granted

by a recognized organization. To learn about some certification programs, see Appendix II.

3. Develop a network of contacts—such as fellow photographers, instructors, and law enforcement officers—who may be able to tell you about staff or contractual positions.

4. Use the Internet to learn more about the field of forensic photography. You might start by visiting the Crime Scene and Evidence Photography Web page at Crime-Scene-Investigator.net. The URL is http://www.crime-scene-investigator.net/csi-photo.html. For more links, see Appendix IV.

FORENSIC VIDEO ANALYST

CAREER PROFILE

Duties: Examine, compare, and evaluate video recordings for clues that may help investigators and attorneys with their cases; perform other duties as required

Alternate Title(s): Forensic Video Expert, Forensic Video Specialist

Salary Range: $27,000 to $93,000 for law enforcement officers

Employment Prospects: Poor

Advancement Prospects: Fair

Prerequisites:

Education or Training—On-the-job training

Experience—Several years of experience in forensic video examination

Special Skills and Personality Traits—Problem-solving, analytical, teamwork, interpersonal, communication, and writing skills; cooperative, dedicated, persistent, observant, creative, trustworthy, and ethical

Special Requirements—Peace officer certificate may be required

CAREER LADDER

```
┌─────────────────────────────────┐
│  Senior Forensic Video Analyst  │
└─────────────────────────────────┘

┌─────────────────────────────────┐
│     Forensic Video Analyst      │
└─────────────────────────────────┘

┌─────────────────────────────────┐
│  Forensic Video Analyst Trainee │
└─────────────────────────────────┘
```

Position Description

Surveillance cameras placed at banks, convenience stores, major intersections, and other strategic locations record the activities of people who pass within their view. When crimes occur, videos of such events are a form of evidence that can be used to prosecute and convict the perpetrators, as well as exonerate innocent suspects. Video evidence is collected and submitted to highly skilled professionals known as Forensic Video Analysts. Their job is to examine, compare, and evaluate video recordings to reveal clues that can help investigators and attorneys with their cases.

Forensic Video Analysts work in both the public and private sectors. Forensic Video Analysts work for law enforcement agencies or in civilian capacities. In local and state law enforcement agencies, Forensic Video Analysts may be civilian employees or sworn officers. Depending on their agency's needs, law enforcement officers may be assigned to their forensic video unit on a full-time or part-time basis.

Many Forensic Video Analysts in law enforcement agencies are also responsible for performing video documenta-

tion services. They take video records of crime scenes, including those in which homicides, assaults, and robberies have taken place. They shoot footage of underground drug labs, at hostage situations, accident scenes, natural disasters, and other police operations. They also document on video any bodily injuries or gunshot wounds on living and dead victims.

Many private Forensic Video Analysts are independent practitioners or employees of consulting firms that offer forensic video analysis services to law enforcement agencies, government agencies, attorneys, insurance companies, corporations, and others. Many of them offer audio and voice identification services as well. In addition to criminal cases, these private forensic specialists may review video evidence for such other legal matters as civil litigation, regulatory violations, and insurance claims.

Forensic Video Analysts are well versed in video terminology as well as possess an understanding of computers and electronics. They work with a variety of equipment including different makes and models of playback devices, processing and enhancement equipment, and output and storage equipment. They are able to work with both analog and digital video equipment, and can convert video tape recordings into digital files, and vice versa. Their technical equipment meets particular standards. For example, video signals display 486 lines of picture; thus, Forensic Video Analysts use equipment that displays pictures at this standard. Equipment that does not display all 486 lines is inadequate because some portions of an image can be lost without that maximum. In addition, these specialists use special software to analyze, evaluate, enhance, and clarify poor-quality videos.

Video is taken from a variety of sources including video cameras, police cars, closed-circuit surveillance systems, and cell phones. It is often recorded on tapes but is increasingly recorded with digital equipment. However, that which is recorded is sometimes blurry, too dark, or characterized by "snow" or "rain" that makes it difficult to use. Individuals or objects on the recordings are sometimes too small or indistinct without enhancement or clarification. Forensic Video Analysts use various image processing techniques to make video recordings useful for resolving crimes, extracting evidence, and displaying to jurors.

Color correction capability allows Forensic Video Analysts to adjust a suspect's clothing or skin tones as well as the color of other objects in view. Filters can be used to sharpen pictures or distinguish objects from backgrounds. Some surveillance equipment simultaneously records and displays multiple views on one screen. Forensic Video Analysts use equipment that can isolate and enhance each view for separate display. On the other hand, they can display two or more separate views on one screen. They can use time and date stamps on videos to indicate the passage of time and coordinate the sequence of separate views.

Forensic Video Analysts can program videos to be searchable so that certain points in the video sequence can be readily accessed. When conversations are videotaped, Forensic Video Analysts can add written transcripts of the dialog for viewing on screen. The transcripts can also be made searchable. Forensic Video Analysts can also highlight certain objects or people on a video so that they stand out in contrast to the rest of the picture.

Forensic Video Analysts closely study video recordings for small details that can be important to a case. By using the full range of their equipment capabilities, these professionals can make such details easily identifiable and meaningful through magnification and sharpening. Digital videos can be examined frame by frame and are more readily enhanced through sharpening, adjusting contrast, and removing snow. Each frame can be printed as a still photograph when needed.

Forensic Video Analysts also routinely perform other video analysis tasks such as decoding digital files into decompressed files and converting recordings from one video standard (or format) to another. Furthermore, they repair and restore damaged videos.

They perform other duties including some that are similar to other forensic professionals. For example, they:

- maintain the chain of custody of the video evidence with which they work by documenting the identity of all personnel who handle the evidence
- provide expert witness testimony at depositions, trials, Congressional meetings, and regulatory hearings
- perform tests to detect tampering or suspicious editing of video recordings
- verify that tapes meet forensic standards
- keep up with the latest developments and technologies in their field
- assist investigations in other jurisdictions

Forensic Video Analysts often work longer than 40-hour weeks to complete tasks or meet deadlines. Forensic Video Analysts in law enforcement agencies may work shifts, and those that are also law enforcement officers are on call 24 hours a day. Private specialists may be required to travel to other cities, states, or countries to meet with clients or perform their assignments.

Salaries

Specific salary information for Forensic Video Analysts is unavailable. In general, their salaries vary, depending on such factors as their education, experience, employer, and geographic location. Civilian employees normally receive lower wages than officers in law enforcement agencies. According to the May 2006 *Occupational Employment Statistics* survey by the U.S. Bureau of Labor Statistics, the estimated annual salary for most police and sheriff patrol officers ranged between $27,310 and $72,450, and for detectives, between $34,480 and $92,590.

Employment Prospects

In general, employers hire Forensic Video Analysts to replace individuals who advance to higher positions, transfer to other jobs, retire, or leave the workforce for various reasons. Employers will create additional positions as long as funding is available.

The forensic video field is young and still small. According to one expert in the field, the demand for these specialists is growing rapidly.

In recent years, increasingly more police agencies have forensic video units. Civilian opportunities in local law enforcement agencies are usually better in large cities and metropolitan areas. Law enforcement officers must normally complete two or more years of patrol duty before they are eligible to apply for the forensic video unit at their agency.

Advancement Prospects

As law enforcement officers, Forensic Video Analysts can advance according to their personal interests and ambitions. They can advance in terms of pay as well as rank. They can apply for voluntary positions on special details within their agency, such as the SWAT team, bomb squad, aviation unit, or crime scene investigation division. They may also pursue a career in criminal investigations. Those interested in supervisory or administrative duties can pursue such positions.

Civilian employees in law enforcements agencies measure advancement through higher incomes, job satisfaction, and professional recognition.

Entrepreneurial individuals can pursue careers as independent contractors or business owners of forensic video services.

Education and Training

Novices generally receive their training on the job while working under the direction and supervision of experienced personnel. Many employers also provide formal instruction. In addition, these forensic specialists obtain training on equipment and software. That training is often provided by the manufacturers and distributors of those items.

Throughout their careers, Forensic Video Analysts enroll in seminars, workshops, and courses to update their skills and keep up with technological advancements.

Special Requirements

In agencies in which Forensic Video Analysts are law enforcement officers, applicants must possess a basic peace officer standards and training certificate. Officers must successfully complete annual training to maintain their certification.

Experience, Special Skills, and Personality Traits

Employers in the private sector prefer to hire candidates who have several years of experience in forensic video examina-tion. Law enforcement agencies also require that candidates for civilian positions have several years of experience.

To perform well at their job, Forensic Video Analysts must have excellent problem-solving, analytical, teamwork, interpersonal, communication, and writing skills. Some personality traits that successful Forensic Video Analysts share include being cooperative, dedicated, persistent, observant, creative, trustworthy, and ethical.

Unions and Associations

Forensic Video Analysts can join professional associations to take advantage of training programs, networking opportunities, and other professional services and resources. Several societies are available at the national level. They include:

- Law Enforcement and Emergency Services Video Association
- National Association of Forensic Video
- International Association for Identification
- American College of Forensic Examiners
  For contact information, see Appendix III.

Tips for Entry

1. Talk with several Forensic Video Analysts to learn about their job and how they entered the field. Ask them to suggest courses that would help prepare you for a career in forensic video analysis.
2. To get an entry-level job with a private firm, be willing to take other jobs so you can get your foot in the door.
3. Keep up with the latest technologies.
4. Learn more about the forensic video analysis field on the Internet. To get a list of relevant Web sites, enter any of these keywords into a search engine: *forensic video*, *forensic video analysis*, or *police forensic video unit*. For some links, see Appendix IV.

FORENSIC AUDIO EXAMINER

Duties: Examine, compare, and evaluate audio evidence; perform duties as required

Alternate Title(s): Audio Forensics Specialist, Forensic Audio Technician, Voiceprint Analyst, Forensic Acoustic Specialist

Salary Range: $27,000 to $93,000 for law enforcement officers

Employment Prospects: Poor

Advancement Prospects: Fair

Prerequisites:

Education or Training—On-the-job training

Experience—Several years of experience in audio forensics

Special Skills and Personality Traits—Listening, analytical, problem-solving, writing, communication, teamwork, and interpersonal skills; be inquisitive, persistent, meticulous, patient, trustworthy, and objective

Special Requirements—Peace officer certificate may be required

Senior Forensic Audio Examiner

Forensic Audio Examiner

Forensic Audio Examiner Trainee

Position Description

Audio forensics is the application of engineering skills and audio science to legal matters. Forensic Audio Examiners work with audio recordings to assist with the investigation of criminal and civil cases and to confirm facts regarding those cases. Their job involves utilizing technical equipment to identify voices, reduce noise, and enhance background sounds on audio recordings. They also compare sounds, analyze the sequence of audio events, and perform other tasks.

Many Forensic Audio Examiners enter this field after working as musicians or studio engineers in the recording industry. Others are law enforcement officers who have received training in audio analysis techniques and the use of specialized technologies.

As forensic specialists, Forensic Audio Examiners apply their abilities and technical expertise to analyzing recorded sounds, particularly voice recordings, for law enforcement agencies and the courts. Their listening abilities and familiarity with computerized sound processing equipment enable them to notice and extract details of audio record-

ings that might escape the attention of ordinary listeners. They can hear or identify subtle differences in vocal intonations, pronunciations, accents, dialects, and other nuances in individual speech patterns that may not be evident to other investigators. Forensic Audio Examiners are also experts in the examination of tape or digital recordings to determine whether recordings are valid and authentic.

These audio specialists use a variety of methods to analyze recordings and provide several important investigative services. One service is voice identification. Forensic Audio Examiners identify an unknown voice by comparing it to a known one. They use the recording of the unknown voice and a recording of a suspect speaking the same words. With a spectrograph and a computer, these analysts analyze the unique characteristics of the two voices that are revealed on the output of voiceprints. A voiceprint provides a graphic representation of vocal intonations, consonant sounds, breath patterns, nasal resonance, and other characteristics of vocal expression. Forensic Audio Examiners combine their use of voiceprints and their listening abilities to confirm that a suspect was indeed recorded, or to prove the suspect's innocence.

Forensic Audio Examiners also employ various techniques using spectrographs, filters, compression technologies, and amplitude adjustment to enhance audios, clarify spoken dialogue, or reveal sounds that were previously unknown. Such unknown or vague background sounds may be voices or other sounds that can provide clues about the source of the recording. In addition, these specialists authenticate tapes by closely examining them to determine what type of recording device was used, if the tape was made with more than one device, or if it was altered in some fashion.

Forensic Audio Examiners also analyze the sequence of events that are recorded to determine the authenticity of the recording. Furthermore, they repair old or damaged recordings and mask or reduce extraneous noises from recordings to clarify their content.

Some Forensic Audio Examiners also conduct video analysis. They may be required to assist with the audio portion of video surveillance recordings, for example. These specialists make sure that such recordings can be played or duplicated to play in useable formats. They perform similar tasks as they would with strictly audio recordings, such as repair, enhancement, voice identification, duplication, and the analysis of background sounds, recording authentication, and the extraction of digital audio information.

Forensic Audio Examiners use a variety of technologies and types of equipment to perform their work, including digital-adaptive enhancement processors that feature graphic equalizers and filtering devices, audio compressors, spectrum analyzers, computer systems, and specialized software. They also utilize various types of voice identification equipment in addition to spectrographs, including specialized software that creates digitally calculated spectrograms as well as tape or digital editing equipment.

Forensic Audio Examiners perform other duties including some that are similar to other forensic professionals. For example, they may:

- maintain the chain of custody of audio evidence by documenting the identity of all personnel who handle the evidence
- give expert witness testimony at depositions, trials, Congressional meetings, and regulatory hearings
- provide evidence analysis services to attorneys for criminal and civil cases
- perform tests to detect tampering or suspicious editing of audio recordings
- verify that tapes meet forensic standards
- keep up with the latest developments and technologies in their field
- assist investigations in other jurisdictions

These specialists work in well-equipped audio and video laboratories. Forensic Audio Examiners often put in more than 40-hour weeks to complete tasks or meet deadlines. Those who serve as law enforcement officers are on call 24 hours a day. Forensic Audio Examiners may work shifts. They may be required to travel to other cities, states, or countries.

Salaries

Salaries for Forensic Audio Examiners vary, depending on such factors as their education, experience, employer, and geographic location. Specific salary information for this occupation is unavailable. In law enforcement agencies, civilian employees normally receive lower wages than law enforcement officers. According to the May 2006 *Occupational Employment Statistics* survey by the U.S. Bureau of Labor Statistics, the estimated annual salary for most police and sheriff patrol officers ranged between $27,310 and $72,450, and for detectives, between $34,480 and $92,590.

Employment Prospects

As with the video forensics field, the audio forensics field is young, small, and emerging. In recent years, the demand for Forensic Audio Examiners has been growing in the private sector as well as with law enforcement agencies.

In general, employers hire Forensic Audio Examiners to replace individuals who advance to higher positions, transfer to other jobs, retire, or leave the workforce for various reasons. Employers will create additional positions as long as funding is available.

Civilian opportunities in local law enforcement agencies are usually better in large cities and metropolitan areas. Law enforcement officers must normally complete two or more years of patrol duty before they are eligible to apply for the forensic audio unit at their agency.

Advancement Prospects

As law enforcement officers, Forensic Audio Examiners can advance according to their personal interests and ambitions. They can advance in terms of pay as well as rank. They can apply for voluntary positions on special details within their agency, such as the SWAT team, aviation unit, or crime scene investigation division. They may also pursue a career in criminal investigations. Those interested in supervisory or administrative duties can seek such positions.

Civilian employees in law enforcement agencies measure advancement through higher incomes, job satisfaction, and professional recognition.

Entrepreneurial individuals can pursue careers as independent contractors or business owners of audio forensics services.

Education and Training

Novices generally receive their training on the job while working under the direction and supervision of experienced personnel. Many employers also provide formal instruction. In addition, they obtain training on equipment and software. That training is often provided by the manufacturers and distributors of those items.

Throughout their careers, Forensic Audio Examiners enroll in seminars, workshops, and courses to update their skills and keep up with technological advancements.

Special Requirements

In agencies in which Forensic Audio Examiners are law enforcement officers, applicants must possess a basic peace officer standards and training certificate. Officers must successfully complete annual training to maintain their certification.

Experience, Special Skills, and Personality Traits

Employers in the private sector prefer to hire candidates who have several years of experience in audio forensics examination. Law enforcement agencies also require that candidates for civilian positions have several years of experience. In addition, employers seek candidates who demonstrate a high level of competence in the operation of audio instruments and equipment.

Forensic Audio Examiners must have critical listening skills, along with excellent analytical, problem-solving, writing, and communication skills. They also need strong teamwork and interpersonal skills, as they must work well with various people from diverse backgrounds. Being inquisitive, persistent, meticulous, patient, trustworthy, and objective are some personality traits that successful Forensic Audio Examiners share.

Unions and Associations

Many Forensic Audio Examiners belong to professional associations to take advantage of networking opportunities, continuing education, and other professional services and resources. Some national societies that they are eligible to join are the Audio Engineering Society, the International Association for Forensic Phonetics and Acoustics, the International Association for Identification, and the American College of Forensic Examiners. Examiners who also engage in forensic video work can become members of the National Association of Forensic Video or the Law Enforcement and Emergency Services Video Association. For contact information, see Appendix III.

Tips for Entry

1. Talk with several Forensic Audio Examiners to learn about their job and how they entered the field. Ask them to suggest courses that would help prepare you for a career in audio forensics.
2. Keep up with the latest technologies.
3. Entry-level jobs are difficult to come by, whether in private firms or law enforcement agencies. Be willing to volunteer in order to get training as well as work experience in audio forensics.
4. Use the Internet to learn more about the audio forensics field. To get a list of relevant Web sites, enter any of these keywords into a search engine: *audio forensics*, *forensic audio*, or *police forensic audio*. For some links, see Appendix IV.

FORENSIC ARTIST

Duties: Create drawings of suspects and victims to help law enforcement agencies solve their cases; prepare demonstrative exhibits for court trials; perform other duties as required

Alternate Title(s): Sketch Artist, Composite Artist, Forensic Sculptor, Police Artist

Salary Range: $18,000 to $80,000

Employment Prospects: Poor

Advancement Prospects: Fair

Prerequisites:

Education or Training—Complete forensic art courses and workshops

Experience—Professional experience usually needed for civilian and contractual positions

Special Skills and Personality Traits—Interpersonal, communication, self-management, teamwork, interviewing, and computer skills; open-minded, compassionate, trustworthy, respectful, courteous, and cooperative

Special Requirements—Peace officer certificate may be required

```
┌─────────────────────────────────┐
│      Senior Forensic Artist     │
└─────────────────────────────────┘

┌─────────────────────────────────┐
│         Forensic Artist         │
└─────────────────────────────────┘

┌─────────────────────────────────┐
│     Forensic Artist Trainee     │
└─────────────────────────────────┘
```

Position Description

Forensic Artists create drawings that are used by law enforcement agencies, forensic laboratories, and the courts to suit a variety of purposes. Their work mainly helps to identify and convict criminals, locate kidnap victims or missing persons, and recognize unidentified dead people.

Forensic Artists may be law enforcement officers or civilians. Many law enforcement officers perform forensic art duties in addition to their primary duties as patrol officers, detectives, crime scene technicians, or criminalists. Agencies may employ civilians on a full-time basis or hire independent Forensic Artists on a contractual basis. Some independent artists offer consulting services or teach forensic art courses; some pursue careers in the fine arts or illustration.

Law enforcement agencies use the skills and talents of Forensic Artists to provide drawings in any of four areas: composite imagery, image modification, reconstructive drawings, and demonstrative evidence. Composite imagery is probably the most familiar forensic art specialty. Com-

posite sketches are used to identify perpetrators of crimes or to eliminate innocent people from a list of suspects. These are not portraits; rather, they are two-dimensional renderings of witnesses' memories. Witnesses or victims may have good memories of what perpetrators look like and can work with Forensic Artists by describing their appearance.

Composite drawings are usually renderings of faces, but may also be full-body images or include such features as clothing, tattoos, cars, or other items used by the perpetrators. Forensic Artists are aware of each witness's or victim's feelings and emotional state. Hence, they are able to interview the witness or victim with care and sensitivity to bring out his or her memories of the suspect's appearance. As they progress with the drawing, they make changes as needed. Most Forensic Artists draw their composite images by hand. Some artists use computer programs that automate this process.

Some Forensic Artists specialize in the area of image modification. This is a method of drawing that Forensic Artists use to alter or add to existing photographs to show how a missing person or fugitive might have aged since they were last seen. This technique is also called age progression. It is particularly useful for creating updated images of missing children. Forensic Artists need training in anatomy, particularly how tissues and bone structures change over time, to enable them to accurately render the growth and aging processes. Forensic Artists create these drawings by hand or with the aid of specialized computer software.

Reconstructive or postmortem drawings make up another type of forensic artwork. These drawings are released to the media and police departments for the identification of corpses that are in various stages of decomposition. Forensic Artists who do reconstructive drawings are trained to understand how flesh covers bone and changes after death. They also confer with and rely on the advice of forensic scientists such as pathologists, anthropologists, and dental specialists to create accurate drawings.

Forensic Artists create these reconstructive drawings from photos that were taken at the morgue. For some cases, they use skulls, partially decomposed skulls, or skull fragments, which they piece together. The artists attach vinyl eraser strips directly on a skull at exactly the precise depth that tissue would occupy according to standard tissue depths that are established for all ethnicities and genders, and that are tabulated for reference. They photograph the skull from a specific angle and the photo is printed life size. Forensic Artists then place paper over the photo and draw the face by using the vinyl strips, teeth, nasal hole, and eye sockets as references. They may use computers to perform this type of work.

Another forensic art specialty is demonstrative evidence. These are exhibits, such as charts, graphs, diagrams, and illustrations that Forensic Artists prepare for attorneys to use in the courts. Each piece of demonstrative evidence depicts specific facts that have been presented in sworn testimony by witnesses or experts. It is the Forensic Artists' job to break down and translate complex concepts into visual aids that communicate the ideas so that judges and juries can clearly understand them.

Forensic Artists are responsible for performing other tasks that may include:

- teaching forensic art workshops or classes to patrol officers, detectives, crime scene investigators, medicolegal death investigators, and others
- providing expert witness testimony in court trials
- consulting about forensic art to law enforcement agencies
- maintaining computerized forensic art databases
- developing and managing quality control standards for forensic art

Law enforcement agencies may send staff artists to other jurisdictions to provide forensic art services to other law enforcement agencies. Independent Forensic Artists travel to various locations to complete assignments.

The work of Forensic Artists can often be stressful and emotional. They may experience exposure to decomposed matter, which may be toxic, as well as be in contact with diseases, strong odors, and hazardous chemicals. They may be required to exert themselves by lifting heavy courtroom exhibits or by bending, stooping, climbing, or crawling when providing assistance at crime scenes. Forensic Artists are expected to be available to work at all hours.

Salaries

Specific salary information for Forensic Artists is unavailable. In general, their annual earnings vary, depending on whether they are employees or independent contractors and on such factors as their education, experience, employer, and geographic location. Business acumen and competition are other aspects that play into earnings of self-employed artists. According to the May 2006 *Occupational Employment Statistics* (OES) survey by the U.S. Bureau of Labor Statistics (BLS), the estimated annual wage for most fine artists ranged between $18,350 and $79,390. The annual mean wage for independent artists was $42,890.

Civilian employees normally receive lower wages than officers in law enforcement agencies. The BLS reported in its 2006 OES survey that the estimated annual salary for most patrol officers ranged from $27,310 to $72,450, and for detectives, from $34,480 to $92,590.

Employment Prospects

Competition is very keen for full-time positions. Civilian staff positions, which are few in number, are typically found in large police forces. Law enforcement officers must usually complete two or more years of patrol duty before they are eligible to apply for volunteer duty as forensic artists.

One expert in the field states that there is a job market for independent artists, but they must be able to promote their abilities to secure work from any agency.

As more law enforcement agencies realize the benefits of using Forensic Artists to aid with investigations, more jobs will become available. However, law enforcement agencies generally have limited budgets, which can restrict their ability to create new positions although the demand is there.

Advancement Prospects

As law enforcement officers, Forensic Artists can advance according to their personal interests and ambitions. They can advance in terms of pay as well as rank. They can apply for voluntary positions on other special details within their agency. They may also pursue a career in criminal investigations. Those interested in supervisory or administrative duties can pursue such positions.

Many Forensic Artists measure advancement through job satisfaction, higher incomes, and professional recognition.

Education and Training

Educational requirements for civilian and contractual positions vary among employers. In general, they prefer to hire candidates who have formal art training. Many employers will allow strong candidates to substitute experience in forensic art, fine arts, medical illustration, or other related areas for one or more years of education.

Independent artists enroll in courses taught by established and recognized Forensic Artists. Law enforcement agencies send officer and civilian artists to FBI forensic art courses as well as to private training programs given by established and recognized Forensic Artists. Independent artists also enroll in private forensic art courses and workshops to gain skills and techniques.

Special Requirements

In agencies in which Forensic Artists are law enforcement officers, applicants must possess a basic peace officer standards and training certificate. Officers must successfully complete annual training to maintain their certification.

Experience, Special Skills, and Personality Traits

Forensic Artists come from various backgrounds. Their primary occupation may be law enforcement officer, crime scene investigator, forensic scientist, forensic anthropologist, medical illustrator, or fine artist, among others.

Although natural talent is important, unit supervisors sometimes select officer candidates with fair drawing ability if they demonstrate a willingness to learn. Candidates for civilian and contractual positions are usually required to have several years of forensic art experience. They may have gained their experience through employment, volunteer work, or internships.

Forensic Artists must have strong interpersonal and communication skills, as they work with law enforcement officers and others as well as with victims and witnesses, who may be emotional, uncooperative, or distressed. In addition, Forensic Artists need effective self-management, teamwork, interviewing, and computer skills. Being open-minded, compassionate, trustworthy, respectful, courteous, and cooperative are some personality traits that successful Forensic Artists share.

Unions and Associations

Forensic Artists can join forensic societies to take advantage of networking opportunities, training programs, professional certification, and other professional services and resources. Some professional associations include the International Association for Identification, the American Academy of Forensic Sciences, and the American College of Forensic Examiners. For contact information, see Appendix III.

Tips for Entry

1. Talk with one or more Forensic Artists to find out more about their work and how they got their training. You might also ask them if you can watch them at work.
2. If you plan to become a law enforcement officer, continue to develop your interest, skills, and talent in art.
3. Are you an artist who is interested in forensic art? Take one or more basic courses in police science or law enforcement to gain an understanding of police operations.
4. Some Forensic Artists obtain professional certification from the International Association for Identification to enhance their employability. For contact information about this program, see Appendix II.
5. Use the Internet to learn more about the forensic art field. You might start by visiting Neville's Forensic Art World Web site (by Wes Neville) at http://www.forensicartist.com. For more links, see Appendix IV.

FORENSIC SCULPTOR

CAREER PROFILE

Duties: Reconstruct a face from a human skull; perform other duties as required

Alternate Title(s): Forensic Artist, Forensic Facial Reconstruction Specialist

Salary Range: $18,000 to $80,000

Employment Prospects: Poor

Advancement Prospects: Fair

Prerequisites:

Education or Training—Forensic sculpting training

Experience—Professional experience may be required

Special Skills and Personality Traits—Communication, interpersonal, teamwork, and self-management skills; patient, compassionate, trustworthy, respectful, cooperative, and open-minded

Special Requirements—Peace officer certificate may be required

CAREER LADDER

```
┌─────────────────────────────────────────┐
│  Forensic Sculptor (Established Expert)  │
└─────────────────────────────────────────┘

┌─────────────────────────────────────────┐
│           Forensic Sculptor             │
└─────────────────────────────────────────┘

┌─────────────────────────────────────────┐
│        Forensic Sculptor Trainee        │
└─────────────────────────────────────────┘
```

Position Description

Forensic sculpture is a type of forensic art that helps law enforcement officers to determine the identity of unknown persons whose skeletal remains cannot be recognized. Forensic Sculptors are the artists who specialize in rendering subjects in three dimensions rather than two. They apply their skills and talent to reconstruct what the deceaseds' faces looked like from their skulls.

Most of these facial reconstruction specialists are independent forensic artists. They offer their services to law enforcement agencies on a contractual basis. Some Forensic Sculptors are law enforcement officers who do forensic sculpture and other types of forensic art in addition to their regular duties. Many of these professionals—both staff and independent artists— create other forms of forensic art for law enforcement agencies, including composite drawings, court exhibits, postmortem sketches, and image modifications.

Forensic sculpting is a mixture of science and fine art. Forensic Sculptors use anthropological information about anatomy such as how muscles and skin adhere to bone and how facial structures differ among the races and between genders. When they create their reconstructions, Forensic Sculptors endeavor to make the faces appear as human as possible by incorporating personality into their end result.

Forensic Sculptors may take several days to craft each sculpture. They follow certain procedures and standards. When they receive a skull, they first clean it and reassemble it if needed. For example, they might need to reattach teeth or the bottom jaw, or they might need to reconstruct a shattered skull. They review information about the deceased individual to learn about where the body was found, what the deceased was wearing, what articles were on the body or nearby. They also examine hair that may still be attached to the skull to determine the exact color. Forensic Sculptors can gain useful perceptions about the deceased's general appearance by studying such items. Furthermore, they study the structure of the skull to discern the deceased's gender, age, and ethnicity.

Their next step is to mount the skull, or a plaster cast of the skull, on a rod, which serves as an improvised neck. They then place small pegs as markers at certain points on the skull. The markers denote the depth of tendons, muscles, and skin; the shape and contours of the face; the placement of the eyes; and the dimensions of the nose and mouth. The tissue depths are assigned according to the gender and ethnicity of the deceased. Forensic Sculptors refer to standardized measurement tables to determine where to place the markers on the skull. These measurements provide a formula for creating very exact detail, including the size and shape of the nose and lips.

Next, Forensic Sculptors place clay on the skull (or cast) to the depths indicated by the markers, and insert artificial eyes into the eye sockets. The clay fills the volumes of the skull such as the cheek cavities. As the clay assumes the shape of the face, the Forensic Sculptors form the mouth and nose according to the width and length of the skull's contours. They use their intuition to determine the facial expression. They estimate the expression by studying whatever items of clothing or personal effects were found with the body. Their goal is to make the sculpture as realistic as possible to make it recognizable. They apply a wig and makeup to create skin tones.

When the sculpture is finished, Forensic Sculptors submit it to the requesting agency, where it is photographed and distributed to the media. Each sculpture is not a precise rendering of the victim's face, but it is suitable for the public to be able to provide a positive identification.

Sometimes law enforcement agencies request that Forensic Sculptors create sculptures of fugitives by using old photographs. Some may use computer technology to reconstruct faces. They scan the skull with lasers to create a holographic image. They use computer software to fill in the flesh and features according to depth and anatomical measurements.

On occasion, Forensic Sculptors are requested to provide expert witness testimony in the courts. They address issues regarding reconstructions they have created or about the methods that are used to craft facial reconstructions.

Some independent Forensic Sculptors also offer consulting services or teach classes about forensic sculpting. Some pursue careers in the fine arts.

Forensic Sculptors may be called upon to work on cases from cities from around the country or even from other nations.

Salaries

Specific salary information for Forensic Sculptors is unavailable. In general, their annual earnings vary, depending on whether they are employees or independent contractors as well as on such factors as their education, experience, employer, and geographic location. Business acumen and competition are other aspects that play into earnings of self-employed artists. According to the May 2006 *Occupational Employment Statistics* survey by the U.S. Bureau of Labor Statistics, the estimated annual wage for most fine artists ranged between $18,350 and $79,390. The annual mean wage for independent artists was $42,890.

Employment Prospects

Some experts say that it is difficult to break into the forensic art field, and in particular forensic sculpting, but the work is rewarding. Opportunities are usually better in large cities and metropolitan areas where crime is more prevalent.

Law enforcement agencies generally employ forensic artists who are able to provide forensic sculpting services as well as fulfill other forensic art needs. A few agencies hire civilian employees, but most agencies assign officers who have the skills and interest to fill forensic artist positions. Law enforcement officers must usually complete two or more years of patrol duty before they are eligible to apply for volunteer duty as forensic artists.

Advancement Prospects

Many Forensic Sculptors measure advancement through job satisfaction, higher incomes, and professional recognition.

As law enforcement officers, forensic artists can advance according to their personal interests and ambitions. They can advance in terms of pay as well as rank. They can apply for voluntary positions on special details within their agency, such as the SWAT team. They may also pursue a career in criminal investigations. Those interested in supervisory or administrative duties can pursue such positions.

Education and Training

There are no standard educational requirements for individuals to meet in order to become a Forensic Sculptor. Many in this field have formal training in sculpture or have taken basic courses in drawing and sculpting. Many also enroll in forensic sculpting courses and workshops that are taught by established and recognized Forensic Sculptors.

Special Requirements

In agencies in which Forensic Sculptors are law enforcement officers, applicants must possess a basic peace officer standards and training certificate. Officers must successfully complete annual training to maintain their certification.

Experience, Special Skills, and Personality Traits

Job requirements vary among employers. Some employers may require no work experience from applicants, while others prefer to hire candidates who have several years of professional sculpting experience. In general, Forensic Sculptors, like all forensic artists, are judged according to their demonstrated proficiency.

To do well at their work, Forensic Sculptors need excellent communication, interpersonal, and teamwork skills. They also must have strong self-management skills, including the ability to work independently, handle stressful situations, and follow and understand directions. Some personality traits that Forensic Sculptors share are being patient, compassionate, trustworthy, respectful, cooperative, and open-minded.

Unions and Associations

Forensic Artists can join forensic societies to take advantage of networking opportunities, training programs, professional certification, and other professional services and resources. Some professional associations include the International Association for Identification, the American Academy of Forensic Sciences, and the American College of Forensic Examiners. For contact information, see Appendix III.

Tips for Entry

1. Some experts suggest taking courses in anatomy, psychology, and criminal justice to help you prepare for a career in forensic sculpting.
2. Be flexible and develop your skills to be able to offer other types of forensic art services, such as composite sketches, age progression drawings, and demonstrative evidence.
3. If you are a law enforcement officer, let your forensic art or forensic services unit supervisor know about your interest. Oftentimes, supervisors select candidates without formal art training who demonstrate natural ability and a willingness to learn.
4. As a freelance artist, develop a marketing plan for yourself. Determine how far you are willing to travel to jobs, and then send out a marketing packet about your services to every law enforcement agency within that radius.
5. Use the Internet to learn more about forensic sculpting. To get a list of pertinent Web sites, enter either of these keywords into a search engine: *forensic sculpting* or *forensic sculptors*. For some links, see Appendix IV.

FORENSIC GRAPHICS SPECIALIST

CAREER PROFILE

Duties: Create charts, diagrams, illustrations, multimedia presentations, and other visual aids for litigation, information, or training purposes; perform other duties as required

Alternate Title(s): Forensic Artist, Litigation Graphics Specialist, Demonstrative Evidence Specialist, Visual Information Specialist; a title that reflects a specialty such as Forensic Animator

Salary Range: $24,000 to $93,000

Employment Prospects: Fair

Advancement Prospects: Good

Prerequisites:

Education or Training—Formal training in art, graphics design, computer graphics, or another related field preferred

Experience—Previous professional experience preferred

Special Skills and Personality Traits—Communication, listening, interpersonal, customer-service, teamwork, self-management, organizational, and problem-solving skills; detail-oriented, flexible, patient, imaginative, positive, and trustworthy

Special Requirements—Peace officer certificate may be required

CAREER LADDER

```
┌─────────────────────────────────────┐
│ Senior Forensic Graphics Specialist  │
└─────────────────────────────────────┘

┌─────────────────────────────────────┐
│    Forensic Graphics Specialist      │
└─────────────────────────────────────┘

┌─────────────────────────────────────┐
│ Forensic Graphics Specialist Trainee │
└─────────────────────────────────────┘
```

Position Description

Legal issues, concepts, and investigations can be difficult to follow and comprehend. Sometimes presenting facts and data in visual form can help audiences understand and remember information. Hence, lawyers, expert witnesses, law enforcement trainers, and others seek the help of Forensic Graphics Specialists to create visual aids that effectively communicate their ideas simply and clearly.

Forensic Graphic Specialists produce charts, maps, diagrams, graphs, illustrations, engineering drawings, computer animations, multimedia presentations, and other visual aids, depending on the needs of their clients. Their work involves utilizing art and graphic design methods and techniques as well as computer technologies, including drawing, graphics processing, presentation, animation, and computer-aided design and drafting (CADD) software applications.

These forensic artists create visual aids for various purposes. The most common purpose is for courtroom presentations. Forensic Graphics Specialists prepare exhibits known as demonstrative evidence. These visual aids are admissible in the courts as long as they depict facts that have been established in sworn testimony by eyewitnesses or expert witnesses such as criminalists, scientists, engineers, or physicians. Forensic Graphics Specialists also prepare visual aids for teaching and informational purposes.

With each project, Forensic Graphics Specialists interview clients—who may be attorneys, medical doctors, law enforcement officers, trainers, or others—to identify their needs. They also work closely with clients to determine what concepts need to be shown in visual form and how they should be presented.

These graphics specialists then review all materials that are given to them to learn about the information they will be illustrating. For example, if they will be producing demonstrative evidence, they might study witness statements, photographs, police reports, and crime scene sketches. These specialists make sure they understand the details to be depicted in visual form. If they are unclear, they consult with their clients or subject matter experts. In addition, Forensic Graphics Specialists make sure the information is accurate and correct. When they have completed all of their research, they analyze the data and plan out the visuals. They create initial sketches, drafts, animations, or presentations for clients to review and approve before they make the final products.

Forensic Graphics Specialists perform a wide range of tasks on their job, such as:

- recommend the most effective media to illustrate the intended material
- make suggestions for visual aids to be used
- prepare time and cost estimates for completing visual aids
- testify as expert witnesses in the courts
- identify, evaluate, and recommend the purchase of software and presentation equipment
- maintain inventory of supplies and equipment
- transport and set up visual aids
- operate or train others in the operation of presentation equipment
- keep up with new developments and technologies

In the private sector, many Forensic Graphics Specialists are independent practitioners or employees of graphics or litigation support firms that offer forensic graphics or demonstrative evidence services. Their services may be contracted by law enforcement agencies, attorneys, insurance companies, government agencies, nongovernmental organizations, and others.

Law enforcement agencies also employ graphics specialists in the role of forensic artist. Along with creating demonstrative evidence, these employees provide composite sketches, age progression drawings of missing persons, postmortem drawings, and other forensic art services. In many local and state agencies, law enforcement officers perform the duties of forensic artist on a part-time or full-time basis. Part-timers carry out forensic art duties when their services are needed. The rest of their time is spent executing their primary duties as patrol officers, detectives, crime scene investigators, criminalists, or other occupations.

Forensic Graphics Specialists usually put in more than 40 hours per week to complete their projects and meet deadlines. Those who are law enforcement officers work shifts that may include working nights, weekends, and holidays. They are typically on call 24 hours a day.

Salaries

Annual incomes for Forensic Graphics Specialists vary, depending on such factors as their experience, education, position (independent contractor or staff member), employer, and geographic location. Specific salary information for this occupation is unavailable, but an approximation can be obtained by looking at the salaries for different visual artists. For example, the U.S. Bureau of Labor Statistics (BLS) reported in its May 2006 *Occupational Employment Statistics* survey that the estimated annual salary for most graphic designers ranged from $24,120 to $69,730, and for multimedia artists and animators, $30,390 to $92,720.

Law enforcement officers earn salaries according to their rank and other factors. The estimated annual salary for most police and sheriff patrol officers ranged between $27,310 and $72,450, and for detectives, between $34,480 and $92,590, according to the BLS survey.

Employment Prospects

In addition to law enforcement agencies, Forensic Graphics Specialists are employed by prosecuting attorneys' offices. In the private sector, law firms sometimes hire Forensic Graphics Specialists.

Forensic graphics (also known as litigation graphics and demonstrative evidence) is a young and growing field. Job opportunities are expected to grow as more visual aids are used in court trials, regulatory hearings, arbitrations, and similar venues to help lay people understand complex concepts and issues.

Advancement Prospects

Many Forensic Graphics Specialists measure advancement through job satisfaction, higher incomes, and professional recognition. For some professionals, the top goal is to become successful independent practitioners or owners of forensic graphics firms.

In private firms, these specialists can advance to lead, supervisory, and administrative positions. Opportunities are usually limited and may require transferring to other workplaces to advance up the ladder.

As law enforcement officers, forensic artists advance according to their personal interests and ambitions. They can move forward in pay as well as in rank. They can apply for voluntary positions on special details within their agency. Those interested in supervisory or administrative duties can pursue such positions.

Education and Training

Educational requirements vary with the different employers. Most prefer candidates who have formal training in art, graphic design, computer graphics, or another related field. Many employers hire candidates with a high school or general equivalency diploma if they have qualifying work experience.

Entry-level specialists receive on-the-job training while working under the direction and supervision of experienced personnel. Some employers provide formal instruction programs.

Throughout their careers, Forensic Graphics Specialists enroll in seminars, workshops, and courses to update their skills and keep up with technological advancements.

Special Requirements

In agencies in which Forensic Graphics Specialists are law enforcement officers, applicants must possess a basic peace officer standards and training certificate. Officers must successfully complete annual training to maintain their certification.

Experience, Special Skills, and Personality Traits

Employers usually seek candidates who have several years of professional experience producing graphics, multimedia presentations, and similar work. Having previous experience creating visual aids for legal purposes is desirable.

To work effectively at their job, Forensic Graphics Specialists must have excellent communication, listening, interpersonal, and customer-service skills. They also need strong teamwork, self-management, organizational, and problem-solving skills. Being detail-oriented, flexible, patient, imaginative, positive, and trustworthy are some personality traits that successful Forensic Graphics Specialists share.

Unions and Associations

Forensic Graphics Specialists can join professional associations to take advantage of networking opportunities, training programs, and other professional services and resources. Some national societies that serve their interests include the Demonstrative Evidence Specialists Association, the American Academy of Forensic Sciences, and the American College of Forensic Examiners. As forensic artists, they are eligible to join the International Association for Identification. For contact information, see Appendix III.

Tips for Entry

1. As a student, obtain an internship with a forensic graphics firm.
2. Contact employers directly to learn about job openings. In addition to permanent positions, be sure to ask about temporary, contractual, or freelance opportunities they might have.
3. Law enforcement officers usually must complete two or more years of patrol duty before they are eligible to apply for volunteer duty as forensic artists.
4. Use the Internet to learn more about what Forensic Graphics Specialists do. To get a list of relevant Web sites, enter any of these keywords into a search engine: *forensic graphics*, *forensic graphics specialists*, *litigation graphics specialists*, or *demonstrative evidence*. For some links, see Appendix IV.

FORENSIC MUSICOLOGIST

CAREER PROFILE

Duties: Provide forensic consulting services to attorneys, recording companies, composers, and others; address legal issues regarding intellectual property issues; perform other duties as required

Alternate Title(s): Forensic Consultant

Salary Range: $30,000 to $94,000

Employment Prospects: Poor

Advancement Prospects: Fair

Prerequisites:

Education or Training—Doctoral degree in music usually preferred

Experience—Several years of work experience in field

Special Skills and Personality Traits—Self-management skills, analytical, organizational, writing, presentation, communication, and interpersonal skills; inquisitive, objective, trustworthy, unbiased, detail-oriented, diligent, and patient

CAREER LADDER

```
┌─────────────────────────────────┐
│     Forensic Musicologist       │
└─────────────────────────────────┘

┌─────────────────────────────────┐
│  Novice Forensic Musicologist   │
└─────────────────────────────────┘

┌─────────────────────────────────┐
│  Music Professor, Musician, or  │
│        Other Profession         │
└─────────────────────────────────┘
```

Position Description

Musicology is the study of music, which includes the history of music and music theory. This discipline also embraces ethnomusicology, which is the study of the musical traditions of different cultures. Most musicologists are academicians who teach college and university students and conduct scholarly research in their particular areas of interest. Other musicologists work in the music publishing industry, or in museums. Many musicologists are also accomplished musicians.

In recent years, some musicologists have become involved in an emerging specialty called forensic musicology. These specialists, known as Forensic Musicologists, apply their expertise to legal matters. They work as consultants, offering their services to attorneys, recording companies, personal artistic managers, composers, artists, and others. In addition to their extensive background in music, these specialists are knowledgeable about intellectual property law and courtroom proceedings. They also understand the importance of being accurate, objective, and unbiased when performing forensic analysis.

These forensic experts primarily address legal issues regarding music copyright. Forensic Musicologists are well versed in the nuances of copyright law in which some uses of older music are protected while other uses are not. For example, using an older song's melody in a new song that deliberately parodies the older song may be permissible. Copyright is a legal document that grants the owner of a piece of creative work, such as a musical composition, the exclusive rights to it. Music copyright owners have complete control over how their works may be used, who may make copies, who may perform them, and who may sell them, among other rights. (Music copyright owners are not necessarily the creators of musical works.) Plagiarizing musical pieces is a copyright infringement, or copyright violation, that can lead to lawsuits as well as criminal charges.

Forensic Musicologists are consulted when a new tune or song appears to use the melody or lyrics of an older musical work. Their job is to help clients establish if a musician deliberately copied another's works and did not simply use an identical melody or lyric by coincidence. They analyze a musical piece in question and determine whether it meets the legal criteria of plagiarism.

Essentially, these forensic specialists analyze and compare two musical works and speculate on whether there is any similarity between the works. This involves careful and thorough analysis of each musical work. They study each aspect of the music such as lyrics, melody, and chord patterns. They examine segments of each work and compare only those segments that have relevance to the suspected issue of plagiarism. For example, four bars of each song may be identical or remarkably similar enough to arouse suspicion of one having been copied from the other.

Many of the plagiarism cases in recent years have involved the musical device known as sampling whereby a segment of one tune is incorporated into a new tune. Samples are directly extracted from a recorded piece and used in another. A musician may sample another musician's work by licensing the use of the sample. The absence of that license is a violation of copyright law.

Forensic Musicologists are hired by diverse clients for different purposes. Attorneys retain these specialists to provide various litigation support services for civil or criminal cases. For example, Forensic Musicologists might:

- review the facts and issues of a case to help attorneys determine if there is sufficient evidence to file a lawsuit or criminal charges
- study a case to identify the technical facts and issues
- instruct lawyers about the technical facts in a case
- conduct research for additional information to support a case
- perform forensic analyses on musical pieces to prove or disprove certain facts or issues
- prepare reports that can be used in settlement negotiations

Attorneys also retain Forensic Musicologists to provide expert witness testimony in depositions, trials, and alternative dispute resolution meetings. They give their professional opinion about specific facts and issues of a case, objectively and without bias. They do not support or oppose the arguments presented by the opposing attorneys or the attorneys that have hired them. In general, when forensic experts perform expert witness services, they do not provide litigation support services.

On occasion, composers as well as artists consult Forensic Musicologists about new compositions. These specialists may be asked to listen to the new work and confirm that the material is in fact original and not in violation of copyright law. Advertising agencies and movie companies also seek Forensic Musicologists when they want to use original music that may sound similar to familiar works. They want these specialists to assure them that their music does not copy another tune, and that the new music fits within the criteria of copyright law.

Very few Forensic Musicologists work full time. Their hours are flexible. They often travel to other cities and states to meet with clients and attend depositions and trials.

Salaries

Specific earnings information for Forensic Musicologists is unavailable. As consultants, they might charge an hourly, daily, or flat rate for assessments, courtroom testimony, and other services that they offer. They might also charge clients for travel time, photocopying, and other out-of-pocket expenses.

Academicians earn salaries that vary, depending on such factors as their ranking, employer, and geographic location. According to the U.S. Bureau of Labor, in its May 2006 *Occupational Employment Statistics* survey, the estimated annual salary for postsecondary music teachers ranged between $29,290 and $94,270.

Employment Prospects

Forensic musicology is a very young but emerging field. It is also a very small occupation, in which practically all Forensic Musicologists offer their services on a part-time basis. Most of these specialists provide forensic consulting services as a sideline to their main occupation as college professors. Some Forensic Musicologists hold down full-time jobs as attorneys, musicians, and other professions.

As more attorneys, music publishing companies, musicians, and others become aware of the benefits of having forensic experts address legal issues, demands will increase for Forensic Musicologists.

Advancement Prospects

As consultants, Forensic Musicologists measure success through job satisfaction, gaining professional recognition, and earning higher incomes.

College and university instructors typically seek tenure-track positions. They advance by rising through the ranks from instructor to full professor. They can also pursue managerial and administrative positions, from department chair to academic dean, and may work their way up to the position of provost or president.

Education and Training

In general, Forensic Musicologists should have an advanced degree, preferably a doctoral (Ph.D.) degree, in music. To teach in academic institutions, individuals must possess a doctorate.

There are no formal training programs in forensic musicology. In general, Forensic Musicologists gain their knowledge in forensic analysis through self-study and essentially learning by doing.

Throughout their careers, Forensic Musicologists enroll in continuing education programs to update their skills and keep up with advancements in their fields.

Experience, Special Skills, and Personality Traits

Typically, music professors and others have worked for many years before becoming forensic consultants.

Potential clients seek Forensic Musicologists who have established themselves as being accomplished in their field. They retain consultants who have the necessary knowledge, skills, and experience to successfully complete their projects.

To do well as consultants, Forensic Musicologists must have strong self-management skills, analytical, organizational, writing, and presentation skills. They also need excellent communication and interpersonal skills, as they must be able to work well with different people from diverse backgrounds. Being inquisitive, objective, trustworthy, unbiased, detail-oriented, diligent, and patient are some personality traits that successful Forensic Musicologists have in common.

Unions and Associations

Forensic Musicologists can join professional associations to take advantage of professional resources and services as well as networking opportunities. In addition to joining societies that serve their particular music field, they can also become members of the American Musicological Society. For contact information, see Appendix III.

Tips for Entry

1. As a high school or college student, get an idea if working in the legal arena might be your forte. For example, you can read books and articles about forensic science. You can also sit in on trials and listen and watch expert witnesses as they give their testimony and are cross-examined.

2. Obtain an advanced degree in music. Education is one of the criteria that courts use when qualifying individuals to be expert witnesses. In general, most expert witnesses (in all fields) possess doctorates in their fields.

3. Contact Forensic Musicologists and talk with them about their work. One of them may be willing to train you.

4. Many Forensic Musicologists get projects through referrals given by colleagues, clients, and other people they know.

5. Use the Internet to learn more about forensic musicology. To get a list of relevant Web sites, enter the keywords *forensic musicology* or *forensic musicologists* into a search engine. For some links, see Appendix IV.

FORENSIC EXPERTS IN HEALTH AND MEDICINE

FORENSIC MEDICAL CONSULTANT

CAREER PROFILE

Duties: Provide forensic consulting services to attorneys, law enforcement agencies, insurance companies, and various other clients; perform duties as required

Alternate Title(s): Forensic Consultant, Forensic Examiner, Forensic Specialist; Forensic Odontologist, Forensic Nurse, or other title that reflects a particular occupation

Salary Range: $100 to $500+ per hour

Employment Prospects: Fair

Advancement Prospects: Poor

Prerequisites:

Education or Training—College degrees and training appropriate to an occupation such as pediatrician or registered nurse

Experience—Several years of experience in occupation

Special Skills and Personality Traits—Self-management, communication, interpersonal, organizational, analytical, writing, and presentation skills; fair, honest, trustworthy, compassionate, respectful, objective, detail-oriented, and meticulous

Special Requirements—Professional license required; certification usually preferred

CAREER LADDER

```
┌─────────────────────────────────┐
│   Forensic Medical Consultant   │
└─────────────────────────────────┘

┌─────────────────────────────────┐
│ Novice Forensic Medical Consultant │
└─────────────────────────────────┘

┌─────────────────────────────────┐
│    Healthcare Practitioner or   │
│        Medical Scientist        │
└─────────────────────────────────┘
```

Position Description

Forensic medicine is the application of medicine to legal issues. Some physicians, dentists, pharmacists, chiropractors, registered nurses, and other health care professionals engage in providing forensic consulting services. Essentially, they apply the knowledge and skills of their particular specialty to the resolution of legal or administrative matters. Collectively, these forensic experts are known as Forensic Medical Consultants. Individually, they hold titles that reflect their particular discipline, such as forensic pharmacist, forensic odontologist, forensic psychiatrist, or forensic nurse.

Forensic Medical Consultants offer their services on a contractual basis to attorneys, law enforcement agencies, medical examiners' (and coroners') offices, the courts, regulatory agencies, insurance companies, hospitals, medical boards, workers' compensation commissions, pharmaceutical companies, private corporations, and other organizations. Most of them perform their consulting services on a part-time basis while working full time in their primary job as health care practitioners, academicians, or medical scientists.

These forensic experts consult on various medicolegal issues related to their specific areas of expertise. These areas are varied and range widely, including emergency medicine, cardiovascular surgery, oncology, pharmacology, alternative medicine, geriatric psychiatry, DNA analysis, infectious diseases, aerospace medicine, industrial hygiene, drug addiction, critical care, child abuse pediatrics, health care management, Medicare fraud, standards of care, reconstructive surgery, and medical products and devices, among many other areas.

Forensic Medical Consultants are probably most well known for being retained by attorneys to provide expert witness testimony in court proceedings for criminal and civil cases. These consultants may work for either the prosecution or defense in a case. As expert witnesses, Forensic Medical Consultants give professional opinions about medical facts and issues that are related to a case. Expert witnesses may also be used to provide technical information about a case so that judges and jurors can understand the facts and issues.

Attorneys also hire Forensic Medical Consultants to provide them with litigation support services. These are different pretrial services that lawyers seek to help them prepare for trials. Some services include reviewing cases to identify medical issues and facts; conducting medical research; educating lawyers about medical facts of a case; performing clinical examinations to prove or disprove facts or issues in a case; interviewing eyewitnesses; and preparing reports to be used in settlement negotiations.

When Forensic Medical Consultants provide litigation support services, they usually do not perform any expert witness services. However, lawyers may ask them to testify as percipient witnesses, which are similar to eyewitnesses. They answer questions about facts related to a case based on their direct observation or work rather than their professional opinion.

Forensic Medical Consultants also offer other types of services for different clients. For example, they may:

- conduct autopsies to determine the cause of death of victims or assist with identifying remains from disaster scenes for medical examiners' offices
- carry out independent medical examinations of disability or worker's compensation claimants for insurance companies
- perform assessments of fellow physicians for medical boards
- evaluate policies and procedures for hospitals or health clinics
- assess medical facts and issues related to administrative hearings with regulatory agencies
- provide expert testimony for nonprofit organizations about medical issues at Congressional hearings

Forensic Medical Consultants are expected to provide independent expert opinions that are impartial and unbiased, and to deliver them on a timely basis. They perform various consulting tasks. They collect data, which may involve performing clinical examinations, gathering literature, interviewing people, and reviewing records and other written materials. They analyze and interpret data and form assessments. In addition, they prepare written reports of their medical findings and conclusions. Their reports must be clear and concise and be presented in language that can be easily understood by nonmedical people. Forensic Medical Consultants also provide expert witness testimony in depositions and trials when needed.

As business owners, Forensic Medical Consultants are responsible for managing their operations. They perform various administrative duties such as paying bills and taxes, col-

lecting clients' fees, bookkeeping, maintaining supplies and equipment, and marketing their services. These consultants also set aside time to generate new business. To be successful, they must work at building up their reputation and credibility. They may write books and articles for professional and trade publications, make guest presentations at professional and trade conferences, and teach workshops and seminars.

Forensic Medical Consultants work flexible hours. Their job requires them to travel frequently to meet with clients, attend depositions and trials, and participate in conferences and other relevant events.

Salaries

Annual gross earnings for Forensic Medical Consultants is based on the total fees that they have earned in a year. Earnings vary yearly, depending on such factors as their occupation, specialties, rates, and the demand for their services in their particular location. Specific earnings information for this occupation is unavailable.

Consultants typically charge an hourly, daily, or flat rate for the different services—such as research, evaluations, and expert witness testimony—that they offer. Hourly fees may range between $100 and $500 or more per hour. Highly reputable consultants can earn as much as $2,000 or more per hour for expert witness services. Consultants may be reimbursed for expenses such as telephone calls, photocopying, and travel time.

Employment Prospects

Opportunities vary for different Forensic Medical Consultants. Some forensic specialties, such as forensic odontology, forensic psychiatry, and forensic nursing are more established than others. In general, though, the job outlook for Forensic Medical Consultants should remain steady over the long term, as lawyers, public agencies, insurance companies, and other organizations and industries rely on outside expertise for their medicolegal cases.

The prospects for forensic consultants within a location depend on the demand for their particular expertise and on the number of similar consultants in the area. Those willing to travel to other locations may have more opportunities to obtain consulting work.

Advancement Prospects

As forensic consultants, healthcare practitioners realize advancement by earning higher incomes and gaining professional recognition. Many also measure success by being sought out for very complex or publicized projects.

Education and Training

Forensic Medical Consultants possess the appropriate education and training that is required for their particular professions. Physicians, for example, possess a bachelor's degree, which may be in any discipline, as well as hold either a doctor of medicine (M.D.) degree or a doctor of osteopathy (D.O.) degree. They have also completed residency training in their specialty (such as pathology) and, if any, subspecialty (such as forensic pathology).

Forensic Medical Consultants may gain forensic training through various ways, depending on their specialty. They might complete residency training, fellowship programs, continuing education courses, on-the-job training, self-study, or a combination of these pursuits.

Throughout their careers, Forensic Medical Consultants enroll in continuing education and training programs to update their skills and knowledge as well as to keep up with advancements in their fields.

Special Requirements

Physicians and registered nurses must be licensed in the jurisdiction where they practice. Licensing requirements vary with each state. For specific information, contact the state board that oversees the licensing of an occupation. For example, contact the appropriate state board of medicine for information about physician licensure.

Attorneys, organizations, and industries usually prefer to retain Forensic Medical Consultants who have obtained board certification or professional certification in their specialties. For example, many forensic psychiatrists are board-certified by the American Board of Psychiatry and Neurology.

Unlike state licenses, professional certifications are not required for physicians, nurses, and other medical professionals to practice in a jurisdiction. Forensic experts obtain professional certification on a voluntary basis from reputable organizations that are recognized within their profession. Applicants must typically pass stringent requirements, including an examination, to become certified. For information about some certification programs, see Appendix II.

Experience, Special Skills, and Personality Traits

Potential clients seek Forensic Medical Consultants who have established themselves as accomplished practitioners. They retain consultants who have the necessary knowledge, skills, and experience to successfully complete their projects. Typically, medical professionals have been in practice for several years before they become forensic consultants.

To perform well as consultants, individuals must have excellent self-management skills, such as the ability to work independently, understand and follow instructions, meet deadlines, and prioritize multiple tasks. They also need exceptional communication and interpersonal skills, as they must be able to handle patients, colleagues, clients, attorneys, officials, and various other people from diverse backgrounds. In addition, Forensic Medical Consultants need strong organizational, analytical, writing, and presentation skills.

Some personality traits that successful Forensic Medical Consultants share include being fair, honest, trustworthy, compassionate, respectful, objective, detail-oriented, and meticulous.

Unions and Associations

Many Forensic Medical Consultants belong to professional associations to take advantage of networking opportunities, continuing education, publications, referral services, and other professional resources and services. They are members of professional societies that serve their profession. For example, many physicians belong to the American Medical Association, while many dentists are members of the American Dental Association.

These consultants can also join forensic societies that serve their particular interests. Registered nurses can belong to the International Association of Forensic Nurses, for example. Two professional associations that serve the general interests of forensic experts are the American Academy of Forensic Sciences and the American College of Forensic Examiners.

For contact information for the above organizations, see Appendix III.

Tips for Entry

1. Talk with experienced Forensic Medical Consultants in your specialty. Try to find someone who is willing to be your mentor.
2. Learn to network. Consultants often learn about potential jobs through word of mouth.
3. Learn more about forensic medicine on the Internet. To find relevant Web sites, enter any of these keywords into a search engine: *forensic medicine*, *forensic medical consulting*, or *medicolegal consulting*.

CHILD ABUSE PEDIATRICIAN

CAREER PROFILE

Duties: Conduct evaluations of children suspected of being abused, neglected, or otherwise maltreated; provide expert assessments; perform other duties as required

Alternate Title(s): Forensic Pediatrician

Salary Range: $66,000 to $146,000

Employment Prospects: Good

Advancement Prospects: Fair

Prerequisites:

    Education or Training—Medical school degree, pediatric residency training, and forensic pediatrics fellowship

    Experience—Work experience gained through a forensic pediatrics fellowship

    Special Skills and Personality Traits—Interpersonal, communication, writing, analytical, observational, and self-management skills; compassionate, friendly, respectful, honest, diligent, and self-motivated

    Special Requirements—Physician licensure; board-certification as a pediatrician may be required

CAREER LADDER

```
┌─────────────────────────────────────┐
│   Senior Child Abuse Pediatrician or │
│  Forensic Pediatrics Program Director│
└─────────────────────────────────────┘

┌─────────────────────────────────────┐
│       Child Abuse Pediatrician       │
└─────────────────────────────────────┘

┌─────────────────────────────────────┐
│             Pediatrician             │
└─────────────────────────────────────┘
```

Position Description

One of the most unfortunate aspects of life is that children are sometimes abused, molested, or neglected. Each year, over a thousand children die from these traumatic incidents. Many more suffer serious or permanent injury and long-lasting emotional difficulties. Pediatric specialists called Child Abuse Pediatricians are the medical experts who are called upon to evaluate children suspected of having been maltreated.

Child abuse pediatrics, or forensic pediatrics, is a new subspecialty of pediatrics, the medical specialty that treats youngsters from infancy through their teenage years. Pediatricians, who are primary care providers, monitor children's growth and development, treat their injuries, and diagnose and prevent their illnesses.

Child Abuse Pediatricians are trained in clinical assessment, research, and advocacy skills. They also have specialized medical skills pertinent to the physical and psychological injuries incurred in child abuse cases. In addition to being familiar with child development, injury biomechanics, pediatric trauma, genetic disorders, and nutrition, they are knowledgeable about child advocacy and protection, mental health evaluation and treatment, forensic autopsy, forensic pathology, the proper handling of criminal and civil child abuse cases, and legislative advocacy.

These forensic specialists cooperate with law enforcement agencies, social agencies such as Child Protective Services, and the courts to identify, evaluate, and treat victims of child abuse and neglect. Child Abuse Pediatricians are confronted with very complex cases that require the input of other experts; hence, they usually work as part of multidisciplinary teams. The makeup of these teams varies with the different forensic pediatrics programs. They may consist of various medical specialists including other physicians, psychiatrists, nurses, and nurse practitioners; social service professionals such as social workers, child development specialists, and family advocates; law enforcement officers; prosecution attorneys; and volunteers.

As experts in child abuse, these pediatric specialists' primary job is to examine and evaluate children who appear to have been abused in one way or another. They consult with others on their team to determine whether the evidence of injury or trauma is in fact the result of criminal negligence, sexual assault, or violent attack, because some diseases may mimic the symptoms of child abuse. Some reported cases of abuse are contrived. Some symptoms may actually be caused by previous illness or previous accidental injury. Consequently, forensic pediatricians use investigative techniques to collect evidence and interview patients to precisely determine the circumstances of the abuse.

Upon completing their evaluations, Child Abuse Pediatricians provide assessments to law enforcement agencies, child protective services, or other entities that are responsible for investigating possible maltreatment, as well as to those agencies that will care for the children. Child Abuse Pediatricians sometimes provide expert testimony in court about facts and issues related to criminal, civil, or custody cases.

Child Abuse Pediatricians are responsible for completing other duties, which vary from one expert to the next. For example, they may:

- prepare written and photographic evidence of injuries resulting from maltreatment
- provide consultation to pediatricians and other primary care providers who suspect that their patients have been mistreated
- perform medical assessments based on reported evidence of all types of child abuse and neglect
- provide treatment and therapy to victims
- conduct research into the causes and consequences of child abuse
- train law enforcement officers, social workers, other doctors and mental health professionals, teachers, day care providers, and parents to recognize evidence of abuse and work against the incidence of child abuse and neglect
- create and sponsor programs designed to educate the public about child abuse and to prevent its occurrence
- participate in child abuse task forces and committees
- establish relationships with and confer regularly with law enforcement agencies, child protection agencies, and other governmental and public organizations
- stay up to date with the latest research and legislative advocacy information regarding child abuse and child prevention topics and issues

Child Abuse Pediatricians work closely with children, their families, and their communities. They may work full time or part time. Many full-time specialists are medical school professors who are part of child abuse programs. Others work with nonprofit, governmental, or nongovernmental child abuse programs. Some Child Abuse Pediatricians run private child abuse and neglected child protection programs.

Salaries
Specific salary information for Child Abuse Pediatricians is unavailable. Their earnings are similar to general pediatri-cians. According to the May 2006 *Occupational Employment Statistics* survey by the U.S. Bureau of Labor Statistics, the estimated annual salary for most general pediatricians ranged between $66,480 and $145,600.

Employment Prospects
Child Abuse Pediatricians usually find employment as academicians in pediatric departments at medical centers, children's hospitals, and hospitals with pediatric residency training programs. Some opportunities are available with child advocacy centers and other child abuse and neglect programs. Some Child Abuse Pediatricians offer forensic pediatric services on a part-time consulting basis, while working in their primary occupation as general pediatricians or emergency room physicians.

Child abuse pediatrics is a new field. According to some experts in the field, there is a growing interest in this subspecialty, as well as an increasing demand for experienced specialists. One expert reports that currently there are more positions available than trained physicians to fill them.

Advancement Prospects
Child Abuse Pediatricians advance according to their interests and ambitions. Those with managerial interests can pursue administrative positions within forensic pediatrics programs or departments in medical centers, for example. Entrepreneurial specialists can become consultants or open a solo practice in addition to offering forensic consulting services.

Many of these forensic pediatricians measure success through job satisfaction, by gaining professional recognition, and by earning higher incomes.

Education and Training
Becoming a Child Abuse Pediatrician involves a long and intense formal education program. Individuals must first earn a bachelor's degree, which may be in any field, then complete four years of medical school to earn a doctor of medicine (M.D.) degree or a doctor of osteopathy (D.O.) degree. They then complete a three-year pediatric residency program, which involves clinical training under the supervision of physicians, to become general pediatricians. To specialize in child abuse pediatrics, pediatricians carry out a fellowship in child abuse pediatrics.

Trainees in child abuse pediatrics learn skills in teaching, community work, expert witness testimony, and research.

Special Requirements
Child Abuse Pediatricians must be licensed physicians in the jurisdictions where they practice. For licensure requirements, contact the appropriate state medical board.

Many employers require that applicants be board-certified pediatricians. This certification is voluntary and is granted by the American Board of Pediatrics. Some employers will hire candidates on the condition that they obtain their certification within a certain time period.

When this book was being written, the American Board of Pediatrics was developing a certification program for child abuse pediatrics. Employers will more likely prefer to hire applicants who possess this certification.

Experience, Special Skills, and Personality Traits

Novice forensic pediatricians gain experience through their fellowship training.

Child Abuse Pediatricians need excellent interpersonal and communication skills, as they must be able to work well with children, families, colleagues, law enforcement officers, social workers, and various others. They also must have effective writing, analytical, observational, and self-management skills.

Some personality traits that successful Child Abuse Pediatricians share include being compassionate, friendly, respectful, honest, diligent, and self-motivated.

Unions and Associations

Some societies that serve the interests of Child Abuse Pediatricians are:

- American Academy of Pediatrics
- American Professional Society for the Abuse of Children
- American Pediatric Society

- Society for Pediatric Research
- American Academy of Forensic Sciences

By joining professional associations, these specialists can take advantage of various professional resources and services as well as networking opportunities. For contact information for the above organizations, see Appendix III.

Tips for Entry

1. While in high school, get an idea if you might like a career helping children. Talk with your school counselor or a local pediatrician to get suggestions on how and where you might volunteer in your community to gain experience working with children.
2. As a student, gain experience working in a medical setting. For example, you might work part time or in the summer for a hospital, doctor's office, health clinic, pharmacy, or skilled nursing facility.
3. As a medical student, take advantage of opportunities to work in child abuse and protection programs.
4. Check out Web sites for children's hospitals and academic medical centers to learn about their pediatrics departments. You may also find postings of job vacancies as well as information about the application process.
5. Use the Internet to learn more about forensic pediatrics. You might start by visiting the Web site for the Child Abuse and Neglect Section that is part of the American Academy of Pediatrics. Its URL is http://www.aap.org/sections/scan. For more links, see Appendix IV.

FORENSIC CHIROPRACTIC EXAMINER

CAREER PROFILE

Duties: Perform independent examinations on patients for insurance companies, government agencies, attorneys, employers, and other entities; perform duties as required

Alternate Title(s): Forensic Chiropractor, Forensic Chiropractic Specialist

Salary Range: $33,000 to $146,000

Employment Prospects: Fair

Advancement Prospects: Poor

Prerequisites:

Education or Training—Chiropractor school training; on-the-job forensic training

Experience—Several years of work experience

Special Skills and Personality Traits—Analytical, organizational, writing, communication, interpersonal, and self-management skills; friendly, truthful, trustworthy, respectful, objective, thorough, reliable, conscientious, and unbiased

Special Requirements—Chiropractor license required; professional certification usually preferred

CAREER LADDER

```
┌─────────────────────────────────────┐
│  Forensic Chiropractic Examiner     │
└─────────────────────────────────────┘

┌─────────────────────────────────────┐
│ Novice Forensic Chiropractic Examiner│
└─────────────────────────────────────┘

┌─────────────────────────────────────┐
│          Chiropractor               │
└─────────────────────────────────────┘
```

Position Description

Most of us have more than a passing familiarity with conventional medical doctors such as general practitioners, surgeons, or various specialists such as pediatricians, cardiologists, or psychiatrists. There are also many alternative medical professions that offer different approaches to healing illnesses or injuries. One of those alternative professions is chiropractic medicine, which concentrates on health problems concerning the body's nervous and musculoskeletal systems. Chiropractors do not perform surgery or prescribe medications. They treat patients by manipulating their joints and spines, as well as by using stretching, massage, and heat therapies. They also counsel their patients to manage their stress and their diet and to exercise regularly. Their patients may need repetitive treatments depending upon the severity of their ailments.

Chiropractic medicine often intersects with legal matters. Some chiropractors, known as Forensic Chiropractic Examiners, perform independent medical evaluation services for such agencies and entities as insurance companies, the legal profession, the Social Security Administration, workers'

compensation commissions, and medical administrators. These organizations handle cases brought before them by people who suffer accidental injuries, some of which occur at their jobs. Forensic Chiropractic Examiners offer their assessment of the injuries, disabilities, or impairments of claimants by objectively examining and testing them in their chiropractic offices. Some of the injured may be under investigation by fraud divisions of the various agencies, or their cases may be part of ongoing legal proceedings. Forensic Chiropractic Examiners do not take sides on the issues. Their role is to determine the truth and provide objective reports of their findings.

When these doctors conduct their forensic examinations, they follow specific steps. They introduce themselves to the examinee, confirm the examinee's identity, and provide an explanation that the examination is by an agency's request and is not for the treatment of symptoms. After further explaining the steps to be taken during the examination, Forensic Chiropractic Examiners conduct the examination in an objective and professional manner. They provide the examinee with an opportunity to request information at the conclusion of the examination. Forensic Chiropractic Examiners prepare thorough written reports regarding their findings, which they submit to the requesting agencies. Their reports include both a diagnosis and prognosis of the examinee's condition and include notes about their opinion of the cause of the injury, the examinee's capacity to return to work, and whether the case is fraudulent.

Forensic Chiropractic Examiners may provide expert witness testimony regarding the results of their examinations. These professionals rely on their training, experience, and expertise in chiropractic medicine to determine the facts of a case. In addition, they utilize their supplementary training in fraud and criminal investigations, occupational assessment, and in their understanding of psychological and physical behavior to determine the facts of a case for presentation as expert witnesses. By law, Forensic Chiropractic Examiners are required to be familiar with court rules of evidence to qualify as expert witnesses.

Forensic Chiropractic Examiners are expected to always act in compliance with laws and regulations governing their profession. Their mission is to provide facts honestly and with integrity. They are bound to ethical standards, which prohibit them from divulging confidential information and from impugning the reputation of any party involved in a case. Above all, they are expected to remain impartial and unbiased when reporting their findings or offering testimony.

These professionals perform duties specific to their forensic services. Forensic Chiropractic Examiners may:

- review medical records provided by both the plaintiff and defense in a case
- conduct independent medical and functional capacity evaluations
- provide affidavits relevant to medical malpractice cases
- assist with the development of questions for interviews and deposition hearings
- make careful decisions regarding their examination discoveries about examinees' impairment, disability, or absence thereof

Most Forensic Chiropractic Examiners work full time as chiropractors. They offer forensic services in addition to their other functions. They work 40-hour weeks but may need to work extra hours to prepare testimony or to conduct examinations on behalf of requesting agencies.

Salaries

Specific earnings information for Forensic Chiropractic Examiners is unavailable. As consultants, they charge an hourly, daily, or flat rate for chart analyses, medical examinations, legal research, courtroom testimony, and other services that they offer.

The estimated annual salary for most chiropractors ranges between $32,670 and $145,600, according to the May 2006 *Occupational Employment Statistics* survey by the U.S. Bureau of Labor Statistics (BLS).

Employment Prospects

Most chiropractors are in solo practice. Some are in group practice or are employed by other chiropractors. The BLS reports an expected 18 to 26 percent increase in employment through 2014. In addition to new jobs, opportunities become available when chiropractors retire. The job market for chiropractors is favorable partly due to the continuing demand for alternative health care.

Opportunities are favorable for highly reputable and credible Forensic Chiropractic Examiners. One expert in the field characterizes the job market as being steady, as many chiropractors do not have a forensic background. The prospects for these specialists within a location depend on the demand for their particular expertise and on the number of similar consultants in the area.

Advancement Prospects

Forensic Chiropractic Examiners realize advancement by building their practices, earning higher incomes, and gaining professional recognition. Many also measure success by being sought out for very complex or publicized cases.

Chiropractors who work for others or are part of a group practice may seek to open a solo practice.

Education and Training

To become a chiropractor, individuals must complete four to five years of study at a chiropractic college to earn a doctor of chiropractic (D.C.) degree. Their education includes such basic health science courses as physiology, anatomy, microbiology, chemistry, physics, and psychology, as well as courses in manipulation and spinal adjustment, physical diagnosis, physiotherapy, and nutrition. In addition, they complete laboratory work as well as clinical training in which they work with patients under the supervision of licensed chiropractors.

The minimum education requirement for entry into chiropractic college may be only two years of college work. Most applicants possess a bachelor's degree.

Chiropractors can complete continuing education courses that teach the skills and knowledge needed to perform independent chiropractic examinations. These courses are sponsored by chiropractic colleges, professional societies, and private educational services.

Throughout their careers, these forensic specialists enroll in courses, workshops, and seminars to update their skills and knowledge.

Special Requirements

Forensic Chiropractic Examiners must be licensed chiropractors in the states where they practice. Licensing requirements vary with each state. For example, some states require that applicants complete two years of an undergraduate program, while others mandate that applicants possess a bachelor's degree. For specific information, contact the appropriate state board of chiropractic examiners.

Experience, Special Skills, and Personality Traits

Chiropractors typically work several years before they begin offering forensic examination services. Some organizations that grant professional certification in this area require that applicants have completed at least three to five years in practice.

Forensic Chiropractic Examiners need excellent analytical, organizational, writing, communication, and interpersonal skills to perform well at their job. In addition, they should have strong self-management skills, such as the ability to work independently, meet deadlines, follow and understand instructions, and prioritize multiple tasks. Being friendly, truthful, trustworthy, respectful, objective, thorough, reliable, conscientious, and unbiased are some personality traits that successful Forensic Chiropractic Examiners share.

Unions and Associations

Forensic Chiropractic Examiners can join professional associations to take advantage of professional services and resources, such as networking opportunities, publications, and continuing education. Some societies that serve their interests include

- American Chiropractic Association
- Academy of Forensic and Industrial Chiropractic Consultants
- International Chiropractors Association
- Academy of Chiropractic Orthopedists
- College on Forensic Sciences
- American College of Forensic Examiners
- American Academy of Forensic Sciences
  For contact information, see Appendix III.

Tips for Entry

1. While in high school, talk with one or more chiropractors in your area to learn more about their profession. Ask if you might visit their practice and watch them at work.
2. Many insurance companies, lawyers, and others prefer to hire Forensic Chiropractic Examiners who have obtained certification from the American Board of Forensic Professionals, the American Board of Independent Medical Examiners, or another recognized organization. To learn about some certification programs, see Appendix II.
3. Gain visibility by teaching workshops at insurance industry trade shows as well as at professional conferences for attorneys or chiropractors.
4. Use the Internet to learn more about the forensic chiropractic field. You might start by visiting these Web sites: Chiro-Legal, http://www.chiro.org/chiro-legal; and College on Forensic Sciences, http://www.forensic-sciences.org. For more links, see Appendix IV.

FORENSIC EPIDEMIOLOGIST

CAREER PROFILE

Duties: Prepare and conduct research studies on public health problems or sudden disease outbreaks; may assist with criminal, civil, or regulatory investigations; perform other duties as required

Alternate Title(s): Forensic Consultant

Salary Range: $37,000 to $87,000

Employment Prospects: Fair

Advancement Prospects: Poor

Prerequisites:

Education or Training—A master's or doctoral degree in epidemiology or another related field

Experience—Several years of work experience

Special Skills and Personality Traits—Writing, computer, self-management, communication, interpersonal, and teamwork skills; trustworthy, analytical, organized, innovative, and flexible

CAREER LADDER

```
┌─────────────────────────────────────┐
│      Forensic Epidemiologist         │
└─────────────────────────────────────┘

┌─────────────────────────────────────┐
│   Novice Forensic Epidemiologist     │
└─────────────────────────────────────┘

┌─────────────────────────────────────┐
│          Epidemiologist              │
└─────────────────────────────────────┘
```

Position Description

Epidemiology is the scientific and medical study of human health and disease. The medical scientists who specialize in this field, epidemiologists, are often referred to as "disease detectives" because they identify health problems and hazards, as well as investigate sudden outbreaks of infectious diseases. They study the patterns and causes of diseases; why disease occurs within a location or population; and why some people contract the disease while others do not. They also conduct research into disease prevention and the effectiveness of treatments. Furthermore, epidemiologists help public health officials to develop guidelines for the promotion of good mental and physical health practices as well as to institute disease prevention measures.

Some epidemiologists are involved with investigating public health problems or disease outbreaks that may result from unlawful or deliberate acts. These specialists are called Forensic Epidemiologists. Their area of expertise is a relatively new one, but it is filling a growing need in society due to increasing threats from terrorist groups who seek to use diseases and disease-causing hazardous materials to attack large populations.

Forensic Epidemiologists provide a connection among such disparate areas of concern as law enforcement, the legal system, medicine, urban planning, pharmaceuticals, and emergency services to protect the public health. They are well versed in the areas of statistics, health surveillance systems, and professional standards. They are also knowledgeable about the proper techniques for gathering evidence and investigation, as well as about how the legal system works.

These forensic experts are mostly consultants who offer epidemiology research and other support services to law enforcement agencies, universities, attorneys, public health departments, and various private industries (such as pharmaceutical manufacturers and biotech companies). Some of them are academicians who offer consulting services on the side, while others are owners, partners, or associates of consulting firms that offer forensic epidemiological services.

Forensic Epidemiologists are increasingly active in law enforcement investigations. Law enforcement agencies consult them on health-related criminal cases. They may try to find evidence that a suspect is deliberately exposing others to HIV/AIDS. They may work with law enforcement agencies to identify disease outbreak patterns, establish which bacterium or virus is causing the disease, restrain it from spreading, and trace the origins of the outbreak to a perpetrator or criminal organization. They may be requested to investigate incidents such as multiple cases of heart attacks within a particular hospital, multiple cases of a food-borne illness, or deliberate exposure to diseases in large groups of people in specific locations. Such occurrences may be attributed to criminal behavior or acts of bioterrorism. Forensic Epidemiologists seek to prove this type of connection by investigating commonality in multiple individual poisoning cases, for example.

Attorneys hire the services of Forensic Epidemiologists to provide litigation support in criminal and civil cases involving fraud, wrongful death, professional licensing, medical malpractice, employment law, personal injury, and environmental regulations, among other areas. Forensic Epidemiologists help attorneys find sufficient evidence to prosecute or defend their cases. These experts might be involved in such tasks as:

- conducting research into the connection between multiple cases of a disease suffered by workers and their workplace
- performing statistical analysis of unfavorable reactions to specific medications
- carrying out comparative studies of local incidents of disease with nationwide rates
- conducting assessments of disease prevention programs
- evaluating and reviewing epidemiological journals
- creating computer models that simulate the cause and spread of disease
- advising lawyers about public health issues
- providing expert witness testimony in courts

Some Forensic Epidemiologists are employed as staff members in medical examiners' and coroners' offices to prepare and coordinate pertinent research activities. For example, they may be involved in the development of procedures to identify emerging infectious diseases.

Forensic Epidemiologists perform a variety of general tasks on their job, regardless of whether they are consultants or staff members. For example, they examine and interpret research data; review and analyze medical and scientific reports; recruit people for project surveys and interviews; prepare written or oral presentations about research projects and results; perform administrative tasks, such as writing correspondence and reports; and attend meetings and conferences.

Many Forensic Epidemiologists travel to other cities, states, and countries to gather research data, attend professional meetings, or make presentations. Their work may require them to spend several days or weeks at a location.

Salaries

Specific earnings information for Forensic Epidemiologists is unavailable. Forensic consultants typically charge an hourly, daily, or flat rate for the various services that they offer. Many of them also receive reimbursements for telephone calls, travel time, and other expenses that they incur on projects.

The U.S. Bureau of Labor Statistics reports in its May 2006 *Occupational Employment Statistics* survey that the estimated annual salary for most epidemiologists ranges between $36,920 and $87,300.

Employment Prospects

Forensic epidemiology is a young but growing field. Opportunities will continue to increase as more law enforcement agencies, attorneys, and others seek epidemiological methods to assist with criminal, civil, and regulatory cases, as well as to protect the public health. The ability of public agencies to hire staff members or consultants depends on the availability of funding.

Some experts report that in general there is growing demand for epidemiologists, particularly those who are trained in infectious diseases.

Advancement Prospects

As forensic consultants, epidemiologists generally realize advancement through job satisfaction, professional recognition, and higher incomes. As staff members, they may be promoted to senior or supervisory positions, but those are limited.

Those with entrepreneurial ambitions seek successful careers as independent practitioners or owners of consulting firms.

Education and Training

Educational requirements vary for different positions as well as with different employers. Forensic Epidemiologists usually possess a master's or doctoral degree in epidemiology, public health, or another related field with major course work in epidemiology.

Those seeking to perform independent research or teach in colleges or universities must hold a doctorate. Individuals who plan to work in hospitals and health care centers usually obtain medical training. After completing a bachelor's degree, they enroll in medical school to earn either a doctor of medicine (M.D.) degree or a doctor of osteopathy (D.O.) degree.

Many universities, public health organizations, and other groups offer training programs in forensic epidemiology.

Throughout their careers, Forensic Epidemiologists enroll in continuing education and training programs to update their skills and keep up with advancements in their fields.

Experience, Special Skills, and Personality Traits

Employers normally prefer to hire staff or consultants who have several years of work experience as epidemiologists.

To perform well at their job, Forensic Epidemiologists must have strong writing, computer, and self-management skills. They also need excellent communication, interpersonal, and teamwork skills, as they must be able to work well with many people from diverse backgrounds. Being trustworthy, analytical, organized, innovative, and flexible are some personality traits that successful Forensic Epidemiologists share.

Unions and Associations

Many Forensic Epidemiologists belong to professional associations to take advantage of networking opportunities, training programs, professional publications, and other professional resources and services. Some national societies that serve their interests are the American College of Epidemiology, the Epidemiology Section of the American Public Health Association, and the American Academy of Forensic Sciences. For contact information, see Appendix III.

Tips for Entry

1. While in high school, begin learning as much as you can about epidemiology. You might read books or talk with epidemiologists in your area, for example.

2. As a college student, obtain an internship in a medical examiner's office or a public health agency that allows you to work with Forensic Epidemiologists, or experts who perform some of their research tasks.

3. Having experience working in forensic research is highly desirable.

4. One way to market your services is to advertise in journals and other publications that your potential clients might read.

5. Use the Internet to learn more about forensic epidemiology. To get a list of relevant Web sites, enter the keywords *forensic epidemiology* or *forensic epidemiologists* into a search engine. For some links, see Appendix IV.

FORENSIC NURSE

CAREER PROFILE

Duties: Investigate cases of abuse, neglect, exploitation, or death; provide care for victims or criminals; perform duties as required

Alternate Title(s): A title that reflects a particular occupation such as Sexual Assault Nurse Examiner, Forensic Nurse Investigator, or Legal Nurse Consultant

Salary Range: $40,000 to $83,000

Employment Prospects: Excellent

Advancement Prospects: Good

Prerequisites:

Education or Training—Possess a degree or diploma in nursing; complete training in forensic nursing specialty

Experience—Several years of nursing experience

Special Skills and Personality Traits—Communication, interpersonal, observational, writing, analytical, and self-management skills; patient, calm, methodical, detail-oriented, objective, and compassionate

Special Requirements—Registered nurse license required

CAREER LADDER

```
┌─────────────────────────┐
│   Senior Forensic Nurse │
└─────────────────────────┘

┌─────────────────────────┐
│     Forensic Nurse      │
└─────────────────────────┘

┌─────────────────────────┐
│     Registered Nurse    │
└─────────────────────────┘
```

Position Description

Registered nurses (RNs) are familiar to all of us. They assist doctors in their offices and in hospitals. They also work in our schools, nursing homes, mental health facilities, and government health agencies. Some of these professionals, who are called Forensic Nurses, work closely with law enforcement, medical examiners' (or coroners') offices, corrections departments, and the courts. More specifically, they apply forensic aspects of their profession to investigate and treat trauma or the death of both the perpetrators and victims of violence, crime, and distressful accidents.

Many Forensic Nurses work with patients who are criminal offenders or victims. Many victims have been involved in sexual assaults or other types of abuse. Some Forensic Nurses work with mentally ill criminals and the victims of traumatic accidents and other violent happenstances. Other Forensic Nurses work with the deceased who were victims of suspicious or unexplained circumstances. They also participate in the investigation of such deaths. In addition, many Forensic Nurses provide care to the families of both victims and perpetrators.

Forensic Nurses undergo additional training to qualify for work in key areas that contribute to the legal system. Their training entails course work in such topics as law enforcement investigation; the observation, collection, and documentation of evidence; the preservation of the chain of custody; wound identification; and court testimony procedures. In addition, they complete laboratory work as well as internships at hospitals.

After their training, Forensic Nurses may continue to work in the usual locations as RNs, but may also find employment in correctional facilities, insurance agencies, medical examiners' offices, psychiatric facilities, or in agencies that provide evidence documentation and information verification services pertinent to abuse, neglect, or fraud cases. Some Forensic Nurses become independent practitioners or start up forensic nursing firms.

Forensic nursing is a relatively new field that emerged during the 1990s. However, there are already several specialties. The three major areas are sexual assault examination, medicolegal death investigation, and legal consulting.

Sexual assault nurse examiners (SANEs) are Forensic Nurses who respond to reports of rape, which are issued by hospital emergency room personnel. These professionals also work in special clinics that handle sexual assault cases. SANEs work closely with the victims in private surroundings and with sensitivity. These nurses interview their patients and obtain their medical history. They document information about the crime and conduct complete physical examinations as well as screenings for sexually transmitted diseases. During the physical examinations, Forensic Nurses obtain evidence of the assaults, which they may present later as testimony in court proceedings.

SANEs work cooperatively with law enforcement and legal systems during the entire process, in which they remain close to the victim. In addition, they provide educational services to victims regarding pregnancy and venereal diseases. They refer their patients to further medical care when needed.

Forensic Nurses who specialize in medicolegal death investigations work in medical examiners' offices or coroners' offices. In that capacity, these professionals, also called forensic nurse investigators, work alongside police investigators to respond to death scenes. These Forensic Nurses are responsible for examining the victims and investigating the circumstances surrounding their deaths. They also take samples of blood and tissue for analysis by forensic pathologists. (These samples may be used as evidence in criminal cases.) In addition, these medicolegal investigators may photograph bodies and arrange for their transport to the morgue for autopsy. At the lab, these Forensic Nurses oftentimes provide assistance during autopsy procedures.

In the area of legal consulting, Forensic Nurses provide help to attorneys in cases where medical issues coincide with legal concerns. When working in this area, these nurses are usually referred to as legal nurse consultants (LNCs). Their cases are more often civil than criminal cases and may entail matters such as personal injury, wrongful death, heart surgery, medical malpractice, negligence, elder abuse, product liability, or workers' compensation, among others. Some LNCs also offer expert witness services and provide testimony relevant to such nursing concerns as intensive care, elder care, or pediatrics.

The following are some other areas in which various Forensic Nurses specialize:

- Clinical forensic nursing entails the inquiry into various medicolegal issues and the treatment thereof. Incidents of trauma or death are the subject of these nurses' investigations in the course of their work in emergency rooms and shelters for domestic violence or abuse victims.
- Forensic correctional nursing is the care of suspected or convicted criminals. These Forensic Nurses might work in jails or prisons, youth centers, and other correctional facilities. Their work is similar to RNs in other sectors of society in that they evaluate and handle injuries and illnesses. These nurses also provide health education to their patients.
- Forensic ER nursing is the care of patients who enter the emergency rooms of hospitals. Forensic Nurses who work in this setting handle sexual assault and violent crime cases. They collect evidence from victims in the ER and may be required to continue this task in operating rooms. Such evidence as bullets or debris that may be relevant to the case is collected. Forensic ER nurses photograph and measure wounds. These nurses also confer with medical examiners in the event of a patient's death.
- Forensic geriatric nursing is the care of senior citizens. These Forensic Nurses are generally involved with cases of the elderly who have been victims of abuse, negligence, or exploitation.
- Forensic pediatric nursing is the care of children. These Forensic Nurses address issues of child abuse, neglect, and exploitation.
- Forensic psychiatric nursing is the care of mentally ill criminal offenders. Forensic Nurses generally handle patients who are incarcerated in state hospitals or in the psychiatric units within prisons. One of their main roles is to determine competency.

The work that Forensic Nurses perform can be difficult because it is often highly emotionally charged. These nurses witness traumatic injuries on a regular basis and frequently deal with distressed and abused patients who are suffering. Nevertheless, Forensic Nurses are very much interested in providing the best of care to their patients.

Forensic Nurses may be employed full time or part time. Some of these nurses work on an on-call basis.

Salaries

Salaries for Forensic Nurses vary, depending on such factors as their education, experience, employer, specialty, and geographic location. Specific salary information for this occupation is unavailable. However, most RNs earned an estimated annual salary that ranged between $40,250 and $83,440, according to the May 2006 *Occupational Employment Statistics* (OES) survey by the U.S. Bureau of Labor Statistics (BLS).

Employment Prospects

Nursing is a large occupation. The May 2006 OES survey states that about 2,417,150 RNs were employed in the United States. The BLS reports that the job outlook for RNs in all specialties is highly favorable. Job growth is expected to increase by more than 27 percent or more through 2014. In addition, opportunities become available as RNs retire, advance to higher positions, transfer to other jobs, or leave the work force for various reasons.

Some experts in the forensic nursing field state that there is a growing interest and demand for Forensic Nurses. In addition, the number of qualified RNs who are available to practice forensic nursing is limited.

Advancement Prospects

Forensic Nurses can advance in any number of ways, depending on their ambitions and interests. They can pursue supervisory and managerial positions, which may require advanced degrees. Those with entrepreneurial interests can become independent contractors or own consulting firms that offer forensic nursing services. Forensic Nurses can also pursue careers as researchers or educators.

Education and Training

Forensic Nurses must first obtain RN training. There are three training options. Individuals can earn an associate degree in nursing, get a bachelor of science degree in nursing, or acquire a diploma after completing a two- or three-year hospital-nursing program.

Many Forensic Nurses have gained their training on the job. As the forensic nursing field grows, more educational programs are becoming established to prepare RNs to enter the different forensic specialties. Some graduate degree and professional certification programs, including online programs, are currently available. In addition, forensic nursing courses may be obtained as electives in undergraduate nursing programs or as continuing education courses that are required for nursing license renewal.

Employers may require that candidates for SANE positions complete a certification-training program that includes classroom instruction and clinical work. They learn such skills as gathering medical histories, wound identification, collecting evidence, basic forensic photography, and interviewing techniques.

Throughout their careers, Forensic Nurses enroll in continuing education programs, as well as training workshops to update their skills and keep up with advancements in their fields.

Special Requirements

Forensic Nurses must be professionally licensed as registered nurses in the states where they practice. To obtain a license, candidates must possess a degree or diploma in nursing and successfully pass a national licensing examination. Nurses must renew their licenses every few years.

Experience, Special Skills, and Personality Traits

Qualifications vary for the different specialties as well as with different employers. In general, nurses enter the forensic nursing field after having worked for several years in hospitals, clinics, doctors' offices, and other settings.

Forensic Nurses need excellent communication and interpersonal skills, as they must be able to deal with victims, families, law enforcement officers, colleagues, and others from diverse backgrounds. In addition, they must have excellent observational, writing, analytical, and self-management skills. Being patient, calm, methodical, detail-oriented, objective, and compassionate are some personality traits that successful Forensic Nurses share.

Unions and Associations

Many Forensic Nurses join professional associations to take advantage of networking opportunities, continuing education, professional certification, and other professional resources and services. They may join general nursing societies, such as the American Nurses Association, as well as forensic societies such as the International Association of Forensic Nurses, the American College of Forensic Examiners, and the American Academy of Forensic Sciences. For contact information, see Appendix III.

Tips for Entry

1. As a student, or even as a new nurse, learn as much as you can about the forensic specialties that interest you. If possible, do volunteer work to get an idea if a particular setting suits you.
2. Many Forensic Nurses obtain professional certification to enhance their employability and creditability. For information about some programs, see Appendix II.
3. Develop a network with forensic nurses and other forensic specialists such as criminalists, forensic scientists, and forensic medical specialists. By networking, you can learn about prospective jobs.
4. Learn more about the forensic nursing field on the Internet. You might start by visiting the International Association of Forensic Nurses Web site at http://www.iafn.org. For more links, see Appendix IV.

FORENSIC ODONTOLOGIST

CAREER PROFILE

Duties: Provide forensic consulting services to law enforcement agencies, medical examiners' offices, and other clients; identify unknown bodies by examining teeth or denture work; perform duties as required

Alternate Title(s): Forensic Dentist, Forensic Consultant

Salary Range: $69,000 to $146,000

Employment Prospects: Good

Advancement Prospects: Poor

Prerequisites:

Education or Training—Dental school training

Experience— Several years of work experience

Special Skills and Personality Traits—Organizational, writing, self-management, communication, interpersonal, teamwork, and small-business skills; trustworthy, reliable, methodical, analytical, and self-motivated

Special Requirements—Dentist license required

CAREER LADDER

```
┌─────────────────────────────────────┐
│      Forensic Odontologist          │
└─────────────────────────────────────┘

┌─────────────────────────────────────┐
│   Novice Forensic Odontologist      │
└─────────────────────────────────────┘

┌─────────────────────────────────────┐
│  Dentist or University Professor    │
└─────────────────────────────────────┘
```

Position Description

No two people have identical teeth. Each of our teeth has a specific dentition; that is to say the shape, markings, size, or position in relation to our other teeth. The number of our teeth and such work as fillings, crowns, bridges, or dentures are also distinctive. Because teeth are unique like fingerprints, they can be used to identify unknown bodies and, on occasion, criminal suspects. In such instances, authorities call upon Forensic Odontologists for assistance.

Odontology is the scientific study of teeth, their structure and growth, and the diseases that affect teeth and mouth tissues. Dentistry is the branch of medicine that applies odontology to practical use by providing health care for our teeth. Forensic Odontologists, also called forensic dentists, apply their knowledge and skills to various legal matters, particularly the identification of suspects and unknown bodies. In addition, Forensic Odontologists have backgrounds in and are knowledgeable about biology, chemistry, and medical subjects regarding illnesses and injuries. They also have special training in forensic investigation methods and in the workings of the law enforcement and judicial systems.

Forensic Odontologists provide consulting services to law enforcement agencies, medical examiners' (or coroners') offices, attorneys, private individuals, insurance companies, and other dentists, among others. Many of their cases involve medicolegal investigations, criminal investigations, and civil litigation. They sometimes examine insurance claims that are suspected of being fraudulent. Some of them also consult with other dentists regarding malpractice or professional liability concerns. They sometimes need to work closely with a variety of other forensic professionals such as criminalists, medical examiners, or forensic anthropologists on certain complex cases.

Forensic Odontologists' most common function is to assist in the identification of unknown bodies. In criminal cases or when people die in such circumstances as automobile accidents, fires, industrial accidents, by drowning, or in disasters when large numbers of people are killed, the victims' remains may be in such a state of decay that they are beyond recognition. However, teeth are the one part of the body that can survive such destruction. In these cases, Forensic Odontologists may be able to identify the victims by comparing their teeth to dental records. These forensic specialists may take molds of the teeth and jaws to create a replica, and then compare the teeth with dental X-rays that are available through the dental records databases.

When dental records are unavailable, Forensic Odontologists may extract DNA samples from the teeth to identify the deceased. They can also establish an identity when only one tooth is available, or when the victim had a total tooth extraction. They do this through the examination of dentures or by making X-rays of the skull and mouth.

In cases where a crime has occurred, the verification of a victim's identity can lead to further investigation into the person's background, the time of death, and a pool of likely suspects. In the absence of dental records, Forensic Odontologists may glean information from the close examination of teeth. They often work with forensic anthropologists to identify dental evidence. The shapes of teeth and skulls reveal ancestral and age characteristics. The condition of the teeth may indicate a victim's age, health habits, or socioeconomic status. The transparency of roots may also indicate a victim's age. All of these factors help these scientists to identify the victim.

Law enforcement agencies sometimes employ Forensic Odontologists to identify bitemark evidence. Criminals may leave bite marks on victim's bodies or on food or on such items as leather belts or pencils found at crime scenes; or victims may bite perpetrators in the course of a struggle. Forensic Odontologists can examine bite marks and compare their impressions with the dentition of the suspects.

When bite marks are found on human skin, Forensic Odontologists must be able to examine them as soon as possible after the biting incident occurs because skin changes rapidly. These professionals take saliva samples, photographs, and molds of the bite marks from living skin and occasionally remove the affected area from corpses for comparison to the suspect's teeth. They make notes about the depth and degree of the impressions as well as the curvature of the mouth arch, the distance between the cuspids (canine teeth), missing teeth, and other features. Bites can leave bruises below the skin. Therefore, if time has elapsed, examination under ultraviolet light may reveal identifiable dentition patterns. Furthermore, DNA evidence may be extracted from bite marks and used to establish identities.

Forensic Odontologists perform many general duties in their work, including:

- preparing reports about their findings and their conclusions regarding forensic examinations
- providing expert witness testimony at depositions and court trials
- certifying the identity of deceased individuals
- designing and overseeing the use of computerized databases of dental records
- instituting forensic dentistry processes
- conferring and cooperating with forensic investigators to collect and analyze evidence
- writing research papers and other documents regarding their findings

Forensic Odontologists occasionally work in unusual environments that expose them to varying climate conditions, dust, smoke, strong smells, or fumes. They are sometimes required to stand or walk for several hours at a time and help with the lifting of bodies or other heavy objects. Their work may be dangerous or they may be exposed to hazardous materials and hence they may be required to wear protective equipment.

Forensic Odontologists usually offer their services as part-time forensic consultants. Most of them continue working in their primary occupation as dentists in private practice or as professors at university dental schools.

Salaries

Specific earnings information for Forensic Odontologists is unavailable. They charge an hourly, daily, or flat rate for initial consultation, examinations, depositions, courtroom testimony, and other services that they offer. Hourly fees generally range from $150 to $250 per hour. Highly experienced consultants earn higher rates. Many consultants charge clients for out-of-pocket expenses such as travel time, telephone calls, and photocopying.

The estimated annual salary for most dentists in general practice ranges between $68,990 and $145,600 per year, according to the May 2006 *Occupational Employment Statistics* survey by the U.S. Bureau of Labor Statistics.

Employment Prospects

Opportunities are favorable for highly reputable and credible Forensic Odonotologists. The prospects for forensic consultants within a location depend on the demand for their particular expertise and on the number of similar consultants in the area. Those willing to travel to other locations have more opportunities to obtain casework.

The job growth for dentists, in general, is expected to increase by 9 to 17 percent through 2014. However, most opportunities will be the result of the large number of dentists who are predicted to retire in these coming years.

Advancement Prospects

Forensic Odontologists realize advancement by earning higher incomes and gaining professional recognition. Many also measure success by being sought out for very complex or publicized cases.

Education and Training

Forensic Odontologists complete four years of dental school to earn a doctor of dental surgery (D.D.S.) degree or a doctor of dental medicine (D.M.D.) degree. Their dental education includes such basic health science courses as physiology, anatomy, microbiology, biochemistry, and histology. Students also complete clinical training under the supervision of licensed dentists, and learn fundamental practice management, such as communicating with patients, managing dental office staff, and professional ethics.

The competition for entry into dental school is intense. The minimum educational requirement for entry is two years of college work, but most applicants possess a bachelor's degree. Dental schools also consider applicants' Dental Admissions Test (DAT) scores, their grade point averages, their recommendations, and other factors when selecting new students.

Dentists can obtain training in forensic odontology from university programs and professional associations.

Throughout their careers, Forensic Odontologists enroll in continuing education and training programs to update their skills and keep up with advancements in their field.

Special Requirements

Forensic Odontologists must be licensed dentists in the state where they practice. Licensing requirements vary with each state. Many states, for example, require that candidates are graduates of a dental school accredited by the Commission on Dental Accreditation, which operates under the American Dental Association.

Experience, Special Skills, and Personality Traits

Forensic Odontologists typically work for several years as dentists or professors before entering this field.

To succeed at consulting work, Forensic Odontologists must have strong organizational, writing, and self-management skills. They also need excellent communication, interpersonal, and teamwork skills, as they must be able to work well with police officers, forensic pathologists, and various others. They also need strong small-business skills.

Some personality traits that successful Forensic Odontologists share include being trustworthy, reliable, methodical, analytical, and self-motivated.

Unions and Associations

Many Forensic Odontologists join professional associations to take advantage of networking opportunities and other professional resources and services. Some forensic societies include the American Society of Forensic Odontology, the American Board of Forensic Odontology, the American College of Forensic Examiners, and the American Academy of Forensic Sciences. Many of these forensic experts also join the American Dental Association, the national society that serves the interests of all dentists. For contact information, see Appendix III.

Tips for Entry

1. High school students who are interested in a dental career need to take courses that prepare them for college. This usually involves taking at least three years of math, two years of science, three years of social sciences, four years of English, and two years of a foreign language.

2. To gain forensic odontology experience, you might volunteer to help experienced forensic experts with their casework.

3. To enhance their employability and professional creditability, Forensic Odontologists obtain professional certification. For information about certification programs, see Appendix II.

4. Many Forensic Odontologists give presentations to health professionals, law enforcement, and forensic colleagues, as well as publish articles in professional journals to help develop their professional reputation.

5. Use the Internet to learn more about Forensic Odontologists. You might start by visiting the ForensicDentistry Online Web site at http://www.forensicdentistryonline.org. For more links, see Appendix IV.

FORENSIC PHARMACIST

CAREER PROFILE

Duties: Provide forensic consulting services to attorneys, law enforcement agencies, insurance companies, pharmaceutical companies, and other clients; perform duties as required

Alternate Title(s): Forensic Consultant

Salary Range: $68,000 to $119,000

Employment Prospects: Fair

Advancement Prospects: Poor

Prerequisites:

Education or Training—Pharmacy school training

Experience—Several years of work experience

Special Skills and Personality Traits— Organizational, writing, communication, interpersonal, and analytical skills; dependable, conscientious, trustworthy, curious, persistent, and detail-oriented

Special Requirements—Pharmacist license required

CAREER LADDER

```
┌─────────────────────────────┐
│     Forensic Pharmacist     │
└─────────────────────────────┘

┌─────────────────────────────┐
│  Novice Forensic Pharmacist │
└─────────────────────────────┘

┌─────────────────────────────┐
│         Pharmacist          │
└─────────────────────────────┘
```

Position Description

When doctors prescribe medicines, pharmacists prepare and dispense those medications to patients. Pharmacists work in the pharmacy departments of hospitals, clinics, and nursing homes, as well as in drug stores and drug manufacturing companies. These health care professionals are highly knowledgeable about the attributes and correct use of both prescription and nonprescription medications and how they interact with food or other medicines. They also understand the chemical properties of medications. Pharmacists draw upon this knowledge to confer with physicians and to counsel patients regarding the proper use of medicines. While most pharmacists dispense manufactured medicines, a few pharmacists compound medications themselves by mixing the ingredients to make the liquids or powders that constitute the medicines.

Pharmacists also specialize in many ways. Their work is needed in the military and other government entities such as the Food and Drug Administration (FDA), the Drug Enforcement Agency, or the Centers for Disease Control and Prevention. They work for heath maintenance organizations and other health insurance providers. Many pharmacists are involved in research with private industrial drug manufacturing companies or at universities, where they also teach. Pharmacists work with terminally ill patients in hospice programs, develop radiopharmaceuticals for cancer treatments, or design nutritional supplements. In addition, pharmacists work in such areas as chemistry, pharmacology, medication management, and pharmacy law.

One particular specialty is forensic pharmacy. Experts in this area, known as Forensic Pharmacists, apply the science of medications to matters pertaining to law such as fraud, litigation, regulatory affairs, and criminal justice. They are knowledgeable in various subjects, including medicine, pharmacy procedure, toxicology, pharmacology, chemistry, psychology, accounting, document examination, and accident reconstruction, among others.

Most Forensic Pharmacists work as part-time consultants who provide forensic services in addition to their full-time clinical, research, or pharmacy work. They offer their services to attorneys, law enforcement agencies, government agencies, insurance companies, hospitals, pharmacies, health care providers, pharmaceutical companies, medical publishers, schools, and other organizations and industries. These forensic specialists are consulted about a number of issues involving drugs and medications. For example, they may be engaged in cases that involve evaluating or investigating:

- medication errors
- prescription forgery
- policies and procedures for the dispensation of drugs
- violations of FDA regulations
- product tampering
- drug patents
- insurance fraud
- workers' compensation claims
- use of drugs or alcohol in car accidents or violent actions
- legal and illegal pharmaceutical evidence in criminal investigations
- use of abused drugs in the workplace
- professional malpractice
- quackery and health care fraud

Many Forensic Pharmacists offer litigation support services to attorneys, who may work for either the defense or the plaintiff. They may be involved in criminal cases, civil litigation, or regulatory matters. Forensic Pharmacists perform such general litigation support tasks as analyzing and evaluating cases to help lawyers determine whether they should be brought to trial, helping lawyers to determine the facts of a case, gathering evidence, interviewing witnesses, formulating lists of questions that lawyers would ask witnesses, and so on. Additionally and more specifically, Forensic Pharmacists may assist and educate attorneys by addressing such topics as chemical and drug toxicity, pharmacy standards, drug interactions, medical malpractice, poisoning, illegal dispensing of controlled substances, and product liability as they pertain to cases involving drugs or medications. They may assist with written reports, depositions, and document reviews.

Forensic Pharmacists perform certain tasks with each project. They collect data, which may involve conducting tests, gathering literature, and interviewing people. They review pertinent records, reports, and other materials that are related to their cases. They analyze and interpret data (such as laboratory tests), and prepare comprehensive reports about their medical and scientific findings. When required, Forensic Pharmacists provide expert testimony in court proceedings.

Some Forensic Pharmacists also offer educational services. For example, organizations may hire them to provide technical instruction such as drug testing information to law enforcement officials, sports officials, industry leaders, or others.

Forensic Pharmacists can choose to apply their expertise and skills in other legal arenas. For example, they may take jobs as forensic toxicologists and work in medical examiners' or coroners' offices. They may work as forensic chemists in crime labs associated with law enforcement agencies, prosecuting attorneys' offices, or other government agencies.

Forensic Pharmacists who work for government agencies inspect pharmacies and drug industry facilities, enforce laws pertaining to the use of medicines, or oversee the adherence to purity standards in drug manufacturing. Some are members of governing pharmacy boards or work for state health departments.

Consulting Forensic Pharmacists work standard 40-hour weeks but may put in additional hours as needed to complete their various tasks. They may be required to travel to other locations to provide forensic services.

Salaries

Specific earnings information for Forensic Pharmacists is unavailable. As consultants, they charge an hourly, daily, or flat rate for initial consultation, assessments, depositions, courtroom testimony, and other services that they offer. In addition, many of them charge clients for out-of-pocket expenses such as travel time, telephone calls, and photocopying.

The estimated annual salary for most pharmacists ranges between $67,860 and $119,480 according to the May 2006 *Occupational Employment Statistics* survey by the U.S. Bureau of Labor Statistics (BLS).

Employment Prospects

Opportunities are favorable for experienced Forensic Pharmacists. The prospects for forensic consultants within a location depend on the demand for their particular expertise and on the number of similar consultants in the area.

Employment for pharmacists, in general, is expected to grow by 18 to 26 percent through 2014, according to the BLS. This is partly due to the aging of the baby boomer population and the rise in their pharmaceutical needs. Additionally, new drugs are being developed and marketed each year.

Advancement Prospects

Forensic Pharmacists realize advancement through job satisfaction, professional recognition, and higher incomes. Those working on a part-time basis might pursue successful full-time careers as independent practitioners or owners of firms that offer forensic services.

Education and Training

To become a pharmacist, individuals must complete four years of pharmacy school to earn a doctor of pharmacy (Pharm.D.) degree. The degree program includes course work in pharmaceutical chemistry, pharmacognosy, pharmacology, business management, and pharmacy practice. Students also complete lab work as well as clinical training under the supervision of licensed pharmacists.

The minimum educational requirement for entry into most pharmacy schools is the completion of two years of college. Some pharmacy schools require that applicants possess a bachelor's degree. Some pharmacy schools have special six-year programs that admit recent high school graduates. If students successfully complete the first two years of pre-pharmacy study, they are then admitted into the pharmacy degree program.

Throughout their careers, Forensic Pharmacists enroll in continuing education programs and training programs to update their skills and keep up with advancements in their fields.

Special Requirements

Forensic Pharmacists must be licensed in the state where they practice. Licensing requirements vary with each state. For specific information, contact the proper state board of pharmacy.

Experience, Special Skills, and Personality Traits

In general, pharmacists should have several years of experience in pharmaceutical practice prior to entering the forensic consulting arena.

To perform well at their work, Forensic Pharmacists must have excellent organizational, writing, communication, interpersonal, and analytical skills. Some personality traits that successful Forensic Pharmacists share include being dependable, conscientious, trustworthy, curious, persistent, and detail-oriented.

Unions and Associations

Forensic Pharmacists typically join professional associations that serve their particular interests at the local, state, or national level. By joining one or more societies, they can take advantage of networking opportunities, professional certification, job referral services, and other professional services and resources. Some national associations include:

- American College of Clinical Pharmacology
- American College of Clinical Pharmacy
- American College of Forensic Examiners
- American Pharmacists Association
- American Society for Pharmacy Law
- National Community Pharmacists Association
  For contact information, see Appendix III.

Tips for Entry

1. As a high school or college student, you can get an idea if the pharmacy field is right for you. For example, you might get a part-time job working in a pharmacy.
2. Many pharmacy colleges prefer to choose applicants who have volunteer or paid experience working with patients in a pharmacy, hospital, nursing home, or another health-related setting.
3. To enhance their credibility, many pharmacists obtain professional certification in the areas in which they specialize. For some certification programs, see Appendix II.
4. As a professional, develop a marketing plan that targets the clientele for whom you wish to work. Consult with marketing experts for help if you lack knowledge or skills in this business area.
5. Use the Internet to learn more about a career in pharmacy in general. You might start by visiting the American Association of Colleges of Pharmacy Web site at http://www.aacp.org. For more links, see Appendix IV.

FORENSIC RADIOLOGIST

CAREER PROFILE

Duties: Provide forensic consulting services to law enforcement agencies, medical examiners' offices, and other clients; use and interpret medical images (such as X-rays) to assist in criminal investigations; perform duties as required

Alternate Title(s): Forensic Consultant

Salary Range: $45,000 to $146,000+

Employment Prospects: Good

Advancement Prospects: Poor

Prerequisites:

Education or Training—Medical school degree, radiology residency training

Experience—Several years of work experience

Special Skills and Personality Traits—Analytical, communication, interpersonal, writing, and organizational skills; observant, methodical, detail-oriented, self-motivated, accurate, and trustworthy

Special Requirements—Physician licensure required; board certification may be required

CAREER LADDER

```
┌─────────────────────────────────┐
│      Forensic Radiologist       │
└─────────────────────────────────┘

┌─────────────────────────────────┐
│   Novice Forensic Radiologist   │
└─────────────────────────────────┘

┌─────────────────────────────────┐
│          Radiologist            │
└─────────────────────────────────┘
```

Position Description

Radiology is a medical specialty. Radiologists are doctors who use medical images such as X-rays, magnetic resonance imaging (MRI), computerized axial tomography (CAT) scans, ultrasound, and other technologies to diagnose and treat injuries or diseases. Some radiologists, known as Forensic Radiologists, use their knowledge and skills to interpret the information gathered from such medical images for purposes that concern the law and the courts. Upon the request of law enforcement investigators, medical examiners and coroners, attorneys, and others, Forensic Radiologists provide input into the investigation of disease, injury, impairment, and death.

These forensic specialists apply their expertise to various types of criminal matters such as spousal, elderly, or child abuse; murders and attempted murders; fraud; theft; forgery; and terrorism. They might work in the areas of bite mark analysis, forensic dental analysis, and the study of gunshot wounds. They also contribute to investigations concerning drug trafficking. For example, their imaging techniques may be used to reveal the presence of drugs inserted into smuggling suspects' body cavities.

Forensic Radiologists provide insight into physical evidence that cannot be seen, unlike such evidence as fingerprints, bullet casings, and bloodstains. For example, these doctors might assist forensic investigators by helping them to locate bullets lodged in victims and track the paths the bullets made within the bodies. In addition, Forensic Radiologists might be called upon to examine guns to determine if they contain bullets or to read altered serial numbers on them.

Many medical examiners' and coroners' offices utilize the services of Forensic Radiologists to help ascertain the cause of death, as well as identify decomposed bodies recovered from the scenes of natural or manmade disasters. These medical specialists can use medical technologies to help determine injuries that were inflicted before and after the death of victims of crime or disasters. They may also be able to establish if bone cancer or other disease may be the cause of death. In addition, Forensic Radiologists may be able to determine the age of skeletal remains and learn if bones are human or non-human.

Like other forensic experts, Forensic Radiologists present their clients with written reports that summarize their findings and conclusions. When required, they provide expert testimony in court proceedings.

Forensic Radiologists generally offer their services as consultants on a part-time basis. Their primary job may be in teaching or in medical practice. They are responsible for completing specific tasks in their general practice as well as in their capacity as Forensic Radiologists. They may:

- work with other physicians, technicians, and specialists
- direct the activities of radiology technologists
- consult with referring physicians to interpret medical images and decide how to use them
- maintain image files for several years for availability to other physicians, patients, or the courts
- stay current with medical and technical advances

Forensic Radiologists work in hospitals or in private medical offices. They may put in long hours and be available to work at any time of the day or night. These doctors use imaging techniques that use radiation. Consequently, their understanding of safety and protective measures is essential. They may be exposed to unpleasant sights and smells when they work on forensic cases.

Salaries

Specific salary information for Forensic Radiologists is unavailable. As consultants, Forensic Radiologists may charge an hourly, daily, or flat rate for examinations, depositions, courtroom testimony, and other services that they offer. Consultants are usually reimbursed for their out-of-pocket expenses such as travel time and telephone calls.

The U.S. Bureau of Labor Statistics reports in its May 2006 *Occupational Employment Statistics* survey that the estimated annual salary for most physicians, who were listed separately, was between $45,160 and $145,600. According to the Salary.com Web site (http://www.salary.com), the median annual salary for radiologists was $279,689 in December 2006.

Employment Prospects

Radiology is an essential tool in the diagnosis and treatment of patients; hence there will always be a need for radiologists. Some experts in the field report that there is a shortage of qualified radiologists, which is expected to continue for the next few years.

Forensic radiology is a young, small field. In general, the job outlook for qualified Forensic Radiologists is favorable.

Advancement Prospects

Forensic Radiologists realize advancement by earning higher incomes and gaining professional recognition. Many also measure success by being sought out for very complex or publicized cases.

Education and Training

Forensic Radiologists complete about 13 years of training before they can practice radiology. They must first earn a bachelor's degree, which may be in any field, then complete four years of medical school to earn a doctor of medicine (M.D.) degree or a doctor of osteopathy (D.O.) degree. This is followed by one year of general residency training and then four years of a diagnostic radiology residency. After completing the residency, they may begin their practice or obtain a fellowship to train in a radiologic subspecialty, such as MRI, musculoskeletal imaging, or pediatric radiology. Fellowship programs are generally one to two years long.

Throughout their careers, Forensic Radiologists enroll in continuing education and training programs to update their skills and keep up with advancements in their fields.

Special Requirements

Forensic Radiologists must be licensed physicians in the jurisdictions where they practice. For licensure requirements, contact the appropriate state medical board.

Many employers prefer to hire consultants who are board-certified radiologists. Medical doctors obtain board certification from the American Board of Radiology, while osteopathic doctors obtain theirs from the American Osteopathic Board of Radiology.

Experience, Special Skills, and Personality Traits

Radiologists have typically been in practice for several years before offering forensic radiology services.

To perform well as Forensic Radiologists, individuals must have excellent analytical, communication, interpersonal, writing, and organizational skills. Being observant, methodical, detail-oriented, self-motivated, accurate, and trustworthy are some personality traits that successful radiologists have in common.

Unions and Associations

Forensic Radiologists can join professional associations to take advantage of networking opportunities, continuing education, and other professional resources and services. Some national societies that serve their interests are the Radiological Society of North America and the American Academy of Forensic Sciences. For contact information, see Appendix III.

Tips for Entry

1. To increase your professional credibility and visibility, you might write articles and make presentations about your specialty.
2. Contact medical examiners' offices, crime labs, and law enforcement agencies to discuss how your forensic services may be helpful and useful for their investigations.
3. Use the Internet to learn more about the field of forensic radiology. To get a list of relevant Web sites, enter either of these keywords into a search engine: *forensic radiology* or *forensic radiologists*. For some links, see Appendix IV.

FORENSIC EXPERTS
IN THE NATURAL SCIENCES

ENVIRONMENTAL FORENSICS EXPERT

CAREER PROFILE

Duties: Provide consulting services to attorneys and various other clients; address legal and liability issues regarding contaminated sites; perform duties as required

Alternate Title(s): Environmental Consultant; Forensic Geochemist, Hydrogeologist, or other title that reflects a particular profession

Salary Range: $35,000 to $136,000

Employment Prospects: Poor

Advancement Prospects: Fair

Prerequisites:

Education or Training—Doctoral degree in a science or engineering field

Experience—Several years of work experience in their field

Special Skills and Personality Traits—Project-management, teamwork, interviewing, computer, writing, interpersonal, and communication skills; cooperative, inquisitive, diligent, detail-oriented, honest, trustworthy, unbiased, and conscientious

CAREER LADDER

```
┌─────────────────────────────────────┐
│   Environmental Forensics Expert     │
└─────────────────────────────────────┘

┌─────────────────────────────────────┐
│ Novice Environmental Forensics Expert│
└─────────────────────────────────────┘

┌─────────────────────────────────────┐
│   Geologist, or Another Profession   │
└─────────────────────────────────────┘
```

Position Description

Over many decades, pollution has emanated from industrial plants, waste disposal sites, fuel storage tanks, pipelines, and other sources to cause millions of dollars of damage to nearby soil or groundwater supplies. In recent years, environmental forensics has emerged in response to legal matters concerning environmental contamination, namely polluted soil and groundwater issues. The scientists and engineers who work in this field—Environmental Forensics Experts—apply scientific analyses to address legal and liability issues in civil disputes, regulatory matters, insurance claims, or criminal investigations.

The role of these forensic specialists is to identify the source of pollutants at a contaminated site and determine how pollutants got to the site, find out when pollutants were released into the environment, and reconstruct past releases. They also establish the extent of the pollution and how it has impacted the area. Furthermore, they determine who is responsible for the contamination of a site, as well as assign costs for cleaning up the contaminated site.

Environmental Forensics is a multidisciplinary field. Experts in this specialty have backgrounds as chemists, geochemists, geologists, hydrologists, environmental scientists, environmental engineers, and biologists, among other professions. They draw upon a broad understanding of various disciplines, including biology, chemistry, geology, hydrology, ecology, physics, statistics, and forensic science, to determine an appropriate and systematic approach to resolving particular problems.

Environmental Forensics Experts use various investigative tools to build a case as to what transpired at a contamination site and which individuals or entities are responsible. They review the history of a contaminated site, study the soil, analyze the flow of groundwater in the area, analyze the source and identity of chemical pollutants (known as the chemical fingerprint), and create a mathematical model to simulate groundwater conditions. They read documents including press releases and corporate records, take aerial photographs, extract samples from the soil and groundwater, and inspect facilities in the course of their investigative work. Furthermore, they trace the course of contaminant spills to determine their origin and permeation into the soil and groundwater.

Forensic Environmental Specialists are retained by attorneys to assist with environmental litigation and insurance claims. They perform various litigation support tasks, such as:

- reviewing cases to identify the technical issues and facts
- teaching lawyers about technical and scientific facts
- collecting soil and groundwater samples as physical evidence
- reviewing environmental reports written by colleagues
- searching records for property transactions, production facility construction data, and other relevant information regarding a contamination site
- conducting research to answer complex scientific and engineering questions
- performing tests to prove or disprove certain facts or issues
- interviewing various professionals, technicians, operators, administrators, and others to obtain data and information
- identifying expert witnesses to testify about certain issues or facts
- addressing strategy issues with attorneys regarding the best way to deal with cases
- developing allocation models for determining financial responsibility
- preparing reports that can be used in settlement negotiations
- creating technical diagrams, charts, databases, models, animations, and other pieces of demonstrative evidence to help judges and juries, regulators, and others understand specific issues or facts
- giving presentations for interrogatory panels or court proceedings

These forensic experts may also serve as expert witnesses at depositions, trials, and administrative hearings. They give sworn professional opinions about facts and issues related to a case. They provide unbiased and impartial testimony; they do not support or oppose the arguments of the lawyers that have hired them, nor those of the opposing attorneys.

These forensic experts are also retained by clients in various industries to perform other services. For example, petroleum and chemical companies might hire Environmental Forensic Experts to determine if they are in compliance with all the proper environmental laws, regulations, and codes.

Environmental Forensics Experts work in offices, laboratories, and in the field. They continually stay up to date with the latest environmental or chemical issues and tactics for confronting them. They also learn and utilize new investigation techniques including computer modeling. They are frequently exposed to toxic chemicals; consequently, they

may be required to wear special clothing or other protective equipment.

Salaries

Specific wage information for Environmental Forensics Experts is unavailable. As consultants, they charge an hourly, daily, or flat rate for initial consultation, depositions, courtroom testimony, and other services that they offer. They may also charge for out-of-pocket expenses, such as travel time, photocopying, and phone calls.

A general idea of their earnings can be gained by looking at wages for the different professionals who work in this specialty. The following are estimated annual salary ranges for some professions, as reported by the U.S. Bureau of Labor Statistics in its May 2006 *Occupational Employment Statistics* survey:

- chemists, $35,480 to $106,310
- environmental scientists, $34,590 to $94,670
- geoscientists, $39,740 to $135,950

Employment Prospects

Since the late 1990s, environmental forensics has been an emerging field. Some experts say that opportunities should grow nationally, as well as worldwide, due to the constant increase in complex environmental regulations.

Many Environmental Forensics Experts work for environmental or geotechnical firms that offer environmental forensics services. Some are independent practitioners. Others are academicians or researchers who offer forensic consulting services on a part-time basis.

Advancement Prospects

In private firms, individuals can advance to senior positions, which may include supervisory and managerial duties. Forensic specialists with entrepreneurial ambitions may become successful independent consultants or owners of firms that offer environmental forensics services and other services.

Many Environmental Forensics Experts measure success by earning higher wages, being assigned more complex cases, and gaining professional recognition.

Education and Training

Although there are no standard requirements for this field, most, if not all, Environmental Forensics Experts possess a doctoral degree. They hold degrees in geology, chemistry, geochemistry, environmental science, environmental engineering, hydrology, or another related field.

Earning a doctorate takes many years of study. Students must first complete a four-year bachelor's degree program, followed by a one- to two-year master's program. They then enter a doctoral program, which requires a few more years of study. Doctoral candidates must write a book-length dissertation that is based on original research. Upon earning their doctorates, many graduates obtain one or more fellowships to continue training and gaining experience in their specialties.

Throughout their careers, Environmental Forensics Experts enroll in continuing education programs and training programs to update their skills and keep up with advancements in their fields.

Experience, Special Skills, and Personality Traits

Typically, Environmental Forensics Experts have many years of work experience in their field before they embark on a career in forensic consulting. Employers hire candidates who have several years of work experience in their field performing environmental consulting or related services. Potential clients seek consultants who are highly accomplished and recognized in their field. In addition, they prefer to retain consultants who have the necessary knowledge, skills, and experience to successfully complete their projects.

Environmental Forensics Experts need excellent project-management, teamwork, interviewing, computer, and writing skills to perform well at their work. In addition, they need strong interpersonal and communication skills, as they must be able to work well with various people from diverse backgrounds. Being cooperative, inquisitive, diligent, detail-oriented, honest, trustworthy, unbiased, and conscientious are some personality traits that successful experts share.

Unions and Associations

Forensic Environmental Specialists can join professional associations to take advantage of networking opportunities, continuing education, publications, and other professional resources and services. One society that specifically serves the interests of these forensic experts is the International Society of Environmental Forensics. For contact information, see Appendix III.

Tips for Entry

1. While in college, obtain an internship with an environmental forensics firm to begin gaining experience.
2. Some employers find that the most desirable candidates are knowledgeable in one or more of the following subjects: programming, geographical information systems (GIS), statistics, analytical chemistry, and environmental chemistry.
3. As of 2006, there were no formal degree programs in environmental forensics in the United States. However, many professional societies, private firms, and other organizations offer training programs in this specialty.
4. Use the Internet to learn more about environmental forensics. To obtain a list of relevant Web sites, enter the keywords *environmental forensics*. For some links, see Appendix IV.

FORENSIC ARCHAEOLOGIST

CAREER PROFILE

Duties: Provide forensic consulting services to law enforcement agencies and others; locate and excavate human remains and material evidence at crime scenes and other sites; perform other duties as required

Alternate Title(s): Forensic Consultant

Salary Range: $29,000 to $109,000

Employment Prospects: Poor

Advancement Prospects: Fair

Prerequisites:

Education or Training—A master's or doctoral degree in anthropology, archaeology, or another related discipline

Experience—Several years of field experience

Special Skills and Personality Traits—Organizational, analytical, teamwork, interpersonal, and communication skills; dedicated, meticulous, trustworthy, curious, and compassionate

CAREER LADDER

Forensic Archaeologist

Novice Forensic Archaeologist

Archaeologist

Position Description

Forensic Archaeologists make up another emerging breed of forensic specialists who apply their science to legal matters. Archaeologists, in general, study human history and prehistory by examining buildings, tools, and other artifacts that they have uncovered from beneath the ground. These scientists use various techniques to locate, map, and excavate ancient sites, as well as to reconstruct historic events that occurred at those sites.

Forensic Archaeologists use their knowledge and skills to help authorities in criminal investigations, particularly with locating clandestine graves as well as recovering human remains and physical evidence at crime scenes. They also help in the investigation of war crimes and genocide by studying mass burials. In addition, they assist at disaster scenes. For example, they might search bomb blast sites or areas hit by violent storms to recover bodies and evidence for analysis in the course of the investigations of these occurrences.

These professionals rely on their archaeological expertise but are also knowledgeable about such other disciplines as anthropology, chemistry, biology, botany, geology, and engineering. They use various technologies to aid them in

their work, including surveying equipment, metal detectors, ground-penetrating radar, satellite imaging, and aerial photography. These forensic experts have specialized training in evidence collection and crime scene analysis. They utilize such forensic techniques as DNA testing, radiocarbon dating, and skull reconstruction.

Forensic Archaeologists follow specific procedures and protocol as they excavate crime scenes, disaster scenes, and other sites. They work carefully and accurately to ensure that evidence is not contaminated and the chain of custody is maintained.

Unless other investigators have uncovered bodies, Forensic Archaeologists need to locate the graves. These forensic scientists prefer that the scene be as undisturbed and secured as possible. They use sensing devices to locate graves or study the terrain for telltale signs of burials. Forensic Archaeologists create a grid at the scene by using string and markers located at specific points. They map the area in detail by sketching and photographing the surroundings with meticulous attention to detail.

When they locate a hidden grave, Forensic Archaeologists carefully open it while noting such details as what tools were used to dig the grave, which strata (layers) of the soil were disturbed, and which artifacts were also left behind. Furthermore, they carefully examine each section of their grid for further evidence that may have been left behind. They use small digging tools and sift the soil through screens to find small artifacts that lie beneath the surface. They collect or tag evidence at the site for further analysis or submission to the authorities.

These professionals use standard archaeological analytical procedures to determine and reconstruct the events that transpired at the scene between the time the graves were created and the time they were discovered. They add details of the uncovered graves to their maps, including cross sections to indicate the depth of the grave and the position of the body and artifacts found therein. Each section of the grid is numbered for reference and all artifacts are listed according to which sections of the grid they were found. Forensic Archaeologists include their maps and illustrations in clearly written reports, which can be easily understood by law enforcement officers, attorneys, and others.

By using the reports that Forensic Archaeologists provide, investigators are able to verify witness testimony, recreate how a victim died, and connect a victim to an assailant or disastrous event. They can also determine whether the decedent died at the scene or elsewhere, as well as establish whether artifacts found at the scene are evidence of a crime. Furthermore, they can finalize their investigations for presentation in court trials or other investigative hearings.

Forensic Archaeologists may be called upon to testify as expert witnesses at court trials. They provide impartial and unbiased testimony on issues related to their analyses as well as the procedures, methods, and techniques that they use.

In every investigation Forensic Archaeologists work closely with other professionals. They work alongside law enforcement officers, crime scene investigators, and medicolegal investigators. They also work with other forensic specialists. For example, forensic artists and photographers might make sketches, maps, and photos of locations under investigation; and forensic botanists and forensic entomologists might assist with the analysis of vegetation and insects that are found at the crime scenes.

Most Forensic Archaeologists are part-time consultants. Many of them are employed full time as academicians or museum employees. They perform duties that are specific to their primary archaeology profession. For example, they may teach, conduct research, and perform fieldwork at archaeological sites; maintain museum collections and design exhibits; serve as museum administrators; publish scholarly papers; or assist government agencies with the management of archaeological resources.

Forensic Archaeologists work in indoor settings such as offices or classrooms. At outdoor burial or disaster sites, they encounter unusual conditions that provide a challenge to their calm and controlled professional manner. Other

investigators, survivors, or victims' families at the scene can provide distraction. The sight of burned corpses or scattered body parts may be disturbing. Forensic Archaeologists need to be physically adept to work meticulously at digging and sifting soil or lifting heavy items. They generally conduct their fieldwork in favorable climate conditions but may be required to work in inclement weather or difficult terrain.

Salaries

Specific salary information for Forensic Archaeologists is unavailable. As consultants, they charge an hourly, daily, or flat rate for initial consultation, depositions, courtroom testimony, and other services that they offer.

Most archaeologists, in general, earn an estimated annual salary that ranged between $28,940 and $81,490, according to the May 2006 *Occupational Employment Statistics* survey by the U.S. Bureau of Labor Statistics (BLS). The estimated annual salary for archaeology professors ranged from $37,590 to $109,330.

Employment Prospects

Forensic archaeology is a young and small occupation; hence, job opportunities are limited. However, the demand for these experts is growing as their services become more widely recognized. Most Forensic Archaeologists are part-time consultants. A few are employed full time by the Federal Bureau of Investigation (FBI), the Joint MIA/POW Accounting Command (JPAC) of the U.S. Army, and other federal agencies.

Most archaeologists are employed by colleges and universities. Other employers of archaeologists include museums and government agencies such as the U.S. National Park Service, U.S. Army Corps of Engineers, state park departments, and state historic preservation offices. Some archaeologists work for private companies that conduct law-mandated archaeological surveys to locate and excavate historic or prehistoric sites on land slated for construction.

Employment for archaeologists, in general, is predicted to increase by 9 to 17 percent through 2014, according to the BLS. Much of the growth is expected to be in the management, scientific, and technical consulting services industry, which includes forensic consulting.

Advancement Prospects

Forensic Archaeologists generally measure success through job satisfaction, professional recognition, and by being sought out for highly complex or publicized cases.

College and university instructors typically seek tenure-track positions. Once they gain tenure at an institution, they cannot be fired without just cause and due process. Academicians advance by rising through the ranks from instructor to full professor. They can also pursue managerial and administrative positions, from department chair to academic dean to the position of provost or president.

Education and Training

Minimally, individuals wishing to become Forensic Archaeologists should possess a master's degree in anthropology or archaeology. Individuals will need a doctoral degree if they plan to teach in universities or colleges or become a museum curator. A master's program generally takes one to two years to complete. After earning a master's degree, doctoral candidates must fulfill another two to three (or more) years of study to earn their degree. They must write a book-length dissertation that is based on original research. With either the master's or doctoral program, future Forensic Archaeologists complete formal course work in field archaeology, laboratory analysis, and osteology. In addition, graduate students are required to do fieldwork in which they participate in excavations under the supervision of their professors.

Throughout their careers, Forensic Archaeologists enroll in continuing education programs to update their skills and keep up with advancements in their fields.

Experience, Special Skills, and Personality Traits

In general, individuals wishing to become Forensic Archaeologists should have several years of field experience, including participation in excavating historic burial sites.

Like other forensic specialists, Forensic Archaeologists need excellent organizational, analytical, teamwork, interpersonal, and communication skills. Being dedicated, meticulous, trustworthy, curious, and compassionate are some personality traits that successful Forensic Archaeologists share.

Unions and Associations

The Society for American Archaeology, the Registry of Professional Archaeologists, the American Anthropological Association, and the American Academy of Forensic Sciences are a few national societies that Forensic Archaeologists are eligible to join. (For contact information, see Appendix III.) By joining professional associations, Forensic Archaeologists can take advantage of job listings, current research data, networking opportunities, and other professional resources and services.

Tips for Entry

1. As a high school student you can begin learning more about archaeology and its specialty areas. You can read books and magazines about the field, watch television programs that feature archaeological subjects, and visit archaeological sites and museums. If possible, volunteer on an archaeological dig.

2. Would you be able to handle human remains? To get an idea, volunteer or obtain a part-time job at your local coroner's or medical examiner's office.

3. One expert in the field recommends taking courses in physical anthropology and human biology, as Forensic Archaeologists need a strong background in the human skeleton.

4. Obtain a research assistantship or volunteer to work on projects for a professor who specializes in forensic archaeology.

5. Learn more about forensic archaeology on the Internet. To find relevant Web sites, enter the keywords *forensic archaeology* or *forensic archaeologists* into a search engine. For some links, see Appendix IV.

FORENSIC BOTANIST

CAREER PROFILE

Duties: Provide forensic consulting services to law enforcement agencies and others; identify, analyze, and interpret botanical evidence; perform duties as required

Alternate Title(s): Forensic Consultant

Salary Range: $38,000 to $146,000

Employment Prospects: Poor

Advancement Prospects: Fair

Prerequisites:

Education or Training—A doctoral degree in botany or another related field

Experience—Several years of experience in field

Special Skills and Personality Traits—Self-management, organizational, communication, and interpersonal skills; patient, objective, diligent, detail-oriented, inquisitive, and trustworthy

CAREER LADDER

```
┌─────────────────────────────┐
│     Forensic Botanist       │
└─────────────────────────────┘

┌─────────────────────────────┐
│   Novice Forensic Botanist  │
└─────────────────────────────┘

┌─────────────────────────────┐
│          Botanist           │
└─────────────────────────────┘
```

Position Description

Botanists are biologists who specialize in the study, identification, and classification of plants—lichens, mosses, ferns, flowers, shrubs, grasses, vines, trees, and so on. These scientists seek to understand the structure and life processes of plants, as well as how plants relate to each other and other living organisms. They also study how plants have developed and changed through time and how plants adapt to their surroundings. Botanists also investigate the practical uses of plants and study the causes and cures of plant diseases. Many botanists devote themselves to studying the biology of particular plant species. Others specialize in such subfields as botany, plant anatomy, physiology, genetics, cytology (cell structure and function), or plant ecology.

Forensic botany is a relatively new subfield. It is a specialty in which scientists apply their botanical expertise to legal matters. Forensic Botanists may be engaged in investigations for criminal or civil cases. Their primary role is to analyze plant evidence to help settle disputes or link criminals to crime scenes or victims.

Forensic Botanists normally work as consultants. They are retained by law enforcement agencies, crime labs, medical examiners' and coroners' offices, attorneys, and other organizations that require expert evaluation of plant evidence.

They might work on such tasks as:

- estimating how long a person has been dead and when the person may have died
- ascertaining if a body had been moved after death or was disturbed in any way
- establishing whether a person had died outdoors and in a particular location
- determining what a person had eaten prior to death
- identifying plant poisons
- detecting secret graves of missing people

Forensic Botanists apply the principles and techniques of their discipline to the analysis of plant evidence. They also utilize an understanding of other biology disciplines, including ecology, molecular biology, palynology (the study of pollen and spores), limnology (the study of fresh water ecology), plant systematics (the relationships between plants and other plants), taxonomy (plant classification), and dendochronology (the study of tree rings), among others.

In addition, they are familiar with forensic principles and methodologies. These scientists, for example, observe a fundamental forensic science principle known as Locard's Exchange Principle that states that whenever a person comes into contact with another person or a place, materials are usually exchanged between contacts. For example, scraps of vegetation from a crime scene may be found on a victim's or suspect's person or attached to other evidence.

Forensic Botanists are able to use various clues from plant material to determine events and timeframes surrounding unexplained deaths and crimes. For example, a suspect might have twigs in his or her hair or a murder victim might grasp a bit of plant material. Forensic Botanists may be able to identify such plant samples and determine where a crime was committed if the samples originated elsewhere. In another example, a body might rest on plant material that is crushed and decayed. By analyzing the decayed material, Forensic Botanists may be able to determine the length of time the body rested in that spot. These scientists can also examine trees or the roots of plants that grow on a clandestine grave, count the growth rings, and estimate when the grave was dug.

Cell walls of plants and the walls around pollen decay very slowly and can remain undamaged for long periods of time. Hence, microscopic plant segments can be identifiable years after a crime was committed or a death occurred. In addition, each plant's cells can be distinguished by their sizes and shapes, which remain unchanged over time, even when digested. By using these facts about plants, Forensic Botanists can help solve crimes in cases where other types of evidence are not available. For example, pollen is always in the air and constantly settles on people and objects. Because pollen content is unique to every geographical area, it can be traced. Forensic Botanists may find traces of pollen on a suspect, murder victim, or other crime scene evidence, and by determining the sources of the pollen, they can establish that a murder took place in another location. In cases of poisoning, Forensic Botanists are able to examine the vegetable contents of a victim's stomach under a microscope and identify the food, measure its level of decay, and determine when the meal was ingested or even where it was consumed.

In most cases, Forensic Botanists analyze plant evidence that has been collected by crime scene investigators. On occasion these forensic specialists go to crime scenes to assist in collecting and processing evidence. They follow specific procedures and preservation techniques to ensure that they have viable samples with which to work. Control samples from the scene and surrounding area are also collected to compare with plant evidence. In addition, Forensic Botanists carefully and accurately document precisely where the plant samples were found while making note of how the samples were associated with their surroundings. Documentation includes written notes, sketches, photographs, and videos, which all complement each other.

Forensic Botanists examine samples in their laboratories, which involves conducting appropriate tests. They are expected to perform their work accurately and correctly. They follow strict procedures and protocols and keep up with current laws of evidence, criminal procedures, and

crime. They make sure that they maintain the chain of custody on every piece of evidence that they handle to ensure that it has not been tampered with or contaminated.

After completing their tests, Forensic Botanists interpret the results of their tests and prepare formal reports that describe their findings and the methods they used to obtain them. Their reports must be comprehensive yet clearly understandable by law enforcement officers, attorneys, judges, and juries.

Forensic Botanists may be called upon to testify as expert witnesses at court trials. They provide impartial and unbiased testimony on issues related to their laboratory analyses as well as about the procedures, methods, and techniques that they use.

Forensic Botanists mostly work in laboratory and office settings. They may travel to reach crime scenes or clandestine gravesites. At these locations, they may endure rough terrain or unfavorable weather, as well as unpleasant sights and odors.

Salaries

Specific salary information for Forensic Botanists is unavailable. As consultants, they charge an hourly, daily, or flat rate for initial consultation, depositions, courtroom testimony, and other services that they offer.

As academicians, botanists earn salaries that vary, depending on such factors as their ranking, employer, and geographic location. The estimated annual salary for most biological science postsecondary teachers ranges between $37,620 and $145,600, according to the May 2006 *Occupational Employment Statistics* survey by the U.S. Bureau of Labor Statistics.

Employment Prospects

Forensic botany is a new field; consequently, the number of opportunities is limited. Currently, most, if not all, Forensic Botanists work on a part-time basis while working full time as college and university professors. As forensic botany becomes more widely recognized, the demand for these experts should increase.

Advancement Prospects

Forensic Botanists generally measure success through job satisfaction, professional recognition, and by being sought for highly complex or publicized cases.

College and university instructors typically seek tenure-track positions. Once they gain tenure at an institution, they cannot be fired without just cause and due process. Academicians advance by rising through the ranks from instructor to full professor. They can also pursue managerial and administrative positions, from department chair to academic dean to the position of provost or president.

Education and Training

Forensic Botanists usually possess a doctoral degree in botany or another biological science discipline. This requires several years of intense training. They first complete a four-year bachelor's degree program, followed by a one- to two-year master's degree program. Upon earning their master's degree, they enroll in a doctoral program, which may take four or more years to finish. To successfully earn their degree, doctoral candidates must write a book-length dissertation based on original research. Upon earning their doctorates, many botanists obtain a postdoctoral position, to continue training in their specialty.

Throughout their careers, Forensic Botanists enroll in continuing education programs to update their skills and keep up with advancements in their fields.

Experience, Special Skills, and Personality Traits

Potential clients seek Forensic Botanists who are highly accomplished and recognized in their field. In addition, they prefer to retain consultants who have the necessary knowledge, skills, and experience to successfully complete their projects.

To succeed at consulting work, Forensic Botanists need excellent self-management, organizational, communication, and interpersonal skills. Being patient, objective, diligent, detail-oriented, inquisitive, and trustworthy are some personality traits that successful Forensic Botanists share.

Unions and Associations

Forensic Botanists can join professional associations to take advantage of networking opportunities, continuing education, professional certification, and other professional resources and services. One national forensic society they might join is the American Academy of Forensic Sciences. Some national societies that serve their particular discipline are the American Society of Plant Biologists, the Botanical Society of America, and the American Institute of Biological Sciences. For contact information, see Appendix III.

Tips for Entry

1. As a high school student, join a youth group that can give you opportunities to learn more about law enforcement or forensic science.
2. Carefully research the graduate schools you might like to attend. Ask questions such as: Does it offer the course work that you want to take? Are there professors with whom you would like to study? Are there Forensic Botanists on staff at a school? Would there be opportunities for you to work on projects with them?
3. If you plan to work for a few years after earning your bachelor's degree, you might apply for a position in a crime lab to gain valuable experience.
4. To gain more visibility for your field and yourself, write articles about forensic botany for trade and professional publications that law enforcement agencies, criminalists, attorneys, judges, and other forensic specialists read.
5. Use the Internet to learn more about forensic botany. To obtain a list of relevant Web sites, enter the keywords *forensic botany* or *forensic botanists* in a search engine. For some links, see Appendix IV.

FORENSIC ENTOMOLOGIST

CAREER PROFILE

Duties: Provide forensic consulting services to law enforcement agencies and others; identify, analyze, and interpret insect evidence; perform duties as required

Alternate Title(s): Forensic Consultant

Salary Range: $38,000 to $146,000

Employment Prospects: Poor

Advancement Prospects: Fair

Prerequisites:

Education or Training—Doctoral degree in entomology, biology, or another related field usually required

Experience—Several years of experience in the field

Special Skills and Personality Traits—Communication, interpersonal, self-management, organizational, analytical, and writing skills; curious, trustworthy, unbiased, meticulous, persistent, and energetic

CAREER LADDER

```
┌─────────────────────────────────┐
│    Forensic Entomologist        │
└─────────────────────────────────┘

┌─────────────────────────────────┐
│  Novice Forensic Entomologist   │
└─────────────────────────────────┘

┌─────────────────────────────────┐
│         Entomologist            │
└─────────────────────────────────┘
```

Position Description

Forensic entomology, or medicocriminal entomology, applies the study of insects and related arthropods (such as spiders, centipedes, and lice) to civil and criminal legal issues. Entomology is a branch of zoology. It is concerned with the classification, distribution, and evolution of all the thousands of insect and related arthropod species. Entomologists, in general, study the structure and life processes of these creatures; their life cycle, behavior, and genetics; their cellular and molecular composition; and their relationships to each other and their surroundings. They also research how insects are beneficial or harmful to humans and the environment. Some of these scientists specialize in the study of specific insects, while others specialize in entomological subfields such as medical, veterinary, conservation, agriculture, or forest entomology.

Forensic entomology is a young subfield, which is the application of this science to medicolegal death investigations. Forensic Entomologists estimate the post-mortem interval (PMI)—the amount of time that passes after the death of the victim. These scientists use insects to make such determinations, as well as to help reveal the probable cause, location, and time of death. Forensic Entomologists are also able to glean other valuable information by studying the insects that live on dead bodies. For example, insect evidence can be used to:

- deduce if a body was disturbed or moved after death
- identify a body by analyzing the DNA of flesh consumed by insects
- determine whether a dead individual used drugs by analyzing accumulated toxins in the insects that fed on the body
- establish whether a suspect was present at the scene of a crime
- ascertain the presence or position of wounds in badly decomposed bodies

Forensic Entomologists have expertise about the life cycle of insects that feed on decomposing flesh. They know that certain insects eat specific parts of bodies at particular intervals. Insects also develop through their life phases from egg to larvae to pupae to adults within a constant timeframe according to each insect species.

These forensic experts also know that variables such as the location of the body and weather conditions can alter the behavior and development cycles of predatory insects. For example, different species live in different geographic areas and consequently devour carcasses at varying rates. Different insects from those found outdoors would consume bodies found in indoor locations. Different insect species consume bodies at different stages of decomposition. Temperature changes and rainfall impact the rate of consumption and decay of a human body as well. A body resting in shade will attract different insects from one left in sunlight. The insects that live underground are different from those that live above the surface. Forensic Entomologists take these factors and more into account when they assist with medicolegal death investigations. Although PMI is at best an estimate, these professionals can determine a fairly accurate PMI by considering the known variables, such as temperature fluctuations and weather conditions at the scene.

Forensic Entomologists occasionally visit death scenes to collect insect evidence. Upon arrival, they observe the scene before entering it and take photographs, record notes on tape and paper, and draw diagrams. They make note of the variables in the local environment. They gather insects directly from the body as well as from the surrounding area and preserve them immediately to ensure that they remain in their current state of development. Forensic Entomologists also obtain more insect samples from the medical examiner or coroner during the autopsy. When they cannot collect evidence directly, they ensure that other investigators make accurate collections.

In addition to medicolegal death investigations, Forensic Entomologists investigate legal issues in the areas of urban pests and stored product pests. They determine monetary damages or physical injuries caused by insects that infest buildings. They investigate crimes committed through the use of insects such as in suspected cases of child neglect or abuse. They assist bloodstain analysts with criminal cases in which insects may have created bloodstains by tracking through blood or leaving flyspecks nearby. Insects have been known to cause automobile and airplane accidents. Forensic Entomologists investigate this type of incident as well. Forensic Entomologists are involved with criminal or civil litigation issues pertaining to food or beverage products contaminated by insects. They determine whether the contamination occurred during or after production.

Forensic Entomologists perform their duties on a consulting basis. They are retained by medical examiners' and coroners' offices, attorneys, the courts, law enforcement agencies, and other organizations.

These experts' general tasks include collecting information, conducting tests, analyzing and interpreting data, and preparing reports of their findings, conclusions, and opinions. They may also provide expert witness testimony in court proceedings and other legal hearings.

Forensic Entomologists are often exposed to unpleasant sights and odors. They mostly work in laboratory and office settings. They may travel to reach crime scenes or clandestine gravesites. At these locations, Forensic Entomologists may endure rough terrain or unfavorable weather.

Salaries

Salary information for Forensic Entomologists is unavailable. As consultants, they charge an hourly, daily, or flat rate for examinations, depositions, courtroom testimony, and other services that they offer. In addition, many of them charge their clients for out-of-pocket expenses such as travel time, telephone calls, and photocopying.

As academicians, entomologists earn salaries that vary, depending on such factors as their ranking, discipline, employer, and geographic location. According to the U.S. Bureau of Labor Statistics in its May 2006 *Occupational Employment Statistics* survey, the estimated annual salary for most biological science postsecondary teachers ranges between $37,620 and $145,600.

Employment Prospects

Forensic entomology is a small but emerging field. Some Forensic Entomologists are independent practitioners. Most others practice on a part-time basis while working in their primary occupation as professors or researchers. Some experts in the field report that opportunities should continue to increase as more law enforcement agencies and medical examiners (and coroners) become aware of this discipline.

Advancement Prospects

Forensic Entomologists generally measure success through job satisfaction, professional recognition, and by being sought for highly complex or publicized cases.

Academicians advance by rising through the ranks from instructor to full professor. They can also pursue managerial and administrative positions, from department chair to academic dean to the position of provost or president.

Education and Training

Forensic Entomologists usually possess a doctoral degree in entomology, biology, zoology, or another related discipline. This requires several years of intense training. They first complete a four-year bachelor's degree program, followed by a one- to two-year master's degree program. Upon earning their master's degree, they enroll in a doctoral program, which may take four or more years to finish. To successfully earn their degree, doctoral candidates must write a book-length dissertation based on original research. Upon earning their doctorates, many entomologists obtain a postdoctoral position to continue training in their specialty.

Throughout their careers, Forensic Entomologists enroll in continuing education programs to update their skills and keep up with advancements in their fields.

Experience, Special Skills, and Personality Traits

Typically, entomologists have practiced for several years in their field before embarking on a career in forensic consulting. Potential clients seek Forensic Entomologists who are highly accomplished and recognized in their field. In addition, they prefer to retain consultants who have the necessary knowledge, skills, and experience to successfully complete their projects.

Forensic Entomologists must have excellent communication and interpersonal skills, as they must be able to work well with law enforcement officers, forensic pathologists, and others. They also need strong self-management, organizational, analytical, and writing skills.

Some personality traits that successful Forensic Entomologists share include being curious, trustworthy, unbiased, meticulous, persistent, and energetic.

Unions and Associations

By joining professional associations, Forensic Entomologists can take advantage of networking opportunities, continuing education, professional certification, and other professional resources and services. Some national societies that serve the general interests of entomologists are the American Entomological Society and the Entomological Society of America. Two forensic societies that these specialists may join are the American Board of Forensic Entomology and the American Academy of Forensic Sciences. For contact information, see Appendix III.

Tips for Entry

1. To gain experience in medicolegal investigations, obtain an internship or part-time job with a medical examiner's or coroner's office.
2. As an expert witness, you must be able to handle the stress of cross-examination. While still a student, attend various criminal and civil trials to get an idea of what different expert witnesses do.
3. Obtain a research assistantship with a professor who does forensic entomology and whose work you respect. If an assistantship is unavailable, then volunteer to work on his or her projects, including casework that comes into his or her lab.
4. To enhance their credibility, many Forensic Entomologists obtain professional certification. For information about some certification programs, see Appendix II.
5. Use the Internet to learn more about forensic entomology. To get a list of relevant Web sites, enter the keywords *forensic entomology* or *forensic entomologists*.

FORENSIC GEOLOGIST

CAREER PROFILE

Duties: Provide forensic consulting services to law enforcement agencies and other clients; identify, analyze, and interpret earth materials evidence; perform duties as required

Alternate Title(s): Forensic Consultant

Salary Range: $37,000 to $136,000

Employment Prospects: Poor

Advancement Prospects: Fair

Prerequisites:

Education or Training—An advanced degree in geology or another related discipline

Experience—Several years of work experience

Special Skills and Personality Traits—Organizational, analytical, self-management, writing, presentation, interpersonal, and communication skills; unbiased, trustworthy, detail-oriented, persistent, inquisitive, and cooperative

CAREER LADDER

```
┌─────────────────────────────┐
│     Forensic Geologist      │
└─────────────────────────────┘

┌─────────────────────────────┐
│  Novice Forensic Geologist  │
└─────────────────────────────┘

┌─────────────────────────────┐
│          Geologist          │
└─────────────────────────────┘
```

Position Description

Forensic Geologists are another group of forensic specialists who apply the principles and techniques of their science to legal matters. Geology is an earth science (also known as a geological science or a geoscience). Geologists examine the materials—rocks, minerals, and soils—that make up the Earth as well as the landforms, such as mountains, volcanoes, valleys, plains, and rivers, on the Earth's surface. These scientists also study the various processes (such as weather, erosion, earthquakes, and tectonics) that shape the Earth, as well as investigate how human activities (such as dredging, mining, and development) affect and change the Earth.

Furthermore, Geologists search for new sources of water, energy, and minerals; they help develop community emergency plans for natural hazards (such as earthquakes, floods, and landslides); and they investigate proposed sites for waste treatment plants, dams, freeways, bridges, harbors, and other structures to make sure they are geologically safe.

Geology is comprised of many subdisciplines, of which forensic geology is one. (Other subdisciplines include mineralogy, hydrology, geophysics, seismology, structural geology, and paleontology, among others.) Forensic geology involves the analysis of soils, rocks, minerals, and fossils and how they impact the investigation of crimes, regulatory violations, insurance claims, and civil disputes.

Forensic Geologists examine earth materials evidence that can be used to help resolve legal or regulatory matters. Basically, Forensic Geologists analyze samples of soil, coal, industrial debris, oils, amber, fossils, sand, inks, paints, and other earth materials found on clothing or property or in groundwater. They attempt to identify their point of origin and whether the samples may offer clues to the identity of crime suspects or help determine how, where, or when disputed events occurred.

Forensic Geologists mostly work in the private sector as consultants. Law enforcement agencies as well as attorneys retain them to examine earth materials evidence in diverse cases such as hit and run vehicle accidents, sexual assaults, murders, or vandalism. These scientists observe a fundamental forensic science principle known as Locard's Exchange Principle, which is attributed to Dr. Edmund Locard, a pioneer in forensic science. Dr. Locard postulated that whenever a person comes into contact with another person or a place, materials are usually exchanged between contacts. Both criminals and victims inadvertently leave soil, grease, or other mineral substances at the scene of a crime, on other evidence, or on clothing. For example, Forensic Geologists might trace stolen crops to the farm from which they were taken by comparing the soil on them to the soil at the farm.

Forensic Geologists can contribute evidence to legal cases that is overlooked by other forensic professionals who do not necessarily look for soil or mineral samples at investigation sites. Geological evidence is of immense value, however, because there are thousands of types of rocks, minerals, and soils, which can all be identified. In the United States alone, there are over 50,000 varieties of soil. Each type of soil was formed and gained its distinctive properties from key factors that vary from one location to another. Consequently, earth material found at any specific point is distinctive.

Forensic Geologists use instruments, particularly specialized microscopes, to closely study earth material samples to identify their unique characteristics. They make note of such features as colors, shapes, and the size and distribution of grains to recognize particular samples. Forensic Geologists make comparisons between samples to determine the point of origin of evidence material. Hence, for example, if a rock or sand found at a crime scene is not normally found at that location, it is quite likely that the suspect can be found at the location of that material's origin.

Forensic Geologists also investigate various issues pertaining to regulatory violations, industrial problems, property claims, environmental hazards, or insurance claims. For example, Forensic Geologists may examine paintings, sculptures, or gems to verify their authenticity for an insurance claim. These professionals may analyze soils or stones used in a construction project to determine the cause of a structural collapse. They may demonstrate how the composition of a road grading material contributed to a car accident. Forensic Geologists may investigate how an occurrence of chemical contamination in soil threatened the health of nearby residents.

Forensic Geologists perform certain tasks when they work on a project. They collect data, which may involve reviewing written materials (such as police reports or insurance claims), testing samples of earth materials, researching literature, and interviewing witnesses. They sometimes visit the crime or incident site. These scientists analyze and interpret the data and form their conclusions. They then prepare well-detailed reports, using clear and concise language to make technical information understandable to lay persons. When requested, they provide expert witness testimony at court proceedings, administrative hearings, or another type of formal event.

Forensic Geologists work in laboratory settings. They also work outdoors at crime scenes, locations where accidents occurred, and at such locations as building sites, groundwater sources, and industrial sites. They may encounter rough terrain and may be required to lift heavy objects.

Salaries

Salary information for Forensic Geologists is unavailable. As consultants, they charge an hourly, daily, or flat rate for initial consultation, depositions, courtroom testimony, and other services that they offer.

According to the May 2006 *Occupational Employment Statistics* survey by the U.S. Bureau of Labor Statistics the estimated annual salary for most geoscientists ranged between $39,740 and $135,950, and for most earth science professors, between $37,330 and $121,500.

Employment Prospects

Some Forensic Geologists are independent practitioners, while others are partners or associates of geological or environmental firms that offer forensic geology services. Some Forensic Geologists are academicians or researchers who offer forensic consulting services on a part-time basis. Public agencies rarely hire Forensic Geologists for staff positions, but with their backgrounds, they may be hired as criminalists or crime scene investigators.

Forensic geology is a small, emerging occupation. Opportunities will continue to grow as the field gains greater familiarity and acceptance by law enforcement agencies, the courts, attorneys, regulatory agencies, and insurance companies.

Advancement Prospects

As forensic consultants, geologists measure success by building their practices, gaining professional recognition, and earning higher incomes. Many also measure success by being sought out for very complex or publicized cases.

Academicians advance by rising through the ranks from instructor to full professor. They can also pursue managerial and administrative positions, from department chair to academic dean to the position of provost or president.

Education and Training

Individuals planning to become Forensic Geologists should have at least a master's degree in geology, physics, or another related field. To teach in four-year colleges and universities, individuals must possess a doctoral degree. Most Forensic Geologists have doctorates.

A master's program generally takes one to two years to complete. After earning a master's degree, doctoral candidates fulfill several more years of study to earn their degree. They must write a book-length dissertation that is based on original research.

Throughout their careers, Forensic Geologists enroll in continuing education programs to update their skills and keep up with advancements in their fields.

Experience, Special Skills, and Personality Traits

Potential clients seek Forensic Geologists who are highly accomplished and recognized in their fields. In addition, they prefer to retain consultants who have the necessary knowledge, skills, and experience to successfully complete their projects. Forensic Geologists are typically at the top of their field and have many years of work experience.

To flourish as a consultant, individuals need excellent organizational, analytical, self-management, writing, and presentation skills. They must also have exceptional interpersonal and communication skills, as they need to work well with attorneys, law enforcement officers, other forensic scientists, and others. Being unbiased, trustworthy, detail-oriented, persistent, inquisitive, and cooperative are some personality traits that successful Forensic Geologists have in common.

Unions and Associations

Forensic Geologists can join professional associations to take advantage of networking opportunities and other professional resources and services. Some organizations that serve their interests are the American Geological Institute, the Geological Society of America, and the American Academy of Forensic Sciences. For contact information, see Appendix III.

Tips for Entry

1. As a student, take advantage of opportunities to gain real experience doing geological work. For example, you might obtain an internship or participate in activities sponsored by a geological organization.
2. Some courses you might take for a well-rounded background include physics, analytical chemistry, biology, math, statistics, and criminal justice.
3. Employers usually require you to give them three references. Choose individuals who can provide information about your work habits and abilities.
4. One expert in the field suggests that interested geologists first take on a case as an expert witness. This can give them an idea if they can handle the pressure of working on short deadlines as well as defending their opinions on the witness stand.
5. Use the Internet to learn more about forensic geology. To obtain a list of relevant Web sites, enter the keywords *forensic geology* or *forensic geologists* into a search engine.

FORENSIC METEOROLOGIST

CAREER PROFILE

Duties: Provide forensic consulting services to attorneys, insurance companies, and other clients; reconstruct and analyze weather patterns during a particular event; perform other duties as required

Alternate Title(s): Forensic Consultant

Salary Range: $39,000 to $120,000

Employment Prospects: Poor

Advancement Prospects: Fair

Prerequisites:

Education or Training—Master's or doctoral degree in atmospheric science or another related field

Experience—Several years of work experience

Special Skills and Personality Traits—Communication, interpersonal, teamwork, self-management, analytical, organizational, writing, and presentation skills; impartial, fair, trustworthy, detail-oriented, curious, and diligent

CAREER LADDER

```
┌─────────────────────────────────────┐
│    Senior Forensic Meteorologist     │
└─────────────────────────────────────┘

┌─────────────────────────────────────┐
│       Forensic Meteorologist         │
└─────────────────────────────────────┘

┌─────────────────────────────────────┐
│            Meteorologist             │
└─────────────────────────────────────┘
```

Position Description

What was the weather like at the time a victim was killed? What were the lighting conditions when a motorcycle accident occurred? How windy was it when a homeowner's fence blew down? These are examples of questions that weather experts known as Forensic Meteorologists might be asked.

Meteorology is the study of the structure and composition of the Earth's atmosphere as well as the continuously changing atmospheric conditions (such as wind, temperature, sunlight, and precipitation) that produce weather on Earth. Many meteorologists, also known as atmospheric scientists, work in the applied field of meteorology. Many of them are involved in forecasting the weather by applying physical and mathematical principles to atmospheric conditions. Broadcast meteorologists (radio and TV weather forecasters) are probably the most familiar type of applied meteorology professionals, while Forensic Meteorologists are less well known.

Forensic Meteorologists are consulting professionals who utilize their meteorological proficiency to help resolve criminal investigations, civil lawsuits, insurance claims, environmental regulatory actions, and other legal matters. They are retained by the courts, by either defense or plain-tiff attorneys, by insurance companies, by law enforcement agencies, by government agencies, and by other entities. These forensic specialists assist with a wide variety of weather-related investigations involving structural collapses, traffic accidents, property damage, aviation mishaps, and crimes.

Forensic Meteorologists reconstruct weather patterns for the area under investigation by reviewing airport weather reports, Doppler radar readings, satellite images, and eyewitness descriptions. They may also turn to atypical data resources such as atmospheric readings taken by air pollution monitors.

By looking back at weather data for incident dates, Forensic Meteorologists analyze the events that were impacted by the weather. They may visit the scene of the accident, injury, or crime to verify that weather conditions prevailed as eyewitnesses reported them. Weather reports are usually regional and do not account for microclimate conditions influenced by local factors such as terrain or other environmental features. For example, icy conditions on roads may not have been indicated by a regional weather report but were reported by eyewitnesses to a vehicle accident in a location that experienced colder temperatures than elsewhere in the region. Forensic Meteorologists may need to interpolate information from several locations to determine conditions at the location in question.

Upon completing their investigations and analyses, Forensic Meteorologists prepare reports that vary in thoroughness according to the needs of their clients. Their reports range from telephone consultations to detailed written information packets to graphic courtroom presentations. A report may detail a few days worth of weather data alone, or may provide additional information such as long-range weather statistics, law enforcement reports, site inspection notes, testimony or depositions provided by adversaries, and expert opinions from other sources. Additionally, these professionals may be requested to appear in courts to provide expert witness testimony.

Like all forensic experts, Forensic Meteorologists are expected to remain objective and unbiased about the details of their cases. They do not assume the role of advocate for either side of a dispute, regardless of who hired them.

Forensic Meteorologists work full time or part time.

Salaries

Salaries for Forensic Meteorologists vary, depending on such factors as their education, experience, employer, and geographic location. Specific salary information for this occupation is unavailable. However, the estimated annual salary for most atmospheric scientists ranged between $39,090 and $119,700, according to the May 2006 *Occupational Employment Statistics* survey by the U.S. Bureau of Labor Statistics (BLS).

Employment Prospects

Many Forensic Meteorologists are employed by meteorological management and consulting firms that offer forensic meteorology services. Some are independent practitioners. Some offer their services on a part-time basis, while working full time at their primary occupation as university professors, researchers, or broadcast meteorologists.

Forensic meteorology is a small field. The competition for staff positions is high. Positions usually become available when Forensic Meteorologists advance to higher positions, transfer to other jobs, or leave the work force for various reasons. Private firms may create additional positions as the demand for their services increases.

The job outlook for meteorologists, overall, is favorable, particularly in the private sector. According to the BLS, employment of this occupation is predicted to grow by 9 to 17 percent through 2014.

Advancement Prospects

In companies, Forensic Meteorologists with administrative and managerial ambitions can pursue such positions, but they are limited. For some meteorologists, their ultimate goal is to become independent consultants or business owners.

Many Forensic Meteorologists realize advancement through job satisfaction, professional recognition, and higher incomes. Many also measure success by being sought for very complex or publicized cases.

Education and Training

Minimally, individuals wishing to become Forensic Meteorologists must have a bachelor's degree in meteorology, atmospheric science, or another related field. To advance in this field, individuals generally need a master's or doctoral degree. Clients, for example, usually prefer to retain Forensic Meteorologists who hold advanced degrees, particularly if they will be providing testimony as expert witnesses.

As of 2006, there were no academic programs available for forensic meteorology studies. According to one expert in the field, training is on-the-job, generally in research or operational meteorology for a significant period of time.

Throughout their careers, Forensic Meteorologists enroll in continuing education programs and training programs to update their skills and keep up with advancements in their fields.

Experience, Special Skills, and Personality Traits

Requirements vary among employers. In general, they prefer to hire candidates who have several years of work experience. Independent consultants must be able to demonstrate to prospective clients that they have the necessary knowledge, skills, and experience to successfully perform their projects.

To be effective consultants, Forensic Meteorologists need excellent communication, interpersonal, and teamwork skills, as they must be able to work well with colleagues, attorneys, law enforcement officers, and others from diverse backgrounds. In addition, they must have strong self-management skills, analytical, organizational, writing, and presentation skills. Being impartial, fair, trustworthy, detail-oriented, curious, and diligent are some personality traits that successful Forensic Meteorologists share.

Unions and Associations

Forensic Meteorologists can join professional associations to take advantage of networking opportunities, continuing education, professional certification, and other professional resources and services. Two national societies that serve their interests include the American Meteorological Society and the National Council of Industrial Meteorologists. For contact information, see Appendix III.

Tips for Entry

1. As a student, join a professional society and participate in its activities. Take advantage of opportunities

to network with experienced professionals, especially Forensic Meteorologists.

2. To succeed as a consultant, you will need strong business and marketing skills. Read books and take courses that can help you develop strong business skills.

3. To enhance their credibility, Forensic Meteorologists become certified by recognized organizations. For information about certification programs, see Appendix II.

4. Contact private firms directly about job openings. If a company does not have any current vacancies, ask if you may send in a résumé or complete an application for future openings.

5. Use the Internet to learn more about forensic meteorology. To get a list of relevant Web sites to visit, enter the keywords *forensic meteorology* or *forensic meteorologists* into a search engine. For some links, see Appendix IV.

FORENSIC MICROBIOLOGIST

CAREER PROFILE

Duties: Provide consulting services to law enforcement agencies and others; apply microbiology knowledge and techniques to legal matters; perform duties as required

Alternate Title(s): Microbial Forensics Expert, Forensic Consultant

Salary Range: $35,000 to $146,000

Employment Prospects: Fair

Advancement Prospects: Poor

Prerequisites:

    Education or Training—Advanced degree usually required

    Experience—Many years of experience in one's field

    Special Skills and Personality Traits—Organizational, self-management, teamwork, communication and interpersonal skills; inquisitive, flexible, self-motivated, trustworthy, objective, and dedicated

CAREER LADDER

```
┌─────────────────────────────────────┐
│  Senior Forensic Microbiologist     │
└─────────────────────────────────────┘

┌─────────────────────────────────────┐
│      Forensic Microbiologist        │
└─────────────────────────────────────┘

┌─────────────────────────────────────┐
│          Microbiologist             │
└─────────────────────────────────────┘
```

Position Description

Microbiology is the study of microbes (or microorganisms) such as bacteria, viruses, molds, yeast, algae, and protozoa. These are very tiny living organisms that can be seen only with the help of microscopes.

Microbiologists seek to understand microbes by studying their characteristics as well as how they function, grow, develop, and reproduce. Additionally, these scientists examine how various microbes interact with other living organisms. Microbiologists are also concerned with understanding how some microbes act as infectious agents and affect the health of plants, animals, and humans.

Some microbiologists specialize in the type of microbes that they study. For example, bacteriologists examine bacteria and virologists investigate viruses that are active inside living cells. Other microbiologists concentrate in a particular specialty of biology. For example, they might study only the physiology, cytology, biochemistry, immunology, or genetics of microorganisms.

A new specialty of microbiology, microbial forensics, focuses on how microbes can be used as weapons. In recent years, for example, terrorists used anthrax enclosed in envelopes to sicken or kill victims. Microbes may also be a factor in cases of medical negligence, the deliberate infection of people with a communicable disease, or intentional food contamination. Such cases are of interest to Forensic Microbiologists.

These scientific specialists face more challenges about the spread of toxic microbial substances because with increasing frequency, unscrupulous individuals deliberately spread diseases. Forensic Microbiologists strive to distinguish microbial substances that occur in nature from those that were concocted in laboratories. Their principal challenge is to prove to judges and juries that dangerous substances were developed by artificial means for the express purpose of doing harm.

As this is being written, Forensic Microbiologists are largely engaged in the process of developing their field. Many of these specialists are involved with conducting research to address such problems as:

- genotyping microbial agents, developing DNA protocols, and developing genomic, molecular, microbiological, and other "fingerprinting" techniques
- recognizing that the incidence of a particular disease is indeed an organized attack

- collecting microbial samples at sites where biological agents are used in criminal or terrorist attacks
- selecting the best analytical methods to use to identify threatening microbial specimens
- training police, ambulance crews, and firefighters to deal with microbial attacks and protect themselves from being affected
- designing and using appropriate tests for suspicious substances as well as standardizing such tests and ensuring quality control for using such tests
- developing plans to respond to threats in order to avert attacks before they occur
- organizing national and international microbial forensics programs
- compiling a microbial DNA database

In addition to these areas of research, Forensic Microbiologists continue to work on ways to deal with political and economic issues in regard to acquiring government funds, balancing the scientific tradition of openness about research with maintaining confidentiality about suspected terrorist threats, and working with law enforcement agencies and the courts.

Forensic Microbiologists mostly work in sterile laboratories and offices. They use computers, electron microscopes, and other sophisticated laboratory equipment. They wear protective clothing and follow strict safety rules and regulations to minimize the risks that are involved in handling microbes, chemicals, and other potentially dangerous substances.

Salaries

Specific salary information for Forensic Microbiologists is unavailable. As consultants, they charge an hourly, daily, or flat rate for initial consultation, courtroom testimony, and other services that they offer.

According to the May 2006 *Occupational Employment Statistics* survey by the U.S. Bureau of Labor Statistics, the estimated annual salary for most microbiologists ranged between $35,460 and $108,270. The estimated annual salary for most bioscience postsecondary teachers, which includes microbiology faculty, ranged between $37,620 and $145,600.

Employment Prospects

Microbial forensics is a very young and small field. The demand for Forensic Microbiologists is greater than the current number of qualified experts. It is expected to stay this way for several years to come.

Forensic Microbiologists are mostly academicians who teach and conduct research in four-year colleges and universities, or are scientists who work for government research labs. Opportunities generally become available as individuals retire, transfer to other jobs, or advance to higher posi-

tions. Employers will create additional positions, as long as funding is available.

Advancement Prospects

Research scientists in government laboratories can be promoted to supervisory and managerial positions, which are limited. Academicians advance by rising through the ranks from instructor to full professor. They can also pursue managerial and administrative positions, from department chair to academic dean to the position of provost or president.

In general, Forensic Microbiologists measure success through job satisfaction, professional recognition, and higher incomes.

Education and Training

Minimally, Forensic Microbiologists should possess a master's degree in microbiology, biology, or another related field. To teach in four-year colleges and universities or to conduct independent research, Forensic Microbiologists must possess a doctoral degree.

It takes several years of committed effort for students to obtain a doctoral degree. First, they complete a four-year bachelor's degree program, followed by a one- or two-year master's degree program. Upon earning their master's degree, they enroll in a doctoral program, which takes several more years to finish. To successfully earn their degree, doctoral candidates must write a book-length dissertation based on original research. Upon earning their doctorates, many postgraduates obtain a fellowship, which may be one or two years long, to continue training in their specialty.

As this is being written, no formal programs to train individuals in microbial forensics are currently available. Microbiologists typically learn on the job, as well as take advantage of training workshops offered by professional associations or other recognized organizations.

Throughout their careers, Forensic Microbiologists enroll in continuing education programs and training programs to update their skills and keep up with advancements in their fields.

Experience, Special Skills, and Personality Traits

Scientific consultants such as Forensic Microbiologists have worked in their fields for many years. They usually have distinguished reputations for their knowledge and skills as well as the research work that they have accomplished.

To work effectively as microbial forensics consultants, microbiologists must have excellent organizational, self-management, and teamwork skills. They also need strong communication and interpersonal skills, as they must be able to work well with colleagues, administrators, government officials, and others. Being inquisitive, flexible, self-motivated, trustworthy, objective, and dedicated are some personality traits that successful Forensic Microbiologists share.

Unions and Associations

Many Forensic Microbiologists belong to professional associations to take advantage of networking opportunities, current research, continuing education, and other professional resources and services. Some national societies that they might join include the American Society for Microbiology, the American Academy of Microbiology, and the American Academy for Forensic Sciences. For contact information, see Appendix III.

Tips for Entry

1. As a college student, seek paid or volunteer assistantships with professors who conduct research in microbial forensics.
2. Many individuals have found jobs through referrals or tips from people they know. Hence, you can contact colleagues, professors, former employers, and others about fellowship opportunities or job vacancies.
3. Use the Internet to learn more about microbial forensics. To obtain a list of relevant Web sites, enter any of these keywords into a search engine: *microbial forensics*, *forensic microbiology*, or *forensic microbiologists*. For some links, see Appendix IV.

FORENSIC PALYNOLOGIST

CAREER PROFILE

Duties: Provide forensic consulting services to law enforcement agencies; identify, analyze, and interpret pollen evidence; perform other duties as required

Alternate Title(s): Forensic Consultant

Salary Range: $38,000 to $146,000

Employment Prospects: Poor

Advancement Prospects: Fair

Prerequisites:

Education or Training—A doctoral degree usually preferred

Experience—Several years of experience in the palynology field

Special Skills and Personality Traits—Self-management, analytical, organizational, report-writing, presentation, communication, and interpersonal skills; objective, trustworthy, unbiased, detail-oriented, inquisitive, meticulous, and creative

CAREER LADDER

```
┌─────────────────────────────────┐
│     Forensic Palynologist       │
└─────────────────────────────────┘

┌─────────────────────────────────┐
│  Novice Forensic Palynologist   │
└─────────────────────────────────┘

┌─────────────────────────────────┐
│         Palynologist            │
└─────────────────────────────────┘
```

Position Description

Forensic palynology is another scientific discipline that can be used to help link criminals to victims and crime scenes. Palynology is the study of pollen and spores, which are microscopic reproductive plant particles that are spread by wind, water, or insects to promote the spread of plant species. These tiny particles are invisible to the naked eye, but when viewed under powerful microscopes, they are infinitely variable in design. Despite their small size, pollen and spores resist decay. They last for years and are even found fossilized within rocks that are millions of years old. Each plant or fungus produces a unique type of pollen or spores, which can be distinguished and identified by palynologists.

Palynology is an interdisciplinary science that is part of both geological and biological sciences. Palynologists apply their studies of pollen and spores to a variety of purposes including understanding allergies; finding oil, gas, and coal deposits; learning what plants prehistoric people used; determining the ages of rocks; and learning about climate changes of the distant past, to name a few.

On occasion, some palynologists, known as Forensic Palynologists, apply their knowledge and skills to criminal investigations in which pollen evidence may be used to help prove or disprove the innocence of suspects. Some plant species, called anemophilous plants, produce pollen or spores in a great quantity that floats in the air and is carried by the wind to fertilize other plants. The dispersal pattern of windborne spores and pollen is called pollen rain. Pollen rain for each region is unique. Pollen and spores from anemophilous plants are present everywhere, and also settle on every indoor and outdoor surface including soils, vegetation, people, objects and fabrics. Other plant species, called zoogamous plants, produce small amounts of pollen that becomes attached to insects, which leave the pollen in other flowers where it fertilizes the plants. Pollen from zoogamous plants is also transferred directly to objects or surfaces in contact with the plants. These microscopic particles, also called palynomorphs, are found at crime scenes and on suspects or victims.

Forensic Palynologists can identify pollen evidence, which may include modern or fossilized pollen specimens. For example, they examine palynomorphs to discover where criminals may have been by comparing pollen rain samples found at crime scenes with those found on the suspect. Even fossilized pollen samples found both on a suspect and at a certain location may incriminate the suspect who claims to have never visited that location.

Forensic Palynologists work on a consulting basis. They are retained by law enforcement agencies (including federal agencies such as the Federal Bureau of Investigation and Drug Enforcement Administration), medical examiners' (and coroners') offices, attorneys, and other entities. They assist with the investigation of a variety of crimes involving burglaries, rapes, assaults, drugs, and murders. Their work helps investigators to link evidence found at crime scenes with other places or to locate clandestine graves. Forensic Palynologists also help investigators determine the country of origin of such items as food, antiques, narcotics, and other merchandise. For example, they may examine pollen within samples of government-subsidized honey to determine how much of it actually originated in other countries.

When Forensic Palynologists are engaged in an investigation, they are among the first to arrive at a crime scene for the purpose of preventing contamination of palynomorphic evidence. They may visit such locations as abduction sites, places where evidence was deposited, homes of victims and suspects, or places where they have been known to visit, and other crime scenes. Pollen and spores adhere to surfaces persistently but may at times be transferred to other objects or surfaces.

These forensic specialists look for palynomorphs on live or decaying plant material, dust deposits, soil, carpets, clothing, ropes, baskets, packing materials, food, furniture, walls, inside automobiles, in graves, and in the stomach and intestinal contents of cadavers. They may take close-up, high-resolution photographs of objects and make detailed maps of the scene for reference, or use photos and maps produced by other investigators. Forensic Palynologists take control samples of plant specimens and soil from the area to compare their pollen with other pollen samples they find at the scene or obtain from evidence recovered by other investigators.

In clean, contamination-free laboratory environments, Forensic Palynologists use special techniques to extract palynomorphic evidence from evidence samples. They may use sticky tape or small vacuum cleaners to collect pollen samples, or they may carefully wash fibrous materials and later extract pollen from the distilled water they use. They employ various techniques, such as using acids, to extract pollen from some samples.

Forensic Palynologists examine pollens and spores through powerful microscopes to determine their unique characteristics and compare with the control samples. They take careful notes about their procedures and observations. Forensic Palynologists are able to provide probable results more often than precise results because of the millions of types of pollen that exist in the world. However, their results can be sufficient to be used as workable evidence to solve crimes or resolve other cases. Forensic Palynologists prepare com-

prehensive reports about their findings, and may be asked to present their results in courts as expert witnesses.

Forensic Palynologists typically offer their consulting services on a part-time basis. Most are full-time academicians and researchers. These scientists perform other tasks pertinent to the field of palynology as well as their forensic work. They build pollen databases that will prove to be helpful with future investigative work. They conduct research on such topics as the comparison of fossil and modern pollens and write scientific papers about their findings. Forensic Palynologists collaborate with other scientists and stay in close contact with police personnel.

Forensic Palynologists work in office and laboratory settings. They also travel to visit crime scenes or collect samples for other types of forensic work.

Salaries

Specific earnings information for Forensic Palynologists is unavailable. As consultants, they charge an hourly, daily, or flat rate for initial consultation, assessments, depositions, courtroom testimony, and other services that they offer. In addition, many of them charge their clients for out-of-pocket expenses such as travel time, telephone calls, and photocopying.

As academicians, palynologists earn salaries that vary, depending on such factors as their ranking, discipline, employer, and geographic location. The estimated annual salary for most postsecondary biological science teachers ranged from $37,620 to $145,600, according to the May 2006 *Occupational Employment Statistics* survey by the U.S. Bureau of Labor Statistics.

Employment Prospects

Forensic palynology is a small but emerging field. This forensic discipline is more widely known and used in New Zealand, Australia, Canada, and the United Kingdom than it is in the United States. As this forensic discipline gains familiarity and acceptance, more opportunities should become available.

Most palynologists teach and conduct research in four-year colleges and universities. Some palynologists are employed by museums, government agencies, and the oil industry.

Advancement Prospects

As forensic consultants, palynologists measure success by building their practice, earning higher incomes, and gaining professional recognition. Many also measure success by being sought for very complex or publicized cases.

College and university instructors typically seek tenure-track positions. Once they gain tenure at an institution, they cannot be fired without just cause and due process. Academicians advance by rising through the ranks from instructor to full professor. They can also pursue managerial and administrative positions, from department chair to academic dean to the position of provost or president.

Education and Training

There were no formal training programs for forensic palynology in the United States as of 2006. Some experts in the field suggest that individuals obtain an education with a strong emphasis in science, particularly in botany and ecology. Many Forensic Palynologists possess a doctoral degree in botany, palynology, or another biological science or geological science field, with a concentration in palynology. To teach in academic institutions, individuals must possess a doctorate.

It takes many years of intense study for students to earn a doctorate. They must first get a bachelor's degree, which is a four-year program, and then finish a one- or two-year master's degree program. This is followed by four to six years in a doctoral program, which includes conducting original research and writing a book-length dissertation in their field of study. Upon earning their doctoral degree, many palynologists complete one or more fellowships, which involves one or more years of additional training in their fields of interest.

Forensic Palynologists enroll in continuing education programs throughout their careers to update their skills and knowledge.

Experience, Special Skills, and Personality Traits

Potential clients seek Forensic Palynologists who have established themselves and are accomplished in their field. They retain consultants who have the necessary knowledge, skills, and experience to successfully complete their projects. Typically, palynologists have many years of work experience before becoming forensic consultants.

To do well as consultants, Forensic Palynologists must have strong self-management, analytical, organizational, report writing, and presentation skills. They also need excellent communication and interpersonal skills, as they must be able to work well with law enforcement officers, attorneys, and others from diverse backgrounds. Being objective, trustworthy, unbiased, detail-oriented, inquisitive, meticulous, and creative are some personality traits that successful Forensic Palynologists share.

Unions and Associations

Forensic Palynologists can join professional associations to take advantage of professional resources and services as well as networking opportunities. Two different organizations that serve their interests are the American Association of Stratigraphic Palynologists, Inc. and the American Academy of Forensic Sciences. For contact information, see Appendix III.

Tips for Entry

1. Research your career options carefully. Choose a school that allows you the opportunity to study under professors who offer forensic consulting services.
2. One expert in the field emphasizes that prospective Forensic Palynologists have a firm understanding of plant ecology, plant communities, and plant geography.
3. Take courses in forensic science, criminology, or criminal justice to gain an understanding of the forensic and law enforcement fields. If possible, obtain an internship in a forensic lab.
4. Get on-the-job training. Contact Forensic Palynologists and ask about opportunities to work with them.
5. Use the Internet to learn more about palynology in general. You might start by visiting the Palynology Web site (maintained by Dr. Owen Davis) at the University of Arizona. The URL is http://www.geo.arizona.edu/palynology. For more links, see Appendix IV.

WILDLIFE FORENSIC SCIENTIST

CAREER PROFILE

Duties: Identify, analyze, and interpret physical evidence for criminal investigations or trials; prepare reports of findings; provide expert witness testimony; perform other duties as required

Alternate Title(s): Wildlife Forensic Specialist, Wildlife Forensic Biologist

Salary Range: $32,000 to $87,000

Employment Prospects: Poor

Advancement Prospects: Fair

Prerequisites:

　Education or Training—Bachelor's degree in biology, chemistry, or another related field

　Experience—Prior work experience in crime labs, preferably in wildlife-related labs

　Special Skills and Personality Traits—Self-management, analytical, writing, communication, interpersonal, and teamwork skills; patient, detail-oriented, unbiased, trustworthy, diligent, and inquisitive

CAREER LADDER

```
┌─────────────────────────────────────┐
│  Senior Wildlife Forensic Scientist │
└─────────────────────────────────────┘

┌─────────────────────────────────────┐
│    Wildlife Forensic Scientist      │
└─────────────────────────────────────┘

┌─────────────────────────────────────┐
│       Criminalist or Wildlife       │
│     Forensic Scientist Trainee      │
└─────────────────────────────────────┘
```

Position Description

Wildlife Forensic Scientists assist law enforcement agencies with criminal investigations that involve protected and endangered animal species. State and federal laws, as well as international treaties, have been established to protect mammals, birds, reptiles, amphibians, and other wildlife in the United States as well as throughout the world. Yet many people continue to hunt protected species for fun or for financial gain. In fact, several billion dollars worth of illegal trade in wildlife and wildlife parts occur each year worldwide. Tusks, internal organs, fur, and antlers, for example, have been sold and used to make leather goods, garments, jewelry, artwork, food, medicinal cures, and other products.

Wildlife Forensic Scientists are responsible for examining physical evidence—which may consist of whole animal bodies, animal parts, or products made from animals, as well as weapons, tools, and other evidence—found at crime scenes. Their job is to provide criminal investigators and prosecuting attorneys with scientific proof that may help them find a link between the suspects and the animal victims or the crime scenes.

Wildlife forensics is a comparatively new law enforcement approach. It is similar to the forensic sciences that deal with human issues, yet different in that it involves the identification of animal species. Wildlife Forensic Scientists work in crime labs that are set up and equipped like any other crime lab. They apply forensic methods and techniques similar to those used to examine physical evidence in human crimes.

Identifying the species of the animal victim is crucial, as that identification determines whether wildlife laws have been broken. Wildlife Forensic Scientists use a variety of methods to identify species, including chemical, DNA, blood testing, and physical comparison techniques. Essentially, they examine evidence samples and match them with known samples. For example, a forensic examiner may have obtained a feather as physical evidence and would try to identify the species by matching it to a sample from a reference library of bird feathers.

Wildlife Forensic Scientists perform autopsies on animal carcasses to determine the cause of the victims' death. The forensic examiners confirm whether victims may have died from natural causes, which included being killed by other animals for food or for territory. If they died of unnatural causes, forensic scientists determine how they were killed, whether by gunshot wounds, pesticide poisoning, environmental pollution, trap wounds, or other forms of trauma.

Wildlife Forensic Scientists examine stomach contents, bullets, shot pellets, poisons, pesticides, soil samples, and trace evidence to find a connection with the victims, criminal suspects, and crime scenes. In small labs, samples of physical evidence may be sent to other crime labs to perform tests, such as DNA analysis, which cannot be done in their labs.

Wildlife Forensic Scientists also examine confiscated products that are suspected of having originated from protected or endangered species. For example, they examine fresh, frozen, or smoked meats; fur coats; reptile leather products such as shoes and purses; loose feathers and down; carved ivory objects; turtle shell jewelry; cosmetics; pharmaceuticals; and so on. Wildlife Forensic Scientists try to determine whether suspected products have characteristics that define them as having originated from certain species.

When these forensic examiners complete their evaluations, they prepare comprehensive reports of their findings and conclusions. They attach photographs, drawings, and other documentation to support their opinions. They are responsible for writing reports that are clear, concise, and easy to understand for investigators, attorneys, and court juries. Wildlife Forensic Scientists are sometimes called upon to provide expert witness testimony at court depositions and trials.

Wildlife Forensic Scientists also perform a variety of other duties. For example, depending on their experience and expertise, they might:

- assist in the development of a lab database or library of visual clues that can be used to identify animal species and individual animals (for instance, a lab might build a collection of tissue and blood samples from various types of reptiles)
- conduct basic research studies on individual animal species to gain knowledge and understanding of the species
- perform analytical work related to wildlife management (for instance, determine the age of an elk)
- conduct genetic, chemical, or blood serum tests on fluid stains or other evidentiary samples
- develop new techniques for identifying various animal species through the examination of eggs, animal parts, blood, cooked meats, oils, or cosmetics
- conduct crime scene investigations or assist crime scene investigators
- lead training workshops for game wardens, park rangers, and others in such topics as wildlife crime scene investigations or interpreting physical evidence
- act as department liaison with law enforcement agencies and other governmental agencies as well as with the general public

- prepare exhibits and evidence for use in the capacity of expert witnesses
- lead or supervise local or statewide wildlife forensic programs

Wildlife Forensic Scientists work in wildlife forensic labs that are part of game and wildlife agencies, law enforcement agencies, private forensic labs, or research labs in academic institutions. Many Wildlife Forensic Scientists are criminalists who perform wildlife forensic examinations as part of their main duties.

Wildlife Forensic Scientists work flexible hours and occasionally travel. They may be on call 24 hours a day.

Salaries

Salaries for Wildlife Forensic Scientists vary, depending on such factors as their education, experience, position, and employer. Federal Wildlife Forensic Scientists receive a salary based on the General Schedule (GS), which is the pay schedule for many federal employees. Employees usually enter at the GS-7, GS-9, or GS-11 level, and can advance to the GS-13 level. In 2007, the basic pay for GS-7 to GS-13 levels ranged from $31,740 to $87,039.

Employment Prospects

The largest employer of full-time Wildlife Forensic Scientists is the National Fish and Wildlife Forensics Laboratory (part of the U.S. Wildlife Service) in Ashland, Oregon. Other full-time opportunities can be found with state wildlife forensic labs.

Wildlife forensics is a small yet emerging field. Most opportunities become available as Wildlife Forensic Scientists advance to higher positions, transfer to other jobs, or retire. State agencies will create additional positions to meet growing needs, as long as funding is available.

Advancement Prospects

Supervisory and administrative positions are available but limited. To advance to management positions, these specialists need a master's or doctorate degree.

Most Wildlife Forensic Scientists pursue advancement by earning higher salaries, receiving greater responsibilities, and gaining professional recognition.

Education and Training

Minimally, applicants for entry-level positions must possess a bachelor's degree in biology, chemistry, biochemistry, forensic science, or another related field.

Novice forensic scientists receive on-the-job training while working under the guidance and supervision of experienced staff members.

Throughout their careers, Wildlife Forensic Scientists enroll in courses, workshops, and seminars to update their skills and knowledge.

Experience, Special Skills, and Personality Traits

Employers usually prefer to hire candidates who have prior experience working in a forensic or wildlife-related laboratory. Entry-level applicants may have gained their experience through internships, research assistantships, or employment in crime, research, or analytical laboratories.

To perform well at their job, Forensic Wildlife Scientists need strong self-management skills, such as the ability to prioritize multiple tasks, handle stressful situations, work independently, and follow and understand directions. In addition, these specialists need excellent analytical, writing, communication, interpersonal, and teamwork skills. Being patient, detail-oriented, unbiased, trustworthy, diligent, and inquisitive are some personality traits that successful Forensic Wildlife Scientists share.

Unions and Associations

Wildlife Forensic Scientists can join several professional associations to take advantage of networking opportunities, continuing education, and other professional services and resources. Many of these scientists join societies that are devoted to their particular fields, such as chemistry, biology, or ornithology. One national forensic society that serves their general interests is the American Academy of Forensic Sciences. For contact information, see Appendix III.

Tips for Entry

1. As a high school student, you can begin gaining experience by working with animals. You might volunteer or get a part-time job at an animal shelter, nature center, zoo, or wildlife park.
2. Check Web sites or call prospective employers on a regular basis for notices about job openings.
3. Carefully read the instructions for applying for a job. Be sure you turn your application in by the deadline and to the proper office. If you send your application to the wrong office, you cannot be guaranteed that it will be forwarded to the correct one.
4. Learn more about wildlife forensics on the Internet. You might start by visiting the National Fish and Wildlife Forensics Laboratory Web site at http://www.lab.fws.gov. For more links, see Appendix IV.

FORENSIC EXPERTS
IN MATHEMATICS AND
COMPUTER SCIENCE

FORENSIC STATISTICIAN

CAREER PROFILE

Duties: Provide forensic consulting services to attorneys and others; analyze and interpret numerical data related to legal matters; perform other duties as required

Alternate Title(s): Forensic Mathematician, Forensic Consultant

Salary Range: $32,000 to $109,000

Employment Prospects: Poor

Advancement Prospects: Fair

Prerequisites:

Education or Training—An advanced degree, preferably a doctoral degree

Experience— Several years of experience in the field

Special Skills and Personality Traits— Problem-solving, organizational, self-management, writing, computer, communication, and interpersonal skills; creative, patient, persistent, inquisitive, detail-oriented, honest, and trustworthy

CAREER LADDER

```
┌─────────────────────────────┐
│    Forensic Statistician     │
└─────────────────────────────┘

┌─────────────────────────────┐
│  Novice Forensic Statistician │
└─────────────────────────────┘

┌─────────────────────────────┐
│  Statistician, Mathematician, or │
│      Other Profession        │
└─────────────────────────────┘
```

Position Description

Forensic Statisticians make up another group of forensic specialists whose field has developed in recent years. Statistics is a branch of mathematics that involves the collection, organization, analysis, and interpretation of large amounts of numerical, or statistical, data about a particular subject. For example, statisticians might derive statistical data from school test scores, temperature readings from a certain location over a number of years, or salary figures for a large corporation. Statistical information is used by a wide variety of people including scientists, engineers, financial analysts, educators, and policy makers for just as wide a variety of reasons—to help solve problems, design projects, evaluate programs, make policy decisions, or predict events, for example.

Forensic statistics is a branch of applied statistics. Applied statisticians use statistical techniques to solve problems in biology, medicine, agriculture, pharmacology, education, psychology, meteorology, engineering, and other fields. In the area of criminal and civil justice, Forensic Statisticians use statistics and probability to help settle such cases as product liability issues, business disputes, trademark disputes, intellectual property theft, fraud, and various forms of discrimination. They are consulted by attorneys, law enforcement agencies, government agencies, and other entities.

Forensic Statisticians use complicated mathematical methods to analyze and interpret crime evidence. Evidence is not always readily identified, nor is it always clear about how it happened to be located at a crime scene, where it originated, or whether it was left there by the suspect or the victim. Many times such unknowns can be clarified by statistical probability methods.

Forensic Statisticians address what is known as probability evidence, which means that they use the mathematical theory of probability to estimate the likelihood that certain events occurred or that certain evidence was left at a scene. For example, Forensic Statisticians may determine that toxic substances found at a crime scene were the probable cause of a victim's injury, or that when a carpet at a burglarized home matches fibers found in a suspect's car it is more than mere coincidence. Evidence samples may be far too numerous to examine thoroughly, as in data stored in hundreds of computer disks. In such cases, Forensic Statisticians examine a small sample and use statistical formulas to calculate the proportion of disks that contain illicit information.

These forensic specialists also apply statistical analysis to match samples of DNA evidence, fingerprints, blood types, handwriting, and more. In addition, Forensic Statisticians work with DNA analysis in civil cases such as paternity suits and in reuniting families separated by political strife, immigration, and other displacement factors. Furthermore, these experts use statistics to help attorneys select jury panels for civil and criminal trials.

In recent years, Forensic Statisticians have been called upon to investigate computerized photo files that contain hidden data. For example, a criminal or terrorist may email a photo of a person or landscape that also contains a photo of a top-secret weapon or a description of a military installation. By using statistical analysis software, Forensic Statisticians can analyze the encrypted data contained in the file and extract the hidden image or text.

Forensic Statisticians also serve as expert witnesses in civil and criminal cases. They are retained by attorneys for either the prosecution or the defense to give their professional opinions about the facts and issues that they are qualified to address. They analyze data concerning a case and arrive at their conclusions about occurrences and evidence. They present their expert opinions to judges and juries in clear concise language and easy-to-understand graphic displays. They do not take sides in cases. Their sworn testimony is objective and unbiased.

Forensic Statisticians perform various tasks apart from their investigative duties. They review and interpret numerical data. They use computers and statistical software to help them organize and analyze data more efficiently. They sometimes need to develop new statistical computer programs in order to complete their projects. They enhance their skills by attending statistical methods conferences.

Forensic Statisticians work flexible hours. Their work environment is primarily in office settings, but they may travel to confer with clients or attend court sessions.

Salaries

Specific salary information for Forensic Statisticians is unavailable. As consultants, they charge an hourly, daily, or flat rate for initial consultation, depositions, courtroom testimony, and other services that they offer.

Most statisticians, in general, earned an estimated annual salary that ranged from $37,010 to $108,630, according to the May 2006 *Occupational Employment Statistics* survey by the U.S. Bureau of Labor Statistics (BLS). The estimated annual salary for mathematics professors ranged between $31,580 and $103,330.

Employment Prospects

Forensic statistics is a small but growing field. Most consultants in this field are employed on a part-time basis, while working in their primary occupations as professors,

researchers, economists, and business analysts, among others. Some Forensic Statisticians work in statistical consulting firms in which they may also perform other types of consulting services.

Job opportunities for statisticians, in general, are expected to be favorable, according to the BLS. It further reports that statistics is widely used and growing in use in many areas. Many employers will not specifically hire statisticians. Rather, they seek those from various disciplines with degrees and backgrounds in statistics for positions in which they will perform analyses and interpretations of data.

Advancement Prospects

Forensic Statisticians generally measure success through job satisfaction, professional recognition, and higher incomes.

Academicians advance by rising through the ranks from instructor to full professor. They can also pursue managerial and administrative positions, from department chair to academic dean to the position of provost or president.

Education and Training

To work in the forensic statistics field, individuals must possess at least a master's degree in statistics, mathematics, or another related field. To teach in universities and four-year colleges, or to conduct basic research, individuals will need a doctoral degree.

Clients usually prefer to retain Forensic Statisticians who hold a doctoral degree, particularly if they will be providing expert witness services. In general, most Forensic Statisticians possess a doctorate.

Throughout their careers, Forensic Statisticians enroll in continuing education programs to update their skills and knowledge.

Experience, Special Skills, and Personality Traits

Potential clients seek Forensic Statisticians who have established themselves as being accomplished in their field. They retain consultants who have the necessary knowledge, skills, and experience to successfully complete their projects. Typically, statisticians and others have many years of work experience before becoming forensic consultants.

To be effective consultants, Forensic Statisticians need excellent problem-solving, organizational, and self-management skills. They also must have strong writing and computer skills. In addition, they must have exceptional communication and interpersonal skills, as they must be able to work well with attorneys and others from diverse backgrounds. Being creative, patient, persistent, inquisitive, detail-oriented, honest, and trustworthy are some personality traits that successful Forensic Statisticians have in common.

Unions and Associations

Many Forensic Statisticians join professional associations to take advantage of networking opportunities, continuing education, and other professional resources and services. Two national societies that serve the general interests of Forensic Statisticians are the American Statistical Association and the Institute of Mathematical Statistics. For contact information, see Appendix III.

Tips for Entry

1. Talk with Forensic Statisticians to learn more about their work. Ask them for suggestions on various ways you can gain experience and training in the forensic statistics field.

2. Enroll in training workshops or programs that teach essential skills for becoming effective expert witnesses.

3. While in college, gain experience by obtaining a research assistantship or volunteering to work with a professor who offers forensic consulting services.

4. Contact lawyers and law enforcement agencies directly. Tell them about yourself and how your services can benefit their investigations.

5. Use the Internet to learn more about forensic statistics. To obtain a list of relevant Web sites enter the keywords *forensic statistics* or *forensic statisticians* into a search engine. For some links, see Appendix IV.

COMPUTER FORENSICS SPECIALIST

CAREER PROFILE

Duties: Identify, collect, preserve, examine, and analyze digital data found on computer media; perform other duties as required

Alternate Title(s): Computer Investigative Specialist, Computer Forensics Investigator, and Digital Forensics Investigator

Salary Range: $34,000 to $103,000+

Employment Prospects: Good

Advancement Prospects: Fair

Prerequisites:

Education or Training—Minimally, a bachelor's degree preferred

Experience—Requirements vary for different positions

Special Skills and Personality Traits—Problem-solving, critical-thinking, organizational, teamwork, interpersonal, communication, and writing skills; inquisitive, detail-oriented, persistent, patient, honest, trustworthy, and self-motivated

Special Requirements—Professional certification or license may be required, depending on the occupation

CAREER LADDER

Senior Computer Forensics Specialist

Computer Forensics Specialist

Computer Forensics Specialist Trainee

Position Description

In recent years, computer forensics has grown to be increasingly important as computers have become more pervasive in modern society. It is, according to some experts, one of the fastest growing areas of forensics. The experts who work in this field are known as Computer Forensics Specialists. Their job is to examine digital evidence. They isolate, remove, preserve, analyze, and keep a record of data that has been stored or encrypted on computer media. They inspect computer hard drives as well as other computer media such as CD-ROMs, zip disks, personal digital assistants (PDAs), flash memory cards, portable media players, and cellular telephones.

Many law enforcement agencies have computer crime units, or high-technology crime units, that are responsible for investigating computer and computer-related crimes. Computer Forensics Specialists who work in these special details may be law enforcement officers or civilians. They examine data from computers found at crime scenes to uncover potential evidence that may lead to the arrest and conviction of suspected criminals.

These specialists are involved in the investigation of such crimes as the theft of computer systems, trade secrets, and information assets (data), as well as the destruction or damage of computer files. They also conduct or assist in investigations in which computers were used to commit, plan, or document crimes such as credit fraud, identity theft, kidnapping, rape, assault, arson, and terrorism. In addition, they provide assistance to other law enforcement officers with preparing search warrants to seize computers, as well as with the proper handling of that equipment. Furthermore, they may assist in collecting and processing evidence at crime scenes.

Some Computer Forensics Specialists work in the private sector, where they offer their forensic services to various individuals and groups. Some of them are employed as staff members of organizations, while others work as forensic consultants or as private investigators.

Insurance companies and other business organizations hire Computer Forensics Specialists to assist them in retrieving evidence of fraud, embezzlement, theft, intellectual property violations, and sexual harassment. Attorneys involved with criminal prosecution or civil litigation enlist the services of these forensic experts to extract computer files in cases involving homicide, child pornography, drug trafficking, divorce, and discrimination, among other cases. Even individual citizens seek the aid of Computer Forensics Specialists to help them handle their workplace issues, such as wrongful termination or age discrimination, or when they are victimized by spam or phishing e-mails. Additionally, these forensic experts assist the government to gather intelligence information about terrorist threats.

Computer Forensic Specialists use some of the same evidence-processing procedures as do other forensic experts but also use software programs and other tools that are unique to computer forensics. Computer Forensics Specialists use their tools and processes to detect security flaws and recover documents, graphics, photos, and other data from computer disk drives and other storage devices. Their specialized software enables these forensic specialists to discover and analyze files that were deleted, overwritten, or encrypted by computer users intent on covering up clandestine activities. Even temporary files, such as those created by word processing software during the creation of documents, for example, can be recovered. Computer Forensics Specialists are able to find and extract e-mails and Web sites from computers used by suspects. These forensic experts also go online and pose as interested parties to entrap criminals suspected of child molestation or pornography crimes.

Computer Forensics Specialists conduct their investigations in computer labs that meet specific standards. They take specific steps and incorporate several methods to conduct their investigations and analyses. They follow particular procedures that enable them to enter permissible evidence at court proceedings.

Their basic approach includes four stages: locating and recognizing data sources, protecting the evidence, analyzing the appropriate data, and preparing the results for reporting and testifying purposes. These professionals are experienced with using all computer platforms and a wide range of software programs, with which they can quickly extract evidentiary material.

When Forensic Computer Specialists conduct their investigations, their first step is to seize the computer equipment, when appropriate, to prevent further use by the suspect. They copy the contents of the hard drive and storage devices; search every file; and identify all files relevant to the case including encrypted, deleted, hidden, and temporary ones. They search for and analyze data found on unallocated disk space; inspect software settings; examine system structures; analyze the suspect's activity and its relevance to the case; and create and print a detailed report containing a log of the investigative activities and full explanation of the analyses.

Throughout this process, Computer Forensics Specialists work to avoid overwriting free space and changing any of the existing data, including date and time stamps. They also take precautions not to introduce viruses. These precautions are necessary to preserve the chain of custody on all computer system and data evidence.

These forensic experts also perform other investigative duties, including interviewing witnesses, victims, and suspects. Law enforcement officers may also engage in performing surveillance or undercover work, participating in evidence searches and seizures, and arresting criminals. Computer Forensics Specialists may be called upon to testify as expert witnesses at depositions, court trials, and other legal hearings. They provide impartial and unbiased testimony about issues related to their laboratory analyses as well as their lab procedures, methods, and techniques.

In addition to their analytical work, these forensic experts perform other duties. For example, they develop new methodologies and techniques for examining digital evidence, and keep up with current research and technologies. Some of them develop training programs as well as teach law enforcement officers and crime scene investigators how to collect digital evidence.

Computer Forensics Specialists work a 40-hour week with many overtime hours. Law enforcement officers are on call 24 hours a day, seven days a week.

Salaries

Salaries for Computer Forensics Specialists vary, depending on such factors as their education, experience, position, employer, and geographic location. Specialists who work in the private sector generally earn higher wages than those who are employed by law enforcement agencies.

Formal salary information for this occupation is unavailable. The U.S. Bureau of Labor Statistics reports in its May 2006 *Occupational Employment Statistics* survey that the estimated annual salary for most computer specialists (not listed separately in other categories) ranged between $35,500 and $103,270. The estimated annual salary for most detectives and criminal investigators in law enforcement agencies ranged between $34,480 and $92,590.

As consultants, Computer Forensics Specialists charge an hourly, daily, or flat rate for their various services, such as initial consultation, examinations, and courtroom testimony. Hourly fees for experienced consultants can range up to $350 and more per hour. Consultants may also charge for telephone calls, travel time, and other out-of-pocket expenses.

Employment Prospects

Computer Forensics Specialists work in local, state, and federal law enforcement agencies. Many agencies hire civilians, but most of these forensic specialists are law enforcement officers. In local and state agencies, the computer crime unit is usually a volunteer detail. Officers perform computer forensics duty in addition to their primary duties as patrol officers, detectives, or other positions. Many agencies require that law officers commit to a minimum number of years when they are chosen for computer forensics duty.

Computer Forensics Specialists are also hired by prosecutor's offices, large corporations, and consulting firms that offer computer forensics services. Some specialists are independent consultants.

Although computer forensics is a young field, the demand is high for qualified experts. Opportunities in both the public and private sectors are expected to increase steadily over the coming years, as computer forensics becomes more important in civil and criminal investigations. In addition, increasingly more businesses and corporations are utilizing the expertise of these professionals to investigate, protect, and preserve their electronic data.

Advancement Prospects

Computer Forensics Specialists can advance in any number of ways, depending on their ambitions and interests. They can rise through the administrative and managerial ranks as technical leaders, unit supervisors, and managers.

Individuals with entrepreneurial ambitions can become independent practitioners or owners of forensic consulting firms. These forensic specialists can also pursue opportunities as instructors and researchers in higher education institutions. They may be required to possess a master's or doctoral degree to advance to higher positions or to obtain teaching jobs in four-year colleges and universities.

Law enforcement officers have additional advancement options. They can rise through the ranks as detectives, sergeants, and so on, up to police chief. They can also seek positions in other law enforcement special details that interest them, such as the SWAT team or air aviation unit. They can also pursue supervisory and managerial positions within their agency.

Education and Training

Educational requirements vary with the different employers. Many employers in the private sector prefer to hire candidates with at least a bachelor's degree in computer science or another related field. Some employers waive the educational requirement for candidates who have qualifying work experience.

Until recently, most Computer Forensics Specialists had learned their skills and knowledge through on-the-job training while working as law enforcement officers or computer security professionals.

Increasingly, formal educational programs are becoming available each year throughout the United States. Individu-

als have the option of enrolling in associate, bachelor's, or master's degree programs in computer forensics. Some colleges and universities also offer professional certification programs in computer forensics. The curriculum in these programs teaches students the computer, forensics, and legal skills and knowledge they need to obtain an entry-level position in computer forensics. Many of these programs also require students to complete an internship.

Throughout their careers, Computer Forensics Engineers enroll in continuing education programs and training programs to update their skills and knowledge, as well as to keep up with technological advancements.

Special Requirements

In agencies in which Computer Forensics Specialists are law enforcement officers, applicants must possess a basic peace officer standards and training certificate. These agencies may hire candidates without a certificate on the condition they complete the necessary law enforcement academy program. Law enforcement officers must successfully complete annual training to maintain their certification.

In the private sector, some specialists offer their services as private investigators. Depending on their location, they must hold either a state or local private investigator's license to practice. For specific information about licensing requirements, contact a local law enforcement agency or the state private investigative licensing agency that covers the jurisdiction where you wish to practice.

Experience, Special Skills, and Personality Traits

Law enforcement agencies generally choose officers for trainee or entry-level positions who have broad computer knowledge and skills in operating systems, programming, software applications, networking, and other areas. They also seek candidates who have the aptitude to learn the necessary skills to perform computer forensics.

For non-officer positions in law enforcement agencies as well as in other work settings, applicants usually need previous work experience in computer forensics. Many Computer Forensics Specialists in the private sector have extensive backgrounds in the field through their work as law enforcement officers and computer security professionals.

To perform well at their job, Computer Forensics Specialists must have excellent problem-solving, critical-thinking, organizational, teamwork, interpersonal, communication, and writing skills. Some personality traits that successful specialists share include being inquisitive, detail-oriented, persistent, patient, honest, trustworthy, and self-motivated.

Unions and Associations

Computer Forensics Specialists can join professional associations to take advantage of networking opportunities, training programs, professional certification, and other professional resources and services. Professional societies are available locally, statewide, regionally, nationally, and worldwide. Some national societies that serve the diverse interests of these experts include:

- High Technology Crime Investigation Association
- International Association of Computer Investigative Specialists
- International Association for Identification
- American Academy of Forensic Sciences
  For contact information, see Appendix III.

Tips for Entry

1. Professional associations and private organizations offer training programs that teach essential skills that individuals need to become Computer Forensics Specialists.

2. If you do plan to enter this career by way of the private sector, be sure to gain a solid understanding of the law and the importance of handling evidence properly. Many community colleges offer courses in criminal justice or police science.

3. Early in your career as a patrol officer, let the computer crime unit supervisor know of your interest in computer forensics investigations.

4. Many Computer Forensics Specialists enhance their employability as well as professional credibility by obtaining professional certifications from recognized organizations. For information about some certification programs, see Appendix II.

5. Use the Internet to learn more about computer forensics. To obtain a list of relevant Web sites, enter any of these keywords into a search engine: *computer forensics*, *forensics computing*, *digital forensics*, or *computer crime unit*. For some links, see Appendix IV.

FORENSIC EXPERTS
IN ENGINEERING AND
CONSTRUCTION

FORENSIC ENGINEER

CAREER PROFILE

Duties: Provide forensic consulting services to attorneys and other clients; perform duties as required

Alternate Title(s): Forensic Consultant, Forensic Expert; a title that reflects their particular engineering specialty such as Forensic Mechanical Engineer or Forensic Electrical Engineer

Salary Range: $46,000 to $121,000+

Employment Prospects: Fair

Advancement Prospects: Good

Prerequisites:

Education or Training—Minimally, a bachelor's degree in an engineering or science discipline

Experience—Several years of work experience in one's field

Special Skills and Personality Traits—Research, writing, presentation, organizational, self-management, interpersonal, and communication skills; curious, innovative, ethical, unbiased, trustworthy, and detail-oriented

Special Requirements—Professional engineer (P.E.) license required

CAREER LADDER

```
┌─────────────────────────────┐
│  Senior Forensic Engineer   │
└─────────────────────────────┘

┌─────────────────────────────┐
│     Forensic Engineer       │
└─────────────────────────────┘

┌─────────────────────────────┐
│         Engineer            │
└─────────────────────────────┘
```

Position Description

Forensic Engineers offer expert evaluations and opinions on engineering issues related to legal and regulatory matters. Engineers from all types of engineering disciplines offer forensic services. Forensic Engineers investigate why buildings, vehicles, machines, manufactured goods, or their material components and parts collapse, break apart, or otherwise fail. They analyze physical evidence to determine the causes of accidents and catastrophes. These professionals seek to answer such questions as: What caused a department store to burn down? Why did an airplane crash? Why did a newly completed high-rise building collapse during an earthquake? What caused workers to fall at a construction site? Was a person's injury caused by a defect in an artificial limb? Did a lawnmower explode because it failed to work properly? What caused toxic waste to leak into a community's water supply?

Most Forensic Engineers are independent consultants or staff consultants with engineering firms that offer foren-sic engineering services. Their forensic skills are sought by attorneys, insurance claims adjusters, various industries, and companies that test products. These professionals apply their engineering expertise to legal concerns rather than to engineering functions such as design or the production of products. Forensic Engineers are well versed in how the legal system works, yet they offer forensic services only in cases that are within their particular realm of engineering expertise, such as civil engineering, mechanical engineering, or materials engineering.

Many Forensic Engineers focus their work in a few specific areas such as certain types of accidents; the causes and origin of fires; mechanical, electrical, chemical, or product design failures; or industrial equipment damage. These engineers investigate operative or functional failures that may be the result of criminal negligence or criminal behavior. Forensic Engineers also work on civil cases, such as injury or product liability claims, as well as intellectual property disputes.

These engineers use several methods and procedures of investigation in much the same manner as other forensic experts. They review police reports, eyewitness statements, expert reports, and other materials for background information. Forensic Engineers inspect sites where accidents, catastrophes, or losses occurred and examine all available physical evidence.

Besides visually inspecting evidence, Forensic Engineers may also use reverse engineering, in which they dissemble a product and examine it closely to learn how it was made. They also conduct close-up examinations by using electron microscopes, spectroscopes, and other optical devices. They may reproduce accidents in laboratory settings to discover what happened. They may perform standardized tests on products to evaluate them for failure or defects. Forensic Engineers document every step of their inspections with written notes, photographs, and videotapes.

Forensic Engineers conduct interviews to determine the course of events that led to equipment failure. They review drawings, schematics, written specifications, and other pertinent documents. They use analytical and testing tools to verify the problems under investigation. These engineers analyze and interpret their data, sometimes with the help of computer models, to show the sequence of events or contributing factors that may have led to an accident or product failure. They are expected to arrive at objective conclusions that, on occasion, may not be favorable for their clients.

Forensic Engineers prepare reports of their findings and conclusions. Their reports are organized clearly and concisely, yet comprehensively, as they may be used for pretrial proceedings, trials, and settlement negotiations. Consequently, they present information in simplified terms so that nontechnical individuals can understand technical and scientific concepts.

Many Forensic Engineers present their findings to courts as expert witnesses for trials and depositions. They may be asked to provide scientific or technical explanations to help judges and juries understand specific issues in a civil or criminal trial. They may be asked for their expert opinions about their specific analysis of the events that took place. These experts avoid taking sides in the issues about which they testify.

Many Forensic Engineers also offer litigation support services to attorneys. Some of their services may include:

- educating lawyers about the subject matter so they can fully understand the issues of a case
- evaluating a case to identify the technical issues and facts
- finding appropriate expert witnesses
- helping lawyers develop effective strategies for a case
- formulating a list of questions that lawyers would use to cross-examine witnesses
- preparing demonstrative evidence (such as diagrams, models, or computer animations)

Forensic Engineers are responsible for keeping abreast of the latest forensic research, techniques, and technologies in their areas of expertise.

Forensic Engineers generally work a 40-hour week. They sometimes work additional hours during evenings and on weekends to complete tasks and meet deadlines. They may travel to different cities and states to meet with clients, survey traffic scenes, or testify in court.

Salaries

Earnings for Forensic Engineers vary, depending on such factors as their education, experience, specialty, position (staff or self-employed), and geographic location. Specific salary information for this occupation is unavailable. According to the May 2006 *Occupational Employment Statistics* survey by the U.S. Bureau of Labor Statistics, most engineers whose discipline was not listed separately in the survey earned an estimated annual salary that ranged between $46,080 and $120,610. However, it is not uncommon for highly experienced and reputable Forensic Engineers to garner higher incomes.

As consultants, Forensic Engineers charge an hourly, daily, or flat rate for their various services, such as initial consultation, examinations, and courtroom testimony. Hourly fees generally range from $100 to $300 per hour or more. Consultants may also charge for telephone calls, travel time, and other out-of-pocket expenses.

Employment Prospects

Most Forensic Engineers work in the private sector where they are employed by small engineering firms or are independent practitioners. Some Forensic Engineers work part time while employed full time as engineers or academicians. Large corporations and government agencies also employ Forensic Engineers.

Job openings for staff positions become available when engineers advance to higher positions, transfer to other jobs, or leave the workforce for various reasons. Private companies will create additional positions as their businesses expand.

Opportunities for experienced and reputable Forensic Engineers are favorable and should continue for years to come. Attorneys and others constantly need their expertise to investigate technical issues for legal matters.

Advancement Prospects

Staff engineers can seek supervisory, administrative, and management positions in their organizations. Engineers in small outfits may have to find employment with other firms in order to obtain such positions. In addition, Forensic Engineers can advance through the ranks from junior consultants to principal consultants.

Entrepreneurial engineers pursue their ambitions by becoming independent consultants or owners of forensic engineering firms.

Education and Training

There are no academic degree programs in forensic engineering as this is being written. Some universities, however, offer forensic engineering courses as electives. Engineers typically learn about forensic applications on the job and through workshops and conferences sponsored by professional associations and other recognized organizations.

Minimally, Forensic Engineers must possess a bachelor's degree in an engineering or science discipline. Most Forensic Engineers have a master's or doctoral degree.

Throughout their careers, Forensic Engineers enroll in continuing education programs and training programs to update their skills and keep up with advancements in their fields.

Special Requirements

Because they offer their services directly to the public, Forensic Engineers must be licensed professional engineers (P.E.) in the states where they practice.

All states—as well as Washington, D.C. and the U.S. territories—have their own unique licensing requirements. For specific information, contact the board of engineering examiners for the jurisdiction where you plan to practice.

Experience, Special Skills, and Personality Traits

Engineers typically have worked for several years in their specialties before embarking on a career as a Forensic Engineer.

Employers generally seek candidates for staff consulting positions who have several years of experience conducting forensic investigations and providing expert witness testimony.

Forensic Engineers must have strong research, writing, presentation, organizational, and self-management skills. In addition, they need excellent interpersonal and communication skills, as they must work well with clients, colleagues, and many others from diverse backgrounds. Being curious, innovative, ethical, unbiased, trustworthy, and detail-oriented are some personality traits that successful Forensic Engineers share.

Unions and Associations

Many Forensic Engineers join professional associations to take advantage of networking opportunities, professional certification, continuing education, professional publications, and other professional services and resources. Societies that serve their diverse interests are available at the local, state, national, and international levels.

The National Academy of Forensic Engineers, the American Academy of Forensic Sciences, and the American College of Forensic Examiners are a few national societies that serve the special interests of these forensic professionals. They also join special focus engineering societies, such as the National Society of Professional Engineers, the Society of Women Engineers, or the Society of Hispanic Professional Engineers.

Additionally, Forensic Engineers may join engineering societies that serve their particular disciplines, such as the American Society of Civil Engineers, the American Institute of Chemical Engineers, the American Academy of Environmental Engineers, ASME International (the American Society of Mechanical Engineers), the Institute of Electrical and Electronics Engineers, SAE International (the Society of Automotive Engineers), or the American Society of Safety Engineers.

For contact information for all of the above organizations, see Appendix III.

Tips for Entry

1. For staff positions, candidates may be allowed to substitute an advanced degree for one or more years of practical experience.
2. Many attorneys, insurance companies, and other prospective clients prefer to retain Forensic Engineers who possess an advanced degree in their engineering discipline.
3. Many Forensic Engineers obtain professional certifications in their specialties to enhance their employability and credibility. For information about specific professional certification programs, contact professional associations.
4. Use the Internet to learn more about forensic engineering. You might start by visiting the National Academy of Forensic Engineers at http://www.nafe.org. For more links, see Appendix IV.

ACCIDENT RECONSTRUCTION SPECIALIST

CAREER PROFILE

Duties: Examine and reconstruct traffic collisions; interpret findings; prepare reports; provide expert witness testimony; perform duties as required

Alternate Title(s): Traffic Accident Reconstructionist, Crash Reconstruction Consultant, Forensic Engineer

Salary Range: $27,000 to $121,000

Employment Prospects: Good

Advancement Prospects: Poor

Prerequisites:

Education or Training—Completion of training programs from recognized institutions; ongoing training and continuing education programs

Experience—Prior accident investigation experience for law enforcement officers

Special Skills and Personality Traits—Analytical, organizational, writing, communication, and interpersonal skills; curious, objective, trustworthy, methodical, detail-oriented, and dedicated

Special Requirements—Law enforcement officers possess peace officer certificate; engineers hold a professional engineer license; private consultants may need a private investigator license

CAREER LADDER

```
┌─────────────────────────────────────┐
│  Accident Reconstruction Consultant  │
└─────────────────────────────────────┘

┌─────────────────────────────────────┐
│  Accident Reconstruction Specialist  │
└─────────────────────────────────────┘

┌─────────────────────────────────────┐
│       Accident Reconstruction        │
│         Specialist Trainee           │
└─────────────────────────────────────┘
```

Position Description

How fast were cars traveling when they collided? Did the glare of the sun contribute to a driver's crossing over the highway median? Did a driver come to a complete stop before turning right? What obstructed a driver from seeing a small child walking in the intersection, as he was turning left? Are the injuries that a passenger reported consistent with how the human body would have moved in a low-impact collision?

Those are a few of the types of questions that Accident Reconstruction Specialists might ask when they examine cases related to insurance claims, civil litigation, criminal investigations, and other legal matters.

Accident Reconstruction Specialists have the knowledge and skills to analyze traffic crash accidents and piece together what occurred. They base their examinations upon physical and factual evidence, and apply geometry, algebra, and calculus principles as well as the laws of physics. They also have an understanding of various subjects such as vehicle dynamics and structural properties, human factors, and weather.

These forensic experts are not to be confused with traffic accident investigators, who are usually police officers. These investigators examine accident scenes soon after collisions have occurred, and are responsible for collecting evidence, interviewing eyewitnesses, and documenting the accident scene. Accident Reconstruction Specialists, on the other hand, reconstruct a traffic crash accident scene to determine pre-existing conditions, hazards, risks, and causes. They analyze and interpret the data that has already been collected. This involves reviewing police reports, eyewitness testimony, photographs, drawings, and other information. From the evidence, these reconstructionists can determine such facts as the speed that vehicles were traveling before and after impact, the distance vehicles were from each other prior to collision, the severity of the impact on pedestrians, and if headlights were functioning properly.

Carefully and thoroughly, Accident Reconstruction Specialists rebuild the events of a traffic crash accident. To help them get a clearer understanding of what took place, they sometimes recreate the accident, including the use of similar vehicles.

These reconstructionists conduct their investigations in labs that meet certain standards. They take specific steps and incorporate several methods to conduct their investigations and analyses. They follow particular procedures that enable them to enter permissible evidence at court proceedings.

Upon completing their investigations, Accident Reconstruction Specialists prepare highly detailed reports about their findings and conclusions. The reports usually include diagrams, models, computer animations, or other visual aids to illustrate their findings. Their reports are expected to be factual, impartial, and unbiased. Attorneys often submit these reports as evidence in civil or criminal trials. They also utilize the reports to negotiate settlements with opposing parties.

When requested, Accident Reconstruction Specialists provide expert testimony at court trials, settlement hearings, alternative dispute resolution meetings, and other formal settings. As expert witnesses at court trials, they address only issues about which they are qualified to provide a professional opinion.

In addition to their analytical work, these forensic experts perform other duties. For example, they develop new methodologies and techniques for examining evidence, develop training programs, teach training workshops, and keep up with current research and technologies.

Accident Reconstruction Specialists work in law enforcement agencies as well as in the private sector. Reconstructionists in law enforcement agencies are law enforcement officers who volunteer for additional duty in their agency's traffic accident unit. Many of them are both traffic accident investigators and reconstructionists. Usually, a traffic accident unit conducts investigations only of traffic crashes that involve deaths or serious physical injuries.

Private crash reconstruction consultants may be independent practitioners or part of consulting firms that offer traffic reconstruction services. Some Accident Reconstruction Specialists are forensic engineers, while others are former law enforcement officers who have served many years as reconstructionists on their forces. These private consultants are typically retained by attorneys and insurance companies to assist with civil litigation, criminal defense cases, and insurance claims.

Accident Reconstruction Specialists generally work a 40-hour schedule. They put in additional hours as needed to complete their tasks and meet deadlines. Law enforcement officers are on call 24 hours a day, seven days a week.

Salaries

Salaries for Accident Reconstruction Specialists vary, depending on such factors as their education, experience, position, employer, and geographic location. Specific salary information for this occupation is unavailable.

Law enforcement officers earn salaries according to their position, rank, and other factors. The U.S. Bureau of Labor Statistics reports in its May 2006 *Occupational Employment Statistics* (OES) survey that the estimated annual salary for most local patrol officers ranged between $27,310 and $72,450, and for most detectives and criminal investigators between $34,480 and $92,590.

According to the 2006 OES survey, the estimated annual salary for most engineers who were not listed in separate categories ranged between $46,080 and $120,610.

As consultants, Accident Reconstruction Specialists charge an hourly, daily, or flat rate for their various services, such as initial consultation, examinations, and courtroom testimony. Their hourly fees generally range from $100 to $200 per hour or more. Consultants may also charge for telephone calls, travel time, and other out-of-pocket expenses.

Employment Prospects

Police departments, sheriffs' offices, and state police departments all have traffic accident units. Depending on the needs of the jurisdiction, a traffic accident unit may have one or several officers working as reconstructionists. Working in a traffic accident unit is a volunteer detail. Many Accident Reconstruction Specialists perform this duty in addition to their primary duties as patrol officers, detectives, or in other positions.

In the private sector, Accident Reconstruction Specialists work for crash reconstruction consulting firms, as well as for forensic engineering practices that offer crash reconstruction consulting services. Some specialists are independent practitioners. These forensic examiners are hired by attorneys, insurance companies, and others on a contractual basis.

Advancement Prospects

Accident Reconstruction Specialists can advance in a number of ways, depending on their ambitions and interests. They can rise through the administrative and managerial ranks as technical leaders, unit supervisors, and managers in their organizations.

Individuals with entrepreneurial ambitions can become independent practitioners or owners of forensic consulting firms. These forensic specialists can also pursue opportunities as instructors and researchers in higher education institutions. They may be required to possess a master's or doctoral degree to advance to higher positions or to obtain teaching jobs in four-year colleges and universities.

Law enforcement officers have additional advancement options. They can rise through the ranks as detectives, sergeants, and so on, up to police chief. They can also seek positions in other law enforcement special details that interest them, such as the SWAT team or air aviation unit.

Independent consultants typically realize advancement through the growth of their businesses, through job satisfaction, and by earning higher incomes.

Education and Training

Accident Reconstruction Specialists obtain their training in various ways. Current law enforcement officers, as well as former officers who are now consultants, receive on-the-job training while working under experienced reconstructionists. They also complete basic and advanced training programs from nationally recognized institutions, such as the Northwestern University Center for Public Safety and the Institute of Police Technology and Management.

Forensic engineers have earned bachelor's and master's degrees in mechanical engineering, automotive engineering, civil engineering, or another engineering field. Many of them learn their reconstructionist skills on the job.

Throughout their careers, Accident Reconstruction Specialists enroll in continuing education programs and training programs to update their skills and knowledge, as well as to keep up with technological advancements.

Special Requirements

Accident Reconstruction Specialists who work in law enforcement agencies must possess a basic peace officer standards and training certificate.

Forensic engineers who specialize in this field must possess a professional engineer license in every state where they practice. For licensing information, contact the board of engineering examiners that governs the jurisdiction in which you wish to work.

Depending on their location, consultants must hold either a state or local private investigator's license to practice. For specific information about licensing requirements, contact a local law enforcement agency or the state private investigative licensing agency that covers the jurisdiction where you wish to practice.

Experience, Special Skills, and Personality Traits

In the private sector, most Accident Reconstruction Specialists are former law enforcement officers who served many years working as traffic accident reconstructionists. Other specialists have years of forensic experience as engineers.

Law enforcement officers must usually complete two to three years of patrol duty before they are eligible to apply for special details such as the traffic accident unit.

To work effectively as traffic accident reconstructionists, individuals must have excellent analytical, organizational, report-writing, communication, and interpersonal skills. Being curious, objective, trustworthy, methodical, detail-oriented, and dedicated are some personality traits that successful Accident Reconstruction Specialists have in common.

Unions and Associations

Accident Reconstruction Specialists can join professional associations to take advantage of networking opportunities, training programs, professional certification, and other professional resources and services. Some national societies that serve the diverse interests of these experts include:

- International Association of Accident Reconstruction Specialists
- National Association of Professional Accident Reconstruction Specialists
- National Association of Traffic Accident Reconstructionists and Investigators
- Society of Accident Reconstructionists
- American Society of Safety Engineers
- National Academy of Forensic Engineers
- American Academy of Forensic Sciences
  For contact information, see Appendix III.

Tips for Entry

1. Early in your career as a patrol officer, let your supervisor know about your interest in traffic accident investigations and reconstruction.
2. Consider obtaining professional certification from recognized organizations to enhance your credibility and employability. For information about certification programs, see Appendix II.
3. For staff positions in the private sector, apply directly to accident reconstruction consulting firms.
4. Use the Internet to learn more about the field of traffic crash reconstruction. You might start by visiting the Accident Reconstruction Network Web site at http://www.accidentreconstruction.com. For more links, see Appendix IV.

CONSTRUCTION FORENSICS EXPERT

CAREER PROFILE	CAREER LADDER

Duties: Provide forensic consulting services to clients; may provide litigation support services to attorneys; perform duties as required

Alternate Title(s): Forensic Construction Consultant; Forensic Engineer, Forensic Architect, Forensic Contractor

Salary Range: Unavailable

Employment Prospects: Fair

Advancement Prospects: Poor

Prerequisites:

Education or Training—College degree and/or on-the-job training appropriate to an occupation

Experience—Extensive work experience in one's field

Special Skills and Personality Traits—Analytical, organizational, self-management, writing, presentation, communication, interpersonal, and computer skills; poised, impartial, trustworthy, fair, inquisitive, detail-oriented, precise, and flexible

Special Requirements—Professional license or certification as required for an occupation

---

Construction Forensics Expert

Novice Construction Forensics Expert

Engineer, Architect, Contractor, or Other Occupation in the Construction Industry

---

Position Description

Did a general contractor fail to complete his obligations in a timely matter? Was poor workmanship the reason for roofs to leak in a new housing development? Were the heating and air conditioning systems in a restaurant installed incorrectly? Did a power tool's design contribute to a person's injury?

Construction Forensics Experts answer questions such as these for litigation, insurance claims, contractual disputes, regulatory hearings, arson investigations, and other legal matters. They are retained by attorneys, insurance companies, developers, contractors, building owners, government agencies, and others who seek their expert assistance.

These forensic consultants are highly experienced practitioners in the planning, design, construction, alteration, operation, and maintenance of all types of buildings, structures, and public works as well as all building systems (plumbing, fire protection, and heating, ventilation and air conditioning systems, for example). They include engineers, architects, construction managers, building contractors, construction trades workers (such as plumbers and electricians), mold specialists, cost estimators, certified public accountants, building and construction inspectors, and others.

Essentially, these consultants' job is to carry out a thorough forensic investigation to identify and define the root causes of and contributing factors to construction problems. They address issues that may involve construction defects, failure of building systems, product safety design, improper maintenance of buildings or building systems, construction work plans, scheduling, construction delays, work safety, building code deficiencies, and management practices, among others.

In addition to detecting the causes of construction problems, Construction Forensics Experts make recommendations for resolving the problems. Sometimes clients also request that these consultants provide an estimate of the cost for correcting construction problems. In many cases, the findings and professional opinions of these forensic experts help clients settle their disputes.

Depending on the complexity of a project, Construction Forensics Experts may work alone or as part of a team. When a project begins, they meet with clients to determine their needs. Throughout the project, they provide clients with regular reports of their progress.

These experts perform a wide range of tasks, which vary with each project. Some tasks are the same in every forensic investigation. For example, they:

- research written materials, such as building codes, for information relevant to a case
- review and analyze shop drawings, photographs, design documents, operating manual instructions, inspection contracts, and various other reports, documents, and files
- conduct site investigations, which include taking visual surveys and performing appropriate tests
- review construction projects for compliance with design documents, building codes, governmental regulations, safety requirements, industry standards, construction practices, or contracts
- interview eyewitnesses
- prepare detailed reports of their findings and professional opinions
- provide expert testimony at depositions, trials, settlement conferences, or alternative dispute resolution meetings

Many Construction Forensics Experts offer litigation support services to attorneys, who may represent either defendants or plaintiffs. These experts help attorneys develop a successful case for their clients by performing such tasks as: reviewing cases to identify the technical issues and facts; helping lawyers understand technical terms and concepts; seeking more evidence to support a case; conducting tests to disprove or prove a fact; finding appropriate expert witnesses; and developing demonstrative evidence (or exhibits) for trials.

Construction Forensics Experts work flexible hours. They put in long hours as needed to complete their tasks and meet deadlines. They frequently travel to meet with clients, attend depositions and trials, and participate in conferences and other relevant events.

Salaries

Specific earnings information for this occupation is unavailable. Annual gross earnings for Construction Forensics Experts is based on the total fees that they have earned in a year. Earnings vary yearly, depending on such factors as their rates, specialties, and the demand for their services.

Forensic consultants charge an hourly, daily, or flat rate for research, examinations, depositions, and other services that they perform. Many consultants receive reimbursements for out-of-pocket expenses such as travel time, telephone calls, and photocopying.

Employment Prospects

In general, opportunities are favorable for experienced and reputable Construction Forensics Experts. Some of these forensic consultants are self-employed. Others are employed by engineering, architectural, or construction firms that offer construction forensics services.

Staff positions usually become available when consultants advance to higher positions, transfer to other jobs, or retire. Employers may create additional positions when the demand for their company's services increases.

Advancement Prospects

Construction Forensics Experts generally measure success through job satisfaction, professional recognition, and by being sought for highly complex or publicized cases.

Staff consultants can be promoted to become supervisors and managers. They can also rise through the ranks, including to partner level. Those with entrepreneurial ambitions can pursue careers as independent practitioners or owners of architectural firms.

Education and Training

Construction Forensic Experts possess the appropriate credentials and training that are required for their particular occupations. For example, engineers have earned at least a bachelor's degree in civil, mechanical, or another engineering discipline, and electricians and other trades workers have completed apprenticeship programs.

Throughout their careers, Construction Forensic Experts enroll in continuing education and training programs to update their skills and knowledge.

Special Requirements

Construction Forensic Experts must have the appropriate professional licenses and certification required for their professions. All engineers, architects, and building contractors must possess the proper licenses to practice in the states where they plan to work. Plumbers and electricians may be required to possess professional licenses.

Experience, Special Skills, and Personality Traits

Building contractors, architects, engineers, and others typically become Construction Forensics Experts after many years of working in their fields.

Employers generally seek candidates for staff consulting positions who have several years of experience conducting forensic investigations as well as providing expert witness testimony.

To succeed at consulting work, individuals need excellent analytical, organizational, self-management, writing, and presentation skills. They also need exceptional communication and interpersonal skills, as they must be able to work well with clients, colleagues, and others from diverse backgrounds. Additionally, they need adequate computer skills. Some personality traits that successful Construction Forensics Experts have in common include being poised, impartial, trustworthy, fair, inquisitive, detail-oriented, precise, and flexible.

Unions and Associations

Construction Forensics Experts can join professional associations to take advantage of networking opportunities, training programs, professional certification, and other professional resources and services. Local, state, and national societies are available to serve the diverse interests of these forensic examiners. Some national groups are:

- National Academy of Forensic Engineers
- American Society of Civil Engineers
- American Institute of Architects
- American Institute of Contractors
- Associated General Contractors of America
- Construction Specifications Institute

- American Society of Professional Estimators
- American Academy of Forensic Sciences
- American College of Forensic Examiners

For contact information, see Appendix III.

Tips for Entry

1. Talk with different Construction Forensics Experts to learn more about their specialties, as well as how they got into the field.
2. Enroll in courses or workshops that teach forensic skills.
3. As an employee, take advantage of opportunities to work on forensic investigations.
4. Many firms who offer construction forensics services maintain a presence on the Internet. Some of them provide information about job openings. To obtain a list of Web sites, enter any of these keywords into a search engine: *construction forensics* or *forensic construction experts*.

FORENSIC ARCHITECT

CAREER PROFILE

Duties: Provide forensic consulting services to attorneys and other clients; perform duties as required

Alternate Title(s): Architect; Forensic Consultant

Salary Range: $39,000 to $105,000

Employment Prospects: Fair

Advancement Prospects: Poor

Prerequisites:

 Education or Training—Bachelor's or master's degree in architecture; on-the-job training

 Experience—Several years of work experience in one's field

 Special Skills and Personality Traits—Communication, interpersonal, project-management, presentation, writing, and computer skills; creative, curious, trustworthy, impartial, detail-oriented, and persistent

 Special Requirements—Architect license required

CAREER LADDER

> **Senior Forensic Architect**

> **Forensic Architect**

> **Architect**

Position Description

Forensic architecture is another forensic specialty in which professionals apply their expertise to legal matters, including civil litigation, contractual disputes, insurance claims, and regulatory violations.

Forensic Architects are professionals with many years of architectural experience. In general, architects are responsible for planning and designing the form and appearance of buildings and structures, including houses, apartment buildings, office complexes, skyscrapers, schools, hospitals, restaurants, shopping malls, warehouses, factories, bridges, and airports, among others. Architects also are responsible for developing plans for building systems such as a structure's plumbing, electrical, heating and cooling, security, and fire protection systems.

When legal problems occur regarding a building or building systems, Forensic Architects are consulted by attorneys, insurance companies, and others. These forensic consultants investigate the architectural facts relating to the development, design, construction, or maintenance of buildings. Their findings and expert opinions help clients resolve or settle their legal cases.

These forensic experts are retained to assist in a wide range of building issues. For example, they may investigate cases involving:

- building failures
- construction defects
- professional negligence or malpractice
- personal injury claims
- compliance with required standards, building codes, and other appropriate laws and regulations
- contractual disputes between a property owner and an architect

Forensic Architects perform a variety of tasks when they conduct their investigations to determine the validity and extent of claims. They inspect work sites, buildings, and building systems. They study pertinent documents, such as design plans, maintenance records, or construction schedules. They interpret contractual requirements. They research industry, governmental, and professional standards, as well as laws, regulations, and building codes.

When they have completed their examinations and analyses, Forensic Architects prepare reports that describe their findings, including the history of the problems, the reasons for their occurrences, and recommendations for resolving the problems. In the case of building failures and defects, Forensic Architects may also provide an estimate of the costs for making repairs. Forensic Architects are expected to write their reports clearly and to express technical concepts in terms that lay people can easily understand. Their clients may use these specialists' reports in settlement negotiations or submit them as evidence in court trials.

On occasion, Forensic Architects may be asked to provide expert testimony about their findings at depositions, court trials, or alternative dispute resolution meetings. They address only issues and facts for which they are qualified to give their professional opinions. Although they are hired to give testimony, they do not advocate for either side in a case. They are expected to give objective and unbiased testimony.

Many Forensic Architects offer litigation support services to attorneys. They perform any number of tasks to help attorneys build a strong and successful case for their clients. For example, Forensic Architects may be retained to help attorneys understand technical documents; review cases to identify the technical issues and facts; photograph evidence; examine incident scenes; conduct tests to prove or disprove certain facts or issues; research professional literature; seek expert witnesses; provide questions for depositions or trials; and prepare exhibits for court trials or alternative dispute resolution hearings.

When Forensic Architects provide litigation support services, they usually do not perform any expert witness services. However, lawyers may ask them to testify as eye-witnesses. They answer questions about facts related to a case based on their direct observation or work rather than their professional opinion.

Forensic Architects may specialize in any number of ways. They may focus on certain structures (such as shopping malls or high-rise towers), specific industries (such as health care or government), and certain types of investigations (such as construction defect litigation).

Many Forensic Architects also continue to offer traditional architectural services, such as design, project management, or construction administration, to clients. Some Forensic Architects are solo practitioners, while others are associates or partners in architectural and engineering firms.

Architects, in general, work full time, but put in additional hours to complete tasks and meet deadlines. Many of them travel to other cities and states to meet with clients or to perform their forensic investigations.

Salaries

Specific salary information for Forensic Architects is unavailable. As consultants, they charge an hourly, daily, or flat rate for initial consultation, depositions, courtroom testimony, and other services that they offer.

The estimated annual salary for most architects ranged between $39,420 and $104,970, according to the May 2006 *Occupational Employment Statistics* survey by the U.S. Bureau of Labor Statistics (BLS).

Employment Prospects

Some architects are employed by government agencies, but overall, most architects work in the private sector.

The competition for jobs is strong. The BLS reports that job growth for this occupation is expected to increase by 9 to 17 percent through 2014. In addition, job openings will become available as architects retire, transfer to other jobs, or advance to higher positions. However, the employment of architects is tied into the health of the economy. For example, job opportunities are usually fewer when the economy is in a downturn.

Opportunities are favorable for experienced Forensic Architects.

Advancement Prospects

Forensic Architects generally measure success through job satisfaction, professional recognition, and by being sought for highly complex or publicized cases.

Staff architects can advance to become supervisors and managers. They can also rise through the ranks, including to partner level. Those with entrepreneurial ambitions can pursue careers as independent practitioners or owners of architectural firms.

Some architects seek opportunities in areas that interest them such as teaching, urban planning, real estate development, or construction management.

Education and Training

Forensic Architects possess a professional degree in architecture, which may be either a bachelor's or master's degree. Some employers prefer to hire candidates who have a master's degree in architecture. Architects typically obtain forensic architecture training on the job.

There are several paths that lead to earning a professional architectural degree. High school graduates can enroll in a five-year bachelor's degree program in which they earn a professional degree in architecture. Upon earning their bachelor's, they can then complete a two-year master's degree program, if they wish. Students who have a non-professional bachelor's degree in architecture or a bachelor's degree in a related field may enroll in a two-year master's degree program in architecture. Students who have earned a bachelor's degree in other disciplines may qualify for a three- or four-year master's degree program.

After graduating from their professional degree program, individuals must then undergo a three-year internship with a licensed architect who supervises and directs their work. Upon successfully completing their internship, they are eligible to take the exam to become licensed architects.

Throughout their careers, Forensic Architects enroll in continuing education programs and training programs to update their skills and keep up with advancements in their fields.

Special Requirements

To practice architecture in the United States (including Washington, D.C. and the U.S. territories), individuals must possess a professional license. Every state has its own licensing requirements. For specific information, contact the board of architecture (or board of architects) that governs the jurisdiction in which you wish to practice. If you plan to practice in more than one state, you must obtain a license for each jurisdiction.

Architects must complete continuing education credits to maintain their professional licenses.

Experience, Special Skills, and Personality Traits

Potential clients seek Forensic Architects who have distinguished themselves in their field. Clients retain consultants who have the necessary knowledge, skills, and experience to successfully complete their projects. Typically, architects have worked for many years in their field prior to becoming forensic consultants.

Prospective employers seek Forensic Architects for staff positions who have several years of work experience, including forensic investigation and expert testimony experience. Strong candidates must also be knowledgeable about the areas (for example, commercial and residential building systems) in which they would work. They should also have a thorough understanding of industry, professional, and governmental standards as well as laws, regulations, and building codes.

Because they must be able to work well with clients, colleagues, attorneys, and many others from diverse back-grounds, Forensic Architects must have excellent communication and interpersonal skills. In addition, their job requires that they have effective project-management, presentation, writing, and computer skills.

Some personality traits that successful Forensic Architects share include being creative, curious, trustworthy, impartial, detail-oriented, and persistent.

Unions and Associations

Forensic Architects can join various professional associations to take advantage of networking opportunities, continuing education, professional certification, and other professional resources and services. Some national societies that serve their different interests include the American Institute of Architects, the Construction Specifications Institute, the American Academy of Forensic Sciences, and the American College of Forensic Examiners. For contact information, see Appendix III.

Tips for Entry

1. Employers sometimes offer full-time positions to interns who have made a strong impression.
2. Some employers and state architectural registration boards require applicants to possess a degree granted from an architectural school accredited by the National Architectural Accrediting Board.
3. Learn how to use computer-aided design and drafting (CADD) programs, as architectural firms are increasingly using these applications.
4. As a junior architect, volunteer to work on projects that involve forensic investigations.
5. Use the Internet to learn more forensic architecture. To find relevant Web sites, enter the keywords *forensic architecture* or *forensic architects* into a search engine. For some links, see Appendix IV.

FORENSIC SURVEYOR

CAREER PROFILE

Duties: Provide forensic consulting services to attorneys, law enforcement agencies, and other clients; conduct accurate and precise surveys; analyze and interpret evidence; perform duties as required

Alternate Title(s): Professional Surveyor; Forensic Consultant

Salary Range: $27,000 to $80,000

Employment Prospects: Fair

Advancement Prospects: Poor

Prerequisites:

Education or Training—Degree or professional certificate in surveying; on-the-job training

Experience—Several years of work experience as a professional surveyor

Special Skills and Personality Traits—Organizational, analytical, self-management, writing, presentation, interpersonal, and communication skills; curious, accurate, precise, unbiased, trustworthy, and dedicated

Special Requirements—Professional surveyor (P.S.) license usually required

CAREER LADDER

```
┌─────────────────────────────┐
│     Forensic Surveyor       │
└─────────────────────────────┘

┌─────────────────────────────┐
│  Novice Forensic Surveyor   │
└─────────────────────────────┘

┌─────────────────────────────┐
│         Surveyor            │
└─────────────────────────────┘
```

Position Description

Professional surveyors measure areas of land that may be in cities or in rural areas, or on mountains or under water (such as oceans and rivers). Typically, they take surveys for clients who need to determine the boundaries and topographical features of real property, to mark out routes (such as roads, channels, and utility transmission lines), and to ensure that buildings and other structures are built both level and plumb (horizontally and vertically even).

Some professional surveyors specialize in performing forensic or investigative surveys for attorneys, insurance companies, contractors, government agencies, and other clients. Forensic Surveyors engage in cases involving property line disputes, insurance claims, vehicular accidents, industrial site mishaps, aircraft collisions, criminal investigations, civil lawsuits, or other legal matters.

Forensic Surveyors apply the principles of mathematics and science to their surveying tasks. They are also familiar with appropriate local, state, and federal laws, such as those that govern their practice and the handling of evidence in legal matters. These professionals are able to prepare accurate maps and written descriptions from the measurements that they take of the topography of a location. Moreover, they are able to interpret technical specifications from written records such as land deeds, construction plans, and accident reports.

Professional surveyors utilize a variety of sophisticated tools to collect and analyze data. Probably their most recognizable tool is the total station, which is a small telescope on a tripod that measures distances with an electronic laser device. Other technologies that these surveyors use include aerial photography, global positioning system (GPS) equipment, geographic information systems (GIS) hardware and software, and 3D laser scanning systems.

Forensic Surveyors perform certain tasks when they work on a project. They collect precise and accurate measurements at the location in question where they measure distances, angles, elevations, and other features that their clients have requested. For example, Forensic Surveyors might take measurements of skid marks, among other evidence, at an automobile accident site. They also review maps, sketches, deeds, and other materials related to a case. In addition, they may interview people to gather more information. For example, in a case involving a property line dispute, Forensic Surveyors might talk to current and former landowners.

Forensic Surveyors analyze and interpret the data that they have collected and form their conclusions. They prepare maps of their surveys as well as highly detailed written reports of their findings and opinions, which their clients may use in settlement meetings or present in court as evidence. Forensic Surveyors are expected to convey technical concepts in terms that lay people can easily comprehend.

When requested, Forensic Surveyors provide expert witness testimony at court proceedings, administrative hearings, or alternative dispute resolution meetings. They may be asked to give their professional opinions about survey issues that are related to a case. They may also be asked to provide technical information about the surveying practice so that judges and jurors can understand the facts and issues of a case.

Forensic Surveyors work in the field as well as in offices. They may conduct research in courthouses and on computer and Internet databases. They generally work alone when compiling and analyzing documentation, but work with assistants and technicians when taking surveys in the field.

Surveying is demanding work. Forensic Surveyors walk long distances or hike up hills while carrying their equipment. They also stand for long periods of time.

Salaries

Salary information for Forensic Surveyors is unavailable. As consultants, they charge an hourly, daily, or flat rate for initial consultation, depositions, courtroom testimony, and other services that they offer.

According to the May 2006 *Occupational Employment Statistics* survey by the U.S. Bureau of Labor Statistics (BLS), the estimated annual salary for most surveyors ranged between $26,690 and $79,910.

Employment Prospects

Many consulting surveyors are employed by architectural and engineering firms. Some are independent practitioners. Surveyors who serve as expert witnesses and have established reputations in forensic surveying are in strong demand.

Opportunities for surveyors overall are favorable. According to the BLS, job growth for this occupation is expected to increase by 9 to 17 percent through 2014. In addition, opportunities will become available as surveyors retire, advance to higher positions, and transfer to other jobs.

Advancement Prospects

As forensic consultants, surveyors measure success by building their practice, gaining professional recognition, and earning higher incomes. Many also measure success by being sought for very complex or publicized cases.

Education and Training

Many two-year colleges offer an associate degree program in surveying, while many four-year colleges and universities offer a bachelor's degree in this discipline. Some colleges and universities also have a professional certificate program for surveyors who are seeking their professional licenses.

With recent advances in surveying, many employers prefer to hire candidates who possess a bachelor's degree in surveying, civil engineering, or another related field. Increasingly, more states are requiring that surveyors have a bachelor's degree to obtain professional licenses.

Forensic Surveyors typically learn their skills on the job. Throughout their careers, they enroll in continuing education programs and training programs to update their skills and knowledge.

Special Requirements

Forensic Surveyors must possess a professional surveyor (P.S.) license in each state (as well as in Washington, D.C. and each U.S. territory) where they practice. In some jurisdictions, it is called the land surveyor (L.S.) or professional land surveyor (P.L.S.) license. For specific licensing information, contact the board of surveying examiners that oversees the jurisdiction where you wish to practice. In general, surveyors must fulfill educational and experience requirements and successfully pass a written examination.

Experience, Special Skills, and Personality Traits

Potential clients seek Forensic Surveyors who are highly accomplished and recognized in their field. In addition, they prefer to retain consultants who have the necessary knowledge, skills, and experience to successfully complete their projects. Forensic Surveyors are typically at the top of their field and have many years of work experience.

To be effective consultants, Forensic Surveyors need excellent organizational, analytical, self-management, writing, and presentation skills. They must also have exceptional interpersonal and communication skills, as they need to work well with colleagues, forensic engineers, attorneys, and others. Being curious, accurate, precise, unbiased, trustworthy, and dedicated are some personality traits that successful Forensic Surveyors share.

Unions and Associations

Forensic Surveyors can join professional associations to take advantage of networking opportunities, continuing education, professional certification, and other professional resources and services. Some national societies that serve their interests include the National Society of Professional Surveyors, the American Congress on Surveying and Mapping, the American Academy of Forensic Sciences, and the American College of Forensic Examiners. For contact information, see Appendix III.

Tips for Entry

1. As a student, obtain a summer job working on a survey crew. This can give you an idea about whether you are suited for a surveying job.

2. As a college student, join a student chapter of a professional society. Participate in its activities, including professional meetings and conferences where you can meet professional surveyors.

3. Many surveyors obtain professional certification to enhance their employability as well as credibility.

4. Learn more about the surveying field on the Internet. You might start by visiting the surveying career Web site created by the National Society of Professional Surveyors. Its URL is http://www.surveyingcareer. com. For more links, see Appendix IV.

FORENSIC EXPERTS IN THE BEHAVIORAL SCIENCES

CRIMINOLOGIST

CAREER PROFILE

Duties: Conduct research on crime and criminal behavior; provide litigation support and expert witness services; perform other duties as required

Alternate Title(s): Forensic Consultant; Professor of Criminology, Professor of Criminal Justice

Salary Range: $31,000 to $116,000

Employment Prospects: Fair

Advancement Prospects: Fair

Prerequisites:

Education or Training—Advanced degree; doctoral degree required for academic teaching

Experience—Many years of work experience in the field

Special Skills and Personality Traits—Self-management, organizational, communication, and interpersonal skills; objective, diligent, detail-oriented, inquisitive, fair, trustworthy, and flexible

CAREER LADDER

```
┌─────────────────────────────────────┐
│  Forensic Consultant/Expert Witness  │
└─────────────────────────────────────┘

┌─────────────────────────────────────┐
│            Criminologist             │
└─────────────────────────────────────┘

┌─────────────────────────────────────┐
│          Doctoral Student            │
└─────────────────────────────────────┘
```

Position Description

Criminology is a subfield of sociology. It is the study of crime, criminal behavior, and how society responds to that behavior. Criminologists research the causes of crime as well as crime laws. Some people, including many in the media, confuse Criminologists with criminalists or forensic scientists. Criminalists are part of the criminology discipline; however, their expertise is in the examination of physical evidence that is found at crime scenes. Criminologists, on the other hand, are primarily academicians or consultants who focus on the study of crime.

There are three major branches of criminology. The first branch, referred to as the sociology of law, involves the history and types of criminal laws and how they are applied or modified to suit the dynamic shifts experienced by societies.

Secondly, Criminologists study criminal etiology. This is the study of the causes of criminality. Criminologists endeavor to explain how people come to engage in criminal acts. They research such questions as: What makes people commit a certain kind of crime? Why does crime happen more often in certain neighborhoods? Why would someone join a gang?

The third main branch of criminology is penology, in which Criminologists study how criminals are arrested or detained. They examine correctional institutions, court systems, and law enforcement entities as well as explore the reasons and motivations why societies perceive and respond to criminals in certain ways. These scholars seek ways to more effectively deal with crime and criminals.

Most Criminologists are employed as professors in the criminology and criminal justice departments of colleges and universities. Academic Criminologists teach courses to undergraduate, graduate, and doctoral students. Their curriculum includes such subjects as criminal law, police ethics, criminal investigation, juvenile delinquency, victimology, and gangs.

These academicians also work on research projects. They probe into such areas as drug addiction; the psychological, physiological, and sociological factors that contribute to criminality; and theories of criminality. Many of these academicians often conduct their research in conjunction with government and law enforcement agencies as well as various criminal justice programs. Academic Criminologists may also be responsible for revising their institution's criminology curriculum, participating as members of various academic committees, or being involved with campus and community programs.

Some Criminologists are directly employed by law enforcement agencies where they apply their research toward helping agency personnel improve their crime-fighting skills and increase their awareness of criminal behavior patterns or crime networks within their jurisdiction. Other Criminologists are private practitioners who offer consulting services to state or federal justice departments. In that capacity, these professionals assist officials with policy issues in the areas of law reform, corrections, juvenile crime, and the use of crime statistics.

Criminologists may specialize in studying one or a few areas of crime. Some of those areas include violent crime, domestic violence, white-collar crime, cyber crime, youth gangs, race and crime, women and crime, victimization, deviance, prison subcultures, correctional rehabilitation, policing, criminal court systems, alternative justice programs, and crime prevention. Some Criminologists devote their time to developing and improving effective research methods for studying evidence in the crime lab as well as at the crime scene.

Criminologists are retained by attorneys to serve as expert witnesses in court trials. As expert witnesses, Criminologists provide testimony that helps judges and juries determine the truth in the judicial process. In civil or criminal cases, they offer opinions on criminal behavior related to the specific issues of the particular cases. However, they can testify only after the judge has ascertained that they have the required expertise, skills, knowledge, training, or education.

Some Criminologists offer litigation support services to attorneys. For example, they might interview defendants and family members to gather evidence for specific issues; review all the records of a case to help lawyers develop trial strategies; review cases to identify issues or facts; or prepare reports that can be used in settlement negotiations.

Criminologists typically have flexible work hours. They divide their time among various activities such as teaching, conducting research, writing, giving presentations, and providing consulting services.

Salaries

Salaries for Criminologists vary, depending on such factors as their education, experience, employer, and geographic location. Specific salary information for this occupation is unavailable. However, they earn wages similar to sociologists. According to the May 2006 *Occupational Employment Statistics* survey by the U.S. Bureau of Labor Statistics, the estimated annual salary for most sociologists ranged between $36,790 and $115,770, and for sociology postsecondary teachers, between $30,880 and $104,820.

As consultants, Criminologists charge an hourly, daily, or flat rate for initial consultation, depositions, courtroom testimony, and other services that they offer.

Employment Prospects

In addition to academic institutions and law enforcement agencies, Criminologists find employment with criminal justice research institutes, correctional facilities, and crime prevention programs.

Job competition is keen in all work settings. In general, job openings become available as Criminologists retire, transfer to other jobs, or advance to higher positions. Opportunities for postsecondary teachers, overall, are expected to increase in the coming years, as a large number of professors are becoming eligible for retirement.

Some private consultants work part time, while holding down full-time positions as teachers and researchers. Some full-time consultants are retired special agents and criminal detectives who decided to start a second career in forensic consulting.

Advancement Prospects

Criminologists generally measure success through job satisfaction, professional recognition, and higher incomes.

Those in staff positions can advance to supervisory, administrative, and managerial positions. Academicians also advance by rising through the ranks from instructor to full professor, as well as by gaining tenure at their institution. Tenured professors are assured a teaching job for life. They cannot be fired without just cause and due process.

Education and Training

Minimally, Criminologists need a master's degree in criminology, criminal justice, sociology, psychology, or another related field. Most Criminologists possess a doctoral degree. A doctorate is the usual requirement for teaching positions in four-year colleges and universities, as well as for advancing to management positions and for performing independent research.

Throughout their careers, Criminologists enroll in continuing education programs to update their skills and knowledge.

Experience, Special Skills, and Personality Traits

Attorneys generally hire Criminologists who have an established reputation in their area of study. They have many years of research experience and have published articles and books about their specialties.

To succeed at their work, Criminologists must have excellent self-management, organizational, communication, and interpersonal skills. Being objective, diligent, detail-oriented, inquisitive, fair, trustworthy, and flexible are some personality traits that successful Criminologists share.

Unions and Associations

Many Criminologists belong to professional associations to take advantage of networking opportunities and other professional resources and services. Some national societies that serve their interests include:

- American Society of Criminology
- Western Society of Criminology
- Academy of Criminal Justice Sciences
- American Sociological Association
- American Academy of Forensic Sciences

For contact information for these organizations, see Appendix III.

Tips for Entry

1. As a college student, obtain an internship to begin gaining experience.

2. Many doctoral graduates obtain postdoctoral fellowships to gain advanced training in their field of interest.

3. Most academic institutions hire part-time faculty. Many schools also offer limited-term contracts for full-time positions to prospective faculty. Such contracts may be renewed.

4. Many professional associations post job listings at their Web sites as well as provide links to other Web sites that offer relevant job listings.

5. Use the Internet to learn more about Criminologists. You might start by visiting the American Society of Criminology Web site at http://www.asc41.com. For more links, see Appendix IV.

FORENSIC HYPNOTIST

Duties: Provide investigative hypnosis services to law enforcement agencies, attorneys, and others; perform duties as required

Alternate Title(s): None

Salary Range: Unavailable

Employment Prospects: Poor

Advancement Prospects: Poor

Prerequisites:

Education or Training—Formal forensic hypnosis training

Experience—Many years of experience in their field

Special Skills and Personality Traits—Organizational, self-management, communication, and interpersonal skills; articulate, fair, trustworthy, unbiased, diligent, and calm

```
┌─────────────────────────────────┐
│      Forensic Hypnotist         │
└─────────────────────────────────┘

┌─────────────────────────────────┐
│   Forensic Hypnotist Trainee    │
└─────────────────────────────────┘

┌─────────────────────────────────┐
│  Hypnotist or Other Profession  │
└─────────────────────────────────┘
```

Position Description

Hypnosis is something we have all seen portrayed on television or in stage shows where people are put in a trance and perform amusing stunts. It seems exotic and mysterious. In fact, hypnosis is quite commonplace. Hypnosis is a state of consciousness that each of us experiences at least twice a day. Our brains operate through the exchange of chemicals that generates minute electrical pulses, which are measured by a unit called the hertz (Hz). Our minds generate different frequencies depending on our state of consciousness. There are four such states: full consciousness (14-35 Hz), the hypnotic state (8-13 Hz), the dream state (4-7 Hz), and the sleep state (.5-3 Hz). Whenever we go to sleep and wake up, we pass through all four states of consciousness. We also experience the hypnotic state when daydreaming, meditating, reading, watching television, or listening to music.

Hypnosis is a state of mind that can also be induced through the guidance of a hypnotist who may use any one of several methods to induce the hypnotic state. Some people use hypnotism to enhance their mental focus, imagination, memory, creativity, and receptiveness to suggestion. Professionals known as hypnotherapists use hypnosis as a therapeutic tool to help patients work through their problems or on self-improvement. Hypnotherapy is contrasted with other forms of counseling that are conducted when the patient is in a state of full consciousness. Hypnosis is a way to help the patient deal with problems or habits subconsciously.

Law enforcement agencies, court systems, and attorneys use hypnosis as a tool to help solve crimes, bring criminals to justice, exonerate the innocent, settle civil suits, and assist witnesses to remember events. The professionals who use hypnosis in these contexts are called Forensic Hypnotists. They differ from hypnotherapists in that they use hypnosis mainly to refresh the subject's memory, not solve problems. Forensic Hypnotists conduct their interviews in the presence of other forensic investigators, such as composite artists. These hypnotists make audio or video recordings of the proceedings, whereas hypnotherapy sessions are conducted in private.

Forensic Hypnotists help witnesses and crime victims remember license plate numbers, the faces of criminals, and other details of events. They follow specific steps and procedures to conduct each investigative hypnosis interview. Their first step is to introduce themselves to the victim or witness. Before the hypnosis begins, Forensic Hypnotists explain the procedure and reassure the subject that the procedure is safe, the subject will retain awareness of the proceedings, and nothing out of the ordinary will occur. These hypnotists take notes, beginning with the introductory stage and continuing throughout the session.

After the introductory stage, Forensic Hypnotists induce hypnosis by using one of several induction methods that include relaxation techniques and visual focusing techniques. When the subject is hypnotized, the hypnotist guides him or her to regress in time to describe events, describe suspects, or to provide relevant information about the case. For example, Forensic Hypnotists may use a technique in which the subject is asked to imagine entering a movie theater where the movie is about the crime or other relevant event. As the subject relives his or her memory of the event, he or she describes the scene. The hypnotist suggests that the "movie" can be fast-forwarded, reversed, or freeze-framed. In the subject's mind, the events may be traumatic, but they are able to observe the proceedings in a relaxed and serene manner.

When the session is finished, the hypnotist brings the subject back to full consciousness and reviews the session. The subject may remember more details at a later date, and the hypnotist encourages follow-up reports. Forensic Hypnotists compile their notes and recordings of their hypnosis sessions, and maintain the chain of custody.

Forensic Hypnotists use their techniques to interview civil defendants, suspects, witnesses, and crime victims as well as people who are involved in accidents, disputes, or other incidents. They cannot guarantee that the information they obtain from their subjects is fully truthful or reliable. Forensic Hypnotists realize that memories are not always recalled accurately. They must also be careful that they do not enable the subject to create false memories. Hence, they always tape their hypnosis sessions to ensure that they do not ask leading questions. For this and other reasons, many states do not allow memories retrieved under hypnosis to be admitted as evidence in court.

Forensic Hypnotists are subject to rigorous scrutiny, particularly by opposing attorneys in a case. They must be able to prove that their background and qualifications are fully documented. False testimony may lead to lawsuits filed against these hypnotists. Forensic Hypnotists may testify in court as fact witnesses, expert witnesses, or consulting experts. Fact witnesses are hypnotists who actually conducted the hypnosis interview. Expert witnesses testify about the hypnosis that someone else conducted. Consulting experts testify that a hypnosis session was conducted properly.

Forensic Hypnotists offer their services on a consultancy basis. Many of them are professional hypnotists and hypnotherapists. Some work in other professions, such as social work, counseling, and psychiatry. Others are law enforcement officers who conduct hypnosis sessions only when needed.

Salaries

As consultants, Forensic Hypnotists may charge an hourly, daily, or flat rate for initial consultation, courtroom testimony, hypnosis sessions, and other services that they offer. Fees vary, depending on their experience, qualifications, geographic location, and other factors. Specific fee information for Forensic Hypnotists is unavailable, but according to Salary.com, fees for hypnotherapists generally range between $50 and $150 per hour.

Employment Prospects

Forensic hypnosis is a voluntary detail for law enforcement officers. They may perform this duty in addition to their primary duty as a patrol officer, criminal investigator, or another position.

The prospects for private Forensic Hypnotists within a location depend on the demand for their expertise and on the number of similar consultants in the area. Those willing to travel to other locations have more opportunities to obtain work. Most private practitioners offer other services, such as counseling and hypnosis training.

Advancement Prospects

Forensic Hypnotists realize advancement through job satisfaction, by gaining professional recognition, and by earning higher incomes. Many also measure success by being sought by attorneys for very complex or publicized cases.

Education and Training

Forensic hypnosis training programs are sponsored by professional hypnosis associations and postsecondary schools. Some professional Forensic Hypnotists offer training workshops at conferences or through their own businesses. Many instructors are former law enforcement officers who provided forensic hypnosis services for their forces.

Throughout their careers, Forensic Hypnotists enroll in continuing education and training programs to update their skills and knowledge.

Experience, Special Skills, and Personality Traits

Prospective clients typically hire Forensic Hypnotists who have many years of experience in the hypnosis field. They are usually highly accomplished and recognized in their field.

To succeed at consulting work, individuals need excellent organizational, self-management, communication, and interpersonal skills. Being articulate, fair, trustworthy, unbiased, diligent, and calm are some personality traits that successful forensic consultants have in common.

Unions and Associations

Professional associations for hypnotists are available. They offer professional certification, training programs, networking opportunities, and other professional resources and services. The National Guild of Hypnotists and the American Council of Hypnotist Examiners are just two examples of societies that Forensic Hypnotists might join. For contact information, see Appendix III.

Tips for Entry

1. Carefully research a forensic hypnosis training program before enrolling in it. Ask questions such as: Is the program recognized by professional associations and reputable Forensic Hypnotists? What is the instructor's background? Where are former students working? If possible, ask former or current students about their experience with the training program.

2. Are you a police officer whose force uses hypnosis services? Let your supervisor know about your interest in learning forensic hypnosis.

3. As a private consultant, contact attorneys and law enforcement agencies directly to let them know that you offer forensic hypnosis services.

4. Use the Internet to learn more about the field of forensic hypnosis. To get a list of relevant Web sites, enter any of these keywords into a search engine: *forensic hypnotists*, *forensic hypnosis*, or *investigative hypnosis*. For some links, see Appendix IV.

FORENSIC PSYCHIATRIST

CAREER PROFILE

Duties: Provide expert opinions on mental health issues related to legal matters; may provide litigation consulting services; perform duties as required

Alternate Title(s): Psychiatrist, Forensic Psychiatrist Consultant

Salary Range: $60,000 to $146,000

Employment Prospects: Fair

Advancement Prospects: Fair

Prerequisites:

Education or Training—A medical degree; psychiatry and forensic psychiatry training

Experience—Several years of clinical experience

Special Skills and Personality Traits—Critical-thinking, organizational, self-management, interpersonal, communication, and presentation skills; honest, trustworthy, unbiased, patient, dedicated, and flexible

Special Requirements—Medical license; board certification usually preferred

CAREER LADDER

```
┌─────────────────────────────────┐
│   Senior Forensic Psychiatrist  │
└─────────────────────────────────┘

┌─────────────────────────────────┐
│      Forensic Psychiatrist      │
└─────────────────────────────────┘

┌─────────────────────────────────┐
│          Psychiatrist           │
└─────────────────────────────────┘
```

Position Description

Psychiatry is a branch of medical science dedicated to the study of mental disorders, their causes, how to treat them, and how to prevent them. Psychiatrists diagnose mental, emotional, or behavioral problems in addition to physical ailments and provide treatment options for their patients, including prescriptions. They keep up to date with new methods and technologies that aid them in their work. Psychiatrists stand in contrast to psychologists, who are not medical doctors.

Forensic Psychiatrists are specialists who focus on legal matters. In the capacity of being expert witnesses, these psychiatrists do not provide therapy or other treatments, as would clinical psychiatrists. Instead, these specialists perform psychiatric evaluations of individuals in the context of legal issues and provide lawyers and courts with their expert opinions. These doctors also help lawyers and juries understand mental disorders relevant to criminal and civil matters. Nevertheless, Forensic Psychiatrists have clinical experience and expertise, which, along with scientific research, they call upon to perform their evaluations or present their opinions.

Forensic Psychiatrists normally deal with cases that are covered by four major areas of law: civil law, criminal law, family law, and regulatory law. In matters of civil law, these professionals provide evaluations and opinions about the mental competence of individuals to do certain things, such as get married, make a will, sign a contract, take care of children, or refuse medical treatment. Forensic Psychiatrists work on behalf of attorneys to address mental health issues in civil lawsuits involving personal injury, product liability, sexual harassment, workers' compensation, or job discrimination.

These medical professionals work in criminal law to conduct evaluations of adult and juvenile defendants and offer opinions about whether such individuals are mentally competent to stand trial, to waive legal representation, to be sentenced, or to be executed. Forensic Psychiatrists also give expert testimony on the mental conditions of such defendants at the time of the trial as well as their mental state at the time the crime took place.

Family law is an area in which Forensic Psychiatrists work on cases involving divorce, children or adults in need of supervision, or other matters brought before family courts.

Forensic Psychiatrists consult in matters pertinent to regulatory law, which includes laws that establish oversight of health care systems or government programs such as Medicare. They work on cases involving the rights of incarcerated or committed individuals. They are involved with regulations pertaining to care and treatment standards.

Some of the areas of expertise that Forensic Psychiatrists utilize in their work include mental health malpractice, criminal justice and public safety, and employment litigation. In malpractice cases, civil or criminal attorneys may call upon Forensic Psychiatrists to testify about the efforts mental health professionals make to provide appropriate care to patients. Forensic Psychiatrists may work with individuals, companies, or government agencies to investigate whether employee claims of emotional or mental disability are the result of stress factors in the workplace. They may work with correctional institutions to evaluate criminal defendants for psychiatric disorders, or to review the testimony of other experts.

In addition to criminal and civil trials, Forensic Psychiatrists provide expert witness services for other types of legal hearings, including juvenile court hearings, family court hearings, administrative hearings, alternative conflict resolution conferences, and legislative hearings. Forensic Psychiatrists are objective when it comes to offering their opinions about their cases. They may work with either plaintiff or defense attorneys but they do not take sides. Their job is to determine facts about the case and deliver their evaluations based upon those facts. Forensic Psychiatrists often fulfill a teaching role in these hearings. They inform the judges, juries, or hearing panels about the medical science of psychiatry and help them to understand emotional disorders, stress syndromes, or mental illnesses, as well as the needs of those suffering from such conditions.

Although Forensic Psychiatrists conduct assessments for legal matters, they are still obligated to maintain confidentiality about the information that individuals give them. They make sure that confidential information is not given to unauthorized persons.

Most Forensic Psychiatrists also offer litigation consulting services to attorneys to help them prepare their cases for trial. They may review and evaluate cases to establish the facts and to help attorneys decide whether the cases should be handled by civil lawsuit or criminal trial. They assist attorneys with understanding mental illnesses and the issues such illnesses may bring to a case. Forensic Psychiatrists help to identify and recruit other expert witnesses as well as suggest questions the attorneys may ask during the course of a trial or hearing. They may help attorneys with jury selection by providing feedback about potential jurors. These forensic experts also may suggest strategies for presenting clear and effective testimony.

Forensic Psychiatrists are ethically bound to provide either litigation consulting or expert witness services for a case, but never both. This is to prevent any conflicts of interest, as well as to ensure that their contribution to a case is objective and unbiased.

Many Forensic Psychiatrists maintain their private practices. Their forensic duties may constitute a small proportion of their normal psychiatric practice. Some of them perform clinical work with parolees, probationers, and crime victims. Other Forensic Psychiatrists are employed in prisons and forensic hospitals where their patients are prisoners.

During their working day, Forensic Psychiatrists read extensively, particularly medical records and legal documents or other information pertinent to their current caseload. They interview people to evaluate their mental health and write reports of their findings. Many cases are settled before they go to court (or other legal hearing) due in large part to the written documentation that Forensic Psychiatrists prepare. These professionals also read books and journals to keep up to date with new developments in the psychiatric profession as well as in forensic psychiatry. Forensic Psychiatrists attend training seminars and professional conferences as part of their continuing career development. They may also teach at these events.

Many Forensic Psychiatrists hold faculty appointments in universities and medical schools where they teach courses in forensics and psychiatry. In addition, they conduct independent research studies, produce scholarly works about their research, and perform other duties as required of their positions as full-time professors.

Forensic Psychiatrists have flexible work schedules. They sometimes travel to other cities and states for their work. These professionals often work with highly disturbed individuals with violent histories. They also work with law enforcement, corrections, and hospital personnel within prisons or mental health facilities.

Salaries

Specific salary information for Forensic Psychiatrists is unavailable. Their earnings are similar to psychiatrists, in general. According to the May 2006 *Occupational Employment Statistics* survey by the U.S. Bureau of Labor Statistics, the estimated annual salary for most psychiatrists ranged between $60,900 and $145,600.

Consultants typically charge an hourly, daily, or flat rate for the different services—such as research, evaluations, and expert witness testimony—that they offer. Hourly fees range between $150 and $500 or more per hour. Consultants may be reimbursed for expenses such as telephone calls, photocopying, and travel time.

Employment Prospects

Staff and academic positions usually become available as Forensic Psychiatrists retire, transfer to other jobs, or advance to higher positions. Employers will create additional positions to meet growing needs if funding is available.

Opportunities are expected to remain favorable for Forensic Psychiatrists. Attorneys, for example, continually seek reputable forensic experts to provide them with expert witness or litigation support services.

Employment prospects for forensic consultants within a location depend on the demand for their particular expertise and on the number of similar consultants in the area. Those willing to travel to other locations may have more opportunities to obtain consulting work.

Advancement Prospects

Forensic Psychiatrists advance according to their interests and ambitions. Staff psychiatrists can pursue administrative and managerial positions within their organizations. Entrepreneurial specialists can become consultants or open a solo practice in addition to offering forensic consulting services.

Many Forensic Psychiatrists measure success through job satisfaction, by gaining professional recognition, and by earning higher incomes.

Education and Training

Preparing for a career in forensic psychiatry involves a long and intense formal education program. Individuals must first earn a bachelor's degree, which may be in any field, then complete four years of medical school to earn a doctor of medicine (M.D.) degree or a doctor of osteopathy (D.O.) degree. They then complete a three- to four-year residency program in psychiatry, which involves clinical training under the supervision of physicians. They learn about inpatient and outpatient treatment, medication management, crisis evaluations, and other subjects. To specialize in forensic psychiatry, psychiatrists carry out a fellowship in that specialty to obtain proper training and practical experience.

Special Requirements

All states, as well as Washington, D.C. and the U.S. territories, require Forensic Psychiatrists to possess a medical license. Requirements vary from state to state. For specific information, contact the medical licensing board that governs the jurisdiction in which you plan to practice.

Attorneys and employers usually prefer to hire board-certified Forensic Psychiatrists. This is a voluntary certification and is granted by the American Board of Psychiatry and Neurology. (See Appendix II for contact information.) To obtain this designation, Forensic Psychiatrists must first be board-certified psychiatrists, which is granted by the same board.

Experience, Special Skills, and Personality Traits

To be expert witnesses, Forensic Psychiatrists must have several years of clinical experience handling issues (such as workers' compensation, violence, or personal injury) that they would be addressing in court. In addition, they must be familiar with laws and regulations that apply to the cases for which they are consulting.

Forensic Psychiatrists need excellent critical thinking, organizational, self-management, and interpersonal skills. They must also have effective communication and presentation skills, as they must be able to convey technical concepts in language that attorneys, judges, and juries can comprehend. Being honest, trustworthy, unbiased, patient, dedicated, and flexible are some personality traits that successful Forensic Psychiatrists share.

Unions and Associations

Many Forensic Psychiatrists belong to various professional associations to take advantage of professional certification, publications, continuing education, networking opportunities, and other professional resources and services. Some national societies that serve their interests include:

- American Academy of Psychiatry and the Law
- American College of Forensic Psychiatry
- American Psychiatric Association
- American Academy of Forensic Sciences
- American Medical Association

For contact information for these societies, see Appendix III.

Tips for Entry

1. Be sure you understand what the forensic psychiatry field is all about before committing yourself to it. Talk with professionals as well as read books and professional journals.
2. Apply to medical schools that offer psychiatry as a clinical specialty.
3. You must be highly competent as a psychiatrist before entering the field of forensic psychiatry.
4. Learn about job vacancies through various sources such as colleagues, professional journals, and professional societies.
5. Use the Internet to learn more about forensic psychiatry. You might start by visiting the Web site for the American Academy of Psychiatry and the Law. Its URL is http://www.aapl.org. For more links, see Appendix IV.

FORENSIC PSYCHOLOGIST

CAREER PROFILE

Duties: Provide expert witness and litigation support services; provide treatment and counseling to criminal suspects and convicts; conduct research; perform other duties as required of their particular position

Alternate Title(s): None

Salary Range: $33,000 to $104,000

Employment Prospects: Good

Advancement Prospects: Fair

Prerequisites:

Education or Training—Doctoral degree in psychology usually required

Experience—Requires several years of work experience to become an expert witness

Special Skills and Personality Traits—Research, analytical, presentation, communication, interpersonal, and teamwork skills; patient, adaptable, curious, trustworthy, unbiased, and compassionate

Special Requirements—Must be a licensed or certified psychologist to provide assessment and treatment services

CAREER LADDER

```
┌─────────────────────────────────────┐
│   Senior Forensic Psychologist       │
└─────────────────────────────────────┘

┌─────────────────────────────────────┐
│       Forensic Psychologist          │
└─────────────────────────────────────┘

┌─────────────────────────────────────┐
│        Doctoral Student              │
└─────────────────────────────────────┘
```

Position Description

Psychologists are scientists who study the human mind and human behavior. They are not to be confused with psychiatrists, who are medical doctors. Psychologists are academicians and scientists who conduct research and who provide nonmedical treatments to patients. Forensic Psychologists are trained in the area of law in addition to the science of psychology. Their expertise lies in such areas as legal psychology, police psychology, correctional psychology, the psychology of crime, and victimology.

Forensic Psychologists apply their scientific knowledge to the legal issues pertinent to civil and criminal cases. They provide treatment and counseling to individuals within a legal or correctional context. Attorneys often retain these professional men and women to provide expert witness testimony on psychological issues relevant to cases involving domestic violence, divorce, child custody, arson, substance abuse, personal injury, or workers' compensation issues. Additionally, attorneys look to Forensic Psychologists to assist them with choosing jurors. Forensic Psychologists also analyze mentally ill criminals. Many of them conduct research and teach in academic institutions. Some work within or contribute to the design of prisons and correctional mental health facilities.

The field of forensic psychology is composed of various subfields. One of these is clinical forensic psychology, which is principally concerned with the evaluation and treatment of individuals who suffer from a broad range of mental illnesses. Forensic Psychologists conduct these procedures in such settings as law enforcement agencies, prisons, state hospitals, mental health clinics, juvenile halls, and academic institutions. Their examination subjects may be involved in civil cases or in the process of being committed to a mental health institution.

Criminal suspects and convicts within adult or juvenile correctional institutions are also evaluated and treated by clinical forensic psychologists for various purposes. For example, these forensic experts examine them to establish their level of competency, to predict or prevent their future potential to be dangerous, or to help them function in society upon release. Those professionals who work in correctional institutions may specialize in individual or group therapy techniques.

Other subfields of forensic psychology include:

- social psychology, in which Forensic Psychologists study jury panels to learn how jurors interact with each other and come to agreement about verdicts
- cognitive psychology, in which Forensic Psychologists study how others involved in legal cases arrive at their decisions
- criminal investigative psychology, in which these professionals study police psychology and criminal psychology
- developmental psychology, in which Forensic Psychologists direct their attention to official policies regarding juveniles or elders with mental problems and their special legal needs

Many Forensic Psychologists work in universities, medical schools, hospitals, research institutes, and clinics where they conduct research or teach. Some of these men and women work with law enforcement agencies where they assist with criminal investigations. They create psychological profiles of typical criminals and of certain crimes. Some Forensic Psychologists perform various duties within the judicial system, such as evaluating defendants for their ability to stand trial or investigating cases of abused or neglected children.

In the capacity of expert witnesses, Forensic Psychologists may testify only on issues for which they have been deemed qualified by the court. Attorneys use these expert witnesses for either one of two purposes: to explain specific psychological concepts in laymen's terms so that judges and juries can fully understand them, and to present their opinions about defendants based on their professional evaluations.

Many Forensic Psychologists offer litigation consulting services as a supplementary activity. However, they are ethically bound to provide either consulting or expert witness services on a case, but not both. This limitation prevents conflicts of interest and also ensures that their expert testimony is objective and unbiased.

Forensic Psychologists attend to specific tasks, depending upon where they work and their subfield. They may:

- mediate divorce cases and child custody agreements
- assist with the selection, placement, and subsequent performance evaluation of law enforcement, military, or security personnel
- consult with organizational managers to establish procedures to deal with violent incidents
- design evaluation and treatment programs for either mentally disturbed criminals or victims

- research the success rate of treatment methods
- attend meetings with attorneys, prison personnel, or police officers to discuss cases
- write scholarly papers about research results for publication in professional journals

Forensic Psychologists work in a variety of environments. They may be self-employed as licensed psychologists who have their own practice. Many, however, work for private or government organizations as employees or contractors. Forensic Psychologists in the public sector are employed by government health agencies, prisons, police departments, court systems, military branches, and government-run mental hospitals. In the private arena, Forensic Psychologists work for hospitals, residential facilities, drug rehabilitation centers, and counseling offices. Some of them work for attorneys or legal advocacy organizations. Others are university instructors or professors who conduct research or teach such classes as psychology and criminal justice.

The work that Forensic Psychologists do can be exciting and rewarding, yet may also involve working with dangerous individuals. The threat of physical intimidation and injury is a very real factor that they must face. Some of the people for whom Forensic Psychologists testify or provide counseling may exhibit behavior or attitudes that they find objectionable or unacceptable. In such cases, Forensic Psychologists need to maintain their professional decorum and conduct their examinations in an objective fashion. Forensic Psychologists may find expert witness testimony a stressful experience when facing the scrutiny of attorneys who seek to discredit their opinions.

Salaries

Salaries for Forensic Psychologists vary, depending on such factors as their experience, the nature of their work, their work setting, and their geographic location. Specific salary information for this occupation is unavailable. However, the estimated annual salary for most clinical psychologists ranged between $35,280 and $102,730, according to the May 2006 *Occupational Employment Statistics* survey by the U.S. Bureau of Labor Statistics. The survey also reports that most postsecondary psychology teachers earned an estimated annual salary that ranged between $32,800 and $104,390.

As consultants, Forensic Psychologists may earn an hourly, daily, or flat rate for initial consultation, depositions, courtroom testimony, and other services that they offer.

Employment Prospects

Staff and academic positions typically become available as individuals transfer to other jobs, advance to higher positions, or retire. Employers will create additional positions to meet growing staff needs, as long as funding is available.

In general, opportunities are expected to be favorable for Forensic Psychologists in the years to come. Some experts in the field expect the greatest number of opportunities will be in the legal industry.

Advancement Prospects

Forensic Psychologists may advance in any number of ways, depending on their ambitions and interests. They can specialize in a particular area. Those with administrative and managerial talents can seek such positions within their organizations. Individuals with entrepreneurial ambitions can become solo practitioners.

Academicians can rise through the teaching ranks from instructor to full professor. Additionally, they can be granted tenure at their institution. Tenured professors are assured a teaching job for life. They cannot be fired without just cause and due process.

Education and Training

To become a Forensic Psychologist, students generally need to obtain a doctoral degree in psychology. Students who want to assess and treat patients usually earn a doctor's degree in psychology (Psy.D.); those who plan to focus on doing research work generally earn a doctor of philosophy degree (Ph.D.) in psychology.

Individuals can also be Forensic Psychologists with only a master's degree in clinical psychology. However, they usually work under the supervision of doctoral degree holders.

Formal training for doctoral degrees takes several years of dedication. Students first complete a four-year bachelor's degree program in psychology or another behavioral science field, and then enter a one- or two-year master's degree program in psychology. Ph.D. candidates complete a three-year program, while clinical psychology candidates complete a four-year program, followed by a one-year internship.

Many doctoral graduates obtain postdoctoral fellowships to continue training in their specialties.

Throughout their careers, Forensic Psychologists enroll in continuing education programs to update their skills and keep up with advancements in their fields.

Special Requirements

Forensic Psychologists who provide forensic assessment and treatment services must obtain licenses or certification in the states where they plan to practice. Those who conduct research, teach, consult, or are involved in policy making are not required to be licensed. However, having a state license may enhance one's credibility as an expert witness.

Experience, Special Skills, and Personality Traits

Employers generally hire candidates who have work experience related to the positions for which they apply. Novice Forensic Psychologists may have gained their experience through research assistantships, postdoctoral training, volunteer work, or employment.

Attorneys typically retain Forensic Psychologists who have several years of experience in their specialties, and who are also familiar with the law and legal procedures.

Forensic Psychologists need strong research, analytical, presentation, communication, interpersonal, and teamwork skills to be effective at their job. Being patient, adaptable, curious, trustworthy, unbiased, and compassionate are some personality traits that successful Forensic Psychologists share.

Unions and Associations

Many Forensic Psychologists join professional associations to take advantage of networking opportunities, continuing education, professional certification, and other professional resources and services. Professional societies are available locally, statewide, regionally, nationally, and worldwide. Some national societies that serve the diverse interests of these forensic experts are the American Psychology-Law Society, the American Academy of Forensic Psychology, the American College of Forensic Psychology, the American Academy of Forensic Sciences, and the American Psychological Association. For contact information, see Appendix III.

Tips for Entry

1. As an undergraduate student, get an idea if forensic psychology is the right field for you. You might, for example, obtain an internship or do volunteer work at a correctional facility.
2. Attend workshops and conferences given by professional associations to broaden your knowledge and understanding about the field.
3. Many Forensic Psychologists enhance their employability and credibility by obtaining professional certification. For information about some certification programs, see Appendix II.
4. Use the Internet to learn more about the field of forensic psychology. To obtain a list of relevant Web sites, enter the keywords *forensic psychology* or *forensic psychologists* into a search engine. For some links, see Appendix IV.

FORENSIC REHABILITATION CONSULTANT

CAREER PROFILE

Duties: Provide forensic consulting services to attorneys and other clients; conduct assessments on individuals; prepare reports; perform duties as required

Alternate Title(s): Vocational Rehabilitation Expert

Salary Range: Unavailable

Employment Prospects: Fair

Advancement Prospects: Poor

Prerequisites:

Education or Training—An advanced degree generally preferred

Experience—Several years of work experience

Special Skills and Personality Traits—Analytical, problem-solving, organizational, self-management, research, writing, communication, and interpersonal skills; believable, trustworthy, unbiased, fair, thorough, and inquisitive

Special Requirements—State license, certification, or registration as a professional counselor may be needed

CAREER LADDER

```
┌─────────────────────────────────────┐
│  Forensic Rehabilitation Consultant  │
└─────────────────────────────────────┘

┌─────────────────────────────────────┐
│   Novice Forensic Rehabilitation     │
│            Consultant                │
└─────────────────────────────────────┘

┌─────────────────────────────────────┐
│ Vocational Rehabilitation Professional│
└─────────────────────────────────────┘
```

Position Description

Forensic Rehabilitation Consultants are experts in vocational rehabilitation. They apply the principles and techniques of their profession to provide expert opinions in legal matters. Their primary role is to assess the employability and the future care needs of individuals as well as the economic damages they suffered due to personal injuries, medical malpractice, lack of spousal support, labor-related issues such as wrongful termination, or other circumstances involving financial loss.

In general, vocational rehabilitation professionals are rehabilitation counselors, registered nurses, and life care planners, among others. They work with clients who have physical, mental, cognitive, or developmental disabilities. Their job is to help clients achieve their goals to lead productive and independent lives. In terms of their clients' vocational needs, vocational rehabilitation professionals evaluate their strengths and limitations, design rehabilitation treatment plans, provide vocational counseling, and arrange for vocational training, job placement, and other services.

Forensic Rehabilitation Consultants may not necessarily work directly with clients, although they use their rehabilitation counseling expertise to contribute to the resolution of disputes in courts, workers' compensation hearings, or other appropriate venues. These professionals are usually private practitioners who offer services directly to attorneys, insurance companies (including workers' compensation insurance agencies), employers, and others.

Forensic Rehabilitation Consultants study injury cases to ascertain the type and amount of loss of present and future earnings suffered by the injured client. Their studies and resulting reports assist courts and alternative dispute resolution panels to evaluate the damages suffered by the client, the effectiveness of rehabilitation treatments, the client's ability to return to the workforce, and the need to award, continue, or terminate compensation and disability claims.

These consultants also acquire facts about injured workers regarding their compliance with the provisions of their insurance or benefits claim. When a claimant evidently strays from a prescribed course of action, Forensic Rehabilitation Consultants must investigate the claimant's status and report the findings to the insurance carrier or government benefits agency. These forensic experts may be called upon to testify in a court setting regarding such findings. At that time, they would present the history of the claimant's case, including the injury and treatments as well as whatever restrictions or job-seeking activities were given to the claimant.

In personal injury or workplace injury cases, Forensic Rehabilitation Consultants are also called upon to complete and report on an objective analysis of a claimant's earning potential. Such an analysis may include interviewing the claimant in addition to reviewing documents pertaining to the claim. They factor such information as the claimant's past work and earnings history, the earnings that were lost due to the injury, the loss of access to work opportunities, the amount of impairment imposed on the claimant by the injury, what new employment the claimant is qualified to perform, and the current offerings in the local job market. In cases of catastrophic injury, Forensic Rehabilitation Consultants also provide their estimates of the cost of future rehabilitative treatments, education, medical expenses, and modifications to the claimant's home, as well as other needs.

Forensic Rehabilitation Consultants follow similar assessment procedures with every case. They:

- assess the injured person's skills
- evaluate the claimant's vocational aptitudes, educational achievements, physical abilities, and career interests
- discuss the issues that concern the attorneys assigned to the case
- request, acquire, and read pertinent medical and tax records
- research local, regional, and national job markets, wage scales, and transferable skills potential
- calculate a vocational disability rating based on the physician's medical impairment rating, the injured person's skill level, availability of suitable employment opportunities, and available pay scales
- write a detailed report including the claimant's family, work, educational, and medical background, as well as present medical circumstances and vocational assessment
- provide expert opinion and witness services to the courts

Forensic Rehabilitation Consultants work in office settings. They may travel to visit insurance company personnel, claimants, or attorneys. These professionals work 40-hour weeks, but may put in extra hours to complete tasks, meet with attorneys or insurance representatives, or participate in training workshops. As expert witnesses, Forensic Rehabilitation Consultants may face intense scrutiny by attorneys of opposing parties, which can be emotionally demanding.

Salaries

Salaries for staff consultants vary, depending on such factors as their education, experience, employer, and geographic loca-

tion. Specific salary information for Forensic Rehabilitation Consultants is unavailable. The Salary.com Web site reported that as of December 2006, most vocational rehabilitation counselors earned between $42,901 and $58,353 per year.

Employment Prospects

Some Forensic Rehabilitation Consultants are independent practitioners, while others are employed by vocational rehabilitation firms that offer forensic services.

Staff positions typically become available as associates advance to higher positions, transfer to other jobs, or leave the workforce for various reasons. Employers create additional positions as their businesses expand.

In general, opportunities are favorable, as litigation lawyers and insurance companies continually seek credible and reputable Forensic Rehabilitation Consultants.

Advancement Prospects

Forensic Rehabilitation Consultants realize advancement by earning higher incomes and gaining professional recognition. Many also measure success by being sought by attorneys for very complex or publicized cases.

Employees in consulting firms can pursue administrative and managerial positions within their organizations. The top goal for entrepreneurial individuals is to start their own consulting business.

Education and Training

Forensic Rehabilitation Consultants normally have master's or doctoral degrees in rehabilitation counseling, counseling psychology, or another related field.

Vocational rehabilitation professionals generally learn about forensic issues and techniques on the job. They also enroll in courses, seminars, and workshops that are offered by professional associations and other organizations.

Throughout their careers, Forensic Rehabilitation Consultants enroll in continuing education and training programs to update their skills and keep up with advancements in their fields.

Special Requirements

Consultants who provide rehabilitation counseling may be required to be licensed, certified, or registered as professional counselors in the states where they work. For specific information, contact the state board that grants licenses to professional counselors in the jurisdiction where you plan to practice.

Experience, Special Skills, and Personality Traits

Attorneys, insurance companies, and others seek Forensic Rehabilitation Consultants who have established themselves as being accomplished in their field. They retain consultants who have the necessary knowledge, skills, and experience to successfully complete their projects. Typically, vocational rehabilitation professionals have many years of work experience before becoming forensic consultants.

To be effective consultants, vocational rehabilitation professionals need strong analytical, problem-solving, organizational, self-management, research, and writing skills. In addition, they must have excellent communication and interpersonal skills, as they must be able to work well with attorneys, clients, and others from diverse backgrounds. Being believable, trustworthy, unbiased, fair, thorough, and inquisitive are some personality traits that successful Forensic Rehabilitation Consultants have in common.

Unions and Associations

Many Forensic Rehabilitation Consultants join various societies to take advantage of such professional resources and services as professional certification, continuing education, and networking opportunities. Some national professional associations include:

- International Association of Rehabilitation Professionals
- American Rehabilitation Economics Association
- American Board of Vocational Experts

- American Academy of Forensic Sciences
- American College of Forensic Examiners

For contact information, see Appendix III.

Tips for Entry

1. As a vocational rehabilitation professional, take advantage of opportunities to work on forensic cases.
2. Many consulting firms maintain a presence on the Internet as a marketing tool to generate new business. Some of them post job vacancies that are currently available.
3. Many Forensic Rehabilitation Consultants have obtained professional certification from recognized organizations to enhance their professional credibility. Typically, applicants for voluntary certification must meet strict requirements. For information about some professional certification programs, see Appendix II.
4. Consultants are often referred to lawyers and insurance companies by former clients.
5. Use the Internet to learn more about the forensic rehabilitation field. To get a list of relevant Web sites, enter any of these keywords into a search engine: *forensic rehabilitation consultants*, *forensic rehabilitation experts*, or *forensic vocational rehabilitation counselors*. For some links, see Appendix IV.

FORENSIC SOCIAL WORKER

CAREER PROFILE

Duties: Conduct forensic evaluations of criminal suspects, criminals, and victims; provide expert assessments to attorneys, courts, and law enforcement agencies; perform other duties as required

Alternate Title(s): Social Worker; Forensic Consultant

Salary Range: $26,000 to $69,000

Employment Prospects: Fair

Advancement Prospects: Fair

Prerequisites:

Education or Training—Bachelor's or master's degree in social work

Experience—Several years of experience in one's field

Special Skills and Personality Traits—Writing, organizational, self-management, teamwork, interpersonal, and communication skills; ethical, trustworthy, patient, objective, detail-oriented, and persistent

Special Requirements—State license, certification, or registration may be required

CAREER LADDER

```
┌─────────────────────────────────┐
│   Senior Forensic Social Worker │
└─────────────────────────────────┘

┌─────────────────────────────────┐
│      Forensic Social Worker     │
└─────────────────────────────────┘

┌─────────────────────────────────┐
│          Social Worker          │
└─────────────────────────────────┘
```

Position Description

Social work is a counseling and guidance profession. It is also a field that involves community action, social planning, research, and administrative work. Social workers help individuals or groups function effectively in society and overcome the obstacles that life may present. These professionals offer their services through various government agencies, charities, health clinics, religious groups, or social advocacy organizations. Social workers may specialize in specific areas of interest such as health care, child welfare, family services, mental health, immigration issues, elder issues, criminal justice, research, advocacy, arbitration, or education. They may also work in the areas of planning and policy making. Whatever their specialty, social workers strive to alleviate social problems such as homelessness, drug addiction, poverty, violence, and crime that impact the lives of people from every strata of society.

One specialty of social work is in the area of forensics. Forensic Social Workers apply their expertise to the legal issues pertinent to crime, civil litigation, and family court disputes. These men and women work in such settings as psychiatric hospitals, prisons, attorney's offices, juvenile detention centers, or social service agencies. Some of them serve as probation officers.

Forensic Social Workers provide social services support to attorneys, the courts, and law enforcement personnel. They may work with either side of a particular court case or they may provide client-based services. The work of Forensic Social Workers entails such functions as serving as expert witnesses, negotiating alternative sentencing for prisoners, educating law enforcement or court personnel about social concerns, or helping to settle employment disputes.

Forensic Social Workers provide social services to criminal suspects, prisoners, and crime victims. They also work with convicts to help them make the transition from prison life to life as parolees and free citizens. Some clients may be mentally ill, marginally educated, or habitual criminals. These professionals do not diagnose mental illness or provide the same sort of counseling as psychologists or psychiatrists. Rather, Forensic Social Workers seek to understand their clients' backgrounds and living circumstances. They help clients work through life problems such as difficulties with marriage, child rearing, or other social responsibilities.

Forensic Social Workers often work with clients who are ill equipped to explain their circumstances to attorneys, judges, or juries. For example, many of their clients are immigrants who faced insurmountable difficulties in their birth nations and continue to negotiate obstacles such as language barriers, cultural differences, or difficulty finding meaningful work.

Forensic Social Workers are skilled with interviewing and investigative techniques, which they use to elicit information from their clients, families, and associates. They establish trust and empathy with their clients and learn as much as they can about the aspects of their clients' lives that pertain to their particular case. These professionals ask their clients questions about their childhood, family life, how they faced life problems in the past, what traumas they suffered, and their feelings about life in general, as well as other life issues.

Forensic Social Workers compile reports of their findings to submit to the courts to enable attorneys, judges, and juries to better understand the clients' motivation for committing crimes, neglecting family duties, failing to report to work, or behaving in ways that create tensions in their communities. Oftentimes attorneys are interested only in the facts of the crime or civil dispute and do not necessarily take a defendant's cultural imperatives or traumatic personal history into account. Forensic Social Workers carefully help their clients to tell their story, which may be their entire life story and involve input from the clients' parents, siblings, and offspring.

The reports that these social workers submit include a thorough rendering of a client's background as well as the social worker's clinical assessment of the life factors that led to the events investigated for the case. With this understanding, the courts may be persuaded to lighten sentences or impose treatment or other rehabilitation processes for the client to complete, for example. As another example, Forensic Social Workers may recommend that children be removed from abusive family settings and placed into foster care.

Forensic Social Workers attend to general social work tasks as well as perform duties that are more specific to their forensic work. They may:

- interview clients, evaluate their problems, provide counseling services, and develop follow-up treatment plans
- keep clear and concise records of each client's case
- provide alternative sources for guidance to clients
- consult with medical health professionals to obtain their clients' medical and psychiatric records
- administer social service programs
- prepare detailed forensic social reports that summarize forensic client cases for use as testimony in courts

- develop and distribute social service information
- work together with law enforcement and legal personnel to reduce recidivism rates
- teach or train university students in domestic violence issues and other areas of concern

These forensic experts also keep up to date with the latest developments in social work, including government rules regarding social service benefits.

Forensic Social Workers mainly work in office environments in a variety of settings. They may travel to provide expert witness services to courts. These professionals work 40 hours per week, but may put in extra hours to complete tasks.

Forensic social work can be stressful and emotionally demanding. Forensic Social Workers may work with clients who have unusual, emotionally charged, or heart-wrenching problems. These professionals must balance their genuine empathy for their clients with a measure of professional detachment.

Salaries

Salaries for Forensic Social Workers vary, depending on such factors as their education, experience, employer, and geographic location. Specific salary information for this occupation is unavailable. According to the May 2006 *Occupational Employment Statistics* survey, by the U.S. Bureau of Labor Statistics (BLS), most social workers who were not listed separately in the survey earned an estimated annual salary that ranged between $25,540 and $68,500.

As consultants, Forensic Social Workers charge an hourly, daily, or flat rate for initial consultation, depositions, courtroom testimony, and other services that they offer. They may also charge for out-of-pocket expenses, such as travel time, photocopying, and phone calls.

Employment Prospects

Many Forensic Social Workers are employed by local and state government agencies, including departments of health and human services, mental health, and social services. They also work for prisons and other correctional facilities, psychiatric hospitals, public defenders' offices, legal assistance programs, and social service agencies. Some Forensic Social Workers, who are clinical social workers, have private practices in which they counsel and treat individuals and families.

Forensic social work is a relatively new field, but according to some experts, the demand for forensic expertise is expected to increase in the coming years. Opportunities are favorable for experienced Forensic Social Workers.

The BLS reports that employment for social workers in general is expected to increase by 18 to 26 percent through 2014. In addition to job growth, social workers will be needed to replace those who advance to higher positions, transfer to other occupations, retire, or leave the workforce for various reasons. Government jobs as well as positions in organizations that receive government funding may be limited due to strict local, state, or federal budgets.

Advancement Prospects

As staff members, individuals can advance to senior positions, which may include supervisory and managerial duties. Forensic Social Workers with entrepreneurial ambitions may start their own forensic consulting business and/or private practice, offering clinical services to individuals and groups. Social workers may also choose to pursue academic careers as teachers and researchers, which requires possession of a doctoral degree.

Education and Training

Forensic Social Workers possess either a bachelor's degree in social work or another related field or a master's degree in social work (MSW). Clinical social workers hold either an MSW or doctoral degree, with a concentration in clinical social work. They also complete a supervised clinical internship and at least two years of postgraduate employment in clinical social work under the supervision of licensed clinical social workers.

There are no formal degree programs for forensic social work, but many social work schools offer an introductory course in the field. Social workers generally learn about forensic issues and techniques on the job. They also enroll in courses, seminars, and workshops that are offered by professional associations and other organizations.

Special Requirements

In the United States, social workers may be required to be licensed, certified, or registered in the jurisdiction where they practice. (This includes all 50 states, Washington, D.C., and the U.S. territories.) A jurisdiction may regulate one, some, or all of these levels of social work practice: social workers with a bachelor's degree, an MSW, an MSW with two years of postgraduate supervised experience, or an MSW with two years of postgraduate clinical social work experience.

Requirements vary with each jurisdiction. For specific information, contact the appropriate board of social work examiners.

Experience, Special Skills, and Personality Traits

Social workers usually work several years before settling into a career in forensic social work. Those who eventually become forensic consultants have worked for many years in their roles as Forensic Social Workers. Potential clients seek consultants who are highly accomplished and recognized in their field. In addition, they prefer to retain consultants who have the necessary knowledge, skills, and experience to successfully complete their projects.

Forensic Social Workers must have excellent writing, organizational, self-management, and teamwork skills for their job. They also need to have effective interpersonal and communication skills, as they must be able to work well with clients, colleagues, attorneys, judges, and others from diverse backgrounds. Being ethical, trustworthy, patient, objective, detail-oriented, and persistent are some personality traits that Forensic Social Workers have in common.

Unions and Associations

Many Forensic Social Workers join professional associations to take advantage of networking opportunities, continuing education programs, and other professional resources and services. Some national societies that serve their interests are the National Organization of Forensic Social Work, the American College of Forensic Examiners, and the National Association of Social Workers. For contact information, see Appendix III.

Tips for Entry

1. Talk with several Forensic Social Workers to get a better idea of what they do. Also ask them for their suggestions for the type of courses and training that would help you prepare for a career in forensic social work.
2. Obtain an internship in a criminal justice setting, such as a correctional facility or public defender's office, to gain valuable experience.
3. To enhance their employability, many social workers obtain professional certification on a voluntary basis from a recognized professional association. For information about some certification programs, see Appendix II.
4. Learn more about the forensic social work field on the Internet. To obtain a list of relevant Web sites, enter the keywords *forensic social work* or *forensic social workers* into a search engine. For some links, see Appendix IV.

FORENSIC EXPERTS IN BUSINESS

FORENSIC ACCOUNTANT

CAREER PROFILE

Duties: Perform investigative and/or litigation support services; analyze and interpret financial evidence; perform duties as required

Alternate Title(s): Forensic Examiner

Salary Range: $34,000 to $94,000+

Employment Prospects: Good

Advancement Prospects: Fair

Prerequisites:

Education or Training—A bachelor's degree; on-the-job training

Experience—Previous accounting and auditing experience needed; investigative experience preferred

Special Skills and Personality Traits—Organizational, analytical, research, writing, interpersonal, and communication skills; curious, objective, detail-oriented, honest, trustworthy, and creative

Special Requirements—CPA license and professional fraud examiner certification may be required

CAREER LADDER

```
┌─────────────────────────────────┐
│   Senior Forensic Accountant    │
└─────────────────────────────────┘

┌─────────────────────────────────┐
│      Forensic Accountant        │
└─────────────────────────────────┘

┌─────────────────────────────────┐
│  Assistant Forensic Accountant  │
└─────────────────────────────────┘
```

Position Description

Accountants generally prepare, analyze, verify, and maintain the financial records of their employers or clients. As they gain experience, many accountants specialize in a particular field of accounting. One such specialty is forensic accounting, in which professionals engage in various legal matters, such as criminal investigations, personal injury lawsuits, divorce cases, contract disputes, product liability claims, and insurance investigations. For example, Forensic Accountants might calculate financial damages in breach of contract scenarios, investigate disputes regarding corporate mergers or acquisitions, or provide assistance in settling fraud cases.

These forensic specialists use accounting, auditing, and investigative skills to analyze and interpret financial records. They have the ability to interpret business information and are knowledgeable about financial reporting systems and accounting procedures. Furthermore, Forensic Accountants understand the processes and procedures for gathering evidence, conducting investigations, and dealing with litigation. They know where to look for evidence and how to obtain relevant information by interviewing suspects and clients.

Many Forensic Accountants are self-employed or work for accounting firms. Some are employed by law enforcement agencies, insurance companies, government agencies, law firms, and banks, among others. Either as employees or contractors, Forensic Accounts perform two major types of services.

One major service that many Forensic Accounts provide is to investigate suspected criminal accounting practices. For example, they might provide their services to parties concerned with violations of generally accepted accounting principles including concealed assets, money laundering, passing bad checks, and fraudulent actions in the areas of bankruptcy, securities, contracts, and credit. Or, for instance, they might investigate employee theft, real estate fraud, or similar cases in which financial records have been destroyed or tampered with.

Essentially, Forensic Accountants review, analyze, and interpret financial evidence, such as bookkeeping records and forged documents. They provide their employers or clients with oral and written reports of their findings and conclusions. They may also offer their recommendations for protecting or recovering assets.

Litigation support is the other major service that many Forensic Accountants provide. This service is offered to attorneys who are engaged in the litigation of civil or criminal cases. Forensic Accountants provide various litigation support tasks. For example, they might:

- review the facts and issues of a case to help attorneys determine if there is sufficient evidence to file a lawsuit or criminal charges
- educate lawyers on the basic concepts of accounting principles
- examine financial records to determine specific facts and issues, such as the accuracy of financial statements
- gather additional evidence to support a case
- interview witnesses
- prepare reports that can be used for negotiation settlements
- develop charts, diagrams, and other demonstrative exhibits for trials

Attorneys may also retain Forensic Accountants to provide expert witness testimony at depositions, trials, or alternative dispute resolution meetings. They give sworn statements about facts or issues about which they are qualified to give professional opinions. When Forensic Accountants provide expert witness services, they do not perform any other type of litigation support services. As expert witnesses, they are expected to provide objective and unbiased opinions that do not support or oppose either party, including the lawyers who have hired them.

Forensic Accountants may provide either investigative or litigation support services, or both. With every project, these forensic specialists perform a variety of basic tasks. For example, they meet with clients; gather information; analyze financial evidence; utilize spreadsheets, databases, and computer models; design special computer applications; write reports and correspondence; and maintain documentation of their case.

Forensic Accountants work indoors in office settings. They may travel to investigate cases. They work 40 hours per week but may put in extra hours to complete their various tasks.

Salaries

Salaries for Forensic Accountants vary, depending on such factors as their education, experience, employer, and geographic location. Formal salary information for this occupation in unavailable. Some experts in the field say that highly experienced Forensic Accountants can earn as much as $100,000 or more per year. According to the May 2006 *Occupational Employment Statistics* survey by the U.S. Bureau of Labor Statistics, the estimated annual salary for most accountants and auditors ranged between $34,470 and $94,050.

Employment Prospects

Accounting firms, insurance companies, banks, financial companies, law firms, private corporations, law enforcement agencies, and government agencies are some organizations that employ Forensic Accountants. Some Forensic Accountants are independent practitioners.

Experts in the field report that forensic accounting has been one of the fastest growing disciplines in accounting since the 1980s. There should be a constant demand for qualified Forensic Accountants through the coming years. Companies, for example, seek these experts to conduct internal investigations to prevent and combat fraud. Law enforcement agencies and attorneys also need Forensic Accountants to assist in such areas as securities investigations, business fraud, intellectual property theft, health care fraud, and terrorist investigations.

Advancement Prospects

Forensic Accountants can advance in any number of ways, depending on their interests, ambitions, and work settings. Forensic Accountants with administrative ambitions can seek positions as supervisors and managers. In accounting firms, Forensic Accountants can rise through the ranks, including partner level. Those with entrepreneurial ambitions can pursue careers as independent practitioners or owners of their accounting firms.

Education and Training

Educational qualifications vary among employers. In general, employers require that candidates possess at least a bachelor's degree in accounting or have completed general accounting courses.

Novice Forensic Accountants receive on-the-job training. They work under the guidance and supervision of experienced personnel.

Throughout their careers, Forensic Accountants enroll in continuing education programs and training programs to update their skills and knowledge.

Special Requirements

Employers may require that applicants possess the following professional certifications: Certified Public Accountant (CPA) and Certified Fraud Examiner (CFE). They may hire strong candidates on the condition that they obtain the proper certification within a certain time period.

The CPA designation is a state license. For more information, contact your state board of accountancy. The CFE certification is granted by the Association of Certified Fraud Examiners.

Experience, Special Skills, and Personality Traits

In general, entry-level applicants must have professional experience in accounting and auditing. They should also have previous experience conducting investigations.

To perform well at their job, Forensic Accountants need excellent organizational, analytical, research, and writing skills. They also need strong interpersonal and communication skills, as they must work well with people from diverse backgrounds. Being curious, objective, detail-oriented, honest, trustworthy, and creative are some personality traits that Forensic Accountants share.

Unions and Associations

Forensic Accountants can join various professional associations to take advantage of networking opportunities, continuing education, professional certification, and other professional resources and services. Some national societies that serve the interests of Forensic Accountants are:

- Forensic Accountants Society of North America
- Association of Certified Fraud Examiners
- American Institute of Certified Public Accountants
- American Academy of Forensic Sciences
- American College of Forensic Examiners

For contact information, see Appendix III.

Tips for Entry

1. Some Forensic Accountants have academic training in criminal justice or law enforcement.
2. Contact employers directly for information about job vacancies as well as their application and job selection process.
3. Use the Internet to learn more about Forensic Accountants. To get a list of relevant Web sites, enter either of these keywords into a search engine: *forensic accountants* or *forensic accounting*. For some links, see Appendix IV.

FORENSIC ECONOMIST

CAREER PROFILE

Duties: Provide forensic consulting services to attorneys and others; perform forensic economic assessment and testimony; perform other duties as required

Alternate Title(s): Forensic Consultant

Salary Range: $39,000 to $137,000

Employment Prospects: Poor

Advancement Prospects: Fair

Prerequisites:

Education or Training—An advanced degree, preferably a doctoral degree

Experience—Several years of work experience

Special Skills and Personality Traits—Communication, interpersonal, self-management, analytical, organizational, report-writing, and presentation skills; fair, honest, trustworthy, objective, diligent, curious, and personable

CAREER LADDER

```
┌─────────────────────────────┐
│     Forensic Economist      │
└─────────────────────────────┘

┌─────────────────────────────┐
│  Novice Forensic Economist  │
└─────────────────────────────┘

┌─────────────────────────────┐
│         Economist           │
└─────────────────────────────┘
```

Position Description

Economists are social scientists who study commercial activity including the manufacturing, allocation, and utilization of goods and services. They study, for example, how wealth is transferred among individuals or corporate entities. They also research business cycles, employment and unemployment statistics, trade, industrial and agricultural output, and the ebbs and flows of the money supply.

When complex economic factors lead to legal issues, specialists called Forensic Economists contribute to their resolution. These experts are consultants who provide various forensic economic services to attorneys, businesses, government agencies, non-profit organizations, and others. They assist on litigious cases that involve either individuals or organizations across the spectrum of economic power. For example, they may provide evidence that an employee suffered loss of earnings through wrongful termination or discrimination. On the other hand, they may show proof that a large corporation lost profits or the value of its business through unfair competition, antitrust violations, or other reasons.

Forensic Economists evaluate corporate losses, which may be incurred through unforeseen interruptions or the theft of property. They analyze the financial impact suffered by organizations in litigious circumstances arising from the wrongful death or injury of an employee. They assess damages and losses that organizations incur in intellectual property cases such as copyright, trade secret, and patent violations. Forensic Economists appraise companies prior to their sale to new owners to help settle shareholder disagreements or to evaluate employee stock option plans. They also review economic damage reports created by the opposing side in a dispute to find inaccuracies.

Many Forensic Economists offer litigation support services to attorneys, who may work for either the defense or the plaintiff. They may be involved in criminal cases, civil litigation, or regulatory matters. They perform such general tasks as:

- analyzing and evaluating cases to help lawyers determine whether they should be brought to trial
- helping lawyers determine the facts and issues of a case
- educating attorneys about the various economic topics involved in a case
- pointing out the scope of economic damage suffered by the plaintiffs or defendants
- gathering evidence

- interviewing witnesses
- preparing detailed reports, including references, information sources, spreadsheets, and other pertinent documentation for lawyers to use in negotiation of settlements as well as court proceedings
- formulating lists of questions that lawyers may ask to cross-examine witnesses

Attorneys may retain Forensic Economists solely for expert witness services. As expert witnesses, they give their professional opinion about facts and issues that they are qualified to address. They give sworn testimony at depositions, trials, or other legal hearings. When hired as expert witnesses, Forensic Economists do not normally perform litigation support services, to ensure objective and unbiased testimony about a case.

Economic issues are often complicated, and Forensic Economists use sophisticated analysis methods to sort out all the facts, which are not readily understood by people who lack their economic expertise. Hence, Forensic Experts make sure they present data and evidence in language and terms that can be easily understood by attorneys and other clients, as well as by judges, juries, and others.

Forensic Economists often work with other experts and resources when analyzing losses and damages. For example, when they deal with individual employment issues, they may work with vocational experts and read medical records to help determine the employee's physical or emotional limitations. They combine this information with current labor statistics to assess the employee's ability to return to work or realize compensatory awards.

Forensic Economists may specialize by working in narrow fields of interest. For example, they may investigate issues in such sectors of the economy as agriculture, labor, or finance. They may work solely with individual employee concerns or take on only large corporate clients.

Many Forensic Economists also provide other economic consulting services that are removed from the legal arena. For example, they may study statistical data in their specialty area; forecast market trends for businesses or business publications; recommend plans or help formulate policies for governments or corporations to resolve economic problems; or testify at legislative sessions about the impact economic legislation may have on the public. All Forensic Economists are responsible for keeping up to date with developments in their profession.

Forensic Economists work in office settings. They work full time or part time. They typically work flexible hours and occasionally travel to meet with clients or attend legal proceedings.

Salaries

Specific salary information for Forensic Economists is unavailable. As consultants, they charge an hourly, daily, or flat rate for initial consultation, depositions, courtroom testimony, and other services that they offer.

Most economists, in general, earn an estimated annual salary that ranged between $42,280 and $136,550, according to the May 2006 *Occupational Employment Statistics* survey by the U.S. Bureau of Labor Statistics (BLS). The estimated annual salary for most economics professors ranged from $38,630 to $130,990.

Employment Prospects

Forensic Economists find employment with economic consulting firms that offer forensic economic services. Some are employed by accounting firms that offer such services in their litigation support departments. Other Forensic Economists work part time, while working full time as educators or business professionals.

Forensic economics is an emerging field. It is only one of several activities that consulting economists might offer to clients.

Employment for economists, in general, is expected to increase by only zero to 8 percent through 2014, according to the BLS. However, much of the growth is expected to be in the management, scientific, and technical consulting services industries, including forensic consulting.

Advancement Prospects

Forensic Economists generally measure success through job satisfaction, professional recognition, and by being sought for highly complex or publicized cases.

College and university instructors typically seek tenure-track positions. Once they gain tenure at an institution, they cannot be fired without just cause and due process. Academicians advance by rising through the ranks from instructor to full professor. They can also pursue managerial and administrative positions, from department chair to academic dean to the position of provost or president.

Education and Training

Minimally, individuals wishing to become Forensic Economists must have a master's degree in economics or in business administration. A doctorate is needed to teach in four-year colleges and universities. Clients usually prefer to retain Forensic Economists who hold a doctoral degree, particularly if they will be providing expert witness services. In general, most Forensic Economists possess a doctorate.

It takes years of committed effort for students to obtain a doctoral degree in economics. First, they complete a four-year bachelor's degree program, followed by a two-year master's degree program. Upon earning their master's degree, they enroll in a doctoral program, which takes several more years to finish. To successfully earn their degree, doctoral candidates must write a book-length dissertation based on original research. Upon earning their doctorates, many economists obtain a postdoctoral position, to continue training in their specialty.

Throughout their careers, Forensic Economists enroll in continuing education programs to update their skills and keep up with advancements in their fields.

Experience, Special Skills, and Personality Traits

Potential clients seek Forensic Economists who have distinguished themselves in their field. Clients hire consultants who have the necessary knowledge, skills, and experience to successfully perform their projects. Typically, economists complete many years of work experience before becoming forensic consultants.

To be effective consultants, Forensic Economists need excellent communication and interpersonal skills, as they must be able to work well with attorneys and others from diverse backgrounds. In addition, they must have strong self-management, analytical, organizational, report-writing, and presentation skills. Some personality traits that successful Forensic Economists share include being fair, honest, trustworthy, objective, diligent, curious, and personable.

Unions and Associations

Forensic Economists can join various professional associations to take advantage of networking opportunities, continuing education, and other professional resources and services. Some national societies that serve the interests of Forensic Economists are the National Association of Forensic Economics, the American Economics Association, the American Rehabilitation Economics Association, and the American Academy of Economic and Financial Experts. For contact information, see Appendix III.

Tips for Entry

1. To learn more about the field, talk with Forensic Economists. One place to meet these professionals is a conference sponsored by professional associations such as the National Association of Forensic Economists.

2. As a college student, obtain a research assistantship with a professor who offers forensic economic consulting services. Let your professor know that you are interested in assisting with his or her forensic cases.

3. Some Forensic Economists have entered the field with professional backgrounds in business, accounting, finance, statistics, or vocational rehabilitation.

4. Contact prospective employers directly about job vacancies.

5. Use the Internet to learn more about forensic economics. To obtain a list of relevant Web sites enter the keywords *forensic economics* or *forensic economists* into a search engine. For some links, see Appendix IV.

FRAUD EXAMINER

CAREER PROFILE

Duties: Detect, investigate, and deter fraud in the workplace; perform duties as required

Alternate Title(s): Fraud Specialist, Fraud Investigator; a title that reflects a specific occupation such as Forensic Accountant, Auditor, Claims Investigator, Security Consultant, or Loss Prevention Specialist

Salary Range: $50,000 to $119,000

Employment Prospects: Good

Advancement Prospects: Good

Prerequisites:

Education or Training — A bachelor's degree; formal or on-the-job training in fraud examination

Experience — Several years of work experience in accounting, auditing, or financial investigations

Special Skills and Personality Traits — Self-management, problem-solving, critical-thinking, organizational, interviewing, research, writing, interpersonal, teamwork, and communication skills; personable, assertive, honest, detail-oriented, persistent, inquisitive, and flexible

Special Requirements — Professional certification may be required

CAREER LADDER

```
┌─────────────────────────────┐
│   Senior Fraud Examiner     │
└─────────────────────────────┘

┌─────────────────────────────┐
│      Fraud Examiner         │
└─────────────────────────────┘

┌─────────────────────────────┐
│   Fraud Examiner Trainee    │
└─────────────────────────────┘
```

Position Description

Fraud in the workplace is a problem that many organizations face, whether they are small businesses, large corporations, government bodies, or nonprofit organizations. Crimes of fraud are not violent crimes but they do cause suffering to the victims and inflict hundreds of billions of dollars in damage to the economy each year. In legal terms, fraud is an act of deception that individuals commit to take funds or other assets from other individuals or organizations. They knowingly and intentionally misrepresent information, such as financial statements, on which victims rely to be accurate and correct. Perpetrators of occupational fraud range from low-level employees to high-ranking executive officers. Fraud may involve vendors, contractors, clients (or customers), or boards of directors.

Because fraud is such a clandestine activity, employers have a difficult time proving how or why it occurs. Hence, they hire Fraud Examiners who are experts in the detection, investigation, and prevention of fraud in the workplace. These specialists work on cases that involve such fraudulent acts as bribery, property or monetary theft, trade secrets or intellectual property theft, falsification of financial statements or claims, failure to divulge financial information, use of company property for personal gain, and conflict of interest.

Along with backgrounds in accounting and auditing, Fraud Examiners have training in criminology and investigative techniques. They are also knowledgeable about laws and regulations relating to fraud. Additionally, they are familiar with common fraud schemes and can spot clues that indicate possible fraudulent acts. Furthermore, Forensic Examiners are aware of the legal consequences of mishandling of evidence and the importance of maintaining the chain of custody.

Fraud Examiners may be directly employed by organizations or they may offer their services on a consultancy basis.

Whether they are employees or contractors, it is their job to resolve accusations of fraud. They also help organizations to prevent fraud from occurring and to implement methods to discover fraudulent activities within their ranks.

With each case, Fraud Examiners follow specific procedures. They evaluate an organization's practices and procedures to identify systemic vulnerabilities that invite fraudulent behavior. They plan their course of action for conducting an examination. They gather evidence, which involves collecting various financial statements, books, records, and other relevant documents; observing the day-to-day organizational activities; and interviewing employees, potential suspects, and others.

Fraud Examiners carefully and thoroughly analyze the data to determine whether the organization's policies are in fact implemented as intended. They report their findings to their employer or client regarding evidence of any fraudulent activity, the identity of suspects, the presence of weaknesses in the system, and which internal controls are not being effectively utilized. When Fraud Examiners uncover a crime, they may be assigned to work with attorneys to build a case.

These forensic experts may help to solve such crimes as mail fraud, extortion, embezzlement, larceny, money laundering, securities fraud, credit card fraud, bankruptcy fraud, and disability fraud.

Fraud Examiners perform various general tasks in their investigations. For example, they may:

- study formal accounting records
- analyze financial statements
- reconstruct accounting records
- conduct business appraisals
- evaluate fraud risks
- locate hidden assets
- trace the path of missing funds
- document their investigations in clearly and concisely written reports
- provide expert witness testimony at depositions, trials and other legal proceedings
- assist in developing and implementing fraud policies and procedures
- work with police officers, FBI agents, or other law enforcement officers
- stay up to date with new developments in their field

Fraud Examiners work in office settings. They use specialized computer software as well as general software such as spreadsheets, databases, and statistical analysis programs to aid in their fraud investigations. Additionally, they may use resources on the Internet to assist in their casework.

In some organizations, Fraud Examiners are employed as auditors, accountants, risk managers, compliance officers, and claims investigators. They perform fraud examination duties in addition to their regular responsibilities. Some private investigators, as well as some law enforcement officers (such as criminal investigators and special agents) are highly trained fraud examiners, and hence perform these services for their clients or employers.

Fraud Examiners work standard 40-hour weeks, but may put in extra hours to complete their various duties.

Salaries

Salaries for Fraud Examiners vary, depending on such factors as their education, experience, position, employer, and geographic location. Fraud Examiners who possess professional certification usually earn higher wages than noncertified examiners. According to PayScale.com, the median annual salaries (in December 2006) for certified Fraud Examiners ranged from $50,000 for internal auditors to $119,100 for chief financial officers. Certified Fraud Examiners working in the insurance and financial services industry earned the highest median annual salary at $75,500 per year, while those in the insurance industry earned the lowest median salary at $51,500 per year.

Employment Prospects

Fraud Examiners are employed in almost all industries. They find employment with private corporations, financial institutions, insurance companies, nonprofit organizations, and other organizations. They are hired by public accounting firms, bookkeeping companies, and management consulting firms. Some professionals are independent practitioners or own firms that offer fraud detection, investigation, and deterrence services.

Local and state law enforcement agencies as well as federal law enforcement agencies (such as the Federal Bureau of Investigation and the U.S. Postal Inspection Service) employ professionals specifically to perform fraud investigations. In addition, Fraud Examiners are hired by other government agencies such as state attorney generals' offices, the U.S. Internal Revenue Service, and offices of the inspector general, which are found in various state and federal government agencies.

Opportunities should continually be favorable for qualified Fraud Examiners, as private companies, government agencies, and other organizations are constantly seeking ways to prevent and reduce fraud. Most positions will become available as individuals retire, transfer to other jobs, or advance to higher positions. Employers will create new positions to meet growing needs.

In general, employment for accountants and auditors is expected to increase by 18 to 26 percent through 2014, according to the U.S. Bureau of Labor Statistics.

Advancement Prospects

Fraud Examiners can advance in any number of ways, depending on their ambitions and interests. They can specialize in particular services or work in certain industries. They can pursue administrative and managerial positions, which may require transferring to other employers. Individuals with entrepreneurial ambitions can become independent practitioners or start their own companies that offer consulting or technical services.

Fraud Examiners can also pursue opportunities as instructors in higher education institutions. They may need master's or doctoral degrees to advance to higher positions or to obtain teaching jobs in colleges and universities.

Education and Training
Minimally, Fraud Examiners should have at least a bachelor's degree in accounting, criminal justice, or another field related to their primary occupation (such as forensic accountant, auditor, or law enforcement officer).

Individuals need on-the-job training, formal training, or a combination of both to become Fraud Examiners. Opportunities for formal training in fraud examination are gradually increasing each year. Professional societies such as the Association of Certified Fraud Examiners and the Institute of Certified Public Accountants offer seminars, workshops, and self-study courses in fraud examination. In addition, several colleges and universities offer degree and certificate programs in this field.

Throughout their careers, Fraud Examiners enroll in continuing education programs to update their skills and knowledge.

Special Requirements
Many employers require that candidates possess the Certified Fraud Examiner (CFE) designation, which is granted by the Association of Certified Fraud Examiners. They may hire candidates on the condition that they obtain the CFE within a certain time frame.

The CFE is a professional certification that individuals obtain on a voluntary basis. In general, applicants must possess a bachelor's degree and two years of professional experience in which they performed duties related to fraud examination. They must also pass an examination that covers accounting, auditing, investigation, law, and criminology. To maintain their certification, CFEs must complete a minimum number of hours of continuing education.

Experience, Special Skills, and Personality Traits
Employers generally seek entry-level candidates who have several years of professional practice in accounting, audit-

ing, or financial investigations, including experience in fraud examinations. Fraud Examiners typically have extensive backgrounds in such fields as accounting, law, criminology, education, or loss prevention.

To perform well at their job, Fraud Examiners need strong self-management, problem-solving, critical-thinking, organizational, interviewing, research, and writing skills. Because they must work well with different people from diverse backgrounds, they need excellent interpersonal, teamwork, and communication skills. Being personable, assertive, honest, detail-oriented, persistent, inquisitive, and flexible are some personality traits that successful Fraud Examiners share.

Unions and Associations
Many Fraud Examiners belong to various professional associations to take advantage of networking opportunities, continuing education, professional certification, and other professional resources and services. Some national societies that serve the interests of these professionals include:

- Association of Certified Fraud Examiners
- Association of Certified Fraud Specialists
- American Institute of Certified Public Accountants
- Institute of Internal Auditors
- National Association of Certified Valuation Analysts
- National Association of Fraud Investigators

For contact information, see Appendix III.

Tips for Entry
1. While in college, take courses in criminal justice if you are an accounting major. If you are a criminal justice major, take courses in accounting and auditing.
2. When you are in the early years of your career as an accountant, auditor, or other profession, let your supervisor or mentor know about your interest in learning to perform fraud examinations.
3. To gain practical experience, volunteer your services to work on fraud investigations in a local law enforcement agency or district attorney's office.
4. Write your résumé so it reflects your qualifications as a Fraud Examiner.
5. Use the Internet to learn more about the fraud examination field. You might start by visiting the Association of Certified Fraud Examiners Web site at http://www.acfe.com. For more links, see Appendix IV.

FORENSIC EXPERTS IN LANGUAGE AND SPEECH

FORENSIC LINGUIST

CAREER PROFILE

Duties: Provide forensic consulting services to attorneys and others; apply linguistic knowledge and skills to legal matters; perform duties as required

Alternate Title(s): Forensic Consultant, Linguist

Salary Range: $38,000 to $83,000

Employment Prospects: Poor

Advancement Prospects: Fair

Prerequisites:

Education or Training—A doctoral degree in linguistics
Experience— Several years of experience in their field
Special Skills and Personality Traits—Communication, interpersonal, self-management, analytical, organizational, report-writing, and presentation skills; curious, honest, trustworthy, objective, persistent, and patient

CAREER LADDER

```
┌─────────────────────────────┐
│     Forensic Linguist       │
└─────────────────────────────┘

┌─────────────────────────────┐
│   Novice Forensic Linguist  │
└─────────────────────────────┘

┌─────────────────────────────┐
│          Linguist           │
└─────────────────────────────┘
```

Position Description

Linguistics is the scientific study of language. There are several approaches that linguists use to understand language: phonetics, the study of speech sounds; phonology, the study of how speech sounds are organized and how that organization differs from language to language; morphology, the study of how words are formed; syntax, the study of the construction of sentences; semantics, the study of the meaning of words; and discourse analysis, the study of how sentences are strung together to create narratives or paragraphs. Each of these approaches is also a linguistic professional specialty. Linguists may focus on one or more of these specialties in their work. Additionally, they may work in subfields of linguistics that more narrowly focus their attention, including historical linguistics, the study of how languages evolve; sociolinguistics, the study of how societies use language in the form of dialects or slang; psycholinguistics, the study of how we mentally process language; and neurolinguistics, the study of how the brain physically processes language.

Another subfield of linguistics is forensic linguistics, which is a relatively new field that has developed within the last several decades. Forensic linguistics is the study and application of how language is used in legal disputes, crime, or courtroom processes. In addition to their exper-

tise in language, Forensic Linguists are well versed and qualified in such other disciplines as mathematics, statistics, the law, and the sciences. Forensic Linguists study written and spoken language in correspondence, business contracts, legal documents, criminal confessions, court proceedings, and documentary crime evidence to interpret or clarify their meanings. They work to clarify the meaning of wills, business communications, and other documents as well. Their studies include electronic communications such as e-mails, text messages, and recorded conversations.

These professionals contribute to linguistic concerns in a variety of ways. For example, they help to improve the readability or comprehensibility of legal documents such as legal briefs or jury instructions. Forensic Linguists study such documents and change complicated or convoluted phrases into simpler formats that say the same thing but can be understood more readily by more people. They also help attorneys to speak clearly in court sessions to explain legal concepts in more commonly used terms. Forensic Linguists may be called to court as expert witnesses to testify on the meaning of spoken or written words relevant to a civil or criminal case.

Forensic Linguists help to settle trademark disputes. For example, they may determine whether or not a trademark becomes so familiar that its use in everyday speech or written usage no longer pertains to a specific brand, thus enabling its usage without penalty.

These professionals investigate what is known as authorship attribution for both written and spoken language, including threatening communications. In this area, Forensic Linguists help law enforcement personnel authenticate bomb threats, suicide notes, libelous articles, or ransom notes and prove or disprove that a certain individual wrote the documents or placed threatening phone calls.

Forensic Linguists look for patterns, similarities, or inconsistencies in speech and written passages. They determine whether the same person made different recordings, or they establish a speaker's regional origin or cultural background by listening to their accent or dialect in their speech. These forensic experts listen to taped confessions or read written confessions to determine whether the confessor was coerced to say certain things. They do this by comparing the suspect's normal speech or writing patterns to what was said or written in the confession. Forensic Linguists read documents to find similarities in syntax and semantics to help identify the author or to determine if several documents were written by the same person. One of their areas of concern is plagiarism. Forensic Linguists compare written materials to determine whether all or part of one is a verbatim copy of another.

Forensic Linguists study and analyze how police officers communicate with suspects or witnesses and help them communicate more effectively by using easily understood vocabulary. They also help judges and attorneys use plainer language rather than their specialized vocabulary of legal terms when addressing a jury. Forensic Linguists also participate in court sessions as expert witnesses when linguistic evidence is relevant to criminal or civil cases.

These professionals sometimes work privately with individuals or parties who are not involved in legal disputes or criminal actions. Such private concerns as plagiarism, incidents of hate speech, or matters of disputed wording in business documents are not settled in court but still fall into the purview of forensic linguistics. In these situations, Forensic Linguists work in the context of private consultation with such clients as university professors, business leaders, or other individuals.

Whether they work in private settings or in the legal arena, Forensic Linguists are increasingly involved in matters that are international in scope. They are becoming more engaged with cases involving terrorism, organized crime, and human rights abuses. They are starting to face the challenge of understanding and conveying the meanings of speech and documents translated from other languages that use different rules of syntax, grammar, and discourse.

These professionals offer their forensic linguistic services on a part-time basis. Most Forensic Linguists work full time researching or teaching in their other linguistic specialties or subfields. They primarily work in universities in office settings.

Salaries

Specific salary information for Forensic Linguists is unavailable. As consultants, they charge an hourly, daily, or flat rate for initial consultation, depositions, courtroom testimony, and other services that they offer.

The median annual salary for faculty in linguistics ranged from $38,326 for instructors to $83,006 for full professors, according to the *2006–07 National Faculty Salary Survey*. This survey was conducted by the College and University Professional Association for Human Resources.

Employment Prospects

Forensic linguistics is a young, small, but growing, field.

Job opportunities for linguists, in general, become available as professionals retire, transfer to other jobs, or advance to higher positions. Because the different fields in which linguists work are small, job competition is strong.

Advancement Prospects

Forensic Linguists generally measure success through job satisfaction, professional recognition, and higher incomes.

College and university instructors typically seek tenure-track positions. Once they gain tenure at an institution, they cannot be fired without just cause and due process. Academicians advance by rising through the ranks from instructor to full professor. They can also pursue managerial and administrative positions, from department chair to academic dean to the position of provost or president.

Education and Training

To teach or conduct research at four-year colleges and universities, linguists must possess a doctoral degree in linguistics. Clients usually prefer to retain Forensic Linguists who hold a doctoral degree, particularly if they will be providing expert witness services. In general, most Forensic Linguists possess a doctorate.

It takes several years of committed effort for students to obtain a doctoral degree in linguistics. First, they complete a four-year bachelor's degree program, followed by a two-year master's degree program. Upon earning their master's degree, they enroll in a doctoral program, which takes several more years to finish. To successfully earn their degree, doctoral candidates must write a book-length dissertation based on original research. Upon earning their doctorates, many linguists obtain a postdoctoral position, to continue training in their specialty.

Throughout their careers, Forensic Linguists enroll in training and continuing education programs to update their skills and knowledge.

Experience, Special Skills, and Personality Traits

Potential clients seek Forensic Linguists who have distinguished themselves in their field. They retain consultants who have the necessary knowledge, skills, and experience to successfully complete their projects. Typically, linguists have many years of work experience, particularly in research, before becoming forensic consultants.

To be effective consultants, Forensic Linguists need excellent communication and interpersonal skills, as they must be able to work well with attorneys and others from diverse backgrounds. In addition, they must have strong self-management, analytical, organizational, report-writing, and presentation skills. Being curious, honest, trustworthy, objective, persistent, and patient are some personality traits that successful Forensic Linguists have in common.

Unions and Associations

Forensic Linguists can join professional associations to take advantage of networking opportunities, continuing education, and other professional resources and services. Some national societies that serve the interests of these specialists are the International Association of Forensic Linguists and the Linguistic Society of America. For contact information, see Appendix III.

Tips for Entry

1. During your college career, work with professors who are involved in doing forensic consulting.
2. Take courses in law, criminal justice, and forensic science to gain a foundation in legal procedures, principles of evidence, forensic techniques, and other subjects.
3. Develop your professional reputation. For example, you might give presentations at conferences and other events for linguists as well as for law enforcement officers, attorneys, or forensic scientists.
4. Learn more about the forensic linguistics field on the Internet. To get a list of relevant Web sites, enter either of these keywords into a search engine: *forensic linguistics* or *forensic linguists*. For some links, see Appendix IV.

FORENSIC PHONETICIAN

Duties: Provide forensic consulting services to attorneys and others; apply phonetics knowledge and skills to legal matters; perform duties as required

Alternate Title(s): Forensic Phonetics Expert, Forensic Consultant

Salary Range: $38,000 to $83,000

Employment Prospects: Poor

Advancement Prospects: Fair

Prerequisites:

Education or Training—A doctoral degree in linguistics

Experience— Several years of experience in one's field

Special Skills and Personality Traits—Analytical, organizational, self-management, communication, interpersonal, writing, and presentation skills; fair, trustworthy, inquisitive, meticulous, and impartial

Forensic Phonetician

Novice Forensic Phonetician

Phonetician

Position Description

Forensic phonetics is a new investigative tool that law enforcement agencies and courts find useful now that audio and video recordings increasingly play an important part in criminal prosecution. Phonetics is the study of the sounds we make when we speak. We use our vocal chords, mouths, and nasal cavities to produce these sounds to form words. Scholars who study phonetics are called phoneticians. They research how we learn to speak and recognize speech as well as how our speech sounds are similar to or differ from one language to another. Phoneticians are linguistics specialists who also draw upon the fields of physics, physiology, medicine, and acoustics to assist them in their studies. Hence, their exploration of speech sounds includes sound wave analysis and research into how our ears, auditory nerves, and brains respond to sound waves to enable us to perceive the spoken word.

Forensic Phoneticians apply the discipline of phonetics to legal and law enforcement issues. Essentially, they perform forensic speech analysis. Some crimes are committed in which the perpetrator may speak but not be seen by the victim. Forensic Phoneticians work with audio speech recordings to help identify suspect speakers, clarify what was said in garbled recorded conversations, authenticate recordings to ensure they were not altered, and conduct voice line-ups to help witnesses pick a perpetrator out of a series of suspects' vocal recordings.

Most of forensic phonetic work is in the area of speaker identification. Forensic Phoneticians use computer equipment to perform some of this work, but they mainly listen intently to audio recordings. They repeatedly listen to the speaker and note certain qualities within the individual's speech. Forensic Phoneticians focus more on how their subject speaks than what he or she says. Their analysis involves four aspects. They analyze the sound the speaker makes with his or her vocal chords aside from the other sounds that constitute speech. For example, they note whether the speaker's voice is rough, strained, or has a breathy quality. Next, Forensic Phoneticians listen to the other sounds made by the speaker's mouth and nasal cavities and make note of the specific vocal qualities expressed. Then they focus on the pronunciation of vowels and other articulations that provide hints to the speaker's geographical and social background. Lastly, Forensic Phoneticians listen to various individual speech characteristics such as the speaker's pronunciation of consonants or whether the speaker slurs certain words or lisps.

In addition to this auditory analysis, Forensic Phoneticians conduct an acoustic analysis. They digitize recordings in order to use specialized software to measure frequencies of pitch and vowel sounds. Unlike forensic audio specialists,

Forensic Phoneticians do not use spectrographic voiceprint analysis to identify speakers. Their use of oscilloscopes and spectrographs serves another purpose. They compare variations in the vocal sound wave frequencies of several speakers to determine which pattern most likely matches the voice of a criminal rather than identify a suspect with a specific voiceprint. Unlike fingerprints or shoe prints, voiceprints are variable or subject to manipulation and are therefore not useful to Forensic Phoneticians.

Forensic Phoneticians also use voice line-ups to help victims or witnesses identify a voice in cases where they cannot visually identify the perpetrator. They listen to a set of recorded voices, which includes the suspect's voice. Forensic Phoneticians select the panel of voices and ensure that their speech patterns are fairly uniform without much variation in voice quality or accents.

Additionally, these professionals work with voice recordings to filter out interference and distortions such as background noises. They also work to authenticate tapes to minimize the use of manipulated recordings as crime evidence. Furthermore, Forensic Phoneticians transcribe recordings that prove difficult for law enforcement personnel to hear in ordinary circumstances. In some cases, background noises may be useful to help investigators determine where or when the suspect spoke. Forensic Phoneticians may assist in this area as well.

Forensic Phoneticians prepare detailed reports of their findings, conclusions, and opinions. They also describe the methods they followed and the equipment and computer software they used. Additionally, they clarify the limitations of forensic speech analysis.

When required, these men and women provide sworn testimony as expert witnesses at depositions and trials. They address only facts and issues in which they are qualified to provide a professional opinion. Like all other forensic consultants, they are expected to provide unbiased and impartial testimony. They do not take sides, including those of the lawyers who have retained them.

These professionals offer their forensic speech analysis services on a part-time basis. Most phoneticians work full time researching or teaching in colleges and universities. Forensic Phoneticians work in office or lab settings equipped with audio equipment and computers. They may travel to confer with law enforcement personnel or to testify in court.

Salaries
Specific salary information for Forensic Phoneticians is unavailable. As consultants, they charge an hourly, daily, or flat rate for initial consultation, depositions, courtroom testimony, and other services that they offer. They may also charge for out-of-pocket expenses such as telephone calls and traveling time.

As academicians, Forensic Phoneticians earn a salary based on their position, experience, employer, and other factors. The College and University Professional Association for Human Resources reports in its *2006–07 National Faculty Salary Survey* that the median annual salary for linguistics (which includes phoneticians) faculty ranged from $38,326 for instructors to $83,006 for full professors.

Employment Prospects
Forensic phonetics is a small field, but opportunities should increase in the coming years as it becomes more familiar and acceptable to law enforcement agencies, attorneys, and others.

Job opportunities for phoneticians, in general, become available as professionals retire, transfer to other jobs, or advance to higher positions.

Advancement Prospects
Forensic Phoneticians generally measure success through job satisfaction, professional recognition, and higher incomes.

Academicians advance by rising through the ranks from instructor to full professor. They can also pursue managerial and administrative positions, from department chair to academic dean to the position of provost or president.

Education and Training
In general, most Forensic Phoneticians possess a doctoral degree in linguistics with an emphasis in phonetics or another related field. Clients usually prefer to retain Forensic Phoneticians who hold a doctoral degree, particularly if they will be providing expert witness services. To teach or conduct research at four-year colleges and universities, phoneticians must possess a doctoral degree in linguistics.

It takes several years of committed effort for students to obtain a doctoral degree in linguistics. First, students complete a four-year bachelor's degree program, followed by a two-year master's degree program. Upon earning their master's degree, they enroll in a doctoral program, which takes several more years to finish. To successfully earn their degree, doctoral candidates must write a book-length dissertation based on original research.

Throughout their careers, Forensic Phoneticians enroll in training and continuing education programs to update their skills and knowledge.

Experience, Special Skills, and Personality Traits
Normally, phoneticians have many years of work experience, particularly in research, before they become forensic consultants. Potential clients seek Forensic Phoneticians who have distinguished themselves in their field. They seek consultants who have the necessary knowledge, skills, and experience to successfully complete their projects.

Forensic Phoneticians need strong analytical, organizational, and self-management skills to be successful at their work. They also must have effective communication and interpersonal skills, as they must be able to work well with attorneys and others from diverse backgrounds. In addition, they need excellent writing and presentation skills. Being fair, trustworthy, inquisitive, meticulous, and impartial are some personality traits that successful Forensic Phoneticians share.

Unions and Associations

Several professional societies serve the interests of Forensic Phoneticians. These include the International Association for Forensic Phonetics and Acoustics and the Linguistic Society of America. (For contact information, see Appendix III.) By joining professional associations, Forensic Phoneticians can take advantage of networking opportunities and other professional resources and services.

Tips for Entry

1. While in high school, find out if the fields of linguistics, and phonetics in particular, fit your interests and ambitions. Along with reading books and articles, you might contact linguistics professors. You can find contact information for faculty at Web sites of university linguistics programs.

2. Upon earning their doctorates, many phoneticians obtain a postdoctoral position to continue training in their specialty.

3. To build your business, contact law enforcement agencies and attorneys. Let them know about your services and how you can help them with their investigations.

4. Use the Internet to learn more about forensic phonetics. To get a list of relevant Web sites enter the keywords *forensic phonetics* or *forensic phoneticians*. For some links, see Appendix IV.

JURISPRUDENCE
EXPERTS

TRIAL LAWYER

CAREER PROFILE

Duties: Represent clients in courts of law; handle legal issues in criminal cases or civil disputes; prepare and file legal documents, collect facts and evidence, negotiate settlements, try cases, and perform other litigation tasks; perform other duties as required

Alternate Title(s): Litigation Attorney, Litigator

Salary Range: $51,000 to $146,000+

Employment Prospects: Good

Advancement Prospects: Good

Prerequisites:

Education or Training—A law (J.D.) degree; on-the-job training

Experience—Some experience desirable

Special Skills and Personality Traits—Organizational, self-management, negotiation, writing, presentation, communication, and interpersonal skills; patient, analytical, quick-witted, persuasive, detail-oriented, and creative

Special Requirements—States require lawyers to be admitted to their state bar; federal courts require registration for lawyers to practice

CAREER LADDER

```
┌─────────────────────────────────┐
│   Senior Associate or Partner   │
└─────────────────────────────────┘

┌─────────────────────────────────┐
│           Associate             │
└─────────────────────────────────┘

┌─────────────────────────────────┐
│        Junior Associate         │
└─────────────────────────────────┘
```

Position Description

Trial Lawyers are experts in litigation, the complex process of resolving criminal or civil disputes in state and federal courts of law. Some Trial Lawyers also handle administrative claims or disputes for clients before local, state, and federal regulatory agencies, such as a planning commission, environmental agency, or transportation board. These attorneys are highly skilled in preparing cases for trial, evaluating evidence, selecting juries, examining and cross-examining witnesses, negotiating settlements, and presenting arguments before juries or judges.

Trial Lawyers may represent the plaintiff, the party filing a lawsuit, or the defendant in a dispute. In criminal cases, the plaintiff is either the state or federal government and is represented by Trial Lawyers known as prosecutors. It is the prosecutors' job to issue criminal charges against suspects and to prove in court that they are guilty of the charges. The suspects are represented by private Trial Lawyers, also known as criminal defense lawyers. When suspects cannot afford an attorney, the court appoints public defenders, who are employed by the government, to represent them.

In civil lawsuits, Trial Lawyers represent clients, who may be individuals, citizen's groups, small business owners, corporations, government agencies, or nonprofit organizations, among others. On behalf of their clients, these lawyers prosecute for them or defend them in court about disputes that may involve business transactions, personal injury, bankruptcy, professional malpractice, product liability, collections, employment matters, landlord issues, or inheritance, to name just a few areas. The plaintiffs' attorneys must prove that their clients' complaints against the defendants are true and that the court should order the defendants to stop or perform certain actions. Additionally, the defendants may be ordered to pay the plaintiffs for damages they may have suffered because of the defendant's actions.

Litigation is a long and complex process; it typically takes several months and oftentimes several years before disputes are settled. Trial Lawyers are usually involved in several cases at a time. They might work on a case alone or as part of a team of attorneys.

Trial Lawyers perform a variety of tasks to prepare for the best defense or prosecution of their cases. They collect and evaluate facts and evidence and make sure to follow specific court procedures for gathering information. They review pertinent documents about their cases, such as police reports, financial records, medical files, and business contracts. They study evidence as well as interview witnesses and others who may provide essential information to support their case. With criminal cases, lawyers might examine crime scenes. Trial Lawyers also seek subject-matter experts to help them understand facts and issues in medicine, science, engineering, human resources, finance, and other technical topics related to a case. In addition, Trial Lawyers arrange depositions to obtain sworn testimony from the plaintiff and the plaintiff's witnesses.

Their job also involves conducting legal research, analyzing legal documents, writing legal correspondence, and drafting legal documents. These lawyers file pretrial motions and attend pretrial hearings and conferences. Throughout the litigation process, Trial Lawyers negotiate settlement for their clients. For example, defense attorneys and prosecutors in criminal cases often agree on plea bargains in which the defendants receive lesser sentencing by pleading guilty to lesser criminal charges. Negotiations can continue up to the moment that a judge or jury makes a verdict. The majority of criminal and civil cases are settled before a case even goes to trial.

If a case goes to trial, a judge or a jury may hear it. In a jury trial, Trial Lawyers participate in the selection of jury members. All trials follow the same procedure, but every court establishes its own set of rules.

A trial begins with opening statements from the Trial Lawyers of both parties, who describe what they expect to prove in the trial. The attorneys then take turns presenting evidence before the court through witness testimony. The Trial Lawyers may cross-examine the other party's witnesses, as well as make appropriate objections to testimony, evidence, and other matters. When both parties have presented all of their evidence, the attorneys take turns presenting their closing arguments. Then the judge or jury deliberates on the evidence and arrives at a verdict.

Once a settlement is made or a judge or jury has made its verdict, the litigation process is done. However, when a plaintiff or defendant does not agree with the verdict, the party may file an appeal in a higher court (an appellate court) to review the trial court proceeding and determine if errors were made in trying the case. Many Trial Lawyers do not specialize in appellate law and hence refer their clients to appellate lawyers.

Like all attorneys, Trial Lawyers establish a confidential relationship with their clients. They are obligated to put their clients' interests above their own and keep their clients

up to date, whether by phone, through e-mail, or in person, throughout the litigation process.

Many Trial Lawyers work in private practice, as law firm associates or partners or as solo practitioners. Some private attorneys focus their practice in one or more areas of law such as criminal, personal injury, intellectual property, or employment law. Some lawyers also choose to represent certain clientele, such as juveniles, commercial businesses, insurance companies, or health-care providers.

Some Trial Lawyers are hired as government attorneys at the local, state, or federal level or as lawyers for public interest organizations. Others are employed as counsel in corporate law departments.

In addition to their legal duties, attorneys perform various non-legal duties. For example, many lawyers supervise and direct the work of junior associates, paralegals, legal secretaries, and other staff members who provide them with legal, administrative, or clerical support. Solo practitioners and many law firm associates generate new clientele for their firms. Solo practitioners are also responsible for their own office management, which includes such duties as paying bills and taxes, as well as purchasing and maintaining office equipment and supplies.

Trial Lawyers typically work long and irregular hours, often putting in 60 hours or more per week to complete their legal tasks and meet strict deadlines. Solo practitioners generally have more flexible hours than law firm associates or government lawyers. Law firm associates are usually under pressure to fulfill a minimum number of billable hours (the number of working hours for which they bill clients).

Salaries

Salaries for Trial Lawyers vary, depending on such factors as their experience, employer, and geographic location. For example, the median annual salaries for first-year associates ranged from $67,000 (in law firms with two to 25 attorneys) to $85,000 (in law firms with 51 to 100 attorneys), according to the NALP 2006 Associate Salary Survey. The survey also reported that the median annual salaries for eighth-year associates ranged from $105,000 (in law firms with two to 25 attorneys) to $110,000 (in law firms with 51 to 100 attorneys).

The U.S. Bureau of Labor Statistics (BLS) reported, in its May 2006 *Occupational Employment Statistics* (OES) survey, that the estimated annual salary for most attorneys ranged between $50,580 and $145,600. Attorneys who worked in legal services earned an estimated annual wage of $119,390. The estimated wages for federal government employees was $116,700; for state attorneys, $77,970; and for local attorneys, $84,570.

Employment Prospects

According to the May 2006 OES survey by the BLS, about 547,710 lawyers were employed in the United States. About two-thirds of all attorneys in the survey worked in the legal services industry.

The BLS reports that employment for attorneys is predicted to grow by 9 to 17 percent through 2014. In addition to job growth, lawyers will be needed to replace those who retire, advance to higher positions, or transfer to other jobs. Due to the large number of law students graduating each year, the competition for jobs is intense.

In general, opportunities for staff positions with law firms, government agencies, and corporations are usually found in metropolitan areas.

Advancement Prospects

Trial Lawyers can advance in any number of ways, according to their interests and ambitions. In law firms, attorneys can advance from associates to partners, which gives them a share in their firm's profits. Some attorneys move from one firm to the next to pursue positions with higher pay, more prestige, or more complex responsibilities. Some attorneys seek positions in corporate law departments, government agencies, or public interest organizations.

Lawyers with entrepreneurial ambitions become solo practitioners or start their own law firms. Other attorneys pursue other legal-related careers by becoming judges, law professors, law librarians, or politicians.

Education and Training

To qualify for entry into a law school, individuals must possess a bachelor's degree, which may be in any field. In addition to their Law School Admission Test (LSAT) scores, a law school considers their undergraduate work, work experience, and other factors to determine their aptitude for the study of law. The competition to get into law school is strong, especially for the top law schools.

Law students complete either a three-year or four-year juris doctor (J.D.) degree program. In their first year of study, they focus on basic courses such as contracts, torts, civil procedure, constitutional law, criminal law, and legal research. In the following years, they choose elective courses in different areas of law as well as gain practical lawyering experience through legal clinics, moot court competitions, and practice trials.

Most employers, as well as state bar associations, require that lawyers possess a J.D. degree from a law school accredited by the American Bar Association or by a proper state authority.

Entry-level attorneys typically receive on-the-job training, in which they work under the supervision and guidance of senior lawyers. Many employers also provide young lawyers with formal educational programs.

Throughout their careers, Trial Lawyers enroll in courses, workshops, and seminars to update their skills and knowledge.

Special Requirements

To practice law in a state (or a U.S. territory or Washington, D.C.), Trial Lawyers must be admitted into that state's bar association. Every jurisdiction has its own eligibility requirements, which usually involve passing a bar examination. For specific information, contact the state bar admission office where you wish to practice.

Once individuals are admitted to a state bar, they receive a certificate or license to practice law in that state. Many states require that attorneys complete continuing legal education courses to maintain their license.

To practice before a federal court, attorneys must apply for admission. Separate registration is required for each federal court.

Experience, Special Skills, and Personality Traits

Most employers prefer to hire candidates who have litigation experience in the practice areas in which they specialize. Some employers will hire recent law graduates who demonstrate a strong interest in litigation work, as well as have gained experience performing litigation tasks through internships, employment, or volunteer work.

To perform well at their job, Trial Lawyers must have excellent organizational, self-management, negotiation, writing, and presentation skills. They also need superior communication and interpersonal skills, as they must be able to work well with clients, colleagues, subject-matter experts, court personnel, and many others from diverse backgrounds.

Some personality traits that successful Trial Lawyers share include being patient, analytical, quick-witted, persuasive, detail-oriented, and creative.

Unions and Associations

In many states, attorneys are required to be members of the state bar association.

Many Trial Lawyers join one or more bar associations or professional societies to take advantage of networking opportunities, educational programs, professional publications, and other resources and services. These organizations are available at the local, state, national, and international levels. Some national organizations that serve the diverse interests of Trial Lawyers include:

- American Association for Justice
- American College of Trial Lawyers
- Section of Litigation, part of the American Bar Association
- DRI
- National Association of Criminal Defense Lawyers
- National District Attorneys Association
- National Legal Aid and Defenders Association
- American Bar Association
- National Lawyers Association

- Federal Bar Association
- National Black Prosecutors Association
- National Hispanic Prosecutors Association
- National Association of Women Lawyers

For contact information for these organizations, see Appendix III.

Tips for Entry

1. Here are a few things you might do to get an idea if litigation law suits you: Read books about attorneys; check out professional magazines that lawyers read; volunteer or intern in a law office; observe criminal or civil trials at nearby courthouses; sit in on a law class; and talk with various attorneys.
2. Gain experience by obtaining an internship in a law firm, corporate law department, legal aid agency, or another legal setting.
3. Many bar associations post job listings at their Web site.
4. Learn more about Trial Lawyers on the Internet. To obtain a list of relevant Web sites, enter any of these keywords into a search engine: *trial lawyers*, *litigation attorneys*, *litigation*, *criminal trials*, or *civil trials*. For some links, see Appendix IV.

PROSECUTING ATTORNEY

CAREER PROFILE

Duties: Conduct criminal proceedings on behalf of the government; may handle civil litigation; perform duties as required

Alternate Title(s): Prosecutor; District Attorney, Assistant U.S. Attorney, or another title that reflects a specific occupation

Salary Range: $44,000 to $121,000+

Employment Prospects: Good

Advancement Prospects: Good

Prerequisites:

Education or Training—A J.D. (law) degree; on-the-job training

Experience—One or more years as a practicing lawyer; litigation experience preferred

Special Skills and Personality Traits—Writing, communication, legal-research, computer, interpersonal, and teamwork skills; analytical, diligent, quick-witted, persistent, flexible, creative, and enthusiastic

Special Requirements— States require lawyers to be admitted to their state bar; federal courts require registration for lawyers to practice

CAREER LADDER

```
┌─────────────────────────────────┐
│         Senior or               │
│ Supervisory Prosecuting Attorney│
└─────────────────────────────────┘

┌─────────────────────────────────┐
│      Prosecuting Attorney       │
└─────────────────────────────────┘

┌─────────────────────────────────┐
│ Prosecuting Attorney (Entry-Level)│
└─────────────────────────────────┘
```

Position Description

In the United States criminal justice system, suspects are assumed innocent until they have been proven guilty beyond a reasonable doubt. It is the job of Prosecuting Attorneys, or prosecutors, to present evidence in courts of law that demonstrates criminal defendants are indeed guilty of their charges. Like all trial lawyers, Prosecuting Attorneys are skilled in evaluating evidence, preparing litigation, selecting juries, examining and cross-examining witnesses, negotiating settlements, and presenting arguments before a jury or judge.

Prosecuting Attorneys are trial lawyers who are employed at the local, state, and federal levels of government. Their duty is to enforce the laws within their jurisdiction and to bring to trial those adults and juveniles who have been accused of committing felony or misdemeanor offenses. Prosecutors try cases in various courts of law, including general jurisdiction (or trial) courts, appellate courts, and special jurisdiction courts such as family, juvenile, and bankruptcy courts.

Prosecuting Attorneys do not represent individuals in criminal cases, although they are advocates for the victims of crime. Instead, prosecutors litigate cases on behalf of the interests of the general public.

These lawyers are responsible for initiating criminal proceedings against criminal suspects. They review the evidence that law enforcement officers have obtained, and determine if there is sufficient proof to file charges against the suspects. Prosecuting Attorneys also establish what felony or misdemeanor charges to file against suspects. In some instances, prosecutors must present their case to a grand jury that has the authority to decide whether the case should go to trial.

Preparing criminal cases for trial is complex and demanding work. Prosecuting Attorneys may be assigned to work alone or with other prosecutors on cases. They work closely with law enforcement officers to build strong cases against the defense. They also supervise and direct the work of paralegals, legal secretaries, and other staff who assist them with legal, administrative, or clerical tasks.

Prosecuting Attorneys are involved in a wide range of legal tasks as they develop their cases. For example, they:

- review police records, medical examiner's files, and reports on physical evidence by forensic scientists
- examine crime scenes
- interview suspects, victims, and witnesses
- conduct legal research for precedents of actions or decisions in similar cases
- analyze the facts and issues of a case
- consult with subject-matter experts, such as psychiatrists, criminologists, or forensic scientists, to understand technical facts and issues related to a case
- develop prosecution strategies
- examine crime scenes
- prepare demonstrative evidence

In addition, Prosecuting Attorneys are responsible for filing appropriate court documents, such as pleadings, answers, and motions on a timely basis, as well as attending pretrial hearings and conferences.

Prosecuting Attorneys settle many of their cases before they reach the trial stage. Throughout the litigation process, prosecutors negotiate plea bargains with the defense lawyers. The prosecutors offer to issue lesser charges to which defendants agree to plead guilty. A plea bargain gives a prosecutor assurance of a conviction, while a defendant receives a shorter jail or prison sentence. Attorneys can continue negotiations up to the moment that a judge or jury makes a verdict.

All criminal trials follow the same procedure; however, each court has its own set of rules which attorneys are expected to follow. A case may be presented before either a judge or a judge and jury. In a jury trial, the attorneys of both sides participate in the jury selection. Every trial begins with opening statements from the prosecutor and the defense attorney, in which the two parties describe what they will prove at the trial. The parties then take turns presenting their case by examining witnesses and introducing evidence. Each side may cross-examine the other party's witnesses, as well as make objections to the other party's line of questioning, evidence, and other matters. The trial ends when both parties make closing statements, in which they present their reasons why the defendant is guilty or innocent of his or her charges.

The judge or jury deliberates upon the facts that were presented at the trial, and then decides on the verdict. If the Prosecuting Attorney or the defense lawyer does not agree with the verdict, the party may petition for an appeal in the appropriate appellate court.

Prosecuting Attorneys work out of local, state, and federal prosecutors' offices. The chief prosecutors are usually known as the Prosecuting Attorneys, while their staff lawyers are called assistant prosecuting attorneys.

Most federal prosecution is done by the U.S. Attorney's Office, which is part of the U.S. Department of Justice. The chief prosecutors are called the U.S. attorneys, while the staff lawyers are known as assistant U.S. attorneys. They are responsible for enforcing the laws of the U.S. Criminal Code. They handle criminal cases such as kidnapping, wire fraud, civil rights abuses, interstate fraud, securities violations, corruption by public officials, immigration violations, and certain violent crimes.

State prosecution is done by Prosecuting Attorneys in state attorney generals' offices. They normally prosecute felony cases that have outcomes that would affect their whole state. Sometimes state prosecutors are assigned to assist district attorneys' offices, which are at the county level, with their cases. Prosecuting Attorneys in the county offices handle felony and misdemeanor offenses that involve state laws or local ordinances. These lawyers also prosecute traffic violations, as well as litigate cases that have to do with child support, paternity, child neglect or abuse, and other family law cases.

Many large cities have a city attorney's office, in which the Prosecuting Attorneys are responsible for handling cases of criminal misdemeanors and violations of city ordinances.

Many Prosecuting Attorneys also engage in civil litigation. On behalf of governmental bodies, they handle lawsuits that involve such issues as employment, personal injury, contracts, land use, or taxes. In local jurisdictions, Prosecuting Attorneys act as legal counsel to government officials, boards, agencies, and departments. They perform any number of duties. For example, they may provide legal advice on transactions; represent county officials at administrative hearings (such as school attendance proceedings or county commissioner meetings); examine public records of officials; and prosecute actions to recover debts or fines for the government.

Local and state chief prosecutors are elected by the voters, while the heads of the various U.S. attorney's offices are appointed by the U.S. president. Chief prosecutors are elected or appointed for a limited number of years. Depending on their job performance, they may be reappointed or re-elected for additional terms. Assistant Prosecuting Attorneys are hired through regular selection processes. Their jobs are usually not affected when new chief prosecutors are appointed or elected.

The work of Prosecuting Attorneys is challenging and can be extremely stressful at times. They juggle a heavy caseload, in which they are handling cases at different pretrial and trial stages. They often put in more than 40 hours per week to complete their duties and work long days, as they get ready to bring a case to trial.

Salaries

Salaries for Prosecuting Attorneys vary, depending on such factors as their experience, employers, and geographic location.

NALP, the association for legal career professionals, reports in its *2006 Public Sector and Public Interest Attorney Salary Report* that the median annual salaries for state Prosecuting Attorneys ranged from $46,374 (for entry-level lawyers) to $67,712 (for lawyers with 11 to 15 years experience). For local Prosecuting Attorneys, the median annual salaries ranged from $43,915 (for entry-level lawyers) to $72,970 (for lawyers with 11 to 15 years experience).

Assistant U.S. attorneys earn salaries based on the Administratively Determined pay scale. Information about this pay scale is unavailable, but it is about equivalent to the General Schedule (GS) scale, another federal pay schedule. Prosecuting Attorneys earn salaries similar to the GS-11 to GS-15 levels. In 2007, the basic pay for these levels ranged from $46,974 to $120,981. Federal employees also receive locality pay that is based on the geographic location where they work. Those living in areas with higher living costs typically earn higher wages.

Employment Prospects

Job opportunities are generally better at the local government level where the turnover rate for prosecutor positions is high. Job openings typically become available as Prosecuting Attorneys retire, advance to higher positions, or transfer to other jobs. On occasion, agencies create additional positions to meet growing needs when funding is available.

Some employers prefer to hire candidates who are willing to make a commitment to work two or more years for them.

Advancement Prospects

Many Prosecuting Attorneys measure advancement by receiving more complex cases, earning higher wages, and gaining professional recognition. Supervisory and managerial positions are available, but are usually limited.

Depending on their interests and ambitions, attorneys can pursue any number of career paths. They can seek other attorney positions with other government agencies, obtain employment as corporate counsels, or work in private practice or in public interest settings. Furthermore, lawyers might choose to pursue such legal-related careers as law professors, judges, law librarians, FBI special agents, lobbyists, or politicians.

Education and Training

Prosecuting Attorneys must possess a juris doctor (J.D.) degree, which is granted after completing a three-year or four-year law school program. Most employers prefer to hire candidates who have graduated from law schools accredited by the American Bar Association or a proper state authority.

Entry-level attorneys typically receive on-the-job training. They perform their duties under the supervision and direction of experienced Prosecuting Attorneys.

Throughout their careers, Prosecuting Attorneys enroll in continuing education courses as well as training workshops and seminars to update their skills and knowledge.

Special Requirements

To practice law in a state (or U.S. territory or Washington, D.C.), lawyers must first gain admission to that state's bar. For specific eligibility information, contact the bar admission office for the jurisdiction where you wish to practice.

To practice in federal courts, attorneys must apply for admission. Each court has its own set of requirements.

Experience, Special Skills, and Personality Traits

Employers generally require that candidates for entry-level positions have one or more years of professional work experience after graduating from law school. In addition, they seek candidates who have litigation experience, as well as demonstrate a strong interest in public service.

Prosecuting Attorneys are expected to possess superior writing, communication, and legal-research skills. Having strong computer skills is also important. In addition, these attorneys need excellent interpersonal and teamwork skills, as they must be able to work well with colleagues, clients, court personnel, support staff, and others from diverse backgrounds. Being analytical, diligent, quick-witted, persistent, flexible, creative, and enthusiastic are some personality traits that successful prosecutors have in common.

Unions and Associations

Prosecuting Attorneys join various bar associations to take advantage of professional resources and services such as educational programs, networking opportunities, and professional publications. Along with local and state bar associations, many prosecutors belong to a national bar association such as the American Bar Association. In some states, attorneys must belong to the state bar association in order to practice law.

Many Prosecuting Attorneys also join associations that serve their particular interests, such as the Federal Bar Association, the National District Attorneys Association, the National Criminal Justice Association, the American Association for Justice, the National Black Prosecutors Association, or the National Hispanic Prosecutors Association. For contact information for these organizations, see Appendix III.

Tips for Entry

1. Are you well suited for a public service career? While in high school or college, volunteer at a community group or public interest organization to get an idea.

2. Gain experience by obtaining an internship, working, or volunteering in a prosecuting attorney's office.

3. Sometimes a prosecutor's office hires lawyers on a part-time or temporary basis.

4. For employment information for the U.S. Attorneys' Office, visit the Office of Attorney Recruitment and Management Web site at http://www.usdoj.gov/oarm.

5. Use the Internet to learn more about prosecutor offices at the different government levels. To find out more about the U.S. Attorneys' Office, visit its Web site at http://www.usdoj.gov/usao. To find Web sites for local and state offices, enter any of these keywords into a search engine: *state attorney general*, *district attorney*, *county prosecutor*, or *city prosecutor*.

FORENSIC CONSULTANT

CAREER PROFILE

Duties: Provide expert witness and/or litigation support services to attorneys; manage business operations; perform duties as required

Alternate Title(s): Expert Witness, Litigation Consultant; Forensic Examiner, Forensic Specialist; a title that reflects a specialty such as Forensic Psychologist or Forensic Sculptor

Salary Range: $100 to $350 + per hour

Employment Prospects: Good

Advancement Prospects: Poor

Prerequisites:

Education or Training—College degrees and training appropriate to an occupation

Experience—Extensive work experience in their field

Special Skills and Personality Traits— Organizational, self-management, communication, interpersonal, and small-business skills; articulate, curious, fair, trustworthy, objective, diligent, and energetic

Special Requirements—Professional license or certification as required for a profession

CAREER LADDER

```
┌─────────────────────────────────┐
│      Forensic Consultant        │
└─────────────────────────────────┘

┌─────────────────────────────────┐
│   Novice Forensic Consultant    │
└─────────────────────────────────┘

┌─────────────────────────────────┐
│   Senior, Administrative, or    │
│ Management Position (in a workplace) │
└─────────────────────────────────┘
```

Position Description

Many forensic scientists, examiners, and analysts work in the private sector as Forensic Consultants. They offer their services on a contractual basis to trial lawyers, medical examiners, law enforcement agencies, regulatory agencies, insurance companies, private corporations, and others that are in need of their particular forensic expertise. Attorneys, for example, typically hire various Forensic Consultants to address facts and issues involved in their criminal and civil cases.

Forensic Consultants come from various scientific, technical, and medical fields. They are former criminalists and law enforcement officers, as well as scientists, physicians, engineers, technicians, physicians, accountants, artists, and academicians, among many others. They typically have years of training and experience in their specialties, such as ballistics, blood splatter analysis, questioned documents, computer forensics, forensic engineering, statistics, forensic accounting, linguistics, entomology, forensic toxicology,

forensic anthropology, forensic nursing, forensic psychology, photography, or video forensics.

Some consultants are experts in one particular area such as forensic linguistics, while others offer consulting services in several areas. For example a Forensic Consultant might specialize in the areas of latent print examination, firearms and tool marks examination, and ballistics analysis.

Trial lawyers often hire different Forensic Consultants to provide expert witness services. As expert witnesses, Forensic Consultants give their professional opinions about particular facts and issues related to civil or criminal cases. They present their opinions as sworn testimony at depositions or in trials or through sworn affidavits (written statements). Forensic Consultants are expected to provide unbiased and impartial testimony. Ethically, they must not support or oppose the arguments of the lawyers that have hired them, nor those of the opposing attorneys.

To testify in court as an expert witness, Forensic Consultants must meet certain qualifications, which vary from judge to judge. They must have the appropriate credentials, experience, skills, knowledge, education, or training that qualifies them to testify about the issues and facts related to a case.

Expert witnesses may also be used for another purpose in court trials: to provide technical information so that judges and jurors can understand the facts and issues of a case. These experts explain technical concepts in terms that are easy to understand.

Many Forensic Consultants offer litigation support services to attorneys. These are various types of pretrial services that lawyers seek to help them prepare for trials. For example, Forensic Consultants might be hired to:

- educate lawyers about the technical, scientific, or medical facts about a case
- review cases to identify the technical issues and facts
- gather physical evidence
- conduct research for additional information to support a case
- conduct tests or experiments to prove or disprove certain facts or issues
- interview eye witnesses
- locate and recruit expert witnesses to testify about certain issues or facts
- prepare reports that can be used in settlement negotiations
- create diagrams, models, or other pieces of demonstrative evidence that can help judges and juries understand specific issues or facts

When Forensic Consultants provide litigation support services, they usually do not perform any expert witness services. However, lawyers may ask them to testify as percipient witnesses, which are similar to eyewitnesses. They answer questions about facts related to a case based on their direct observation or work rather than their professional opinion.

Many Forensic Consultants are solo practitioners. Some are in partnership with other consultants. Some consultants own firms with a staff of associates and administrative and clerical employees. Some Forensic Consultants offer their services as a supplemental activity to their primary occupation, such as professor, physician, dentist, scientist, or engineer.

As business owners, Forensic Consultants are responsible for managing their operations. They perform various administrative and financial duties to keep their business running successfully. For example, they are responsible for paying bills and taxes, collecting clients' fees, balancing financial accounts, maintaining supplies and equipment, and marketing their services. If they hire staff, they must take care of paying employees and provide them with training and supervision.

In addition to constantly generating new business, Forensic Consultants continue to build their reputation and credibility. To accomplish both goals, they network with colleagues, attorneys, law enforcement agencies, crime labs, community organizations, associations, and others to develop contacts for future work projects. Many consultants write books and articles for professional and trade publications and make guest presentations at professional and trade conferences. Some consultants offer educational services, such as training workshops to law enforcement agencies, or obtain positions as lecturers or adjunct instructors at colleges and universities.

Forensic Consultants work flexible hours. Their job requires them to travel frequently to meet with clients, attend depositions and trials, and participate in conferences and other relevant events. Many consultants offer their services statewide, regionally, or nationally.

Salaries

Annual gross earnings for Forensic Consultants is based on the total fees that they have earned in a year. Earnings vary yearly, depending on such factors as their rates, specialties, and the demand for their services. Specific earnings information for this occupation is unavailable.

Forensic Consultants charge an hourly, daily, or flat rate for research, examinations, depositions, and other services that they perform. Hourly fees generally range between $100 and $350 or more per hour. Highly reputable consultants can earn as much as $2,000 or more per hour for expert witness services. Many Forensic Consultants also charge clients for out-of-pocket expenses such as travel time, telephone calls, and photocopying.

Employment Prospects

In general, opportunities are favorable for Forensic Consultants. Litigation lawyers continually seek credible and reputable Forensic Consultants. Public crime labs and other governmental agencies also hire consultants to assist with backlogs, when funding is available.

Advancement Prospects

Forensic Consultants realize advancement by earning higher incomes and gaining professional recognition. Many also measure success by being sought by attorneys for very complex or publicized cases. Becoming a Forensic Consultant is usually the ultimate career goal for many professionals.

Education and Training

Forensic Consultants typically acquire the appropriate credentials and training that are required for their particular professions. For example, most criminalists possess at least a bachelor's degree in chemistry, biology, or another related field; forensic anthropologists have doctoral degrees in physical anthropology; and forensic radiologists hold medical doctor degrees and have completed the proper medical training.

Throughout their careers, Forensic Consultants enroll in continuing education and training programs to update their skills and knowledge.

Special Requirements

Forensic Consultants have the appropriate professional licenses and certification required for their professions. For example, engineers hold a professional engineer license and physicians possess a medical license in the states where they practice.

Experience, Special Skills, and Personality Traits

Criminalists, scientists, physicians, and others normally become Forensic Consultants after many years of working in their fields.

To succeed at consulting work, individuals need excellent organizational, self-management, communication, and interpersonal skills. They also need strong small-business skills. Being articulate, curious, fair, trustworthy, objective, diligent, and energetic are some personality traits that successful Forensic Consultants share.

Unions and Associations

Many Forensic Consultants belong to societies to take advantage of networking opportunities, continuing education, publications, and other professional resources and services. Two professional associations that serve the general interests of many forensic experts are the American Academy of Forensic Sciences and the American College of Forensic Examiners. For contact information, see Appendix III.

Tips for Entry

1. You might volunteer to do an occasional project for public organizations for free. This can help you build up your experience, as well as make valuable contacts.
2. Many Forensic Consultants obtain professional certification from recognized organizations to enhance their credibility. For information about certification programs, see Appendix II.
3. Take one or more small-business courses or workshops to make sure you have the proper skills to develop a successful business.
4. Maintain a portfolio of your publications, presentations, prior testimony work, and other relevant work, and show it to prospective clients.
5. Use the Internet to learn more about what Forensic Consultants do. Many experts maintain a Web site on the Internet. Visit some of these sites to learn about what different Forensic Consultants do. To get a list of Web sites, enter the keywords *forensic consultants*, *forensic consulting*, *expert witnesses*, or *litigation support services*. For some links, see Appendix IV.

JUDGE

CAREER PROFILE

Duties: Preside over court hearings and trials; conduct legal research, review court documents, and perform other legal duties; perform other duties as required

Alternate Title(s): Trial Judge, Appellate Judge, Bankruptcy Judge, or another title that reflects a particular position

Salary Range: $123,000 to $212,000

Employment Prospects: Poor

Advancement Prospects: Poor

Prerequisites:

Education or Training—J.D. (law) degree may be required; orientation training

Experience—Several years of experience as practicing lawyer usually required

Special Skills and Personality Traits—Case-management, analytical, interpersonal, and communication skills; hardworking, patient, respectful, trustworthy, and ethical

Special Requirements—Admission to a state bar association may be required

CAREER LADDER

```
┌─────────────────────────────────────┐
│   Presiding Judge or Judge in a      │
│   higher state or federal court      │
└─────────────────────────────────────┘

┌─────────────────────────────────────┐
│   Trial or Appellate Court Judge     │
│   (state or federal court)           │
└─────────────────────────────────────┘

┌─────────────────────────────────────┐
│  Attorney or Judge (in a lower court)│
└─────────────────────────────────────┘
```

Position Description

Judges preside over hearings and trials in local, state, federal, and tribal courts. They listen to legal cases concerning a wide range of issues, including criminal actions, contractual disagreements, financial disputes, tax violations, personal injury claims, divorce, inheritance, property rights, child custody, and traffic violations, among others. Judges are responsible for overseeing hearings and trials and making sure they run smoothly, efficiently, and fairly. They also interpret and apply laws accordingly to each case, as well as ensure that the legal rights of the parties involved in a case are met. Judges are expected to perform their duties objectively and without bias. They cannot in any way influence the outcome of a trial.

The U.S. judicial system is composed of the federal judiciary and 50 state court systems. Different courts handle different types of cases. Judges hear legal cases that are appropriate to the type of courts over which they preside. Federal court judges deal with cases that concern constitu-

tional issues, the federal government, federal law violations, or lawsuits between citizens of different states. State court judges handle cases that involve state laws and regulations.

The majority of Judges serve in trial courts, in which the facts of criminal and civil cases are determined and judgments are made based on the evidence and witness testimony that are presented in these courts. Many trial judges work in general jurisdiction courts where they handle all types of civil and criminal cases.

Trial judges usually hold pretrial hearings to establish if cases are worth going to trial. In criminal cases, Judges may decide that defendants be held in jail or released until their trials begin.

Trial judges conduct two types of trials. In bench trials, Judges listen to both sides of a case and determine the outcome of the trial. In criminal cases, Judges decide whether criminal defendants are innocent or guilty; and in civil cases, they decide which party is right and if compensation should be awarded to the winning party.

In jury trials, jurors are selected to hear the evidence and testimony presented by both sides of a case and then make a decision. Before the jury makes its decision, the presiding Judge explains relevant laws to jurors and instructs them how to evaluate the facts that they have heard in the trial.

In both bench and jury trials, Judges are responsible for sentencing guilty parties in criminal cases as well as determining the settlement awards in civil cases.

Bench and jury trials may take several days, weeks, or months to complete. Judges establish the procedures for their courtrooms, and they make sure that lawyers, witnesses, and jurors comply. If situations occur during trials for which there are no standard procedures, Judges have the power to interpret the law and determine appropriate procedures. In addition, Judges determine the facts surrounding a case and rule on the admissibility of physical evidence and witness testimony that is submitted in court. Judges stop lawyers if their questions are inappropriate, and they settle disagreements between the opposing lawyers.

Some trial judges work in limited jurisdiction courts—such as municipal, traffic, juvenile, family, small claims, and bankruptcy courts—in which they hear only certain types of cases. For example, family court judges oversee legal proceedings that focus on child custody, legal guardianships, adoption, domestic violence, child abuse, and other issues concerning families and children.

When litigants do not agree with the results of their trial, they may appeal their cases to higher-level courts known as appellate courts. Appellate judges do not retry cases nor do they hear new evidence. They review the petitions made by the litigants and determine if errors have been made during the trial procedure that resulted in a miscarriage of justice.

These Judges generally review arguments as written briefs. They sometimes listen to oral arguments that are limited to 30 minutes or less. After appellate judges review a case, they make one of three decisions. They may agree with the decision of the trial judge; they may reverse the decision; or they may request that the case be retried. If litigants disagree with the appellate judges' decision, they may appeal to the next higher court, and all the way up to the U.S. Supreme Court, which is the highest court in the nation.

There are also Judges known as administrative law judges, who are employed by government agencies that are responsible for administering a particular set of laws and regulations, such as health, environmental, tax, workplace safety, or professional licensure. These Judges settle disputes and complaints that individuals, businesses, and groups have with government agencies.

In addition to their courtroom duties, all Judges perform various legal duties in their private offices (or chambers). For example, they research legal issues, review court documents such as pleadings and motions, write opinions and decisions, and draft legal correspondence. Some Judges have the authority to marry people. Additionally, Judges direct the work of staff attorneys, paralegals, and other legal and administrative support staff.

Judges are usually appointed by executive bodies or elected to the bench by voters within their jurisdiction. Federal trial and appellate judges serve a life term; that is, until they retire or die. They can be removed from office only through impeachment. Some federal judges, such as bankruptcy judges, are appointed by other federal judges. State and local judges serve limited terms, which may be renewed through reappointment or reelection.

Judges usually wear robes when they are presiding in court. Their work can oftentimes be demanding and stressful. They must sometimes deal with situations in court in which people are highly emotional.

Most Judges have a 40-hour work schedule, but some put in additional hours to complete their duties. Some Judges in limited jurisdiction courts work part time.

Salaries

Salaries for Judges vary, depending on such factors as their employer and geographic location. The National Center for State Courts reported in its July 2006 *Survey of Judicial Salaries* the following median annual salary for state court judges:

- general jurisdiction trial court judges, $122,559
- intermediate appellate court judges, $132,102
- highest court associate justices, $136,810
- highest court chief justices, $142,264

The annual salaries for federal court judges in 2006 were:

- district court trial judges, $165,200
- circuit court appellate judges, $175,100
- Supreme Court associate justices, $203,000
- Supreme Court Chief Justice, $212,100

Employment Prospects

There are a limited number of judgeships at the state and federal levels, which are established by state legislatures and the U.S. Congress. From time to time, a legislative body may authorize the creation of new judgeships to handle increasing caseloads in courts, as long as funding is available.

In general, judgeship openings become available when Judges retire, advance to higher positions, or resign. In recent years, there has been a trend wherein Judges resign or retire early and take private practice jobs because of higher pay, which may create more opportunities, according to some experts in the field. However, the competition should continue to be strong due to the prestige of the position.

The appointment process is intense and difficult; it involves obtaining necessary political support to become appointed or elected to office. Nominees are thoroughly screened before they are appointed or elected to a judgeship. Federal judges are nominated by the president of the United States and then confirmed by the U.S. Senate. State judges may be appointed by executive bodies or elected by voters.

Advancement Prospects

Advancement opportunities are limited. Judges can serve as supervisory or presiding judges of their court for restricted terms. Judges can also seek appointments to positions in higher courts at the state or federal level.

Most Judges measure their success through job satisfaction, professional recognition, and pay increases.

Education and Training

Educational requirements vary with the different courts. State courts usually prefer that Judges possess a juris doctor (J.D.) degree, the professional degree in law. Federal courts have no formal requirement; but most federal judges possess a J.D. degree.

Judges typically receive orientation training when they first serve. Throughout their careers, they enroll in continuing education and training programs to update their skills and knowledge. In many states, Judges are required to complete continuing education courses.

Special Requirements

Judges may be required to be licensed lawyers. This entails maintaining current membership in a state attorney bar association. Some states require that candidates for judgeships have been a bar association member for a minimum number of years.

Experience, Special Skills, and Personality Traits

Requirements vary with the different courts. Most state courts prefer that candidates be practicing lawyers or have practiced for a minimum number of years.

Candidates for federal judgeships are not required to be attorneys. However, most federal judges had been practicing attorneys when they were nominated for judgeships.

To perform well at their work, Judges must have excellent case-management, analytical, interpersonal, and communication skills. Some personality traits that successful Judges share include being hardworking, patient, respectful, trustworthy, and ethical.

Unions and Associations

Judges join professional associations and bar associations to take advantage of networking opportunities and other professional resources and services. Two national organizations in which many Judges are members are the American Bar Association and the American Judges Association. Many federal judges belong to the Federal Bar Association. For contact information, see Appendix III.

Tips for Entry

1. Talk with various Judges about their jobs and how they became Judges.
2. Get experience working in a court setting by obtaining a judicial law clerkship or a staff attorney position.
3. For state judgeships, contact the courts in which you wish to work for information about the selection process.
4. Use the Internet to learn more about state and federal courts. You might start by visiting these Web sites: the National Center for State Courts, http://www.ncsconline.org; and The U.S. Courts, http://www.uscourts.gov. For more links, see Appendix IV.

FORENSIC SCIENCE EDUCATORS, RESEARCHERS, AND REPORTERS

FORENSIC TRAINING SPECIALIST

CAREER PROFILE

Duties: Plan, develop, and/or coordinate training programs; may develop courses and design instructional materials; may teach courses, workshops, or seminars; perform duties as required

Alternate Title(s): Forensic Training Coordinator, Forensic Training Manager

Salary Range: $27,000 to $141,000

Employment Prospects: Fair

Advancement Prospects: Fair

Prerequisites:

Education or Training—A bachelor's degree in one's field

Experience—Work experience in forensic specialty; experience working with training programs

Special Skills and Personality Traits—Leadership, organizational, problem-solving, teamwork, writing, presentation, interpersonal, and communication skills; inspirational, energetic, flexible, creative, and self-motivated

CAREER LADDER

```
┌─────────────────────────────────────┐
│   Senior Training Specialist or      │
│  Training Program Coordinator        │
└─────────────────────────────────────┘

┌─────────────────────────────────────┐
│        Training Specialist           │
└─────────────────────────────────────┘

┌─────────────────────────────────────┐
│    Training Program Instructor       │
└─────────────────────────────────────┘
```

Position Description

Throughout their careers, criminalists and other forensic examiners as well as crime scene investigators, law enforcement officers, medicolegal investigators, and others involved in legal matters sign up for forensic training programs to maintain their professional competence. They complete training programs that are provided by their employers, either internally or through outside sources. Many of them also voluntarily enroll in courses, workshops, and seminars that are given or sponsored by government agencies, academic institutions, professional associations, or private firms.

Training programs for forensic professionals are designed and managed by Forensic Training Specialists. Along with having expertise in instructional design, these men and women have extensive training and background in the forensic specialties in which they work. They are involved in various types of training programs, including:

- technical training in forensic specialties (such as latent print analysis, sexual assault examination, computer forensics, or traffic crash investigation) for entry-level as well as for experienced professionals
- evidence handling training (such as the chain of custody and the collection and preservation of evidence)
- legal training in rules of evidence, evidence authentication, criminal law procedures, expert witness testimony, and other areas
- training in administrative and laboratory policies (such as quality assurance, security, and standard operating procedures)
- safety training including chemical, biological, and physical hazards

Forensic Training Specialists may be involved in any or all aspects of the planning, development, instructional design, deliverance, and management of training programs. Some of them hold job titles that reflect their particular responsibilities; for example, forensic training managers oversee the daily administration of training programs for their employers.

Forensic Training Specialists consider many elements when they design a training program. They determine its purpose, learning objectives, and performance goals. They also decide on the most effective way to deliver instruction. Training programs may be implemented in such forms as classroom instruction, workshops, seminars, individual coaching, on-the-job training, interactive video training, computer-based training, or intranet instruction. In addition, these specialists establish what requirements students must have to enroll in a program, as well as determine what qualifications they seek in prospective instructors.

Training specialists work closely with subject matter experts as they design training programs. The experts help the specialists determine the content of the program—the topics to teach, types of practice exercises, and so on. They also discuss evaluation strategies for measuring performance upon completion of training. Forensic Training Specialists utilize the experts' advice to develop a program syllabus that outlines the topics and the sequence by which they would be taught. They also settle on the types of assessments (such as written exams, laboratory exercises, and mock trials) that should be used to measure the learning of trainees. Many Forensic Training Specialists are also involved in creating print, visual, and/or technology-based instructional materials. In designing programs and materials, developers integrate adult learning principles and take into account the different abilities and learning styles of a program's participants.

Many Forensic Training Specialists are responsible for teaching courses, workshops, or seminars. Although the curriculum and instructional materials are established, they bring their own teaching styles to the training sessions. As experienced teachers, they plan for the most effective means of delivering instruction based on the topic, learning objectives, number of participants, length of training, and other factors. They lecture and lead discussions; they supervise class activities and lab exercises. To help reinforce and enrich their instruction, they use various teaching aids, including multimedia, computer programs, and the Internet. In preparation for their training sessions, they gather all necessary materials, equipment, and supplies and set up their classrooms appropriately.

Training programs are generally less structured than formal academic courses. Depending on the purpose and contents of a training program, it may last one or two hours or be taught once or twice a week for several weeks. Instructors are expected to document attendance and fulfill other required recordkeeping tasks. Program managers make sure that programs adhere to schedules, come under budget, and meet appropriate policies and standards as well as local, state, and federal laws and regulations.

Forensic Training Specialists perform various other duties, which vary according to their experience and position. For example, they may also be responsible for any of the following tasks:

- evaluating curriculum for currency and trends
- collaborating with government officials and professional interest groups to identify training needs
- reviewing the effectiveness of training programs and preparing feedback for training coordinators and instructional designers
- updating courses and instructional materials
- coaching training session participants who need additional help in learning skills and concepts
- formulating training policies
- developing training evaluation methods and criteria
- coordinating and administering contracts with vendors and independent instructors
- coordinating schedules of various training programs
- selecting and hiring contractual instructors
- assigning work and providing supervision to instructors and other training staff

Some Forensic Training Specialists are staff members in law enforcement agencies, state crime laboratories, and medical examiners' (or coroners') offices. Others work for forensic training centers affiliated with government agencies and academic institutions. Still others work for private firms and nonprofit organizations that offer forensic training services.

Forensic Training Specialists work part time or full time. Those who provide instruction may be scheduled to teach evenings or weekends. Some Forensic Training Specialists travel to other cities or states to teach or to meet with clients or subject matter experts.

Salaries

Salaries for Forensic Training Specialists vary, depending on such factors as their education, experience, position, employer, and geographic location. According to the May 2006 *Occupational Employment Statistics* survey by the U.S. Bureau of Labor Statistics, the estimated annual salary for most training and development specialists ranged between $27,450 and $80,630. The estimated annual salary for most training and development managers ranged between $43,530 and $141,140.

Employment Prospects

With advancements in the different forensic areas occurring each year, opportunities for experienced training specialists should continue to grow. Job openings become vacant as Forensic Training Specialists are promoted, transfer to other jobs, or leave the workforce for various reasons. Employers will create additional positions to meet growing needs as long as funding is available.

Advancement Prospects

Forensic Training Specialists can be promoted to senior, supervisory, and management positions, which may require moving to other organizations. Those with entrepreneurial ambitions can become independent practitioners or business owners that offer forensic training services.

Education and Training

Educational requirements vary with the different employers. In general, employers prefer to hire applicants who have at least a bachelor's degree in criminal justice, forensic science, or another discipline that is related to their forensic specialty. Many Forensic Training Specialists possess a master's degree in their field of interest.

Experience, Special Skills, and Personality Traits

Requirements vary, depending on the employer and the position. In general, employers seek candidates who have extensive forensic backgrounds in their specialties. They also have previous experience in the development, coordination, and/or teaching of forensic training programs. Candidates should also be knowledgeable about adult learning principles, instructional methods, training techniques, and the creation of learning materials.

To do their work effectively, Forensic Training Specialists must have strong leadership, organizational, problem-solving, teamwork, writing, and presentation skills. They also need excellent interpersonal and communication skills, as they must work well with colleagues, forensic professionals, law enforcement officers, managers, governmental officials, and various others with diverse backgrounds.

Some personality traits that successful Forensic Training Specialists share include being inspirational, energetic, flexible, creative, and self-motivated.

Unions and Associations

Forensic Training Specialists can join professional associations to take advantage of networking opportunities, training programs, professional certification, and other professional resources and services. Professional societies are available locally, statewide, regionally, nationally, and worldwide. One national association that serves the interests of training professionals is the American Society for Training and Development. The American Academy of Forensic Sciences is a key society that serves the general interests of many forensic professionals. For contact information for these groups, see Appendix III.

Tips for Entry

1. Take one or more courses that are aimed at teaching adult learners.
2. Build up your public speaking and teaching skills by making presentations or teaching workshops at professional meetings and conferences.
3. As a practitioner in the field, volunteer to help with the planning and development of training programs at your workplace.
4. Use the Internet to learn about different organizations and private firms that offer forensic training services. For relevant Web sites, enter the keywords *forensic training services* into a search engine. For some links, see Appendix IV.

FORENSIC SCIENCE INSTRUCTOR

CAREER PROFILE

Duties: Teach undergraduate and graduate students; prepare courses and lessons; may conduct scholarly research; perform other duties as required

Alternate Title(s): Lecturer, Assistant Professor, Associate Professor, Professor; a title that reflects a particular discipline such as Forensic Science Professor or Chemistry Professor

Salary Range: $29,000 to $146,000

Employment Prospects: Good

Advancement Prospects: Fair

Prerequisites:

Education or Training—A doctoral degree usually required

Experience—Practical experience in their field as well as teaching experience required

Special Skills and Personality Traits—Organizational, self-management, communication, presentation, and interpersonal skills; creative, inquisitive, flexible, dedicated, and inspirational

CAREER LADDER

```
+-------------------------+
|    (Full) Professor     |
+-------------------------+

+-------------------------+
|   Associate Professor   |
+-------------------------+

+-------------------------+
|   Assistant Professor   |
+-------------------------+

+-------------------------+
|       Instructor        |
+-------------------------+
```

Position Description

In two-year colleges, four-year colleges, and universities, Forensic Science Instructors teach courses that prepare students for careers in criminalistics, computer forensics, forensic anthropology, and other forensic specialties. Most, if not all, of these educators have many years of practical experience working as forensic scientists and administrators; and many of them continue to work in the field while they are teaching.

Forensic Science Instructors work in different types of academic programs. In two-year colleges, they instruct students who are pursuing associate degrees, while instructors in four-year colleges and universities teach students who are seeking bachelor's, master's, and doctoral degrees. These educators may be part of forensic science departments or among the faculty in chemistry, biological sciences, psychology, and other academic departments. In schools that do not have forensic science degree programs, students earn a degree in a particular discipline (such as criminal justice, chemistry, or entomology) with an emphasis in forensic science.

Some Forensic Science Instructors are part of professional certificate programs that provide a foundation for careers in particular forensic areas such as crime scene investigation, medicolegal death investigation, or forensic toxicology. Professional certificate programs may be offered in two-year colleges as well as in four-year colleges and universities.

Most academic faculty members hold one of four ranks—instructor, assistant professor, associate professor, and (full) professor. Full-time Forensic Science Instructors may be hired on a tenure or non-tenure track. Tenured staff members are assured of a job at their institution until they retire, resign, or die. With tenure, they cannot be fired without just cause and due process. Instructors on the non-tenure track generally receive limited-term appointments of one to three years, which may be renewed by the institution.

Some Forensic Science Instructors are adjunct (or part-time) instructors. Many adjunct faculty members are forensic scientists, medical examiners, and other forensic professionals who work full time or part time at their occupations.

Some adjunct instructors in forensic science departments are members of other academic programs such as a chemistry department or a school of health sciences.

Forensic Science Instructors may be assigned to teach one or several courses in a term. In four-year colleges and universities, they may teach undergraduate or graduate students, or both. Some of them teach evening or weekend classes.

Instructors are responsible for developing a syllabus for each course, which outlines the sequence of topics to be taught throughout a term. They also prepare class lessons, activities, experiments, and examinations. They deliver their instruction in various ways. They give lectures, lead small-group discussions, and supervise laboratory experiments and classroom exercises. Some instructors conduct lessons on cable or closed-circuit television, while others teach online courses.

College and university instructors perform other teaching duties. For example, they create student assignments, administer exams, grade exams and student papers, and evaluate students' performances. They also complete necessary administrative tasks such as keeping attendance records. In addition, instructors establish certain office hours for students who seek advice on academic and career matters. Adjunct instructors usually have limited administrative and student-advising duties.

Many full-time instructors supervise graduate students with their teaching assignments and research projects. Many instructors also supervise assistants who provide them with instructional, administrative, or research support.

Forensic Science Instructors at four-year colleges and universities are responsible for conducting scholarly research in topics that interest them. They may engage in basic research to broaden the body of knowledge in their forensic science field such as criminalistics, forensic entomology, forensic psychiatry, or forensic anthropology. They may be involved in applied research to develop new or improved techniques, procedures, products, technology, or systems for forensic examinations. Professors are responsible for obtaining funds to pay for their research projects, which include overhead costs, purchases of equipment and supplies, and financial support for themselves and their assistants. Moreover, these professors are expected to share the results of their research work by publishing their findings in academic publications or books.

Full-time faculty members also perform various administrative duties. For example, they participate in departmental meetings to discuss and handle matters regarding curriculum, budgets, policy matters, and the selection and hiring of new instructors. Forensic Science Instructors also serve on academic and administrative advisory committees that address institutional policies and issues, as well as act as advisors to student organizations. In addition, professors are obligated to perform community service, such as offer voluntary consulting services to law enforcement agencies or serve on committees or commissions established by criminal justice agencies.

Furthermore, Forensic Science Instructors keep up with developments in their field. They read current literature, network with colleagues, and attend professional conferences.

Forensic Science Instructors typically work long hours to complete their various teaching, research, and other duties. Some adjunct instructors teach at two or more institutions, including courses for extension programs.

Salaries

Salaries for Forensic Science Instructors vary, depending on such factors as their ranking, discipline, employer, and geographic location. Faculty in four-year colleges and universities typically earn higher salaries than those in two-year colleges.

Specific salary information for this occupation is unavailable. A general idea of earnings for Forensic Science Instructors can be obtained by looking at the wages of similar professionals. The U.S. Bureau of Labor Statistics reports in its May 2006 *Occupational Employment Statistics* survey the following estimated salary ranges for most postsecondary teachers in these disciplines:

* chemistry, $36,160 to $116,910
* biological sciences, $37,620 to $145,600
* psychology, $32,800 to $104,390
* anthropology and archaeology, $37,590 to $109,330
* criminal justice and law enforcement, $29,450 to $89,850

Employment Prospects

Forensic Science Instructors are hired by public and private two-year colleges, four-year colleges, and universities.

Opportunities are favorable for qualified Forensic Science Instructors, and should continue to be favorable for the coming years. Throughout the country, more and more academic institutions are developing forensic science degree programs and adding forensic science courses to meet the growing number of students who are interested in pursuing a forensic science career. In addition, increasingly more employers are seeking entry-level candidates who have a strong academic background in forensic science, chemistry, or other natural science disciplines. As more colleges and universities create forensic science programs, the demand for forensic science educators should intensify.

Advancement Prospects

College faculty members rise through the ranks as instructors, assistant professors, associate professors, and full professors. Those in tenure-track positions usually attain tenure upon reaching the associate professor rank. Appointments and promotions for faculty are based on their job performance, including their records of teaching, research, and community service. Receiving a promotion is separate from attaining tenure.

Forensic Science Instructors with managerial ambitions can pursue two career paths. Academically, they can advance up the ladder from department chair to dean to provost to president. Those interested in the administrative aspects can pursue such positions as dean of students, director of student activities, and development director. The administrative track can also lead to the top position of college or university president.

Education and Training

Candidates for positions in four-year colleges and universities typically need a doctoral degree in forensic science, chemistry, biochemistry, or another related field. Employers may hire candidates, particularly for adjunct positions, with a master's degree, if they have qualifying work experience. To teach in two-year colleges, candidates must possess at least a master's degree in their field.

It takes several years of committed effort for students to obtain a doctoral degree. First, students complete a four-year bachelor's degree program, followed by a one- or two-year master's degree program. Upon earning their master's degree, they enroll in a doctoral program, which takes several more years to finish. To successfully earn their degree, doctoral candidates must write a book-length dissertation based on original research. Upon earning their doctorates, many students complete an additional two or more years in postdoctoral research and study.

Experience, Special Skills, and Personality Traits

Employers generally prefer to hire candidates for entry-level positions who have practical experience in their forensic specialties. They may have gained their experience through employment, fellowships, or research projects. They also seek candidates who have previous teaching experience, preferably in adult settings.

To be effective educators, Forensic Science Instructors must have excellent organizational, self-management, communication, presentation, and interpersonal skills. Being creative, inquisitive, flexible, dedicated, and inspirational are some personality traits that successful instructors share.

Unions and Associations

Many Forensic Science Instructors belong to professional associations to take advantage of networking opportunities, continuing education programs, and other professional services and resources. They may join general-interest forensic societies in their field, such as the American Academy of Forensic Science and the Council on Forensic Science Education. In addition, they may join societies that serve their particular forensic area, such as the Society of Forensic Toxicologists, the Association of Firearms and Tool Mark Examiners, or the American Board of Forensic Entomology. Instructors who perform consulting work might join the American College of Forensic Examiners.

In addition, Forensic Science Instructors belong to professional associations that serve the interests of the academic faculty, such as the National Association of Scholars and the American Association of University Professors. Those in public institutions are eligible to join the higher education divisions of the National Education Association or the American Federation of Teachers, which are labor unions.

For contact information for the above organizations, see Appendix III.

Tips for Entry

1. While in college, gain teaching experience by obtaining tutoring or teaching assistant positions.
2. You usually need to provide three references to prospective employers. Be sure you have current contact information for your references.
3. Many schools require a statement of research and teaching interests. Have you thought about your goals and objectives? Have you listed them?
4. Contact schools directly to learn about current or future openings.
5. Get an idea of the variety of forensic science programs that are available in the United States. Many of these academic programs maintain a presence on the Internet. To find relevant Web sites, enter any of the following keywords into a search engine: *college forensic science program*, *university forensic science program*, or *community college forensic science program*.

FORENSIC SCIENCE RESEARCHER

CAREER PROFILE

Duties: Plan and conduct applied or basic research projects; perform duties as required

Alternate Title(s): Research Scientist; a title that reflects a specialty, such as Forensic Chemist

Salary Range: $35,000 to $145,000

Employment Prospects: Fair

Advancement Prospects: Fair

Prerequisites:

Education or Training—Doctoral degree required to conduct independent research, teach in academic institutions, or to hold top management positions

Experience—Work and research experience related to the desired position is required

Special Skills and Personality Traits—Interpersonal, communication, organizational, problem-solving, and self-management skills; patient, persistent, detail-oriented, curious, enthusiastic, and dedicated

CAREER LADDER

```
┌─────────────────────────────┐
│   Senior Researcher or      │
│   Principal Investigator    │
└─────────────────────────────┘

┌─────────────────────────────┐
│         Researcher          │
└─────────────────────────────┘

┌─────────────────────────────┐
│     Research Associate      │
└─────────────────────────────┘
```

Position Description

Forensic science plays an important role in the delivery of justice in legal matters. Law enforcement officers, attorneys, and the courts use forensic evidence to assist in convicting suspects or proving them innocent. Attorneys, government agencies, insurance companies, and other entities rely on forensic examinations to help settle civil, regulatory, arbitration, and other legal-related cases. In addition, various individuals and groups utilize forensic analysis to reconstruct accidents and other casualties, to locate missing people in mass disasters, and to identify victims from their remains, among other purposes.

Every year, new and improved forensic practices and tools are being introduced to increase the types of forensic evidence that can be used, as well as to boost the quality and speed of processing evidence. Much of this is due to the work and dedication of Forensic Science Researchers who work in academic, government, and private laboratories. Because forensic science is an interdisciplinary field, Forensic Science Researchers have diverse backgrounds. They are criminalists, chemists, biological scientists, geoscientists, medical scientists, social scientists, behavioral scientists, mathematicians, engineers, and others.

Many Forensic Science Researchers are involved in applied research to develop new or improved forensic methods, procedures, and technologies. They utilize fundamental principles and techniques of forensic science and other disciplines in their studies. They seek practical applications in a wide range of areas. For example, depending on their interests and backgrounds, forensic research scientists might be involved in creating:

- techniques for the analysis of physical evidence (such as DNA, fire debris, or explosives)
- tools to conduct forensic tests at crime scenes
- software to automatically search databases, such as latent print or dental X-ray databases, for evidence
- databases of materials (such as soils, pollens, or animals) for determining the origin of physical evidence
- statistical methods for the reliability of evidence identification
- procedures to examine different types of computer hardware (such as portable electronic devices) or computer systems (such as the Macintosh operating system)

Some Forensic Science Researchers conduct basic research to expand further knowledge and understanding in their forensic areas. For example, researchers might investigate questions such as these: How does forensic evidence impact the criminal justice processes? What is the most effective way to manage and run crime labs? Can DNA databases help prevent crimes from occurring? The results of basic research are used in further investigations of practical applications.

Depending on their research projects, forensic research scientists work alone or collaborate with other researchers. Independent researchers are responsible for obtaining grants from government and private sources to fund their projects. This involves preparing proposals that describe the purpose, goals, objectives, methodologies, personnel, and other aspects of their projects. They also include detailed budgets and submit other required forms.

Forensic Science Researchers are responsible for the design and management of their research projects. They perform a wide range of tasks that vary each day. For example, they design and conduct experiments, tests, and surveys; gather, analyze, and interpret data; review scientific literature; prepare correspondence, forms, reports, and other required paperwork; attend meetings; and perform administrative tasks such as maintaining equipment, ordering supplies, paying bills, and planning work schedules. These researchers also monitor laboratory practices to ensure that standards as well as laws and regulations are being met. In addition, they keep up to date with current developments and technologies in forensic science as well as in their particular disciplines. Furthermore, they supervise research assistants, technicians, and other support staff.

Academic researchers are usually employed as instructors who teach courses to undergraduate or graduate students. Their teaching duties include preparing course outlines, lecturing and leading discussions, supervising class activities and lab work, and grading tests and papers, among other tasks. In addition, they are responsible for advising students on academic and career matters. Many of them also supervise graduate students with their research projects. Moreover, academic researchers perform various administrative and community service duties.

Forensic Science Researchers mostly work indoors in offices and laboratories. Academic researchers usually have more flexible hours than government and private researchers. Researchers in all settings put in extra work hours to complete their various tasks.

Salaries

Salaries for Forensic Science Researchers vary, depending on such factors as their experience, employer, and geographic location. Specific salary information for this occupation is unavailable. A general idea of earnings for Forensic Science Researchers can be obtained by looking at earnings for different professionals who engage in forensic science research. The U.S. Bureau of Labor Statistics reports in its May 2006

Occupational Employment Statistics survey the following estimated salary ranges for most of these professionals:

- chemists, $35,480 to $106,310
- clinical psychologists, $35,280 to $102,730
- medical scientists, $35,490 to $117,520
- microbiologists, $35,460 to $108,270
- research computer scientists, $53,590 to $144,880
- sociologists, $36,790 to $115,770
- statisticians, $37,010 to $108,630

Employment Prospects

Forensic Science Researchers find employment in government and private research laboratories. Academic research opportunities are found in public and private four-year colleges and universities. Academic opportunities are usually for teaching positions.

Opportunities in general are favorable for qualified Forensic Science Researchers and should continue to be favorable for the coming years. Most job openings are created to replace individuals who retire, resign, or transfer to other positions. Employers will create additional positions to meet growing needs if funding is available.

Advancement Prospects

Forensic Science Researchers can be promoted to supervisory and managerial positions, which may require moving to another workplace. A doctorate is usually required to obtain top management positions.

Academic faculty members can rise through the ranks as instructors, assistant professors, associate professors, and full professors.

Education and Training

To become an academic researcher, a doctoral degree in one's field is required. Government and private labs also prefer to hire candidates with doctorates, but are willing to hire applicants with master's or bachelor's degrees if they have qualifying work experience.

It takes several years of dedication for students to obtain a doctoral degree. First, they complete a four-year bachelor's degree program, followed by a one- or two-year master's degree program. Upon earning their master's degree, they enroll in a doctoral program, which takes several more years to finish. To successfully earn their degree, doctoral candidates must write a book-length dissertation based on original research. Upon earning their doctorates, many students complete an additional two or more years in postdoctoral research and study.

Experience, Special Skills, and Personality Traits

Employers generally hire candidates who have work and research experience related to the positions for which they apply. They may have gained their experience through internships, student research projects, and employment. Doctoral candidates may be required to have several years of postdoctoral experience.

Forensic Science Researchers need strong interpersonal, communication, organizational, and problem-solving skills. In addition, they must have self-management skills, such as the ability to work independently, meet deadlines, handle stressful situations, and prioritize multiple tasks. Being patient, persistent, detail-oriented, curious, enthusiastic, and dedicated are some personality traits that successful Forensic Science Researchers share.

Unions and Associations

Many Forensic Science Researchers are members of various professional societies. They join general-interest forensic societies, such as the American Academy of Forensic Science and the American College of Forensic Examiners. They also join societies that serve their particular forensic or science discipline, such as the American Chemical Society, the Society of Forensic Toxicologists, the Association of Firearms and Tool Mark Examiners, or the American Academy of Psychiatry and the Law. (For contact information for the above organizations, see Appendix III.) By joining professional associations, these research scientists can take advantage of networking opportunities, continuing education programs, and other professional services and resources.

Tips for Entry

1. Gain research experience during your undergraduate years by obtaining a research assistantship or volunteering to work on a professor's research project.
2. If possible, get an internship in a forensic laboratory to gain practical experience.
3. Professional societies, such as the American Academy of Forensic Science, post job listings at their Web sites that include announcements for research opportunities.
4. You can use the Internet to learn more about the various types of forensic science research that is being conducted. To obtain a list of relevant Web sites, enter either of these key words into a search engine: *forensic science research* or *forensic science researchers*. For some links, see Appendix IV.

CRIME REPORTER

CAREER PROFILE

Duties: Provide objective and accurate news reports about crime and crime-related matters; perform duties as required

Alternate Title(s): Crime Journalist, Crime Beat Reporter, Police Beat Reporter

Salary Range: $19,000 to $74,000

Employment Prospects: Fair

Advancement Prospects: Fair

Prerequisites:

Education or Training — A bachelor's degree in journalism, English, or another related field; on-the-job training

Experience — News reporting experience required

Special Skills and Personality Traits — Researching, note-taking, interviewing, writing, story-telling, interpersonal, communication, organizational, problem-solving, teamwork, and self-management skills; inquisitive, quick-witted, enthusiastic, energetic, persistent, objective, and creative

CAREER LADDER

```
┌─────────────────────────────────────┐
│        Senior Crime Reporter         │
└─────────────────────────────────────┘

┌─────────────────────────────────────┐
│            Crime Reporter            │
└─────────────────────────────────────┘

┌─────────────────────────────────────┐
│         Novice Reporter or           │
│    General Assignment Reporter       │
└─────────────────────────────────────┘
```

Position Description

Every day, we read and hear news accounts about crime that has occurred locally, statewide, nationally, or around the world. The journalists who are responsible for covering crime beats (or police beats) are called Crime Reporters. Their reports range from the routine to the most lurid. They write about vandalism, burglaries, theft, robberies, larceny, fraud, kidnapping, sexual assaults, murders, terrorism, and other incidents. They also report about missing persons, traffic accidents, airplane collisions, fires, natural disasters, and other types of casualties and tragedies. In addition, these journalists write features, analyses, or investigatory reports about crime trends, crime prevention strategies, policing, forensic science, the criminal court system, the legal process, and criminal justice issues (such as juvenile justice, organized crime, corrections, the death penalty, and crime victims).

Crime Reporters are employed by newspapers, magazines, and online publications as well as by radio and television broadcast stations. Their job is to seek out stories that would interest their publication's or station's audience. They usually work on several stories for every issue or broadcast.

At some newspapers, Crime Reporters contribute to a daily police column for which they compile brief accounts about local criminal incidents, arrests, and suspects who are most wanted by authorities.

Crime Reporters have a hectic and difficult job. They work in offices, but a large amount of their time is spent in the field, where they cover stories or conduct research for stories. Additionally, reporters investigate leads for potential stories. For example, a Crime Reporter might learn that there has been an upsurge in youth gang activity or that the city budget deficit may force a cut in public safety staff.

Their job requires them to quickly gather accurate and correct information about people, places, and events for a story. They observe events, such as crime scene investigations, fires, or court trials. They interview eyewitnesses, local authorities, and others who may provide relevant information about an incident. In addition, they read press releases, official papers, and other pertinent documents that they have obtained from reliable sources. Print and online reporters may have the additional duty of taking photographs for their stories.

Furthermore, Crime Reporters conduct research for background information for their stories. They talk with subject-matter experts to gain an understanding of difficult facts and issues. For example, a Crime Reporter might talk with forensic anthropologists or forensic dentists to learn how unknown remains can be identified. These journalists also look up facts and figures at courthouses, public offices, and libraries, as well as on electronic databases and the Internet.

Crime Reporters are able to organize their notes quickly and choose the best structure for their stories. They follow specific formats and standards to compose succinct yet comprehensive articles. Unless they are doing an opinion piece, Crime Reporters write objective stories. That is, they state only the factual details about an event, person, or place. Reporters also write their articles clearly so that their audience can easily understand their stories. Before submitting their stories, journalists double-check dates and figures, the spelling of names and places, the titles of people, and other facts to ensure they are correct and accurate.

Reporters are always under pressure to meet deadlines. Thus, it is common for reporters to write their stories on laptop computers while in the field and then electronically transmit their stories to their editors. Broadcast reporters may present their stories live or on tape that will be broadcast at a later time.

Crime Reporters usually work on their stories alone. On occasion, they work with other reporters, including those from other beats, to compile a comprehensive investigative or feature report, such as a story about why local prosecutors have a low conviction rate or a biography of the first woman sheriff in a county.

Part of a Crime Reporter's job is to develop dependable sources within law enforcement agencies, prosecuting attorneys' offices, the coroners' (or medical examiners') offices, crime labs, courts, and other organizations. They contact their sources on a regular basis to learn about breaking news as well as to get ideas for potential stories.

Entry-level reporters are typically given routine writing assignments. They also assist senior reporters by conducting research for their stories. As reporters gain experience, they are assigned increasingly difficult stories, as well as begin to specialize in a particular news area such as the crime beat.

At some publications and broadcast stations, the crime beat is used as a test of a reporter's flexibility, courage, and dedication, and hence novice reporters are assigned to it. Some Crime Reporters cover the police beat for a few years, while others work this beat throughout their journalistic career.

Crime Reporters have stressful jobs. Along with constantly meeting deadlines, they often deal with conflict situations and highly emotional people. Their personal safety is sometimes at risk. For example, Crime Reporters have been arrested or injured while covering raids, riots, demonstrations, robberies, and other incidents; and some Crime Reporters have received death threats as they investigated stories.

Crime Reporters are employed full time or part time. Some are freelancers, or self-employed. These journalists work long hours. They may work early mornings, evenings, or nights, depending on when their newspapers are published or their stations are on the air. They may also work weekends and holidays. All Crime Reporters are expected to be available at any time of the day or night.

Salaries

Salaries for Crime Reporters vary, depending on such factors as their education, experience, employer, and geographic location. According to the May 2006 *Occupational Employment Statistics* survey by the U.S. Bureau of Labor Statistics (BLS), the estimated annual salary for most reporters ranged between $19,180 and $73,880.

Employment Prospects

In general, job opportunities for Crime Reporters become available as individuals advance to higher positions, transfer to other jobs, or leave the workforce for various reasons. The turnover rate for Crime Reporters is high because of the nature of the subject matter.

Novice reporters typically start at newspapers and broadcast stations in small towns and the suburbs. As they gain experience, many of them seek opportunities at larger publications and stations. In general, the competition is high for jobs at large metropolitan and national newspapers, magazines, broadcast stations, and broadcast networks.

Most reporting opportunities will become available as reporters transfer to other positions or move into occupations in related fields such as advertising or public relations. The employment growth for reporters, in general, is expected to increase by zero to 8 percent through 2014, according to the BLS. This is partly due to the continuing consolidation of newspaper and broadcast companies. Jobs may be more favorable with online newspapers and magazines as well as with cable television stations.

Job opportunities in the publishing and broadcast industries are also dependent on the health of the economy. During slow economic periods, companies generally hire fewer reporters.

Advancement Prospects

Reporters can advance in various ways, depending on their interests and ambitions. Some reporters seek positions in large metropolitan or national newspapers and broadcast stations. Some reporters become columnists, news analysts, special correspondents, news anchors, talk show hosts, and book authors. Other reporters pursue related careers by becoming editors, news bureau directors, broadcast producers, program managers, and publishers. Still others follow their educational interests and become college and university professors.

Many reporters realize advancement by earning higher wages, receiving more complex assignments, and being recognized for the quality of their work.

Education and Training

Employers normally hire applicants for entry-level positions who have at least a bachelor's degree in journalism, communications, English, or another related field.

Novice reporters typically receive on-the-job training. They perform research and other routine tasks under the supervision and direction of editors and experienced reporters.

Experience, Special Skills, and Personality Traits

Employers generally hire candidates for entry-level reporting positions who have previous reporting experience. They may have gained their experience on school newspapers or television stations, or through internships or employment.

Applicants for crime beat positions may be expected to have several years of reporting experience, which includes some crime reporting.

Along with exceptional researching, note-taking, interviewing, and writing skills, Crime Reporters need strong storytelling skills. They must also have excellent interpersonal, communication, organizational, problem-solving, teamwork, and self-management skills. Being inquisitive, quick-witted, enthusiastic, energetic, persistent, objective, and creative are some personality traits that successful Crime Reporters share.

Unions and Associations

Crime Reporters can join professional associations to take advantage of networking opportunities, job listings, and other professional services and resources. Some of the different societies that are available for print and broadcast reporters are:

- Criminal Justice Journalists
- Investigative Reporters and Editors
- The Society of Professional Journalists
- Radio-Television News Directors Association (open to electronic journalists in broadcasting, cable, and other electronic media)
- American Society of Journalists and Authors (open to all freelance reporters)
- Association for Women in Communications
- Asian American Journalists Association

For contact information, see Appendix III.

Tips for Entry

1. While in high school or college, work on your school newspaper or broadcasting station to begin gaining experience.
2. Take one or more basic courses in criminal justice, law enforcement, or police science. Be sure to list those courses on your résumé and application.
3. Do your research before you go to a job interview. Along with learning about the newspaper or broadcasting station, get an idea about the geographic area and the people that it serves.
4. Be willing to take a general assignment position or to cover another beat, if a crime-reporting beat is not immediately available.
5. Use the Internet to learn more about becoming a journalist and a Crime Reporter, in particular. You might start by visiting these Web sites: Society of Professional Journalists, http://www.spj.org; and Institute for Justice and Journalism (University of Southern California Annenberg School for Communication), http://www.justicejournalism.org. For more links, see Appendix IV.

APPENDIXES

APPENDIX I
EDUCATION AND TRAINING RESOURCES ON THE INTERNET

In this appendix, you will find World Wide Web sources for education and training programs pertaining to some of the occupations in this book. To learn about programs for other occupations, talk with school or career counselors as well as with professionals. You can also look up schools in college directories produced by the Princeton Review or other publishers, which may be found in your school or public library.

Note: All Web site addresses were current at the time this book was written. If a URL is no longer valid, enter the title of the Web site or the name of the organization or individual into a search engine to find the new URL.

PAYING FOR YOUR EDUCATION
Scholarships, grants, student loans, and other financial aid programs are available to help you pay for your college education. These programs are sponsored by government agencies, professional and trade associations, private foundations, businesses, and other organizations. (You can find contact information for many professional associations in Appendix III.)

To learn more about financial assistance programs, talk with your high school guidance counselor or college career counselor. You might also consult college catalogs, as they usually include financial aid information. In addition, you might visit or contact the financial aid office at the college where you plan to attend or are attending now. Lastly, check out these Web sites for financial aid information:

FinAid, http://www.finaid.org; and Student Aid on the Web (U.S. Department of Education Federal Student Aid), http://studentaid.ed.gov.

GENERAL RESOURCES
The following Web sites provide links to various academic programs at colleges and universities in the United States.
- Peterson's, http://www.petersons.com
- The Princeton Review, http://www.princetonreview.com
- "Web U.S. Higher Education," a listing of two-year colleges, four-year colleges, and universities (maintained by the University of Texas at Austin), http://www.utexas.edu/world/univ
- WorldWideLearn (a directory of online degree programs), http://www.worldwidelearn.com

ACCOUNTING
The American Institute of Certified Public Accountants has a listing of accounting degree programs at http://www.startheregoplaces.com.

ANTHROPOLOGY/FORENSIC ANTHROPOLOGY
- The American Association of Physical Anthropologists provides a listing of physical anthropology programs at http://physanth.org/gradprogs.
- A listing of forensic anthropology programs can be found at ForensicAnthro.com, http://www.forensicanthro.com/forensic-programs; or OsteoInteractive Web site, (sponsored by the Eccles Health Sciences Library at the University of Utah, Salt Lake City), http://library.med.utah.edu/kw/osteo/resources/resources.html.

ARCHAEOLOGY
The Society for American Archaeology provides a listing of academic institutions in the United States that have at least one archaeologist on each of their faculties. Its URL is http://www.saa.org/careers/academic.html.

ARCHITECTURE
The National Architectural Accrediting Board has a database of accredited professional programs in architecture, bachelor, master's, and doctoral degrees. Its URL is http://www.naab.org.

CHILD ABUSE PEDIATRICS
A listing of fellowship programs in child abuse and neglect can be found at these Web sites:
- Ray Helfer Society, http://helfersociety.org/Fellowships.htm
- American Academy of Pediatrics Section on Child Abuse and Neglect, http://www.aap.org/sections/scan/fellow.htm

CHIROPRACTIC MEDICINE
A listing of chiropractic schools can be found at these Web sites:
- American Chiropractic Association Web, http://www.amerchiro.org

- Association of Chiropractic Colleges, http://www.chirocolleges.org

COMPUTER SCIENCE/ COMPUTER FORENSICS

A database of computer science and information programs is provided at the Accreditation Board for Engineering and Technology Web site at http://www.abet.org.

CRIME SCENE INVESTIGATION

Crime-Scene-Investigator.net provides a list of degree and certificate programs in crime scene investigation and other forensic fields at http://www.crime-scene-investigator.net/csi-training.html.

CRIMINOLOGY/CRIMINAL JUSTICE

The American Society of Criminology has a listing of schools at these Web sites:

- undergraduate programs, http://www.asc41.com/UNDER-GRAD.html
- graduate programs, http://www.asc41.com/GRADLINKS.html

DENTISTRY

The American Dental Association provides a listing of dental schools at its Web site. The URL is http://www.ada.org.

ENGINEERING

To find academic programs for all of the different engineering disciplines, check out the following links:

- ABET, Inc., http://www.abet.org
- All Engineering Schools, http://www.allengineeringschools.com

ENTOMOLOGY

Dr. Louis Bjostad at Colorado State University provides a listing of entomology departments at http://www.colostate.edu/Depts/Entomology/colleges.html.

ENVIRONMENTAL SCIENCE/ ENVIRONMENTAL ENGINEERING

A database of college programs in environmental science, environmental engineering, and related environmental programs can be found at EnviroEducation.com: The Environmental Education Directory. The URL is http://www.enviroeducation.com.

FIRE INVESTIGATION/FIRE SCIENCE

- CFITrainer.net is an online resource of training programs for fire investigators. The URL is http://www.cfitrainer.net.

- The U.S. Fire Administration provides a listing of academic programs in fire science and fire prevention programs at http://www.usfa.dhs.gov/nfa/higher_ed/degree_programs/index.shtm.

FORENSIC ART

Neville's Forensic Art World maintains a listing of educational programs that are currently available in forensic art. The URL is http://www.forensicartist.com/education.html.

FORENSIC PSYCHIATRY

American Academy of Psychiatry and the Law provides a directory of forensic psychiatry fellowship programs at http://www.aapl.org/fellow.htm.

FORENSIC PSYCHOLOGY

The following Web sites provide a listing of forensic psychology degree programs:

- All About Forensic Psychology, http://www.all-about-forensic-psychology.com
- American Psychology-Law Society, http://www.unl.edu/ap-ls/student/graduate_programs.html

FORENSIC SCIENCE

The following Web sites provide listings for degree and continuing education programs in forensic science and other forensic disciplines.

- American Academy of Forensic Sciences, http://www.aafs.org
- Henry C. Lee Institute of Forensic Science (affiliated with the University of New Haven), http://www.henryleeinstitute.com
- Reddy's Forensic Page, http://www.forensicpage.com

JOURNALISM

The following Web sites offer information about current training programs that are available:

- JournalismTraining.Org, http://www.journalismtraining.org
- Access—The News University Training Blog, http://access.newsu.org

JUDICIAL EDUCATION AND TRAINING

The National Judicial College offers education and training programs for judges. For information, go to its Web site at http://www.judges.org.

LAW

The following Web sites provide a listing of law schools:

- American Bar Association, http://www.abanet.org/legaled/approvedlawschools/approved.html

- Association of American Law Schools, http://www.aals. org/about_memberschools.php

LAW ENFORCEMENT TRAINING

Policetraining.net provides a listing of law enforcement classes and seminars that are currently available. Its URL is http://www.policetraining.net.

LINGUISTICS/PHONETICS

The Linguist List has a database of linguistics programs (including phonetics) at http://linguistlist.org/teach/programs/index.html.

MEDICINE

- The Association of American Medical Colleges provides a listing of medical schools at http://www.aamc.org/medicalschools.htm.
- The Accreditation Council for Graduate Medical Education provides a listing of graduate medical education programs, or residency programs, at http://www.acgme.org.
- The American Association of Colleges of Osteopathic Medicine has a listing of schools that offer the doctor of osteopathic medicine (D.O.) degree at http://www.aacom.org/colleges.

MEDICOLEGAL DEATH INVESTIGATION

The American Board of Medicolegal Death Investigators offers a current listing of training opportunities at its Web site, http://www.slu.edu/organizations/abmdi.

METEOROLOGY

The National Weather Association has a listing of degree programs in meteorology and atmospheric science. Its URL is http://www.nwas.org.

MUSICOLOGY

American Musicological Society provides a listing of graduate programs in musicology at its Web site, http://www.ams-net.org.

NURSING/FORENSIC NURSING

- All Nursing Schools.com has a database of the various types of nursing programs, including forensic nursing programs. The URL is http://www.allnursingschools.com.
- The American Association of Colleges of Nursing has a database of bachelor's and graduate-degree nursing pro-

grams at its Web site. The URL is http://www.aacn.nche.edu.

PATHOLOGY/FORENSIC PATHOLOGY

The Intersociety Council for Pathology Information, Inc. maintains a directory of pathology programs for residency and fellowship training programs. The URL is http://www.pathologytraining.org.

PHARMACY

The following Web sites provide a listing of pharmacy schools and colleges:
- American Association of Colleges of Pharmacy, http://www.aacp.org
- RXinsider.com, http://www.rxinsider.com/schools_of_pharmacy.htm

POLICE ACADEMIES

A listing of some police academies in the United States is available at the CopCareer.com Web site, http://www.copcareer.com/academy/policeacademy.htm.

POLYGRAPH

The following Web sites have a listing of polygraph schools:
- American Association of Police Polygraphists, http://www.policepolygraph.org/polyschools.htm
- American Polygraph Association, http://www.polygraph.org/schools.cfm

SOCIAL WORK

The Council on Social Work Education provides a database of bachelor's and master's degree programs in social work. Its URL is http://www.cswe.org.

STATISTICS

The American Statistical Association has a database of schools offering degrees in statistics. Its URL is http://www.amstat.org.

SURVEYING

The American Congress on Surveying and Mapping has a list of surveying programs at http://www.acsm.net/college.html.

TOXICOLOGY

The Society of Toxicology provides a listing of academic and post-doctoral programs in toxicology. Its URL is http://www.toxicology.org.

APPENDIX II
PROFESSIONAL CERTIFICATION PROGRAMS

Professional certifications are granted by professional associations or other recognized organizations on a voluntary basis. Unlike occupational licensure, professional certification is not a mandatory state or local requirement for professionals to practice in their field. Employers may require or strongly prefer to hire candidates who possess particular professional certifications. Many individuals obtain professional certifications to enhance their employability.

To be eligible for professional certification, individuals are usually required to have several years of work experience. They may need to complete courses, seminars, or workshops as well as pass professional examinations.

This appendix lists professional certification programs for some of the occupations in this book. To learn about other programs, talk with professionals, employers, and professional associations in the fields that interest you.

Note: All Web addresses were accessible while this book was being written. If a URL no longer works, you might find the new one by entering the name of the certification program or organization into a search engine.

ACCIDENT RECONSTRUCTION SPECIALIST

The Accreditation Commission for Traffic Accident Reconstruction offers professional certification. For information, write to P.O. Box 5436, Hudson, FL 34674, or call (800) 809-3818. Information can be found online at http://www.actar.org.

BLOODSTAIN PATTERN ANALYST

The International Association for Identification offers a bloodstain pattern certification program. For information write Grant D. Graham Sr. at 3119 Shadow Wood Drive, Ocean Springs, MS 39564, or call him at (601) 506-7093. Information can be found online at http://www.theiai.org/certifications/bloodstain/index.php.

CHILD ABUSE PEDIATRICIAN

The American Board of Pediatrics (ABP) offers a board certification program in child abuse pediatrics. For information, write to 111 Silver Cedar Court, Chapel Hill, NC 27514, or visit the ABP Web site at http://www.abp.org.

COMPUTER FORENSICS SPECIALIST

The International Association of Computer Investigative Specialists (IACIS) offers certification programs for Certified Electronic Evidence Collection Specialist (CEECS) and Certified Forensic Computer Examiner (CFCE). For information, write to P.O. Box 1728, Fairmont, WV 26555; or call (888) 884-2247; or visit the IACIS Web site at http://www.iacis.info.

CORONER

The American Board of Medicolegal Death Investigators offers a certification program to qualifying medical death investigators. For information, write to 1402 South Grand Boulevard, St. Louis, MO 63104; or call (314) 977-5970. Information can be found online at http://www.slu.edu/organizations/abmdi.

CRIME SCENE INVESTIGATOR

- The International Association for Identification offers the following certification programs: Certified Crime Scene Investigator, Certified Crime Scene Analyst, and Certified Senior Crime Scene Analyst. For information, write to Curtis Shane, Secretary, 1193 West Shore Drive, Brunswick, GA 31523; or call (912) 261-0990. Information can also be found online at http://www.theiai.org/certifications/crime_scene/index.php.
- The American College of Forensic Examiners offers a Certified Medical Investigator (CMI) program. For information, write to 2750 East Sunshine Street, Springfield, MO 65804; or call (800) 423-9737 or (417) 881-3818. Information can also be found online at http://www.acfei.com/programs_cmi.php.

CRIMINALIST

The American Board of Criminalistics (ABC) has a certification program that offers three levels of certification: Diplomate D-ABC; Fellow F-ABC; and Technical Specialist S-ABC. It grants certification in forensic biology, drug analysis, fire debris analysis, trace evidence, and forensic molecular biology. For information, write to P.O. Box 1123, Wausau, WI 54402; or visit the ABC Web site at http://www.criminalistics.com.

DNA ANALYST

The American Board of Criminalistics (ABC) has a program in forensic biology with three levels of certification: Diplomate D-ABC; Fellow F-ABC; and Technical Specialist S-ABC. For information, write to P.O. Box 1123, Wausau, WI 54402; or visit the ABC Web site at http://www.criminalistics.com.

EVIDENCE CUSTODIAN

The International Association for Property and Evidence offers these certification programs: Certified Property and Evidence Specialist (CPES) and Corporate Certified Property and Evidence Specialist (CCPES). For information, write to 903 North San Fernando Boulevard, Suite 4, Burbank, CA 91504; or call (800) 449-4273 or (818) 846-2926. Information can be found online at http://www.iape.org.

FINGERPRINT TECHNICIAN

The International Association for Identification offers a tenprint fingerprint certification program. For information, write to Barbara A. Powell, Secretary, Tenprint Print Certification Board, P.O. Box 10464, Phoenix, AZ 85064; or call (602) 818-3524. Information can be found online at http://www.theiai.org/certifications/tenprint/index.php.

FIRE INVESTIGATOR

- The National Association of Fire Investigators offers the following certification programs: Certified Fire and Explosion Investigator (CFEI), Certified Fire Investigation Instructor (CFII), and Certified Vehicle Fire Investigation (CVFI). For information, write to 857 Tallevast Road, Sarasota, FL 34243; or call (877) 506-NAFI or (941) 359-2800. More information can be found online at http://www.nafi.org/Certification.htm.
- The International Association of Arson Investigators offers the Certified Fire Investigator (CFI) program. For information, write to 2151 Priest Bridge Drive, Suite 25, Crofton, MD 21114; or call (410) 451-3473. More information can be found online at http://www.firearson.com/cfi.
- The American Board of Criminalistics (ABC) has a program in fire debris analysis with three levels of certification: Diplomate D-ABC; Fellow F-ABC; and Technical Specialist S-ABC. For information, write to P. O. Box 1123, Wausau, WI 54402; or visit the ABC Web site at http://www.criminalistics.com.

FORENSIC ACCOUNTANT

The American College of Forensic Examiners offers a Certified Forensic Accountant (Cr.FA) program. For information, write to 2750 East Sunshine Street, Springfield, MO 65804; or call (800) 423-9737 or (417) 881-3818. Information can also be found online at http://www.acfei.com/programs_crfa.php

FORENSIC ANTHROPOLOGIST

- The American Board of Forensic Anthropology grants the Diplomate of the American Board of Forensic Anthropology (DABFA) certification. For information about this certification program, visit the board's Web site at http://www.csuchico.edu/anth/ABFA.
- The American College of Forensic Examiners offers a Certified Medical Investigator (CMI) program. For information, write to 2750 East Sunshine Street, Springfield, MO 65804; or call (800) 423-9737 or (417) 881-3818. Information can be found online at http://www.acfei.com/programs_cmi.php.

FORENSIC ARTIST

The International Association for Identification offers a forensic art certification program. For information, e-mail Charles Jackson, Forensic Art Certification Secretary, forensicartctj@aol.com. Information can be found online at http://www.theiai.org/certifications/artist/index.php.

FORENSIC BIOLOGIST

The American Board of Criminalistics (ABC) has a program in forensic biology with three levels of certification: Diplomate D-ABC; Fellow F-ABC; and Technical Specialist S-ABC. For information, write to P. O. Box 1123, Wausau, WI 54402; or visit the ABC Web site at http://www.criminalistics.com.

FORENSIC CHEMIST

- The American Board of Criminalistics (ABC) has a certification program that offers three levels of certification: Diplomate D-ABC; Fellow F-ABC; and Technical Specialist S-ABC. For information, write to P. O. Box 1123, Wausau, WI 54402; or visit the ABC Web site at http://www.criminalistics.com.
- The American Board of Forensic Toxicology grants diplomate certification to forensic toxicology specialists. For information about this program, write to 410 North 21st Street, Colorado Springs, CO 80904; or call (719) 636-1100. Information can be found online at http://www.abft.org.

FORENSIC CHIROPRACTIC EXPERT

The American Board of Forensic Professionals offers the diplomate certification in the field of chiropractic forensics (DABFP). For information about this certification program, write to 208 Syracuse Avenue, Oswego, NY 13126; or call (315) 343-5713. Information can be found at http://www.forensic-sciences.org/abfp/abfp_certification.htm.

FORENSIC CONSULTANT

The American College of Forensic Examiners offers a Certified Forensic Consultant (CFC) program. For information, write to 2750 East Sunshine Street, Springfield, MO 65804; or call (800) 423-9737 or (417) 881-3818. Information can be found online at http://www.acfei.com/programs_cfc.php.

FORENSIC DRUG CHEMIST

The American Board of Criminalistics (ABC) has a program in drug analysis with three levels of certification: Diplomate D-ABC; Fellow F-ABC; and Technical Specialist S-ABC. For more information, write to P. O. Box 1123, Wausau, WI 54402; or visit the ABC Web site at http://www.criminalistics.com.

FORENSIC ECONOMIST

The American Rehabilitation Economics Association offers a certification program to forensic economic experts. For information, write to 127 North Westwind Drive, El Cajon, CA 92020; or call (800) 317-2732. Information can be found online at http://www.a-r-e-a.org.

FORENSIC ENGINEER

The Council of Engineering and Scientific Specialty Boards is the recognized accreditation body for engineering and scientific certification and specialty certification programs. They have a listing of certification programs online at http://www.cesb.org.

FORENSIC ENTOMOLOGIST

• The Entomological Society of America offers the following certification programs: Associate Certified Entomologist (ACE) and Board Certified Entomologist (BCE). For information, write to 10001 Derekwood Lane, Suite 100, Lanham, MD 20706; or call (301) 731-4535. Information can be found online at http://www.entsoc.org.
• American Board of Forensic Entomology grants the diplomate certification (ABFE) to qualified candidates. For information about this certification program, write to Dr. Richard Merritt, Department of Entomology, Michigan State University, East Lansing, MI 48824; or call (517) 355-8309. Information can be found online at http://www.research.missouri.edu/entomology.

FORENSIC MEDICAL CONSULTANT

• American Board of Medical Specialties (ABMS) oversees the certification of physicians in various medical specialties, such as pathology, pediatrics, and radiology. For information about the ABMS board certification programs, write to 1007 Church Street, Suite 404, Evanston, IL 60201; call (847) 491-9091; or visit the ABMS Web site at http://www.abms.org.
• The American College of Forensic Examiners offers a Certified Medical Investigator program. For information, write to 2750 East Sunshine Street, Springfield, MO 65804; or call (800) 423-9737 or (417) 881-3818. Information can be found online at http://www.acfei.com/programs_cmi.php.

FORENSIC METEOROLOGIST

The American Meteorological Society offers the Certified Consulting Meteorologist (CCM) program. For information, write to 45 Beacon Street, Boston, MA 02108; or call (617) 227-2425. Information can be found online at http://www.ametsoc.org/amscert/index.html.

FORENSIC NURSE

• The American Association of Legal Nurse Consultants offers the Legal Nurse Consultant Certified (LNCC) program. For information, write to 401 North Michigan Avenue, Chicago, IL 60611; or call (877) 402-2562, or fax (312) 673-6655. Information can be found online at http://www.aalnc.org.
• The American College of Forensic Examiners offers a Certified Forensic Nurse (CFN) program. For information, write to 2750 East Sunshine Street, Springfield, MO 65804; or call (800) 423-9737 or (417) 881-3818. Information can be found online at http://www.acfei.com/programs_cfn.php.
• The American Board of Medicolegal Death Investigators offers a certification program to qualifying medical death investigators. For information, write to 1402 South Grand Boulevard, St. Louis, MO 63104; or call (314) 977-5970. Information can be found online at http://www.slu.edu/organizations/abmdi.

FORENSIC ODONTOLOGIST

• The American Board of Forensic Odontology, Inc. offers a professional certification program to forensic dentists. For information, write to 410 North 21st Street, Colorado Springs, CO 80904; or call (719) 636-1100. Information can be found online at http://www.abfo.org.
• The American College of Forensic Examiners offers a Certified Medical Investigator (CMI) program. For information, write to 2750 East Sunshine Street, Springfield, MO 65804; or call (800) 423-9737 or (417) 881-3818. Information can be found online at http://www.acfei.com/programs_cmi.php.

FORENSIC PATHOLOGIST

• The American Board of Pathology offers a board certification program to pathologists. For information, write to P.O. Box 25915, Tampa, FL 33622; or call (813) 286-2444. Information can be found online at http://www.abpath.org.
• The American College of Forensic Examiners offers a Certified Medical Investigator (CMI) program. For information, write to 2750 East Sunshine Street, Springfield, MO 65804; or call (800) 423-9737 or (417) 881-3818.

Information can be found online at http://www.acfei.com/programs_cmi.php.

FORENSIC PATHOLOGY TECHNICIAN

The American Society for Clinical Pathology offers the Pathologist's Assistant PA (ASCP) certification program. For information, write to 33 West Monroe Street, Suite 1600, Chicago, IL 60603; or call (312) 541-4999. Information can be found online at http://www.ascp.org.

FORENSIC PHARMACIST

- The American College of Forensic Examiners offers a Certified Medical Investigator (CMI) program. For information, write to 2750 East Sunshine Street, Springfield, MO 65804; or call (800) 423-9737 or (417) 881-3818. Information can also be found online at http://www.acfei.com/programs_cmi.php.
- The American Board of Forensic Toxicology grants diplomate certification to forensic toxicology specialists. For information about this program, write to 410 North 21st Street, Colorado Springs, CO 80904; or call (719) 636-1100. Information can be found online at http://www.abft.org.

FORENSIC PHOTOGRAPHER

- The International Association for Identification offers a forensic photography certification program. For information, write to David T. Gamble, Monmouth County Prosecutor's Office, 132 A Jerseyville Avenue, Freehold, NJ 07728; or call (732) 294-5906. Information can be found online at http://www.theiai.org/certifications/imaging/index.php.
- The Evidence Photographers International Council has a board-certified evidence photographer program. For information, write to 229 Peachtree Street NE, #2200, Atlanta, GA 30303. Information can be found online at http://www.evidencephotographers.com/EPICertification.html.

FORENSIC PSYCHIATRIST

- The American Board of Psychiatry and Neurology offers a board certification program in forensic psychiatry. For information, write to 500 Lake Cook Road, Suite 335, Deerfield, IL 60015; or call (847) 945-7900. Information can be found online at http://www.abpn.com.
- The American College of Forensic Examiners offers a Certified Medical Investigator (CMI) program. For information, write to 2750 East Sunshine Street, Springfield, MO 65804; or call (800) 423-9737 or (417) 881-3818. Information can also be found online at http://www.acfei.com/programs_cmi.php.

FORENSIC PSYCHOLOGIST

- The American Board of Professional Psychology offers a board-certification program in forensic psychology. For

information, write to 300 Drayton Street, Third Floor, Savannah, GA 31401; or call (800) 255-7792 or (912) 234-5477. Information can be found online at http://www.abpp.org.
- The American College of Forensic Examiners offers a Certified Medical Investigator (CMI) program. For information, write to 2750 East Sunshine Street, Springfield, MO 65804; or call (800) 423-9737 or (417) 881-3818. Information can be found online at http://www.acfei.com/programs_cmi.php.

FORENSIC RADIOLOGIST

- The American Board of Radiology offers a board certification program in radiology. For information, write to 5441 East Williams Boulevard, Suite 200, Tucson, AZ 85711; or call (520) 790-2900. Information can be found online at http://www.theabr.org.
- The American College of Forensic Examiners offers a Certified Medical Investigator (CMI) program. For information, write to 2750 East Sunshine Street, Springfield, MO 65804; or call (800) 423-9737 or (417) 881-3818. Information can also be found online at http://www.acfei.com/programs_cmi.php.

FORENSIC REHABILITATION CONSULTANT

The Commission on Rehabilitation Counselor Certification has professional certification programs for rehabilitation counselors. For information, write to 300 North Martingale Road, Suite 460, Schaumburg, IL 60173; or call (847) 944-1325. Information can be found online at http://www.crccertification.com.

FORENSIC SOCIAL WORKER

The National Association of Social Workers offers the following certification programs: Academy of Certified Social Workers (ACSW), Diplomate in Clinical Social Work (DCSW), and Qualified Clinical Social Worker (QCSW). It also has certification programs for gerontology, health care, school social work, case management, and other specialties. For information, write to 750 First Street NE, Suite 700, Washington, DC 20002; or call (202) 408-8600. Information can be found online at http://www.naswdc.org.

FORENSIC TOXICOLOGIST

- The American Board of Forensic Toxicology grants diplomate certification to forensic toxicology specialists. For information, write to 410 North 21st Street, Colorado Springs, CO 80904; or call (719) 636-1100. Information can be found online at http://www.abft.org.
- The American College of Forensic Examiners offers a Certified Medical Investigator (CMI) program. For information, write to 2750 East Sunshine Street, Springfield, MO 65804; or call (800) 423-9737 or (417) 881-3818.

Information can also be found online at http://www.acfei. com/programs_cmi.php.

FORENSICS VIDEO ANALYST
- The National Association of Forensic Video offers the Certified Forensic Videographer (CFV) program. For information, write to 15235 Brand Boulevard, Suite A-110, Mission Hills, CA 91345; or call (818) 231-1038. Information can be found online at http://www.natasfv.org.
- The Law Enforcement and Emergency Services Video Association offers a forensic video analyst certification program. For information, write to P.O. Box 547, Midlothian, TX 76065; or call (972) 291-5888. Information can be found online at http://www.leva.org.

FRAUD EXAMINER
The Association of Certified Fraud Examiners offers the Certified Fraud Examiner (CFE) program. For information, write to 716 West Avenue, Austin, TX 78701; or call (800) 245-3321 or (512) 478-9000; or fax (512) 478-9297; or visit its Web site at http://www.acfe.com.

HISTOLOGIST
The American Society for Clinical Pathology offers the following certification programs: Histotechnician HT (ASCP) and Histotechnologist HT (ASCP). For information, write to 33 West Monroe Street, Suite 1600, Chicago, IL 60603; or call (312) 541-4999. Information can be found online at http://www.ascp.org.

LATENT PRINT EXAMINER
The International Association for Identification offers a latent fingerprint certification program. For information, write to James E. Bush, Secretary, IAI Latent Print Certification Board, Mississippi Crime Laboratory, P.O. Box 4450, Meridian, MS 39304; or call (601) 483-5273. Information can be found online at http://www.theiai.org/certifications/fingerprint/index.php.

MEDICAL EXAMINER
- The American Board of Independent Medical Examiners offers professional certification for independent practitioners. For information, write to 1338 Third Avenue, Huntington, WV 25701; or call (877) 523-1415 or (304) 523-1415. Information can be found online at http://www.abime.org.
- The American College of Forensic Examiners offers a Certified Medical Investigator (CMI) program. For information, write to 2750 East Sunshine Street, Springfield, MO 65804; or call (800) 423-9737 or (417) 881-3818. Information can be found online at http://www.acfei.com/programs_cmi.php.

MEDICOLEGAL DEATH INVESTIGATOR
- The American Board of Medicolegal Death Investigators offers a certification program to qualifying medical death investigators. For information, write to 1402 South Grand Boulevard, St. Louis, MO 63104; or call (314) 977-5970. Information can be found online at http://www.slu.edu/organizations/abmdi.
- The American College of Forensic Examiners offers a Certified Medical Investigator (CMI) program. For information, write to 2750 East Sunshine Street, Springfield, MO 65804; or call (800) 423-9737 or (417) 881-3818. Information can be found online at http://www.acfei.com/programs_cmi.php.

POLYGRAPH EXAMINER
The American Association of Police Polygraphists offers the Certified Forensic Law Enforcement Polygraph Examiner (CFLEPE) program. For information, write to P.O. Box 657, Waynesville, OH 45068; or call (888) 743-5479. Information can be found online at http://www.policepolygraph.org/certification.htm.

QUESTIONED DOCUMENT EXAMINER
The American Board of Forensic Document Examiners offers a diplomate certification program. For information, write to 7887 San Felipe, Suite 122, Houston, TX 77063; or call (713) 784-9537. Information can be found online at http://www.abfde.org.

TRACE EVIDENCE EXAMINER
The American Board of Criminalistics (ABC) has a program in trace evidence with three levels of certification: Diplomate D-ABC; Fellow F-ABC; and Technical Specialist S-ABC. For more information, write to P. O. Box 1123, Wausau, WI 54402; or visit the ABC Web site at http://www.criminalistics.com.

APPENDIX III
PROFESSIONAL UNIONS
AND ASSOCIATIONS

You can contact the following organizations, or visit their Web sites, to learn more about careers, job opportunities, training programs, conferences, professional certification, and other topics. Many of these organizations have student chapters. Most have branch offices throughout the United States. Contact an organization's headquarters to find out if a branch is in your area.

To learn about other local, state, regional, and national professional organizations, talk with local professionals.

Note: Web site addresses change from time to time. If you come across an address that no longer works, you may be able to find an organization's new URL by entering its name into a search engine.

CRIME SCENE AND CRIMINAL INVESTIGATION PERSONNEL

American Association of Police Polygraphists
P.O. Box 657
Waynesville, OH 45068
Phone: (888) 743-5479
Fax: (937) 488-1046
http://www.policepolygraph.org

American Deputy Sheriffs' Association
3001 Armand Street, Suite B
Monroe, LA 71201
Phone: (800) 937-7940
Fax: (318) 398-9980
http://www.deputysheriff.org

American Federation of Police and Concerned Citizens
6350 Horizon Drive
Titusville, FL 32780
Phone: (321) 264-0911
http://www.aphf.org/afp_cc.html

American Polygraph Association
P.O. Box 8037
Chattanooga, TN 37414
Phone: (800) APA-8037 or
(423) 892-3992
Fax: (423) 894-5435
http://www.polygraph.org

Association for Crime Scene Reconstruction
http://www.acsr.org

Federal Criminal Investigators Association
P.O. Box 23400
Washington, DC 20026
Phone: (800) 403-3374 or
(630) 969-8537
Fax: (800) 528-3492
http://www.fedcia.org

Federal Law Enforcement Officers Association
P.O. Box 326
Lewisberry, PA 17339
Phone: (717) 938-2300
Fax: (717) 932-2262
http://www.fleoa.org

Fraternal Order of Police
National Headquarters
701 Marriott Drive
Nashville, TN 37214
Phone: (615) 399-0900
Fax: (615) 399-0400
http://www.grandlodgefop.org

High Technology Crime Investigation Association
4021 Woodcreek Oaks Boulevard, Suite 156, PMB 209
Roseville, CA 95747
Phone: (916) 408-1751
Fax: (916) 408-7543
http://www.htcia.org

International Association for Identification
2535 Pilot Knob Road, Suite 117
Mendota Heights, MN 55120

Phone: (651) 681-8566
Fax: (651) 681-8443
http://www.theiai.org

International Association for Property and Evidence
903 North San Fernando Boulevard, Suite 4
Burbank, CA 91504
Phone: (800) 449-4273 or
(818) 846-2926
Fax: (818) 846-4543
http://www.iape.org

International Association of Arson Investigators
2151 Priest Bridge Drive, Suite 25
Crofton, MD 21114
Phone: (410) 451-3473
Fax: (410) 451-9049
http://www.firearson.com

International Association of Women Police
http://www.iawp.org

International Crime Scene Investigators Association
PMB 385
15774 South LaGrange Road
Orland Park, IL 60462
Phone: (708) 460-8082
http://www.icsia.org

International Homicide Investigators Association
10711 Spotsylvania Avenue
Fredricksburg, VA 22408

Phone: (877) 843-4442
Fax: (540) 898-5594
http://www.ihia.org

National Association of Fire Investigators
857 Tallevast Road
Sarasota, FL 34243
Phone: (877) 506-NAFI or
  (941) 359-2800
Fax: (941) 351-5849
http://www.nafi.org

National Black Police Association
3251 Mt. Pleasant Street NW, Second
  Floor
Washington, DC 20010
Phone: (202) 986-2070
Fax: (202) 986-0410
http://www.blackpolice.org

National Fire Protection Association
1 Batterymarch Park
Quincy, MA 02169
Phone: (617) 770-3000
Fax: (617) 770-0700
http://www.nfpa.org

National Troopers Coalition
http://www.ntctroopers.com

**North American Wildlife Enforcement
  Officers Association**
http://www.naweoa.org

CRIME LAB PERSONNEL

**American Academy of Forensic
  Sciences**
410 North 21st Street
Colorado Springs, CO 80904
Phone: (719) 636-1100
Fax: (719) 636-1993
http://www.aafs.org

**American College of Forensic
  Examiners**
2750 East Sunshine Street
Springfield, MO 65804
Phone: (800) 423-9737 or
  (417) 881-3818
Fax: (417) 881-4702
http://www.acfei.com

**American Society of Crime Laboratory
  Directors**
139K Technology Drive
Garner, NC 27529
Phone: (919) 773-2044

Fax: (919) 773-2602
http://www.ascld.org

**American Society of Questioned
  Document Examiners**
P.O. Box 18298
Long Beach, CA 90807
Fax: (562) 901-3378
http://www.asqde.org

**Association of Firearms and Tool Mark
  Examiners**
http://www.afte.org

**Association of Forensic DNA Analysts
  and Administrators**
http://www.afdaa.org

**Association of Forensic Quality
  Assurance Managers**
http://www.afqam.org

**International Association for
  Identification**
2535 Pilot Knob Road, Suite 117
Mendota Heights, MN 55120
Phone: (651) 681-8566
Fax: (651) 681-8443
http://www.theiai.org

**International Association of Bloodstain
  Pattern Analysts**
http://www.iabpa.org

CRIMINALISTS

**American Academy of Forensic
  Sciences**
410 North 21st Street
Colorado Springs, CO 80904
Phone: (719) 636-1100
Fax: (719) 636-1993
http://www.aafs.org

American Chemical Society
1155 16th Street NW
Washington, DC 20036
Phone: (800) 227-5558 or
  (202) 872-4600
Fax: (202) 872-4615
http://www.chemistry.org

**American College of Forensic
  Examiners**
2750 East Sunshine Street
Springfield, MO 65804
Phone: (800) 423-9737 or
  (417) 881-3818
Fax: (417) 881-4702
http://www.acfei.com

**American Society of Questioned
  Document Examiners**
P.O. Box 18298
Long Beach, CA 90807
Fax: (562) 901-3378
http://www.asqde.org

**Association for Crime Scene
  Reconstruction**
http://www.acsr.org

**Association of Firearms and Tool Mark
  Examiners**
http://www.afte.org

**Association of Forensic DNA Analysts
  and Administrators**
http://www.afdaa.org

**International Association for
  Identification**
2535 Pilot Knob Road, Suite 117
Mendota Heights, MN 55120
Phone: (651) 681-8566
Fax: (651) 681-8443
http://www.theiai.org

**International Association of Bloodstain
  Pattern Analysts**
http://www.iabpa.org

MEDICOLEGAL DEATH INVESTIGATION PERSONNEL

**American Academy of Forensic
  Sciences**
410 North 21st Street
Colorado Springs, CO 80904
Phone: (719) 636-1100
Fax: (719) 636-1993
http://www.aafs.org

**American Anthropological
  Association**
2200 Wilson Boulevard, Suite 600
Arlington, VA 22201
Phone: (703) 528-1902
Fax: (703) 528-3546
http://www.aaanet.org

**American Association of Pathologists'
  Assistants**
Rosewood Office Plaza, Suite 300N
1711 West County Road B
Roseville, MN 55113
Phone: (800) 532-AAPA or
  (651) 697-9264
http://www.pathologistsassistants.org

American Association of Physical Anthropologists
http://www.physanth.org

American Board of Medicolegal Death Investigators
1402 South Grand Boulevard
St. Louis, MO 63104
Phone: (314) 977-5970
Fax: (314) 977-5695
http://www.slu.edu/organizations/abmdi

American College of Forensic Examiners
2750 East Sunshine Street
Springfield, MO 65804
Phone: (800) 423-9737 or
    (417) 881-3818
Fax: (417) 881-4702
http://www.acfei.com

American Medical Association
515 North State Street
Chicago, IL 60610
Phone: (800) 621-8335
http://www.ama-assn.org

American Society for Clinical Pathology
33 West Monroe Street, Suite 1600
Chicago, IL 60603
Phone: (800) 267-2727 or
    (312) 541-4999
Fax: (312) 541-4998
http://www.ascp.org

International Association of Coroners and Medical Examiners
http://www.theiacme.com

College of American Pathologists
325 Waukegan Road
Northfield, IL 60093-2750
Phone: (800) 323-4040 or
    (847) 832-7000
Fax: (847) 832-8000
http://www.cap.org

International Association of Forensic Toxicologists
http://www.tiaft.org

National Association of Medical Examiners
430 Pryor Street SW
Atlanta, GA 30312
Phone: (404) 730-4781
http://www.thename.org

National Society for Histotechnology
10320 Little Patuxent Parkway, Suite 804
Columbia, MD 21044
Phone: (443) 535-4060
Fax: (443) 535-4055
http://www.nsh.org

Society of Forensic Toxicologists
1 North MacDonald Street, Suite 15
Mesa, AZ 85201
Phone: (888) 866-7638
http://www.soft-tox.org

Society of Toxicology
1821 Michael Faraday Drive, Suite 300
Reston, VA 20190
Phone: (703) 438-3115
Fax: (703) 438-3113
http://www.toxicology.org

FORENSIC EXPERTS IN ART AND MULTIMEDIA

American Academy of Forensic Sciences
410 North 21st Street
Colorado Springs, CO 80904
Phone: (719) 636-1100
Fax: (719) 636-1993
http://www.aafs.org

American College of Forensic Examiners
2750 East Sunshine Street
Springfield, MO 65804
Phone: (800) 423-9737 or
    (417) 881-3818
Fax: (417) 881-4702
http://www.acfei.com

American Musicological Society
6010 College Station
Brunswick, ME 04011
Phone: (877) 679-7648 or
    (207) 798-4243
http://www.ams-net.org

Audio Engineering Society
60 East 42nd Street, Room 2520
New York, NY 10165
Phone: (212) 661-8528
Fax: (212) 682-0477
http://www.aes.org

Demonstrative Evidence Specialists Association
http://www.desa.org

Evidence Photographers International Council
229 Peachtree Street NE, #2200

Atlanta, GA 30303
Phone: (866) 868-3742
http://www.epic-photo.org

International Association for Forensic Phonetics and Acoustics
http://www.iafpa.net

International Association for Identification
2535 Pilot Knob Road, Suite 117
Mendota Heights, MN 55120
Phone: (651) 681-8566
Fax: (651) 681-8443
http://www.theiai.org

Law Enforcement and Emergency Services Video Association
P.O. Box 547
Midlothian, TX 76065
Phone: (972) 291-5888
http://www.leva.org

National Association of Forensic Video
15235 Brand Boulevard, Suite A-110
Mission Hills, CA 91345
Phone: (818) 231-1038
Fax: (818) 838-1667
http://www.natasfv.org

Professional Photographers of America
229 Peachtree Street NE, Suite 2200
Atlanta, GA 30303
Phone: (404) 522-8600
Fax: (404) 614-6400
http://www.ppa.com

FORENSIC EXPERTS IN MEDICINE AND HEALTH

Academy of Chiropractic Orthopedists
P.O. Box 400
Norwalk, IA 50211
Phone: (515) 981-9654
Fax: (515) 981-9427
http://www.dcorthoacademy.com

Academy of Forensic and Industrial Chiropractic Consultants
http://www.aficc.com

American Academy of Forensic Sciences
410 North 21st Street
Colorado Springs, CO 80904
Phone: (719) 636-1100
Fax: (719) 636-1993
http://www.aafs.org

American Academy of Pediatrics
141 Northwest Point Boulevard
Elk Grove Village, IL 60007
Phone: (847) 434-4000
Fax: (847) 434-8000
http://www.aap.org

American Board of Forensic Odontology
410 North 21st Street
Colorado Springs, CO 80904
http://www.abfo.org

American Chiropractic Association
1701 Clarendon Boulevard
Arlington, VA 22209
Phone: (703) 276-8800
Fax: (703) 243-2593
http://www.amerchiro.org

American College of Clinical Pharmacology
3 Ellinwood Court
New Hartford, NY 13413
Phone: (315) 768-6117
Fax: (315) 768-6119
http://www.accp1.org

American College of Clinical Pharmacy
13000 West 87th Street Parkway
Lenexa, KS 66215
Phone: (913) 492-3311
Fax: (913) 492-0088
http://www.accp.com

American College of Epidemiology
1500 Sunday Drive, Suite 102
Raleigh, NC 27607
Phone: (919) 861-5573
Fax: (919) 787-4916
http://www.acepidemiology2.org

American College of Forensic Examiners
2750 East Sunshine Street
Springfield, MO 65804
Phone: (800) 423-9737 or
   (417) 881-3818
Fax: (417) 881-4702
http://www.acfei.com

American Dental Association
211 East Chicago Avenue
Chicago, IL 60611
Phone: (312) 440-2500
http://www.ada.org

American Medical Association
515 North State Street
Chicago, IL 60610
Phone: (800) 621-8335
http://www.ama-assn.org

American Nurses Association
8515 Georgia Avenue, Suite 400
Silver Spring, MD 20910
Phone: (800) 274-4262 or
   (301) 628-5000
Fax: (301) 628-5001
http://www.nursingworld.org

American Pediatric Society
3400 Research Forest Drive, Suite B7
The Woodlands, TX 77381
Phone: (281) 419-0052
Fax: (281) 419-0082
http://www.aps-spr.org

American Pharmacists Association
1100 15th Street NW, Suite 400
Washington, DC 20005
Phone: (800) 237-2742 or
   (202) 628-4410
Fax: (202) 783-2351
http://www.aphanet.org

American Professional Society on the Abuse of Children
P.O. Box 30669
Charleston, SC 29417
Phone: (877) 402-7722 or
   (843) 764-2905
Fax: (803) 753-9823
http://apsac.fmhi.usf.edu

American Society for Pharmacy Law
3085 Stevenson Drive, Suite 200
Springfield, IL 62703
Phone: (217) 529-6948
Fax: (217) 529-9120
http://www.aspl.org

American Society of Forensic Odontology
13048 North Research Boulevard, Suite B
Austin, TX 78750
http://www.asfo.org

College on Forensic Sciences
208 Syracuse Avenue
Oswego, NY 13126
Phone: (315) 343-5713
Fax: (315) 343-5714
http://www.forensic-sciences.org

Epidemiology Section
American Public Health Association
800 I Street NW
Washington, DC 20001
Phone: (202) 777-2742
Fax: (202) 777-2533
http://www.apha.org

International Association of Forensic Nurses
1517 Ritchie Highway, Suite 208
Arnold, MD 21012
Phone: (410) 626-7805
Fax: (410) 626-7804
http://www.iafn.org

International Chiropractors Association
1110 North Glebe Road, Suite 650
Arlington, VA 22201
Phone: (800) 423-4690 or
   (703) 528-5000
Fax: (703) 528-5023
http://www.chiropractic.org

National Community Pharmacists Association
100 Daingerfield Road
Alexandria, VA 22314
Phone: (800) 544-7447 or
   (703) 683-8200
Fax: (703) 683-3619
http://www.ncpanet.org

Radiological Society of North America
820 Jorie Boulevard
Oak Brook, IL 60523
Phone: (800) 381-6660 or
   (630) 571-2670
Fax: (630) 571-7837
http://www.rsna.org

Society for Pediatric Research
3400 Research Forest Drive, Suite B7
The Woodlands, TX 77381
Phone: (281) 419-0052
Fax: (281) 419-0082
http://www.aps-spr.org

FORENSIC EXPERTS IN THE NATURAL SCIENCES

American Academy of Forensic Sciences
410 North 21st Street
Colorado Springs, CO 80904
Phone: (719) 636-1100

Fax: (719) 636-1993
http://www.aafs.org

American Academy of Microbiology
1752 N Street NW
Washington, DC 20036
http://www.asm.org/Academy

**American Anthropological
Association**
2200 Wilson Boulevard, Suite 600
Arlington, VA 22201
Phone: (703) 528-1902
Fax: (703) 528-3546
http://www.aaanet.org

**American Association of Stratigraphic
Palynologists**
http://www.palynology.org

**American Board of Forensic
Entomology**
http://research.missouri.edu/entomology

American Entomological Society
1900 Benjamin Franklin Parkway
Philadelphia, PA 19103
Phone: (215) 561-3978
Fax: (215) 299-1028
http://www.ansp.org/hosted/aes

American Geological Institute
4220 King Street
Alexandria, VA 22302
Phone: (703) 379-2480
Fax: (703) 379-7563
http://www.agiweb.org

American Institute of Biological Sciences
1444 I Street NW, Suite 200
Washington, DC 20005
Phone: (202) 628-1500
Fax: (202) 628-1509
http://www.aibs.org

**American Institute of Professional
Geologists**
1400 West 122nd Avenue, Suite 250
Westminster, CO 80234
Phone: (303) 412-6205
Fax: (303) 253-9220
http://www.aipg.org

American Meteorological Society
45 Beacon Street
Boston, MA 02108
Phone: (617) 227-2425
Fax: (617) 742-8718
http://www.ametsoc.org

American Society for Microbiology
1752 N Street NW
Washington, DC 20036
Phone: (202) 737-3600
http://www.asm.org

American Society of Plant Biologists
15501 Monona Drive
Rockville, MD 20855
Phone: (301) 251-0560
Fax: (301) 279-2996
http://www.aspb.org

Botanical Society of America
P.O. Box 299
St. Louis, MO 63166
Phone: (314) 577-9566
Fax: (314) 577-9515
http://www.botany.org

Entomological Society of America
10001 Derekwood Lane, Suite 100
Lanham, MD 20706
Phone: (301) 731-4535
Fax: (301) 731-4538
http://www.entsoc.org

Geological Society of America
P.O. Box 9140
Boulder, CO 80301
Phone: (303) 357-1000
Fax: (303) 357-1070
http://www.geosociety.org

**International Society of Environmental
Forensics**
150 Fearing Street, Suite 21
Amherst, MA 01002
Phone: (413) 549-5170
Fax: (413) 549-0579
http://www.environmentalforensics.org

**National Council of Industrial
Meteorologists**
P.O. Box 721165
Norman, OK 73070
Phone: (405) 329-8707
Fax: (405) 329-8717
http://www.ncim.org

**Register of Professional
Archaeologists**
5024-R Campbell Boulevard
Baltimore, MD 21236
Phone: (410) 933-3486
Fax: (410) 931-8111
http://www.rpanet.org

Society for American Archaeology
900 Second Street NE, #12
Washington, DC 20002
Phone: (202) 789-8200
Fax: (202) 789-0284
http://www.saa.org

FORENSIC EXPERTS IN MATHEMATICS AND COMPUTER SCIENCE

**American Academy of Forensic
Sciences**
410 North 21st Street
Colorado Springs, CO 80904
Phone: (719) 636-1100
Fax: (719) 636-1993
http://www.aafs.org

American Statistical Association
732 North Washington Street
Alexandria, VA 22314
Phone: (888) 231-3473 or
(703) 684-1221
Fax: (703) 684-2037
http://www.amstat.org

**High Technology Crime Investigation
Association**
4021 Woodcreek Oaks Boulevard,
Suite 156 #209
Roseville, CA 95747
Phone: (916) 408-1751
Fax: (916) 408-7543
http://www.htcia.org

Institute of Mathematical Statistics
P.O. Box 22718
Beachwood, OH 44122
Phone: (216) 295-2340
Fax: (216) 295-5661
http://www.imstat.org

**International Association for
Identification**
2535 Pilot Knob Road, Suite 117
Mendota Heights, MN 55120
Phone: (651) 681-8566
Fax: (651) 681-8443
http://www.theiai.org

**International Association of Computer
Investigative Specialists**
P.O. Box 1728
Fairmont, WV 26555
Phone: (888) 884-2247
http://www.iacis.info

FORENSIC EXPERTS IN ENGINEERING AND CONSTRUCTION

American Academy of Environmental Engineers
130 Holiday Court, Suite 100
Annapolis, MD 21401
Phone: (410) 266-3311
Fax: (410) 266-7653
http://www.aaee.net

American Academy of Forensic Sciences
410 North 21st Street
Colorado Springs, CO 80904
Phone: (719) 636-1100
Fax: (719) 636-1993
http://www.aafs.org

American College of Forensic Examiners
2750 East Sunshine Street
Springfield, MO 65804
Phone: (800) 423-9737 or
  (417) 881-3818
Fax: (417) 881-4702
http://www.acfei.com

American Congress on Surveying and Mapping
6 Montgomery Village Avenue, Suite 403
Gaithersburg, MD 20879
Phone: (240) 632-9716
Fax: (240) 632-1321
http://www.acsm.net

American Institute of Architects
1735 New York Avenue NW
Washington, DC 20006
Phone: (800) AIA-3837 or
  (202) 626-7300
Fax: (202) 626-7547
http:///www.aia.org

American Institute of Chemical Engineers
3 Park Avenue
New York, NY 10016
Phone: (800) 242-4363 or
  (212) 591-8100
Fax: (212) 591-8888
http://www.aiche.org

American Society of Civil Engineers
1801 Alexander Bell Drive
Reston, VA 20191
Phone: (800) 548-2723 or
  (703) 295-6300
Fax: (703) 295-6222
http://www.asce.org

American Society of Professional Estimators
2525 Perimeter Place Drive, Suite 103
Nashville, TN 37214
Phone: (888) EST-MATE or
  (615) 316-9200
Fax: (615) 316-9800
http://www.aspenational.com

American Society of Safety Engineers
1800 East Oakton Street
Des Plaines, IL 60018
Phone: (847) 699-2929
Fax: (847) 768-3434
http://www.asse.org

American Institute of Contractors
P.O. Box 26334
Alexandria, VA 22314
Phone: (703) 683-4999
Fax: (703) 683-5480
http://www.aicnet.org

ASME International (American Society of Mechanical Engineers)
3 Park Avenue
New York, NY 10016
Information Central Orders/Inquiries:
P.O. Box 2300
Fairfield, NJ 07007
Phone: (800) 843-2763 or (973) 882-1167
Fax: (973) 882-1717
http://www.asme.org

Associated General Contractors of America
2300 Wilson Boulevard, Suite 400
Arlington, VA 22201
Phone: (703) 548-3118
Fax: (703) 548-3119
http://www.agc.org

Construction Specifications Institute
99 Canal Center Plaza, Suite 300
Alexandria, VA 22314
Phone: (800) 689-2900
Fax: (703) 684-8436
http://www.csinet.org

Institute of Electrical and Electronics Engineers
Corporate Office
3 Park Avenue, 17th Floor
New York, NY 10016
Phone: (212) 419-7900
Fax: (212) 752-4929
http://www.ieee.org

International Association of Accident Reconstruction Specialists
P.O. Box 534
Grand Ledge, MI 48837
Phone: (517) 622-3135
http://www.iaars.org

National Academy of Forensic Engineers
174 Brady Avenue
Hawthorne, NY 10532
Phone: (866) NAF-EORG
Fax: (877) 741-0633
http://www.nafe.org

National Association of Professional Accident Reconstruction Specialists
P.O. Box 65
Brandywine, MD 20613
Phone: (301) 843-0048
http://www.napars.org

National Association of Traffic Accident Reconstructionists and Investigators
P.O. Box 2588
West Chester, PA 19382
Phone: (610) 696-1919
http://www.natari.org

National Society of Professional Engineers
1420 King Street
Alexandria, VA 22314
Phone: (703) 684-2800
Fax: (703) 836-4875
http://www.nspe.org

National Society of Professional Surveyors
6 Montgomery Village Avenue, Suite 403
Gaithersburg, MD 20879
Phone: (240) 632-9716
Fax: (240) 632-1321
http://www.nspsmo.org

SAE International (Society of Automotive Engineers)
400 Commonwealth Drive
Warrendale, PA 15096
Phone: (877) 606-7323 or
  (724) 776-4841
Fax: (724) 776-0790
http://www.sae.org

Society of Accident Reconstructionists
4891 Independence Street, Suite 140
Wheat Ridge, CO 80033
Phone: (303) 403-9045
Fax: (303) 403-9401
http://www.accidentreconstruction.com/
  soar

**Society of Hispanic Professional
Engineers**
5400 East Olympic Boulevard, Suite 210
Los Angeles, CA 90022
Phone: (323) 725-3970
Fax: (323) 725-0316
http://oneshpe.shpe.org

Society of Women Engineers
230 East Ohio Street, Suite 400
Chicago, IL 60611
Phone: (312) 596-5223
Fax: (312) 596-5252
http://www.swe.org

FORENSIC EXPERTS IN THE BEHAVIORAL SCIENCES

Academy of Criminal Justice Sciences
P.O. Box 960
Greenbelt, MD 20768-0960
Phone: (800) 757-2257 or (301) 446-6300
Fax: (301) 446-2819
http://www.acjs.org

**American Academy of Forensic
Psychology**
http://www.aafp.ws

**American Academy of Forensic
Sciences**
410 North 21st Street
Colorado Springs, CO 80904
Phone: (719) 636-1100
Fax: (719) 636-1993
http://www.aafs.org

**American Academy of Psychiatry and
the Law**
One Regency Drive
P.O. Box 30
Bloomfield, CT 06002
Phone: (800) 331-1389 or
(860) 242-5450
Fax: (860) 286-0787
http://www.aapl.org

American Board of Vocational Experts
3540 Soquel Avenue, Suite A
Santa Cruz, CA 95062
Phone: (831) 464-4890
Fax: (831) 576-1417
http://www.abve.net

American College of Forensic Examiners
2750 East Sunshine Street
Springfield, MO 65804

Phone: (800) 423-9737 or (417) 881-3818
Fax: (417) 881-4702
http://www.acfei.com

**American College of Forensic
Psychiatry**
P.O. Box 5870
Balboa Island, California 92662
Phone: (949) 673-7773
Fax: (949) 673-7710
http://www.forensicpsychonline.com

**American College of Forensic
Psychology**
P.O. Box 5870
Balboa Island, California 92662
Phone: (949) 673-7773
Fax: (949) 673-7710
http://www.forensicpsychology.org

**American Council of Hypnotist
Examiners**
700 South Central Avenue
Glendale, CA 91204
Phone: (818) 242-1159
Fax: (818) 247-9379
http://www.hypnotistexaminers.org

American Medical Association
515 North State Street
Chicago, IL 60610
Phone: (800) 621-8335
http://www.ama-assn.org

American Psychiatric Association
1000 Wilson Boulevard, Suite 1825
Arlington, VA 22209
Phone: (703) 907-7300
http://www.psych.org

American Psychological Association
750 First Street NE
Washington, DC 20002
Phone: (800) 374-2721 or (202) 336-5500
http://www.apa.org

**American Rehabilitation Economics
Association**
127 North Westwind Drive
El Cajon, CA 92020
Phone: (800) 317-2732
http://www.a-r-e-a.org

American Society of Criminology
1314 Kinnear Road, Suite 212
Columbus, Ohio 43212
Phone: (614) 292-9207
Fax: (614) 292-6767
http://www.asc41.com

American Sociological Association
1307 New York Avenue NW, Suite 700
Washington, DC 20005
Phone: (202) 383-9005
Fax: (202) 638-0882
TDD: (202) 638-0981
http://www.asanet.org

American-Psychology Law Society
http://www.ap-ls.org

**International Association of
Rehabilitation Professionals**
1926 Waukegan Road, Suite 1
Glenview, IL 60025
Phone: (847) 657-6964
Fax: (847) 657-6963
http://www.rehabpro.org

National Association of Social Workers
750 First Street NE, Suite 700
Washington, DC 20002
Phone: (202) 408-8600
http://www.naswdc.org

National Guild of Hypnotists
P.O. Box 308
Merrimack, NH 03054
Phone: (603) 429-9438
Fax: (603) 424-8066
http://www.ngh.net

**National Organization of Forensic
Social Work**
460 Smith Street, Suite K
Middletown, CT 06457
Phone: (860) 613-0254
Fax: (860) 613-1650
http://www.nofsw.org

Western Society of Criminology
Criminology and Criminal Justice
Division
Mark O. Hatfield School of Government
Portland State University
P.O. Box 751
Portland, OR 97207
http://www.sonoma.edu/cja/wsc

FORENSIC EXPERTS IN BUSINESS

**American Academy of Economic and
Financial Experts**
http://www.aaefe.org

American Academy of Forensic Sciences
410 North 21st Street
Colorado Springs, CO 80904

Phone: (719) 636-1100
Fax: (719) 636-1993
http://www.aafs.org

American College of Forensic Examiners
2750 East Sunshine Street
Springfield, MO 65804
Phone: (800) 423-9737 or (417) 881-3818
Fax: (417) 881-4702
http://www.acfei.com

American Economic Association
2014 Broadway, Suite 305
Nashville, TN 37203
Phone: (615) 322-2595
Fax: (615) 343-7590
http://www.vanderbilt.edu/AEA

American Institute of Certified Public Accountants
1211 Avenue of the Americas
New York, NY 10036
Phone: (212) 596-6200
http://www.aicpa.org

American Rehabilitation Economics Association
127 North Westwind Drive
El Cajon, CA 92020
Phone: (800) 317-2732
Fax: (619) 593-9989
http://www.a-r-e-a.org

Association of Certified Fraud Examiners
716 West Avenue
Austin, TX 78701
Phone: (800) 245-3321 or (512) 478-9000
Fax: (512) 478-9297
http://www.acfe.com

Association of Certified Fraud Specialists
P.O. Box 348777
Sacramento, CA 95834
Phone: (866) HEY-ACFS or (916) 419-6319
Fax: (916) 419-6318
http://www.acfsnet.org

Forensic Accountants Society of North America
4248 Park Glen Road
Minneapolis, MN 55416
Phone: (952) 928-4668
Fax: (952) 929-1318
http://www.fasna.org

Institute of Internal Auditors
247 Maitland Avenue
Altamonte Springs, FL 32701
Phone: (407) 937-1100
Fax: (407) 937-1101
http://www.theiia.org

National Association of Certified Valuation Analysts
1111 Brickyard Road, Suite 200
Salt Lake City, UT 84106
Phone: (801) 486-0600
Fax: (801) 486-7500
http://www.nacva.com

National Association of Forensic Economics
P.O. Box 394
Mount Union, PA 17066
Phone: (866) 370-6233 or (814) 542-3253
http://nafe.net

Association of Fraud Investigators
2519 NW 23rd Street, Suite 204
Oklahoma City, OK 73107
Phone: (405) 833-2327
http://www.nafraud.com

FORENSIC EXPERTS IN LANGUAGE

International Association for Forensic Phonetics and Acoustics
http://www.iafpa.net

International Association of Forensic Linguists
http://www.iafl.org

Linguistic Society of America
1325 18th Street NW, Suite 211
Washington, DC 20036
Phone: (202) 835-1714
Fax: (202) 835-1717
http://www.lsadc.org

JURISPRUDENCE EXPERTS

American Academy of Forensic Sciences
410 North 21st Street
Colorado Springs, CO 80904
Phone: (719) 636-1100
Fax: (719) 636-1993
http://www.aafs.org

American Bar Association
321 North Clark Street

Chicago, IL 60610
Phone: (800) 285-2221 or (312) 988-5000
http://www.abanet.org

American College of Forensic Examiners
2750 East Sunshine Street
Springfield, MO 65804
Phone: (800) 423-9737 or (417) 881-3818
Fax: (417) 881-4702
http://www.acfei.com

American College of Trial Lawyers
19900 MacArthur Boulevard
Suite 610
Irvine, CA 92612
Phone: (949) 752-1801
Fax: (949) 752-1674
http://www.actl.com

American Judges Association
300 Newport Avenue
Williamsburg, VA 23185
Phone: (757) 259-1841
Fax: (757) 259-1520
http://aja.ncsc.dni.us

American Association for Justice
1050 31st Street NW
Washington, DC 20007
Phone: (800) 424-2725 or (202) 965-3500
http://www.justice.org

DRI
150 North Michigan Avenue
Suite 300
Chicago, IL 60601
Phone: (312) 795-1101
Fax: (312) 795-0747 or (312) 795-0749
http://www.dri.org

Federal Bar Association
2011 Crystal Drive, Suite 400
Arlington, VA 22202
Phone: (703) 682-7000
Fax: (703) 682-7001
http://www.fedbar.org

National Association of Criminal Defense Lawyers
1150 18th Street NW, Suite 950
Washington, DC 20036
Phone: (202) 872-8600
Fax: (202) 872-8690
http://www.nacdl.org

**National Association of Women
Lawyers**
American Bar Center, MS 15.2
321 North Clark Street
Chicago, IL 60610
Phone: (312) 988-6186
Fax: (312) 988-5491
http://www.abanet.org/nawl

**National Black Prosecutors
Association**
1507 East 53rd Street, Suite 108
Chicago, IL 60615
Phone: (877) 588-1656
http://www.blackprosecutors.org

National Criminal Justice Association
720 Seventh Street NW, Third Floor
Washington, DC 20001
Phone: (202) 628-8550
Fax: (202) 628-0080
http://www.ncja.org

**National District Attorneys
Association**
99 Canal Center Plaza, Suite 510
Alexandria, VA 22314
Phone: (703) 549-9222
Fax: (703) 836-3195
http://www.ndaa.org

**National Hispanic Prosecutors
Association**
P.O. Box 4856
Chicago, IL 60680
http://www.hispanicprosecutors.org

National Lawyers Association
17201 East 40 Highway, Suite 207
Independence, MO 64055
Phone: (800) 471-2994
Fax: (816) 229-8425
http://www.nla.org

**National Legal Aid and Defenders
Association**
1140 Connecticut Avenue NW,
Suite 900
Washington, DC 20036
Phone: (202) 452-0620
Fax: (202) 872-1031
http://www.nlada.org

Section of Litigation
American Bar Association
Phone: (312) 988-5662
http://www.abanet.org/litigation

FORENSIC SCIENCE, EDUCATORS, RESEARCHERS, AND REPORTERS

**American Academy of Forensic
Sciences**
410 North 21st Street
Colorado Springs, CO 80904
Phone: (719) 636-1100
Fax: (719) 636-1993
http://www.aafs.org

**American Academy of Psychiatry and
the Law**
One Regency Drive
P.O. Box 30
Bloomfield, CT 06002
Phone: (800) 331-1389 or
(860) 242-5450
Fax: (860) 286-0787
http://www.aapl.org

**American Association of University
Professors**
1012 14th Street NW, Suite 500
Washington, DC 20005
Phone: (202) 737-5900
Fax: (202) 737-5526
http://www.aaup.org

**American Board of Forensic
Entomology**
http://www.research.missouri.edu/
entomology

American Chemical Society
1155 16th Street NW
Washington, DC 20036
Phone: (800) 227-5558 or
(202) 872-4600
Fax: (202) 872-4615
http://www.chemistry.org

**American College of Forensic
Examiners**
2750 East Sunshine Street
Springfield, MO 65804
Phone: (800) 423-9737 or
(417) 881-3818
Fax: (417) 881-4702
http://www.acfei.com

American Federation of Teachers
555 New Jersey Avenue NW
Washington, DC 20001
Phone: (202) 879-4400
http://www.aft.org

**American Society for Training and
Development**
1640 King Street, Box 1443
Alexandria, VA 22313
Phone: (703) 683-8100
Fax: (703) 683-8103
http://www.astd.org

**American Society of Journalists and
Authors**
1501 Broadway, Suite 302
New York, NY 10036
Phone: (212) 997-0947
Fax: (212) 937-2315
http://www.asja.org

Asian American Journalists Association
1182 Market Street, Suite 320
San Francisco, CA 94102
Phone: (415) 346-2051
Fax: (415) 346-6343
http://www.aaja.org

**Association for Women in
Communications**
3337 Duke Street
Alexandria, VA 22314
Phone: (703) 370-7436
Fax: (703) 370-7437
http://www.womcom.org

**Association of Firearms and Tool Mark
Examiners**
http://www.afte.org

Council on Forensic Science Education
http://www.criminology.fsu.edu/COFSE/
default.html

Criminal Justice Journalists
720 Seventh Street NW, Third Floor
Washington, DC 20001
Phone: (202) 448-1717
http://reporters.net/cjj

Investigative Reporters and Editors
138 Neff Annex
Missouri School of Journalism
Columbia, MO 65211
Phone: (573) 882-2042
Fax: (573) 882-5431
http://www.ire.org

National Association of Scholars
22 Witherspoon Street, Second Floor
Princeton, NJ 08542
Phone: (609) 683-7878
http://www.nas.org

National Education Association
1201 16th Street NW
Washington, DC 20036
Phone: (202) 833-4000
Fax: (202) 822-7974
http://www.nea.org

**Radio-Television News Directors
    Association**
1600 K Street NW, Suite 700

Washington, DC 20006
Phone: (202) 659-6510
Fax: (202) 223-4007
http://www.rtnda.org

Society of Forensic Toxicologists
1 North MacDonald Street, Suite 15
Mesa, AZ 85201
Phone: (888) 866-7638
http://www.soft-tox.org

Society of Professional Journalists
Eugene S. Pulliam National Journalism
    Center
3909 North Meridian Street
Indianapolis, IN 46208
Phone: (317) 927-8000
Fax: (317) 920-4789
http://www.spj.org

APPENDIX IV
RESOURCES ON THE WORLD WIDE WEB

In this appendix, you will find a listing of Web sites that can help you learn more about the occupations that were profiled in this book. In addition, you will find some Web resources that offer career and job search information.

Note: All Web site addresses were current at the time this book was written. If a URL is no longer valid, enter the Web page title or the name of the organization or individual into a search engine to find the new address.

GENERAL INFORMATION

Bureau of Justice Statistics
U.S. Department of Justice
http://www.ojp.usdoj.gov/bjs

Crime Spider
http://www.crimespider.com

National Criminal Justice Reference Service
http://www.ncjrs.org

National Institute of Justice
U.S. Department of Justice
http://www.ojp.usdoj.gov/nij

Office of Justice Programs
U.S. Department of Justice
http://www.ojp.usdoj.gov

Prentice Hall's Cybrary
by Frank Schmalleger, Ph.D.
http://talkjustice.com/cybrary.asp

U.S. Department of Homeland Security
http://www.dhs.gov

U.S. Department of Justice
http://www.usdoj.gov

Wikipedia
http://www.wikipedia.org

CAREER AND JOB INFORMATION

CareerJournal.com
The *Wall Street Journal* Executive Career Site
http://www.careerjournal.com

CareerOneStop
http://www.jobbankinfo.org

Career Prospects in Virginia
http://www.ccps.virginia.edu/career_prospects

ISEEK
http://www.iseek.org

Monster
http://www.monster.com

Occupational Employment Statistics
U.S. Bureau of Labor Statistics
http://www.bls.gov/oes

Occupational Outlook Handbook
U.S. Bureau of Labor Statistics
http://www.bls.gov/oco

O*NET OnLine
http://online.onetcenter.org

USA Jobs
U.S. Office of Personnel Management
http://www.usajobs.opm.gov

FORENSIC SCIENCE—GENERAL INFORMATION

All-About-Forensic-Science.Com
http://www.all-about-forensic-science.com

Anil Aggrawal's Websites
http://www.geradts.com/anil/index.html

Canadian Society of Forensic Science
http://www.csfs.ca

Criminal Justice Resources: Forensic Science
by Jon Harrison
http://www.lib.msu.edu/harris23/crimjust/forsci.htm

crimeline
crime222.net
http://www.crime222.net/forensic_history/index.htm

Dr. Zeno's Forensic Site
by Dr. Zeno Geradts
http://forensic.to

Forensic-Evidence.com
http://www.forensic-evidence.com

Forensic Science Resources
by R. Scott Carpenter
http://www.tncrimlaw.com/forensic

Forensic Science Resources on the Internet
by Cynthia Holt
http://www.istl.org/03-spring/internet.html

History of Forensic Science
by Online Learning Haven
http://www.learninghaven.com/articles/history-of-forensic-science.html

In the Spotlight: Forensic Science
http://www.ncjrs.gov/spotlight/forensic/summary.html

Internet Resources for Medicolegal Forensics
http://www.apsu.edu/oconnort/3210/3210links.htm

NecroSearch International
http://www.necrosearch.org

Reddy's Forensic Page
by Reddy P. Chamakura
http://www.forensicpage.com

Young Forensic Scientists Forum
http://www.aafs.org/yfsf/index.htm

ACCIDENT RECONSTRUCTION SPECIALIST

National Highway Traffic Safety Administration
http://www.nhtsa.dot.gov

Traffic Accident Reconstruction Origin
http://www.tarorigin.com

Web Site Links
by the Accreditation Commission for Traffic Accident Reconstruction
http://www.actar.org/links.html

BLOODSTAIN PATTERN ANALYST

Bloodstain Pattern Analysis Tutorial
by J. Slemko Forensic Consulting
http://www.bloodspatter.com/BPATutorial.htm

Carolina Forensics
http://www.carolinaforensics.org

Scientific Working Group on Bloodstain Pattern Analysis
http://www.swgstain.org

CHILD ABUSE PEDIATRICIAN

American College of Pediatricians
http://acpeds.org

ChildAbuseMD.com
http://www.childabusemd.com

National Children's Advocacy Center
http://www.nationalcac.org

Ray Helfer Society
http://helfersociety.org

COMPUTER FORENSICS SPECIALIST

Computer Forensics Inc.
http://www.forensics.com

Computer Forensics World
http://www.computerforensicsworld.com

Computer Crime and Intellectual Property Section (U.S. Department of Justice)
www.cybercrime.gov

File System Forensic Analysis
by Brian Carrier
http://www.digital-evidence.org

Scientific Working Group on Digital Evidence
http://swgde.org

CONSTRUCTION FORENSICS EXPERT

Construction Claims Online
http://www.constructionclaims.com

Construction Trends.com
http://www.constructiontrends.com

PE Construction Weblog
http://communicators.typepad.com/peconstruction

The Construction Contractor's Digest
http://www.contractorsblog.com

CORONER

Industry Links
by International Association of Coroners and Medical Examiners
http://theiacme.com/links.html

Los Angeles County Department of Coroner
http://coroner.co.la.ca.us/htm/Coroner_Home.htm

Medical Examiner and Coroner Information Sharing Program
http://www.cdc.gov/epo/dphsi/mecisp/index.htm

Pan American Coroners Office
http://coronersweb.cloudmakers.org

CRIME LAB DIRECTOR

ASCLD/LAB-Legacy
http://www.ascld-lab.org/legacy/indexlegacy.html

Crime Lab Project
http://www.crimelabproject.com

Ethics in Science
http://www.chem.vt.edu/chem-ed/ethics/index.html

Kruglick's Forensic Resource and Criminal Law Search Site
http://www.bioforensics.com/kruglaw/forensic.htm

Laboratories Accredited by ASCLD/LAB
http://www.ascld-lab.org/legacy/aslablegacylaboratories.html

CRIME REPORTER

Caroline's Crime Scene Blog
by Caroline Lowe
http://wcco.com/crimesceneblog

A Journalist's Guide to the Internet
by Christopher Callahan
http://reporter.umd.edu

JournalismJobs.com
http://www.journalismjobs.com

Poynter Online
http://www.poynter.org

USC Annenberg Institute for Justice and Journalism
http://www.justicejournalism.org

CRIME SCENE INVESTIGATOR

Crime Scene Investigations
by M/Sgt. Hayden B. Baldwin, ISP
http://www.feinc.net/cs-inv-p.htm

The Crime Scene
by Katherine Ramsland, Crime Library
http://www.crimelibrary.com/criminal_mind/forensics/crimescene/1.html

CRIME SCENE SUPERVISOR

Crime Scene Evidence Files
http://www.crimescene.com

"How Crime Scene Investigation Works"
by Julia Layton, Howstuffworks.com
http://science.howstuffworks.com/csi.htm

ICSIA Useful Links
http://www.icsia.org/usefulllinks.htm

CRIMINAL INVESTIGATOR

Crime and Clues
http://www.crimeandclues.com

Crime Library
http://www.crimelibrary.com

Federal Bureau of Investigation
http://www.fbi.gov

True Crime and Justice
by Kari Sable Burns
http://www.karisable.com/crime.htm

CRIMINALIST

American Board of Criminalistics
http://www.criminalistics.com

**American Society for Clinical
Laboratory Science**
http://www.ascls.org

**An Introduction to Criminalistics and
Physical Evidence**
by Dr. Tom O'Connor
http://faculty.ncwc.edu/toconnor/315/
315lect02.htm

Dr. Henry Lee
http://www.drhenrylee.com

FBI Laboratory
http://www.fbi.gov/hq/lab/labhome.htm

Forensic Web Links/FAQ's
by Northeastern Association of Forensic
Scientists
http://www.neafs.org/faqs.htm

Links
by National Center for Forensic Science
http://ncfs.ucf.edu/links.html

CRIMINOLOGIST

Academy of Criminal Justice Sciences
http://www.acjs.org

Criminal Justice Links
by Cecil Greek
http://www.criminology.fsu.edu/cjlinks

Criminal Justice Mega Links
by Dr. Tom O'Connor
http://www.apsu.edu/oconnort

DNA ANALYST

DNA Resource.com
http://www.dnaresource.com

The President's DNA Initiative
http://www.dna.gov

ENVIRONMENTAL FORENSICS EXPERT

EcoWorld
http://www.ecoworld.com

**EnviroNetBase: Environmental
Resources Online**
http://www.environetbase.com

Environmental Forensics
by Environmental Health Sciences
Center, Oregon State University
http://www.ehsc.orst.edu/outreach/
forensics.html

EVIDENCE CUSTODIAN

List-O-Links
by International Association for Property
and Evidence
http://www.iape.org/Links/index.htm

Property-Evidence Unit
Washington County Sheriff's Office
http://www.co.washington.or.us/sheriff/
investig/evidence.htm

The Property Unit Manager
by Bob Huestis
http://www.capet.com/property_unit_
manager.htm

FINGERPRINT TECHNICIAN

Fingerprint Identification
by Federal Bureau of Investigation
http://www.fbi.gov/hq/cjisd/ident.htm

**Michele Triplett's Fingerprint
Dictionary**
http://www.fprints.nwlean.net

FIRE INVESTIGATOR

Firehouse.com
http://www.firehouse.com

InterFIRE Online
http://www.interfire.org

**National Association of State Fire
Marshals**
http://www.firemarshals.org

U.S. Fire Administration
http://www.usfa.dhs.gov

FIREARMS EXAMINER

ATF Laboratories
http://www.atf.gov/labs/index.htm

Firearms ID.com
http://www.firearmsid.com

**Scientific Working Group for Firearms
and Toolmarks**
http://www.swggun.org

**U.S. Bureau of Alcohol, Tobacco,
Firearms and Explosives**
http://www.atf.gov

FORENSIC ACCOUNTANT

Forensic Accounting Demystified
by Alan Zysman
http://www.forensicaccountant.com

Forensic Accounting Information
by Florida Atlantic University
http://www.forensic-accounting-
information.com

Start Here. Go Places.com
by American Institute of Certified Public
Accountants
http://www.startheregoplaces.com

FORENSIC ANTHROPOLOGIST

**American Board of Forensic
Anthropology**
http://www.csuchico.edu/anth/ABFA

**Biological Anthropology Resources on
the World Wide Web**
by Karen B. Supak
http://www.geocities.com/CapeCanaveral/
Lab/9893/index.html

ForensicAnthro.com
http://www.forensicanthro.com

Forensic Anthropology
http://library.med.utah.edu/kw/osteo/
forensics/index.html

Forensic Sciences
by Kathy Reichs
http://www.kathyreichs.com/forensics.htm

FORENSIC ARCHAEOLOGIST

Archaeology Fieldwork.com
http://www.archaeologyfieldwork.com

**National Park Service Archeology
Program**
http://www.cr.nps.gov/archeology

The Archaeology Channel
http://www.archaeologychannel.org

FORENSIC ARCHITECT

Careers in Architecture
by American Institute of Architects
http://www.aia.org/ed_careers

e-Architect
http://www.e-architect.com

FORENSIC ARTIST

Forensic Faces Institute
http://www.forensicart.org

Neville's Forensic Art World
http://www.forensicartist.com

**Orange County Sheriff's Office
    Forensic Artist**
by Detective Stephen A. Fusco
http://www.ocsoartist.com

FORENSIC AUDIO EXAMINER

Owl Investigations
http://www.owlinvestigations.com

Team Audio
http://www.audiorestoration.com

FORENSIC BIOLOGIST

**American Institute of Biological
    Sciences**
http://www.aibs.org

Forensic Biology Section
Georgia Bureau of Investigation Division
    of Forensic Science
http://www.state.ga.us/gbi/fsdna.html

FORENSIC BOTANIST

American Society of Plant Taxonomists
http://www.aspt.net

Forensic Botany
by Jennifer Van Dommelen
http://myweb.dal.ca/jvandomm/
    forensicbotany

**The Virtual Library of Botany/Plant
    Biology**
http://www.ou.edu/cas/botany-micro/
    www-vl

FORENSIC CHEMIST

**International Association for Chemical
    Testing**
http://www.iactonline.org

World Wide Resources in Chemistry
by Hiram College Library
http://library.hiram.edu/sub_chem.htm

FORENSIC CHIROPRACTIC EXPERT

College on Forensic Sciences
http://www.forensic-sciences.org/index.
    htm

**The Chiropractic Resource
    Organization**
http://www.chiro.org

FORENSIC CONSULTANT

Expert Communications
http://www.expertcommunications.com

Expert Witness Marketing and Training
http://expertcommunications.blogspot.
    com

ExpertPages
http://expertpages.com

Forensic Expert Witness Association
http://www.forensic.org

The Forensic Panel
http://forensicpanel.com

ForensisGroup
http://www.forensisgroup.com

FORENSIC DRUG CHEMIST

Alcohol and Drug Information
by U.S. Substance Abuse and Mental
    Health Services Administration
http://ncadi.samhsa.gov

**U.S. Drug Enforcement
    Administration**
http://www.dea.gov

FORENSIC ECONOMIST

Forensic Economics Database
by Thomas R. Ireland
http://www.denison.edu/economics/
    forensics

**Resources for Economists on the
    Internet (RFE)**
http://www.aeaweb.org/RFE

The Essential Economic Resource
by Don Frankenfeld
http://www.frankenfeld.com

FORENSIC ENGINEER

A Sightseer's Guide to Engineering
http://www.engineeringsights.org

Junior Engineering Technical Society
http://www.jets.org

Links
by National Academy of Forensic
    Engineers
http://www.nafe.org/link.html

**National Council of Examiners for
    Engineering and Surveying**
http://www.ncees.org

Progressive Engineer Online
http://www.progressiveengineer.com

**Society of Forensic Engineers and
    Scientists**
http://www.forensic-society.org

FORENSIC ENTOMOLOGIST

Forensic Entomology
by Stephen W. Bullington, Ph.D.
http://www.forensic-ent.com

Forensic Entomology.com
http://www.forensic-entomology.com

Insect Investigations
http://www.insectinvestigations.com

**Iowa State Entomology Index of
    Internet Resources**
http://www.ent.iastate.edu/List

FORENSIC EPIDEMIOLOGIST

EpiMonitor.Net
http://www.epimonitor.net

Forensic Epidemiology
by Public Health Law Clearinghouse
http://www.publichealthlaw.info/
    forensicepi-more.htm

**The WWW Virtual Library: Medicine
    and Health: Epidemiology**
http://www.epibiostat.ucsf.edu/epidem/
    epidem.html

U.S. Centers for Disease Control and Prevention
http://www.cdc.gov

FORENSIC GEOLOGIST

American Geophysical Union
http://www.agu.org

Earth Science World—Gateway to the Geosciences
http://www.earthscienceworld.org/index.html

National Association of State Boards of Geology
http://www.asbog.org

Raymond C. Murray, Forensic Geologist
http://www.forensicgeology.net

U.S. Geological Survey
http://www.usgs.gov

FORENSIC GRAPHICS SPECIALIST

The Art Engineering Company
http://members.aol.com/macbloom/index.html

Graphic Artists Guild
http://www.gag.org

Trial Exhibits
http://www.demonstrativeevidence.net

FORENSIC HYPNOTIST

American Society of Clinical Hypnosis
http://www.asch.net

"Forensic Hypnosis"
by Katherine Ramsland, Crime Library
http://www.crimelibrary.com/forensics/hypnosis

"How Hypnosis Works"
by Tom Harris, Howstuffworks.com
http://www.howstuffworks.com/hypnosis.htm

Hypnosis Online.com
http://hypnosisonline.com

Marx Howell and Associates
http://www.marxhowell.com

FORENSIC LINGUIST

Forensic Linguistics Institute
http://www.thetext.co.uk

Forensic Linguistics Project
Hofstra University
http://www.hofstra.edu/Academics/HCLAS/FLP/index_FLP.cfm

Language and Law.org
by Peter Tiersma
http://www.languageandlaw.org

The Linguist List
http://linguistlist.org

Roger W. Shuy
http://rogershuy.com

FORENSIC MEDICAL CONSULTANT

Accreditation Council for Graduate Medical Education
http://www.acgme.org

American Board of Medical Specialties
http://www.abms.org

American Osteopathic Association
http://www.osteopathic.org

Federation of State Medical Boards
http://www.fsmb.org

Forensic Medicine Jobs
http://www.forensicmedicinejobs.com

Medical Expert Witness and Consultant Directory
http://expertpages.com/medical.htm

The Student Doctor Network
http://www.studentdoctor.net

FORENSIC METEOROLOGIST

National Weather Association
http://www.nwas.org

National Weather Service
National Oceanic and Atmospheric Administration
http://www.nws.noaa.gov

Internet weather Web site, links, and bookmarks
http://www.sbcomputer.com/great_weather_links.html

FORENSIC MICROBIOLOGIST

Microbes.info: The Microbiology Information Portal
http://www.microbes.info

Microbeworld
http://www.microbeworld.org

"Microbial Forensics"
by Abigail A. Salyers
http://www.actionbioscience.org/newfrontiers/salyerspaper.html

Microbiology: A Resource for Research Microbiologists
http://www.horizonpress.com/gateway/micro.html

FORENSIC MUSICOLOGIST

J. Marshall Bevil, Ph.D.
http://home.earthlink.net/~llywarch/forns.html.htm

Recorded Sound Reference Center
The Library of Congress
http://www.loc.gov/rr/record

U.S. Copyright Office
http://www.copyright.gov

FORENSIC NURSE

Discover Nursing.com
http://www.discovernursing.com

Forensictrak
http://www.forensictrak.com

Legal Nurse Consultants, Nursing Entrepreneurs
http://www.legalnursingconsultant.org

FORENSIC ODONTOLOGIST

Bureau of Legal Dentistry
http://www.boldlab.org

Forensic Dentistry Online
http://www.forensicdentistry.online.org

FORENSIC PALYNOLOGIST

Forensic Botany: Palynology
by Jennifer Van Dommelen

http://myweb.dal.ca/jvandomm/
   forensicbotany/palynology.html

Forensic Palynology
by Crime and Clues
http://www.crimeandclues.com/
   palynology.htm

Palynology at the University of Arizona
by Dr. Owen Davis
http://www.geo.arizona.edu/palynology/
   index.html

FORENSIC PATHOLOGIST

**Anatomic Pathology: Welcome to the
   Morgue**
http://www.geocities.com/Tokyo/
   Island/6653/morgue.htm

**The Internet Pathology Laboratory for
   Medical Education**
by Edward C. Klatt, M.D.
http://library.med.utah.edu/WebPath/
   webpath.html

PathMax: Forensic Pathology Links
by Shawn E. Cowper
http://www.pathmax.com/forensiclink.html

FORENSIC PATHOLOGY TECHNICIAN

Clark County Coroner
http://www.co.clark.nv.us/CORONER/
   unid.htm

"How Autopsies Work"
by Robert Valdes, Howstuffworks.com
http://health.howstuffworks.com/
   autopsy1.htm

FORENSIC PHARMACIST

**American Association of Colleges of
   Pharmacy**
http://www.aacp.org

Rx Career Center
http://www.rxcareercenter.com

What is a Forensic Pharmacist?
by Peter D. Anderson, Pharm.D.
http://hometown.aol.com/PAnder7291/
   forensic-pharmacist.index.html

FORENSIC PHONETICIAN

Dr. Helen Fraser
http://www.one.edu.au/lcl/staff/hfraser.php

**International Phonetic Association
   Links**
http://www.arts.gla.ac.uk/IPA/links.html

FORENSIC PHOTOGRAPHER

Crime Scene and Evidence Photography
http://www.crime-scene-investigator.net/
   csi-photo.html

Crime Scene Photography 1.01
http://www.brazoria-county.com/sheriff/
   id/photography

FORENSIC PSYCHIATRIST

Forensic Psychiatry On-Line
http://www.priory.com/forpsy.htm

Forensic Psychiatry Resource Page
by James F. Hooper, M.D., DFAPA
http://bama.ua.edu/~jhooper

**International Academy of Law and
   Mental Health**
http://www.ialmh.org

FORENSIC PSYCHOLOGIST

All About Forensic Psychology
http://www.all-about-forensic-
   psychology.com

American Board of Forensic Psychology
http://www.abfp.com

Forensic Psychology
http://www.psychologyinfo.com/forensic

Psych Web
by Russ Dewey
http://www.psywww.com/index.html

**Psychology and Law Resources for
   Students**
by American Psychology-Law Society
http://www.ap-ls.org/students/
   careersIndex.html

FORENSIC RADIOLOGIST

American College of Radiology
http://www.acr.org

**American Association for Women
   Radiologists**
http://www.aawr.org

Radiology Info
http://www.radiologyinfo.org

FORENSIC REHABILITATION CONSULTANT

**American Rehabilitation Counseling
   Association**
http://www.arcaweb.org

Forensic Special Interest Section
International Association of
   Rehabilitation Professionals
http://www.rehabpro.org/forensics_
   frameset.html

Vocational Diagnostics Inc.
http://www.legaldamages.com

**World Wide Web Resources for
   Rehabilitation Counselors**
http://luna.cas.usf.edu/~rasch

FORENSIC SCIENCE INSTRUCTOR

**Chronicle Careers: Jobs in Higher
   Education**
http://chronicle.com/jobs

HigherEdJobs.com
http://www.higheredjobs.com

PhDs.org
http://www.phds.org

Postdoc Jobs.com
http://www.postdocjobs.com

Preparing Future Faculty Program
http://www.preparing-faculty.org

FORENSIC SCIENCE RESEARCHER

Forensic Science Initiative
http://www.wvu.edu/~forsci/index.htm

International Forensic Research Institute
http://www.ifri.fiu.edu

National Center for Forensic Science
http://ncfs.ucf.edu

FORENSIC SCULPTOR

Forensic Sculpting
by Seth Wolfson
http://www.forensicsculpting.com

International Sculptor Center
http://www.sculpture.org

Forensic Art
by Karen T. Taylor
http://www.karenttaylor.com/
FORENSIChome.html

Sculptural Forensics
by George C. Vail
http://www.sculpturalforensics.com

FORENSIC SEROLOGIST

Forensic Serology
by Dr. Tom O'Connor
http://faculty.ncwc.edu/toconnor/425/
425lect13.htm

FORENSIC SOCIAL WORKER

Association of Social Work Boards
http://www.aswb.org

Help Starts Here
by National Association of Social
Workers
http://www.helpstartshere.org

FORENSIC STATISTICIAN

Forensic Statistics and Mathematics
by Reddy P. Chamakura
http://www.forensicpage.com/new30.htm

Forensic Mathematics
by Charles H. Brenner, Ph.D.
http://dna-view.com/index.html

FORENSIC SURVEYOR

**Land Surveying and Geomatics:
On-Line Resources**
http://surveying.mentabolism.org

Land Surveyor Reference Page
http://www.lsrp.com

**National Council of Examiners for
Engineering and Surveying**
http://www.ncees.org

FORENSIC TOXICOLOGIST

**Alan Barbour's Forensic Toxicology
Page**
http://www.abarbour.net

American Board of Forensic Toxicology
http://www.abft.org

ToxiLinks
by Society of Forensic Toxicologists
http://www.soft-tox.org/?pn=toxilinks

FORENSIC TRAINING SPECIALIST

Learnativity.com
http://www.learnativity.com

**Virginia Institute of Forensic Science
and Medicine**
http://www.vifsm.org

**Western Forensic Law Enforcement
Training Center**
Colorado State University–Pueblo
http://partners.colostate-pueblo.edu/
wfletc

FORENSIC VIDEO ANALYST

**Forensic Audio, Video and Image
Analysis Unit**
FBI Laboratory
http://www.fbi.gov/hq/lab/org/faviau.htm

Forensic Tape Analysis, Inc.
by Stephen Cain
http://www.videoexpert.com

Police Video Analysis
http://www.policeone.com/police-
technology/software/video-analysis

**Scientific Working Group on Imaging
Technology**
http://theiai.org/guidelines/swgit/index.php

FORENSIC WILDLIFE SCIENTIST

Wildlife DNA Services
http://www.wdnas.com

Wildlife Forensic DNA Laboratory
Trent University, Ontario
http://www.forensicdna.ca

Wildlife Forensics Unit
Northeast Wildlife DNA Laboratory, East
Stroudsburg University
http://www3.esu.edu/dna/wildlife/
forensics.asp

FRAUD EXAMINER

National Fraud Awareness Week
http://www.fraudweek.com

The FRAUDfiles Blog
by Tracy Coenen
http://www.sequence-inc.com/fraudfiles

Workplace Fairness
http://www.workplacefairness.org

HISTOLOGIST

Histology
by Southwest Environmental Health
Science Center, University of Arizona
http://swehsc.pharmacy.arizona.edu/
exppath/micro/histology.html

**Histosearch: The Histology Search
Engine**
http://www.histosearch.com

JUDGE

Judicial Branch
http://usinfo.state.gov/usa/infousa/
politics/judbranc.htm

Supreme Court of the United States
http://www.supremecourtus.gov

Useful Links
by National Judicial College
http://www.judges.org/links.html

LATENT PRINT EXAMINER

Complete Latent Print Examination
http://www.clpex.com

Latent Print Examination
by Ed German
http://www.onin.com/fp

Ridges and Furrows
http://www.ridgesandfurrows.homestead.
com

MEDICAL EXAMINER

**Allegheny County Medical Examiner's
Office**
http://www.county.allegheny.pa.us/me

**American Board of Independent
Medical Examiners**
http://www.abime.org

HBO: Autopsy
http://www.hbo.com/autopsy/index.html

National Board of Medical Examiners
http://www.nbme.org

MEDICOLEGAL DEATH INVESTIGATOR

American Board of Medicolegal Death Investigators
http://www.slu.edu/organizations/abmdi

Forensic Talk: Medicolegal Death Investigation
http://harfordmedlegal.typepad.com/
forensics_talk/medicolegal_death_
investigation/index.html

MORGUE ASSISTANT

Death—The Last Taboo
http://www.deathonline.net

Visible Proofs: Forensic Views of the Body: Exhibition
http://www.nlm.nih.gov/visibleproofs/
exhibition

PATROL OFFICER

CopSeek.com
http://www.copseek.com

Exploring: Law Enforcement
(Law Enforcement Explorers)
http://www.learning-for-life.org/
exploring/lawenforcement

National Association of Police Organizations
http://www.napo.org

Officer.com
http://www.officer.com

PoliceOne.com
http://www.policeone.com

POLYGRAPH EXAMINER

"How Lie Detectors Work"
by Kevin Bonsor, Howstuffworks.com

http://people.howstuffworks.com/lie-
detector.htm

National Polygraph Association
http://www.nationalpolygraph.org

Polygraph Frequently Asked Questions
by American Polygraph Association
http://www.polygraph.org/faq.cfm

The Polygraph Place
http://www.polygraphplace.com

PROSECUTING ATTORNEY

American Prosecutors Research Institute
http://www.ndaa.org/apri

FindLaw
http://www.findlaw.com

International Association of Prosecutors
http://www.iap.nl.com

Prosecutor Info Website
http://www.prosecutor.info

United States Attorneys
U.S. Department of Justice
http://www.usdoj.gov/usao

QUALITY MANAGER

Forensic Quality Services
http://www.forquality.org

QA and QC in Forensic Science
by Reddy P. Chamakura
http://www.forensicpage.com/new40.
htm

QUESTIONED DOCUMENT EXAMINER

Emily J. Will, Forensic Document Examiner
http://www.qdewill.com

Guidelines for Forensic Document Examination
http://www.fbi.gov/hq/lab/fsc/backissu/
april2000/swgdoc1.htm

Questioned Document Examination
by Dr. Tom O'Connor
http://faculty.ncwc.edu/toconnor/425/
425lect05.htm

Southeastern Association of Forensic Document Examiners
http://www.safde.org

TRACE EVIDENCE EXAMINER

International Association for Microanalysis
http://www.iamaweb.com

Trace Evidence
http://www.westchestergov.com/
labsresearch/ForensicandTox/forensic/
trace/fortraceframeset.htm

Trace Evidence Recovery Guidelines
by the Scientific Working Group
on Materials Analysis Evidence
Committee
http://www.fbi.gov/hq/lab/fsc/backissu/
oct1999/trace.htm

TRIAL LAWYER

Daubert on the Web
by Peter Nordberg
http://www.daubertontheweb.com

HG.org—Worldwide Legal Directories
http://www.hg.org

Law.com
http://www.law.com

Legal Career Center Network
http://www.thelccn.com

Legal Education and Student Resources
by the American Bar Association
http://www.abanet.org/legaled.html

GLOSSARY

academician A teacher and scholar who works in a higher education institution.

acoustics The scientific study of sound and sound waves.

administrative Relating to the daily management of an organization such as a law firm or law school.

administrative hearing A legal proceeding held before a government agency regarding violations of the laws that the agency enforces.

advanced degree A college degree beyond a bachelor's degree.

advocacy Support for a particular cause, policy, idea, or person.

advocate (v.) To be in favor of something or someone; (n.) a person who supports a cause.

affidavit A written statement that one swears is true under oath.

AFIS Automated fingerprint identification system; a computerized database containing millions of fingerprints that is used to identify the owner of fingerprints left at crime scenes.

alternative dispute resolution A way to settle a dispute without going through a court trial.

analysis A detailed examination of something in order to better understand it.

analyst A specialist who conducts a detailed examination of something in order to explain what it is.

analytical skills The abilities that a worker needs to critically examine and solve problems.

anatomy The scientific study of the internal structure of living organisms.

anthropology The scientific study of human society and cultures.

appeal A written request to a higher court to review and overturn a judgment made in a lower court.

application The act of using the knowledge and skills of one's discipline for a practical and specific purpose.

arson A crime in which a fire was intentionally set.

assault A violent physical attack on a person or animal.

assessment An evaluation of the nature or quality of something; for example, a forensic examiner makes an assessment about whether threads found on a victim come from a suspect's shirt.

associate degree The degree earned upon fulfilling the requirements of a two-year college program.

audit To conduct an organized review of formal records.

autopsy A medical examination of a dead body to determine its cause and manner of death.

bachelor's degree The degree earned upon fulfilling the requirements of a four-year college program.

bacteria Microorganisms that can cause disease.

ballistics The study of bullets and other projectiles in motion.

behavioral sciences The various disciplines, such as psychology, that study human conduct.

bench trial A court trial in which a judge, rather than a jury, decides the facts.

biohazard Any dangerous biological material, such as bacteria and viruses, that presents a risk or possible risk to the health of people and animals or to the environment.

biological evidence Any type of matter that originates with tissue, such as hair, skin, blood, saliva, sweat, dental pulp, and fingernails.

biology The scientific study of humans, animals, plants, and one-celled organisms.

bioterrorism The use of germs, bacteria, or other biological material to terrorize or intimidate a group of people, usually for political purposes.

BLS Bureau of Labor Statistics; the agency within the U.S. Department of Labor that is responsible for collecting, processing, analyzing, and disseminating statistical data about labor economics.

cadaver A dead body.

candidate A person whom an employer is interested in hiring.

career An individual's profession or occupation.

case A subject, incident, or situation that is examined by a law enforcement officer, forensic scientist, or another professional.

chain of custody The method used to track every person who handles a piece of evidence and to record his or her purpose for handling it.

chemistry The scientific study of substances (or chemicals) that make up all living things and nonliving matter.

child abuse The physical or mental mistreatment of a child by his or her parent or legal guardian, or by another adult.

claim The request or demand for money, property, or other benefits from an organization or government agency.

claimant A person who is receiving or claiming insurance benefits or other types of benefits.

clandestine Hidden; secret.

client An individual or organization that uses the services of a professional.

code A system of laws and regulations that govern a particular activity such as traffic or taxation.

communicable disease A disease that can easily be spread from one person to another, either through direct or indirect contact.

communication skills The speaking and listening abilities that workers need to perform their job.

comparative Involving comparisons between two or more subject matters.

compliance Meeting the conditions required by a specific law, regulation, or policy.

consultant An expert in a particular field who charges a fee for his or her professional advice and services.

contaminate To make something unclean and harmful.

continuing education Organized learning experiences, such as courses and seminars, that professionals take after earning their degree to improve or strengthen their career goals.

contractual Being part of a formal legal agreement.

controlled substance Any type of drug or substance (such as narcotics and stimulants) that is regulated by law.

convict (n.) A criminal; (v.) to judge someone guilty of committing a crime.

coroner A public official who is responsible for investigating the cause and manner of unexplained deaths within his or her jurisdiction.

correctional facility A jail, prison, or other institution where criminals fulfill their court sentence for breaking a law.

corrections The program of treating and rehabilitating criminals that may include a jail or prison sentence, probation, and/or parole.

court A government body that has the power to resolve legal disputes.

court exhibit Demonstrative evidence; a visual aid, such as a chart or animation, that attorneys use in court to help the judge and jurors understand complex or technical issues and facts.

court proceeding Any hearing or court appearance related to making a decision about a civil or criminal case.

crime lab Crime laboratory or forensic laboratory; a facility where scientific methods and techniques are used to process, examine, and analyze physical evidence (such as fingerprints and DNA).

crime scene A location where a crime has taken place.

crime scene investigation A thorough examination at a crime scene to locate and collect all items of evidence that may link a criminal suspect to a victim or the crime scene.

criminal defendant A person who is accused of committing a crime and defends himself or herself against criminal charges in a court of law.

criminal investigation A thorough examination of a crime to determine who committed the crime, and when, where, how, and why it was committed.

criminal investigator A law enforcement officer whose job is to find sufficient proof that a suspect committed a crime in order to try him or her in court.

criminalist A forensic scientist; he or she uses scientific methods and techniques to examine and analyze physical evidence.

criminalistics A forensic science discipline; the application of science to the identification, analysis, and evaluation of physical evidence for legal purposes.

criminal justice The system that involves arresting, convicting, sentencing, and imprisoning criminals.

criminologist One who studies crime and criminals.

critical-thinking skills The ability to examine and analyze a situation and make sensible judgments on how to handle it.

cross-examine To question witnesses of the opposing side in a trial.

cross-trained Being trained to perform more than one job.

CSI Crime scene investigator; one who locates and collects physical evidence at a crime scene.

damage The compensation awarded by a court to a person who has suffered a loss or injury due to the unlawful act of another party.

data Information, including facts and figures.

database An organized collection of facts and figures that is stored in a computer.

death scene The location where a person died.

decision The judgment, or opinion, that is made at the end of a case in a court of law.

defend To speak on behalf of a person or group accused of wrongdoing.

defendant In a criminal trial, the person charged with committing a crime; in a civil trial, the person or group who is charged with wrongdoing against another party.

defense attorney The lawyer who represents the defendant.

demonstrative evidence A visual aid, such as a chart or animation, that attorneys use in court to help the judge and jurors understand complex or technical issues and facts.

deposition A verbal statement that a witness makes under oath in an authorized place outside of a courtroom.

detail-oriented Able to pay close attention to the various aspects of a task, project, or job.

discipline A field of study, such as biology, chemistry, or forensic science.

dispute A disagreement between two parties.

DNA Deoxyribonucleic acid; the genetic code of all living organisms.

doctorate (or doctoral degree) An advanced degree; the degree earned upon fulfilling the requirements of a postgraduate program.

document (n.) A formal or legal record; (v.) to provide proof that something is true.

domestic violence Assault, psychological abuse, murder, or other form of violence that takes place within a family or a close relationship between two people.

emerging Starting to develop.

entomology The scientific study of insects and related arthropods such as spiders and centipedes.

entrepreneurial Willing to take the risks of starting a new business.

entry-level position A job that individuals can obtain with little or no experience.

estimated wages An amount that is close to the actual pay a worker earns.

ethical Behaving justly and honestly.

ethics A system of principles that governs how individuals or groups should behave within an organization.

evidence The testimony, documents, and other information presented in a court of law to prove one's case; also: items left at a crime scene.

exonerate To acquit; to formally declare that a person is not guilty of a crime.

experience Paid and volunteer work that an individual has done that is related to the position for which he or she applies.

expert opinion An evaluation about a legal issue given by a person who has professional knowledge and experience in the subject matter.

expert witness An individual whom a court recognizes as having the required knowledge, education, experience, and credentials to address specific issues in a court trial.

fellowship An award given to professionals or doctoral-degreed scientists to further their study and training in their field.

felony A serious crime such as murder, arson, kidnapping, or drug dealing; a person convicted of a felony may be sentenced to prison for several years or to death.

fibers Fine threads of cloth.

findings Conclusions that one forms after completing an investigation.

first responder The first police officer that arrives at a crime scene.

flexible Able to handle changes.

forensic The application of science to the examination of legal issues.

forensic anthropology The application of anthropological principles and techniques to medicolegal death investigations.

forensic laboratory Crime laboratory; a facility where scientific methods and techniques are used to process, examine, and analyze physical evidence (such as fingerprints and DNA).

forensics The application of science to the study of legal or regulatory matters.

fraud The criminal act of taking money or other benefits from a person through deception.

hearing A formal proceeding before a judge, administrative agency, or legislature in which evidence and arguments are presented to resolve a dispute about issues of law or fact.

homicide The crime of killing a person.

human remains Dead body.

independent practitioner A self-employed individual who performs contractual work for a person or organization.

internship The period of employment as a trainee or a low-level assistant in order to gain experience.

interpersonal skills The abilities a worker needs to communicate and work well with others on the job.

issue A point of disagreement between parties in a lawsuit.

judiciary The judicial branch of government.

jurisdiction The area in which certain laws and regulations are applicable.

juror A member of the jury who is sworn to give a verdict on a legal case.

jury A group of people who have sworn to listen objectively to the facts and issues of a case and then to provide a verdict.

juvenile An individual under the age of 18.

latent prints An impression of a set of fingerprints, palm prints, or footprints that have been taken from a surface of an object.

law The system of rules and principles that a community recognizes as being enforceable by proper authorities.

lawsuit A legal action that one party (the plaintiff) has brought against another party (the defendant) in a court of law.

leadership skills The abilities a worker needs to provide supervision and direction to other workers on a project or in a unit.

liability A financial obligation for which someone is responsible.

licensing board A state agency responsible for regulating the issuance of licenses to attorneys or another profession.

licensure The act of issuing a professional license.

literature Books, government reports, newspapers, and other resources that a professional consults when doing research on a topic.

litigation A lawsuit.

litigation consultant A professional who offers his or her expert services to attorneys involved in lawsuits.

local Within a certain geographical area.

malpractice The failure of a physician or other professional to do his or her professional duties due to illegal or unethical behavior.

maltreatment Abuse of a person or animal.

master's degree An advanced degree that is earned upon fulfilling the requirements of a one- or two-year graduate program.

medical examiner A physician who is officially responsible for conducting death investigations within his or her jurisdiction.

medicolegal Relating to both the law and medicine.

microorganism A tiny organism, such as a virus, that can be seen only under a microscope.

misdemeanor A minor crime, such as vandalism or disorderly conduct; a person guilty of a misdemeanor may be required to pay a fine and/or serve a short sentence in jail.

morgue A room or building where dead bodies are stored and examined.

multimedia The combination of two or more media (such as graphics, video, and animation) for a presentation.

natural sciences The science disciplines (such as chemistry) that study natural phenomena.

negligence Failure to provide proper care which results in a person or property becoming harmed or injured.

negotiate To reach an agreement through discussion and compromise.

networking Making contacts with colleagues and other people who may be able to provide information about job openings.

novice A new or inexperienced worker.

odontology The scientific study of teeth.

offender An individual who has committed a crime.

party One of two sides in a lawsuit.

pathology The scientific study of how cells and tissues are changed by disease; a medical practice that diagnoses diseases as well as the cause of death.

pediatrics The medical practice of diagnosis and treatment of children's diseases.

physical evidence Any object, such as fingerprints, blood, bullets, documents, and computer files, used as proof that a suspect has committed a crime.

plaintiff The party who brings a lawsuit against an individual or group.

postdoctoral Relating to academic work or research done after a doctoral degree has been awarded.

postmortem After death.

practice A business.

practitioner A person who pursues a specific profession, such as law.

principle A basic law, rule, or truth.

problem-solving skills The abilities an individual needs to analyze and evaluate problems and find ways to solve them.

prosecute To put an individual or group on trial.

prosecutor A prosecuting attorney; he or she represents the government in a criminal or civil trial.

quality Having all the required characteristics and being free of all defects.

regulation A rule that a government agency establishes in order to fulfill the requirements of a law.

regulatory agency A government agency that enforces a specific set of laws and regulations.

rigor mortis The stiffening of the body that occurs within several hours after its death.

self-management skills The abilities a worker needs to perform his or her duties without constant supervision.

sentence The punishment a judge orders that a person convicted of a crime must serve.

serology The scientific study of blood serum.

settlement An agreement made between two parties in a dispute.

statute A law created by a legislative body.

subject-matter expert An individual who is highly knowledgeable about and experienced with a particular topic.

subordinate A person who is lower in rank or status in a workplace.

suspect A person who is believed to have committed a crime.

task A duty or job that an employee must perform.

teamwork skills The abilities an employee needs to work effectively as part of a group on a work project or in a unit.

technician A worker who provides technical support to scientists or other professionals.

technique A technical method for performing a task.

technologist A scientist or engineer who is involved in the practical application of his or her discipline.

testify To answer questions in a court of law.

testimony A statement that a person makes and swears under oath to be true.

toxic Poisonous.

toxicology The scientific study of poisons and how they affect the human body.

trace evidence Any very small items of physical evidence such as hair, soil, paint chips, and explosives residue.

trial A formal examination of the facts and issues in a criminal or civil case before a court of law.

try To conduct a legal case in a court of law.

URL Universal Resource Locator: the address of a Web site on the Internet

vendor A business that sells services and/or products.

verdict The decision made by a judge or jury about a case.

verify To prove that something is true.

witness A person who has direct knowledge about a suspect, crime, or crime scene.

BIBLIOGRAPHY

A. PERIODICALS

Print and online publications are available that target many of the various occupations described in this book. These include magazines, journals, newspapers, newsletters, webzines, and electronic news services. Listed below are just a few publications that serve the interests of forensic scientists, forensic experts, crime scene investigators, and other occupations that are described in this book.

To learn about other print and online publications, talk with librarians, educators, and professionals for recommendations. Also check out professional and trade associations. Many of them publish journals, newsletters, magazines, and other publications.

You may be able to find some of the print publications at a public, school, or academic library. Many of the print magazines also allow limited free access to their articles on the Web. Some of the Web-based publications are free, whereas others require a subscription to access certain issues and other resources. Some publications offer free subscriptions to students or professionals.

Note: Web site addresses were current when this book was written. If a Web site address no longer works, you may be able to find its new address by entering the name of the publication into a search engine.

The Adjunct Advocate
(for part-time academic instructors)
http://www.adjunctnation.com

American Journal of Forensic Medicine and Pathology
http://www.amjforensicmedicine.com

American Journal of Forensic Psychiatry
P.O. Box 5870
Balboa Island, CA 92662
Phone: (949) 673-7773
Fax: (949) 673-7710
http://www.forensicpsychonline.com/jrnl.htm

American Journal of Forensic Psychology
P.O. Box 5870
Balboa Island, CA 92662
Phone: (949) 673-7773
Fax: (949) 673-7710
http://www.forensicpsychology.org/journalpg.html

The American Lawyer
Phone: (800) 755-2773
http://www.americanlawyer.com

American Police Beat
http://www.apbweb.com

The Chronicle of Higher Education
Phone: (800) 728-2803 or (815) 734-1216
http://chronicle.com

Clinical and Forensic Toxicology News
American Association for Clinical Chemistry
http://www.aacc.org/AACC/publications/toxicology

Crime Times
Wacker Foundation
http://www.crime-times.org

Criminology: An Interdisciplinary Journal
American Society of Criminology
Phone: (614) 292-9207
Fax: (614) 292-6767
http://www.asc41.com/publications.htm

Evidence Technology Magazine
http://www.evidencemagazine.com

The FBI Law Enforcement Bulletin
http://www.fbi.gov/publications/leb/leb.htm

The Forensic Examiner
American College of Forensic Examiners Institute
http://acfei.com/examiner.php

Forensic Magazine
Vicon Publishing, Inc.
4 Limbo Lane
Amherst, NH 03031
Phone: (603) 672-9997
Fax: (603) 672-3028
http://www.forensicmag.com

Forensic Nurse
http://www.forensicnursemag.com

Forensic Science Communications
U.S. Federal Bureau of Investigation
http://www.fbi.gov/hq/lab/fsc/current/index.htm

Forensic Science International
IngentaConnect Publication
http://www.ingentaconnect.com/content/els/03790738

Fraud Magazine
Association of Certified Fraud Examiners
Phone: (800) 245-3321 or (512) 478-9000
http://www.cfenet.com/fraud/mag.asp

International Journal of Forensic Engineering
Inderscience Publishers
http://www.inderscience.com/browse/index.php?journalID=159

International Journal of Forensic Mental Health
International Association of Forensic Mental Health Services
http://www.iafmhs.org/iafmhs.asp?pg=journal

Journal of Forensic Accounting
http://www.edwardspub.com/journals/JFA

Journal of Digital Forensics, Security and Law
Association of Digital Forensics, Security and Law
http://www.jdfsl.org

Journal of Forensic Document Examination
Association of Forensic Document Examiners
http://www.afde.org/journal.html

Journal of Forensic Identification
International Association for Identification
https://www.theiai.org/publications

Journal of Forensic Nursing
International Association of Forensic Nurses
http://www.iafn.org/publication/jfnDefault.cfm

Police: The Law Enforcement Magazine
http://www.policemag.com

Police Times
American Federation of Police & Concerned Citizens
http://www.aphf.org/pt.html

Professional Surveyor Magazine
http://www.profsurv.com

Psychiatric News
American Psychiatric Association
http://pn.psychiatryonline.org

Psychology, Public Policy, and Law
American Psychological Association
Phone: (202) 336-5600
Fax: (202) 336-5568
http://www.apa.org/journals/law

Radiology
Radiological Society of North America
http://radiology.rsnajnls.org

B. BOOKS

Listed below are some books that can help you learn more about the different occupations in the forensic sciences. To learn about other books that may be helpful, ask professionals—individuals and organizations—as well as librarians for suggestions.

Arrigo, Bruce A. and Stacey L. Shipley. *Introduction to Forensic Psychology, 2d ed.* Boston: Elsevier/Academic Press, 2005.

Axelrod, Alan and Guy Antinozzi. *The Complete Idiot's Guide to Criminal Investigation.* Indianapolis, Ind.: Alpha Books, 2003.

Baden, Michael, M.D. and Marion Roach. *Dead Reckoning: The New Science of Catching Killers.* New York: Simon and Schuster, 2001.

Bell, Suzanne. *The Facts On File Dictionary of Forensic Science.* New York: Facts On File, Inc., 2004.

Breeze, Roger, Bruce Budowle, and Steven Schutzer. *Microbial Forensics.* Boston: Elsevier/Academic Press, 2005.

Brodsky, Stanley L. *The Expert Expert Witness: More Maxims and Guidelines for Testifying in Court.* Washington, D.C.: American Psychological Association, 1999.

Burns, Karen Ramey. *Forensic Anthropology Training Manual.* Upper Saddle River, N.J.: Prentice Hall, 1999.

Camenson, Blythe. *Opportunities in Forensic Science Careers.* Lincolnwood, Ill.: VGM Career Books, 2001.

Dix, Jay. *Handbook for Death Scene Investigators.* Boca Raton, Fla.: CRC, 1999.

Dix, Jay, and Robert Calaluce. *Guide to Forensic Pathology.* Boca Raton, Fla.: CRC, 1998.

Dominick, Joseph T. et al. *Crime Scene Investigation.* Pleasantville, N.Y.: Reader's Digest Association, 2004.

Echaore-McDavid, Susan. *Career Opportunities in Education and Related Services, 2d ed.* New York: Ferguson, Infobase Publishing, 2006.

Echaore-McDavid, Susan. *Career Opportunities in Law and the Legal Industry, 2d ed.* New York: Ferguson, Infobase Publishing, 2007.

Echaore-McDavid, Susan. *Career Opportunities in Law Enforcement, Security, and Protective Services, 2d ed.* New York: Checkmark Books, Facts On File, Inc., 2006.

Echaore-McDavid, Susan. *Career Opportunities in Science.* New York: Checkmark Books, Facts On File, Inc., 2003.

Evans, Colin. *A Question of Evidence: The Casebook of Great Forensic Controversies, from Napoleon to O.J.* Hoboken, N.J.: John Wiley and Sons, 2003.

Farmer, Dan, and Wietse Venema. *Forensic Discovery.* Upper Saddle River, N.J.: Addison-Wesley, 2005.

Farr, J. Michael, and Laurence Shatkin, eds. *The O*NET Dictionary of Occupational Titles, 3rd ed.* Indianapolis, Ind.: JIST Publishing, 2004.

Ferllini, Roxana. *Silent Witness.* Buffalo, N.Y.: Firefly Books, 2002.

Fletcher, Connie. *Every Contact Leaves a Trace: Crime Scene Experts Talk about Their Work from Discovery through Verdict.* New York: St. Martin's Press, 2006.

Friedlander, Mark P., Jr. *Outbreak: Disease Detectives at Work.* Minneapolis, Minn.: Lerner Publications, 2003.

Genge, N.E. *The Forensic Casebook: The Science of Crime Scene Investigation.* New York: Ballantine Books, 2002.

Golden, Thomas, Steven Skalak, and Mona Clayton. *A Guide to Forensic Accounting Investigation.* Hoboken, N.J.: Wiley, 2005.

Houck, Max M., and Jay A. Siegel. *Fundamentals of Forensic Science.* Boston: Elsevier/Academic Press, 2006.

Innes, Brian. *Bodies of Evidence.* Pleasantville, N.Y.: Reader's Digest, 2000.

———. *Forensic Science.* Broomall, Pa.: Mason Crest Publishers, Inc., 2003.

James, Stuart H., and Jon J. Nordby, eds. *Forensic Science: An Introduction to Scientific and Investigative Techniques, 2d ed.* Boca Raton, Fla.: CRC, 2005.

Lee, Henry C., and Frank Tirnady. *Blood Evidence: How DNA is Revolutionizing the Way We Solve Crimes.* Cambridge, Mass.: Perseus Publishing, 2003.

Loue, Sana. *Case Studies in Forensic Epidemiology.* New York: Kluwer Academic/Plenum Publishers, 2002.

Lyle, D. P. *Forensics for Dummies.* Indianapolis, Ind.: Wiley Publishing, Inc., 2004.

McDavid, Richard A. and Susan Echaore-McDavid. *Career Opportunities in Engineering.* New York: Ferguson, Infobase Publishing, 2007.

Munneke, Gary A. *Careers in Law.* Lincolnwood, Ill.: VGM Career Books, 2004.

Murray, Raymond C. *Evidence from the Earth: Forensic Geology and Criminal Investigation.* Missoula, Mont.: Mountain Press Publishing Company, 2004.

Nafte, Myriam. *Flesh and Bone: An Introduction to Forensic Anthropology.* Durham, N.C.: Carolina Academic Press, 2000.

Owen, David. *Hidden Evidence.* Buffalo, N.Y.: Firefly Books, 2000.

Ramsland, Katherine. *The Criminal Mind: A Writer's Guide to Forensic Psychology.* Cincinnati, Ohio: Writer's Digest Books, 2002.

———. *The Forensic Science of C.S.I.* New York: Berkeley Boulevard Books, 2001.

Rhine, Stanley. *Bone Voyage: A Journey in Forensic Anthropology.* Albuquerque, N.Mex.: University of New Mexico Press, 1998.

Roach, Mary. *Stiff: The Curious Lives of Human Cadavers.* New York: W. W. Norton and Co., 2003.

Sachs, Jessica Snyder. *Corpse: Nature, Forensics, and the Struggle to Pinpoint Time of Death.* Cambridge, Mass.: Perseus Books Group, 2002.

Saferstein, Richard. *Criminalistics: An Introduction to Forensic Science, 8th ed.* Upper Saddle River, N.J.: Pearson Prentice Hall, 2004.

Stephens W. Richard Jr. *Careers in Criminal Justice.* Needham Heights, Mass.: Allyn & Bacon, 1999.

Stevens, Serita. *Forensic Nurse.* New York: Thomas Dune Books, 2004.

Taylor, Karen T. *Forensic Art and Illustration.* Boca Raton, Fla.: CRC, 2000.

U.S. Department of Labor. *Career Guide to Industries, 2006-2007 Edition.* Washington, D.C.: Bureau of Labor Statistics, 2006. Available online at http://www.bls.gov/oco/cg.

U.S. Department of Labor. *Occupational Outlook Handbook 2006-2007 Edition.* Indianapolis, Ind.: JIST Publishing, Inc., 2006.

U.S. Department of Labor. *Occupational Outlook Handbook 2006-2007 Edition.* Washington, D.C.: Bureau of Labor Statistics, 2006. Available online at http://www.bls.gov/oco.

Vacca, John R. *Computer Forensics: Computer Crime Scene Investigation.* Hingham, Mass.: Charles River Media, 2002.

Walker, Maryalice. *Entomology And Palynology: Evidence from the Natural World.* Philadelphia: Mason Crest Publishers, 2005.

Ward, Jenny. *Crimebusting: Breakthroughs in Forensic Science.* New York: Bradford Press, 1998.

Wecht, Cyril, and Greg Saitz with Mark Curriden. *Mortal Evidence: The Forensics Behind Nine Shocking Cases.* Amherst, N.Y.: Prometheus Books, 2003.

Wells, Joseph T. *Principles of Fraud Examination.* Hoboken, N.J.: John Wiley and Sons, 2004.

Wilkinson, Caroline. *Forensic Facial Reconstruction.* New York: Cambridge University Press, 2004.

Zelicoff, Alan P., M.D., and Michael Bellomo. *Microbe: Are We Ready for the Next Plague?* New York: Amacom, 2005.

C. ONLINE PUBLICATIONS

Listed below are some reports, guides, and other valuable materials that can help you learn more about forensic science and related fields. They are available online and can be downloaded as PDF files.

American Academy of Forensic Sciences. *So You Want to be a Forensic Scientist!* Available online at http://www. aafs.org.

American Academy of Pediatrics. *Pediatrics 101.* Available online at http://www.aap.org/profed/career.htm.

American Institute of Architects. *Careers in Architecture.* Available online at http://www.aia.org.

American Prosecutors Research Institute. *Crash Reconstruction Basics for Prosecutors.* Alexandria, Va.: American Prosecutors Research Institute, 2003. Available online at http://www.ndaa.org/apri.

American Society for Engineering Education. *Engineering, Go For It!* Washington, D.C.: American Society for Engineering Education. Available online at http://www. cnginccring-goforit.com.

Association of Certified Fraud Examiners. *2004 Report the Nation on Occupational Fraud and Abuse.* Austin, Tex.: Association of Certified Fraud Examiners, 2004. Available online at http://www.acfe.com/fraud/report.asp.

Bryant, Vaughn M., and Gretchen D. Jones. "Forensic Palynology: Current Status of a Rarely Used Technique in the United States of America." *Forensic Science International* 163 (2006): 183–197. Available online at http://anthropology.tamu.edu/faculty/Bryant/publications.htm.

Collins, Donald. *The Dentist's Role in Forensic Identification.* Chicago: American Dental Association, 2004. Available online at http://www.ada.org/prof/prac/disaster/recover/volunteering.asp.

Criminal Justice Journalists. *Covering Crime and Justice: A Guide for Journalists.* Columbia, Mo.: Investigative Reporters and Editors, Inc., 2003. Available online at http://www.justicejournalism.org/crimeguide.

Forensic Engineering Task Force, The. *Report on The Practice of Forensic Engineering.* Denver, Colo.: Colorado State Board of Licensure for Professional Engineers and Professional Land Surveyors, 2006. Available online at http://www.dora.state.co.us/aes/library.htm.

Kentucky State Police Forensic Laboratories Section. *Physical Evidence Handbook (Rev. June 2001).* Frankfort, Ky.: Kentucky State Police Forensic Laboratories Section, 2001. Available online at http://www.firermsid.com

National Center for State Courts. *Survey of Judicial Salaries. Vol. 31, No. 1.* Williamsburg, Va.: National Center for State Courts, July 2006. Available online at http://www.ncsconline.org/D-KIS/index.html.

National Medicolegal Review Panel. *Death Investigation: A Guide for the Scene Investigator* (NCJ167568). Washington, D.C.: National Institute of Justice, U.S. Department of Justice, November 1999. Available online at: http://nij.ncjrs.gov/publications/pubs_db.asp.

Society of Toxicology. *Resource Guide to Careers in Toxicology.* Available online at http://www.toxicology.org/AI/APT/careerguide.asp.

Technical Working Group for Education and Training in Forensic Science. *Education and Training in Forensic Science: A Guide for Forensic Science Laboratories, Educational Institutions, and Students* (NCJ 203099). Washington, D.C.: National Institute of Justice, U.S. Department of Justice, June 2004. Available online at: http://nij.ncjrs.gov/publications/pubs_db.asp.

Technical Working Group for the Examination of Digital Evidence. *Forensic Examination of Digital Evidence: A Guide for Law Enforcement* (NCJ199408). Washington, D.C.: National Institute of Justice, U.S. Department of Justice, April 2004. Available online at: http://nij.ncjrs.gov/publications/pubs_db.asp.

Technical Working Group on Crime Scene Investigation. *Crime Scene Investigation: A Guide for Law Enforcement* (NCJ 178280). Washington, D.C.: National Institute of Justice, U.S. Department of Justice, January 2000. Available online at http://www.nij.ncjrs.gov/publications/pubs_db.asp.

Wade, Colleen, ed. *FBI Handbook of Forensic Services.* Quantico, Va.: Federal Bureau of Investigation, 2003. Available online at http://www.fbi.gov/publications.htm.

INDEX